OBSCENE PEDAGOGIES

OBSCENE
PEDAGOGIES

TRANSGRESSIVE TALK AND SEXUAL
EDUCATION IN LATE MEDIEVAL BRITAIN

Carissa M. Harris

CORNELL UNIVERSITY PRESS
Ithaca and London

First published 2018 by Cornell University Press

Printed in the United States of America

Library of Congress Cataloging-in-Publication Data

Names: Harris, Carissa M., author.
Title: Obscene pedagogies : transgressive talk and sexual
    education in late medieval Britain / Carissa M. Harris.
Description: Ithaca : Cornell University Press, 2018. |
    Includes bibliographical references and index.
Identifiers: LCCN 2018022917| ISBN 9781501730405
    (cloth) | ISBN 9781501730412 (pdf) |
    ISBN 9781501730429 (ret)
Subjects: LCSH: English literature—Middle English,
    1100-1500—History and criticism. | Obscene words in
    literature. | Sex in literature. | Misogyny in literature. |
    Sex instruction—Great Britain—History—To 1500. |
    Sex role—Great Britain—History—To 1500.
Classification: LCC PR275.O27 H37 2018 |
    DDC 820.9/3538—dc23
LC record available at https://lccn.loc.gov/2018022917

For G. G. Rose,
who always told me that I would write a book someday

Contents

Acknowledgments

It takes a village to dress a drag queen, and I am so very grateful to everyone who helped me bring the Matchless Orinda into being.

My first thanks go to Northwestern University's English Department and Medieval Studies Cluster, the communities in which this project was born. Words cannot express how indebted I am to Susie Phillips, an unfailingly generous and astute reader, teacher, and mentor who never gave up on me. This book would not exist without Susie's brilliance, guidance, wisdom, compassion, and understanding. Barbara Newman and Katy Breen forged me into a medievalist and taught me how to hone my arguments, and Julia Stern was warmly supportive from my earliest days at Northwestern. Melissa Daniels-Rauterkus, Greg Laski, and Wanalee Romero provided fictive kinship. Maggie Mascal and I had countless generative conversations about medieval single-women's songs, gendered sexual subjectivity, rape culture, and embodiment. I am grateful to Rachel Blumenthal, Vanessa Corredera, Meghan Daly Costa, Kathy Daniels, Becky Fall, Jackie Hendricks, Zack Jacobson, Maha Jafri, Nathan Mead, Laura Passin, Raashi Rastogi, Whitney Taylor, Simone Waller, Sarah Wilson, and so many more people than I can name in this space, for being my Evanston family.

This book was made possible through the collective efforts of countless medievalist colleagues, friends, and mentors. Foremost is Tara Mendola, editrix extraordinaire, who was the first person to behold the Matchless Orinda in her entirety and whose sharp but kind eye helped me to prepare her to be beheld by others. Rita Copeland, Anne Klinck, Nicole Nolan Sidhu, and David Wallace gave thoughtful, generous feedback on individual chapters, and Rita and Nicole served as my mentors for the Ford Postdoctoral and Woodrow Wilson Early Career Enhancement Fellowships in 2016–17. Donna Aza Weir-Soley was a kind, gracious mentor at the 2016 Woodrow Wilson Retreat. Suzanne Edwards and Elly Truitt provided mentorship and counsel regarding the book-writing process. Tekla Bude, Tony Edwards, Tom Farrell, Susanna Fein, Lucy Hinnie, Monica Green, Imani Kai Johnson, S. C. Kaplan, Sally

Mapstone, David Raybin, Cindy Rogers, and Taylor Sims shared leads and unpublished material; they and Lucy Allen, Sarah Baechle, Candice Briggs, Dyan Elliott, Mary Flannery, Anna Lyman, Kathleen Kennedy, Liza Strakhov, and countless others shared insights and engaged in stimulating conversations with me about these topics. Michael Cornett, Martha Driver, and the anonymous readers for the *Journal of Medieval and Early Modern Studies* and *Journal of the Early Book Society* gave instrumental feedback on early portions of chapters 3 and 5 and helped me to develop and clarify my ideas. Carolyn Dinshaw provided encouragement and inspiration, and Sara Ahmed wrote *Living a Feminist Life* at just the right time. Joseph Derosier and Joshua Byron Smith furnished Old French and Latin guidance and friendship. There are many more people who have had a hand in this book, more than I can name in this space, and I am so grateful to every one of you for helping bring her into being. Thank you for your conviviality, collegiality, and brainpower.

The University of Arkansas's Mellon-RBS Symposium, the University of Connecticut's Methodologies of Difference Colloquium, and the University of Virginia's Medieval Colloquium were engaged, thoughtful audiences for portions of this book. The University of Pennsylvania's Medieval-Renaissance community treated me as one of their own from the moment I moved to Philadelphia, and I am so grateful for their fellowship, friendship, and intellectual generosity. Penn's Gen/Sex and Med/Ren reading groups kindly workshopped portions of chapters 1 and 3 and provided invaluable feedback. The Philly Faculty of Color writing retreats organized by Jennifer Harford Vargas and Nina Johnson were instrumental to this book's early stages. I am especially grateful to my two writing groups, who read large portions of this book in its crudest forms: Kinohi Nishikawa and Rebbeca Tesfai provided weekly accountability and perspective from beyond my field, while Claire Falck, Marissa Nicosia, and Thomas Ward shared premodern expertise and prosecco.

Temple University supported my research at every turn as I developed this project into a book. Suzanne Gauch provided extraordinary mentorship and wrote letters of support; Joyce Ann Joyce believed in me from the beginning; Talissa Ford, Kate Henry, Sue-Im Lee, Steve Newman, Jena Osman, James Salazar, Brian Teare, Shannon Walters, and Gabe Wettach provided guidance and kind support in various ways; Stephanie Morawski's Concur wizardry and infinite patience made my research and conference travel possible; and Larry Venuti was a wise, attentive research mentor. My Temple students deserve special mention for reading these texts with me, challenging me to articulate their ongoing relevance, never ceasing to ask questions, reminding me why I write, and giving me life. You are my legendary children.

The research for this book was generously funded by the Ford Foundation, the Medieval Academy of America, Northwestern University's Graduate School, Temple University's College of Liberal Arts, a Temple University research sabbatical, and the Woodrow Wilson National Fellowship Foundation. I am indebted to the kind and helpful staff in the rare books and manuscripts rooms at the British Library, Cambridge University Library, London College of Arms, National Library of Wales, New York Public Library, and Weston Library. Colin Harris at the Weston Library deserves special mention for his assistance in helping me search for background information on MS Ashmole 176. Mohamed Graine at the Municipal Library of Lyon kindly gave me permission to use this book's memorable cover image, and Joseph Derosier's French expertise was instrumental in facilitating our communication. An early version of chapter 3 was published as "Rape Narratives, Courtly Critique, and the Pedagogy of Sexual Negotiation in the Middle English Pastourelle" in *Journal of Medieval and Early Modern Studies* 46, no. 2 (2016): 263–87, and an early version of part of chapter 5 appeared as "'All the Strete My Voyce Shall Heare': Gender, Voice, and Female Desire in the Lyrics of Bodleian MS Ashmole 176" in *Journal of the Early Book Society* 20 (2017): 29–58. I gratefully acknowledge Duke University Press and Pace University Press for allowing me to use that work here.

I could not have asked for a better editor than Mahinder Kingra at Cornell University Press, who has been warm, encouraging, and willing to let me take risks. He always supported the more unconventional aspects of this project, and I appreciate his constructive input. The two anonymous readers for Cornell University Press read this manuscript in its entirety and shared feedback that was rigorous, thorough, and kind, and I am so grateful for their insight, wisdom, and generosity. Sara R. Ferguson was the keen-eyed final stylist who prepared the Matchless Orinda to walk the runway, Mary Ribesky at Westchester Publishing Services took Orinda's hand and led her out into the world, and Carmen Torrado Gonzalez provided useful marketing assistance.

Jami Ake and George Pepe first inspired me to become a professor when I was a freshman and provided invaluable mentorship during and beyond my undergraduate years, and Jessica Rosenfeld introduced me to the joys of medieval literature during my final semester at Wash U. The staff at the Shot Tower provided the best iced coffee in Philadelphia and a welcoming space to write. Coach Kane and Bill Eisenstadt challenged me physically and mentally, and I had many revelations about this book in their spin classes. Eternal thanks are due to Margery Kempe for making me a medievalist. Hillary Rodham Clinton, Andrea Constand, Emily Doe, Anita Hill, Audre Lorde, Sojourner Truth, Harriet Tubman, Maxine Waters, and my foremothers inspired me and gave me strength while I was writing this book. I am indebted to all those who came before me and fought against gender- and race-based injustice so that I could be a mixed-race woman with a Ph.D. in America, and I hope I have honored their sacrifices here. Finally, I thank my family, spouse, friends, and cats for their unflagging support and encouragement throughout this whole process.

And to all you motherfuckers who reminded me what rape culture and misogyny look like while I was writing this book, I thank you for keeping the fire alive.

LIST OF ABBREVIATIONS

DIMEV *Digital Index of Middle English Verse,* http://www.dimev.net.

DMLBS *Dictionary of Medieval Latin from British Sources,* http://logeion.uchicago.edu/.

DOST *Dictionary of the Older Scottish Tongue,* http://www.dsl.ac.uk.

MED *Middle English Dictionary,* https://quod.lib.umich.edu/m/med/.

ODNB *Oxford Dictionary of National Biography,* http://www.oxforddnb.com.

OED *Oxford English Dictionary,* http://www.oed.com.

OFED Hindley, Alan, Frederick W. Langley, and Brian J. Levy, eds. *The Old French-English Dictionary.* Cambridge: Cambridge University Press, 2000.

TM Ringler, Jr., William A. *Bibliography and Index of English Verse in Manuscript, 1501–1558.* London: Mansell, 1992.

TP Ringler, Jr., William A. *Bibliography and Index of English Verse Printed 1476–1558.* London: Mansell, 1988.

Libraries and Repositories

BL British Library, London

Bodleian Bodleian Library, University of Oxford

CUL Cambridge University Library, Cambridge

NLS National Library of Scotland, Edinburgh

NLW National Library of Wales, Aberystwyth

NYPL New York Public Library

OBSCENE PEDAGOGIES

Introduction
The Pedagogy of Obscenity

In *The Castle of Perseverance* (c. 1425), a morality play featuring personifications of the seven deadly sins, characters repeatedly use obscenities like "cunte" and "serdyn" as tools for sexual education. Gluttony teaches his friend Mankind how to indulge his bodily appetites with a step-by-step script: he orders him to enjoy "mete and drynkys goode" (1149) and rich spices, then urges, "And thanne mayst thou bultyn in thi boure / And serdyn gay gerlys" (then you must copulate in your bedroom, / And fuck pretty girls) (1159–60).[1] Gluttony's use of "bultyn" takes a verb normally applied to the sifting of grain and transforms it into a descriptive sexual term indicating repetitive back-and-forth bodily movement.[2] The explicit verb "serdyn" means "to fuck" in Old and Middle English, and John Florio lists "sard" alongside "fucke" and "swive" in his 1598 Italian-English dictionary.[3] In mobilizing the shock value of "bultyn" and "serdyn" and instructing his friend to turn word

---

1. David N. Klausner, ed., *The Castle of Perseverance* (Kalamazoo, MI: Medieval Institute Publications, 2010). Text references are to lines in this edition.

2. *MED* s.v. "bulten" (v.), 1–2. It has similar double connotations in Old French: *OFED* s.v. "buleter" (v.): "bolt, sieve; (fig.) to engage in sexual intercourse."

3. *OED* s.v. "sard" (v.); *MED* s.v. "serden" (v.); John Florio, *A Worlde of Wordes, or Most copious, and exact dictionarie in Italian and English* (London: Arnold Hatfield for Edward Blount, 1598), 137, s.v. "fottere"; Melissa Mohr, *Holy Shit: A Brief History of Swearing* (Oxford: Oxford University Press, 2013), 88–89, 145–56.

into action, Gluttony uses obscenity to teach Mankind about masculine sexuality.

Gluttony's lewd lecture is significant for two reasons. First, it demonstrates how medieval religious writers harnessed obscenity's powers for didactic purposes to teach individuals about sex and sin. Mankind points to the educational dimensions of his friend's speech when he replies, "Soth and sad it is, thy sawe" (your words are true and wise) (1162), drawing on the valences of "sawe" as "a teaching, doctrine" and "a rule, law, commandment."[4] Gluttony instructs Mankind regarding not only with whom ("gay gerlys") but also where ("in thy boure") and how ("bultyn[g]") he will copulate. Gluttony's use of the verb form "mayst" reinforces his statement's pedagogical thrust, as it can connote obligation, meaning "should" or "must."[5] His instructions are successful, as Mankind tells Gluttony's sister Lechery, "To bedde thou muste me brynge" (1207). She responds with a lesson of her own when she orders, "In my cunte thou schalt crepe" (1190). She links genital obscenity with the didactic verb "schalt"—which "express[es] an order, a commandment, direction"—to issue instructions regarding her "cunte," illustrating obscenity's efficacy for articulating female desire.[6] Gluttony's speech teaches his fellow man how to copulate, as he breaks down the sexual script into discrete steps: pampering the body, retreating to the bedroom with pretty girls, then vigorously "bultyn[g]" and "serdyn[g]." This scene stages same-sex peer pedagogy with effective results, as one man's bawdy, instructive words result in another's deeds.

Obscenity is a useful teaching tool because of its inherent transgression and capacity to agitate, and Gluttony is only one of many speakers to deploy its pedagogical potency in late medieval England and Scotland. Mary Caputi states that "we recognize the obscene in its determined violation of established norms, its eagerness to proclaim from beyond the acceptable."[7] Obscenity sheds light on cultural taboos and anxieties because it "challenges the accepted limits of culture, not always with a view toward redefining these limits but toward revisiting their reasons for being, and toward underscoring their ultimate tenuousness."[8] Obscenity defies assumptions and sensibilities; it horrifies, scandalizes, entices, offends; and it incites laughter. Through its insistence on violating the rules of polite expression, it reaches listeners with its galva-

---

4. *MED* s.v. "sau" (n.[2]), 4.

5. *MED* s.v. "mouen" (v.[3]), 7c.

6. *MED* s.v. "shulen" (v.[1]), 4a.

7. Mary Caputi, *Voluptuous Yearnings: Toward a Feminist Theory of the Obscene* (Lanham, MD: Rowman and Littlefield, 1993), 7.

8. Caputi, *Voluptuous Yearnings*, 6.

nizing power and shocks them into reconsidering how they think about gender, sex, and power.

With its transgression of taboos governing bawdy talk, obscenity provokes two main axes of response: the irresistible pull of arousal and titillation and the revulsive push of shame and disgust. The former response is due to medieval culture's frequent conflation of sexual words and deeds. It is reflected in Linda Williams's emphasis on "pornography's solicitation of the bodies of its viewers" and Jeffrey Henderson's claim that obscenity can "excite amusement or pleasure."[9] The latter response, in contrast, entails recoil, revolt, loathing, nausea, horror. Obscenity operates similarly to the abject theorized by Julia Kristeva, which "simultaneously beseeches and pulverizes the subject," operating as "a vortex of summons and rejection."[10] We are simultaneously drawn in and repulsed by the obscene; we cannot stay put. In many cases, as in Gluttony's speech teaching Mankind "how to serd" and asserting the centrality of "serdyn[g] gay gerlys" to Mankind's performance of masculinity, speakers mobilize obscenity's powers of compulsory response to educate audiences about sexuality.

Some men deploy obscenity when teaching their peers how to dominate and dehumanize women, while others use it to challenge dominant narratives about masculinity and to propose alternatives, a practice that scholars and activists have identified as one of the key sites of rape prevention more generally.[11] Obscenity enables women to voice their dissatisfaction with the sexual status quo, to instruct their partners about pleasure, and to teach each other strategies for negotiation. It is this capacity of obscenity to educate and change minds that I investigate throughout *Obscene Pedagogies*, in order to understand its meanings in the later Middle Ages and to uncover its present-day implications. Starting with an examination of obscenity's role in authorizing masculine aggression and fostering misogyny before turning to explore its potential for facilitating sexual negotiation and encouraging empathy for rape survivors,

---

9. Linda Williams, *Hard Core: Power, Pleasure, and the "Frenzy of the Visible,"* 2nd ed. (Berkeley: University of California Press, 1999), xiii; Jeffrey Henderson, *The Maculate Muse: Obscene Language in Attic Comedy,* 2nd ed. (Oxford: Oxford University Press, 1991), 7; see also Drucilla Cornell, "Pornography's Temptation," in *Feminism and Pornography,* ed. Drucilla Cornell (Oxford: Oxford University Press, 2000). For more on the range of potential reactions to explicit medieval visual representations of sexuality, see Sarah Salih, "Erotica," in *A Cultural History of Sexuality in the Middle Ages,* ed. Ruth Evans (New York: Berg, 2011).

10. Julia Kristeva, *Powers of Horror: An Essay in Abjection,* trans. Leon S. Roudiez (New York: Columbia University Press, 1982), 5, 1; William Ian Miller, *The Anatomy of Disgust* (Cambridge, MA: Harvard University Press, 1997).

11. Nicola Henry and Anastasia Powell, "Framing Sexual Violence Prevention," in *Preventing Sexual Violence: Interdisciplinary Approaches to Overcoming a Rape Culture,* ed. Nicola Henry and Anastasia Powell (New York: Palgrave Macmillan, 2014), 7.

Obscene Pedagogies investigates how medieval lyric voices mobilize the obscene to teach their peers about violence, power, and desire.

"Histories that are still": Feminist Frameworks

Feminists have long argued that the personal is political. I follow Judith M. Bennett, Sara Ahmed, Carolyn Dinshaw, and others in suggesting that the personal and political are also historical.[12] Individual experiences of gendered embodiment not only have larger political causes and import but also are shaped by a long history of ideologies so entrenched that they have calcified and come to be viewed as "natural." *Obscene Pedagogies* seeks to uncover a usable past in the literature of premodern England and Scotland that can help us understand current cultural discourses and lived realities with greater perspicacity. I am a mixed-race woman of color. My body, and the meanings it carries in this world, is an ineluctable condition of my existence as a human and as a scholar. I approach these texts as an embodied subject, and I incorporate both contemporary material and occasional personal anecdote into my scholarly analysis. I use a black feminist framework even though many of these texts are not explicitly about race, because it enables me to approach these texts in generative ways.[13] I ground *Obscene Pedagogies* in several key features of black feminist thought articulated by Patricia Hill Collins, most notably an awareness of the long legacy of struggle against sexual violence, connections to lived experience, and the merging of intellectual work and activism.[14] A black feminist framework is aware of how different inequalities intersect—in the case

---

12. Judith M. Bennett argues for "the feminist potential of this particular sort of women's history [that is] focused on feminist issues, aware of the distant past, attentive to continuities, and alert to the workings of patriarchal power," declaring that "women's history, especially when viewed across many centuries, can . . . stimulate feminist outrage and revolutionary fervor." *History Matters: Patriarchy and the Challenge of Feminism* (Philadelphia: University of Pennsylvania Press, 2006), 5, 153–55. While my focus is on literature in addition to history, my aims are similar to Bennett's. See also Sara Ahmed, *Living a Feminist Life* (Durham, NC: Duke University Press, 2017); Carolyn Dinshaw, *How Soon Is Now? Medieval Texts, Amateur Readers, and the Queerness of Time* (Durham, NC: Duke University Press, 2012), 1–39.

13. I use Patricia Hill Collins's definition of "black feminist thought": "Black feminist thought works on behalf of Black women, but does so in conjunction with other similar social justice projects." *Black Feminist Thought: Knowledge, Consciousness, and the Politics of Empowerment*, 2nd ed. (New York: Routledge, 2009), xi. For other examples of black feminist frameworks applied to premodern and ancient texts, see Kim F. Hall, *Things of Darkness: Economies of Race and Gender in Early Modern England* (Ithaca, NY: Cornell University Press, 1996), esp. 254–68, and "'These Bastard Signs of Fair': Literary Whiteness in Shakespeare's Sonnets," in *Post-Colonial Shakespeares*, ed. Ania Loomba and Martin Orkin (New York: Routledge, 1998); Nyasha Junior, *An Introduction to Womanist Biblical Interpretation* (Louisville, KY: Westminster John Knox Press, 2015).

14. Collins, *Black Feminist Thought*, 24–48.

of peasant women in the pastourelle, or unmarried urban working women in singlewomen's songs, or tapsters in clerk-and-serving-maid ballads—to produce violence that falls more heavily on some bodies than others. The medieval attitudes outlined in this book have shaped my life in profound and indelible ways, and I am committed to probing the roots of those attitudes by using "words as tools" to "hammer away at the past," to use Ahmed's evocative phrasing.[15] I use an intersectional framework, which Kimberlé Crenshaw names as "account[ing] for multiple grounds of identity when considering how the social world is constructed" and which Brittney Cooper calls "an account of power," to examine the violence inflicted on women disadvantaged by gender, class, age, profession, and unmarried status, including "wenches," brewhouse workers, milkmaids, and penniless peasant girls.[16]

I was always aware of race-based sexual violence's insistent presence in my family history, and I bring that keen awareness of violence's manifold forms to my analysis here. My great-great-great-grandfather was a plantation owner in Hearne, Texas. My great-great-great-grandmother was his kitchen slave. We do not know her name. He raped her, and she gave birth to my great-great-grandmother Kate.

When I was a child, my great-grandmother Rose told me stories about our foremothers. "Just call me G. G. Rose," she always said. "'Great-Grandma' makes me sound like an old lady." She told me about her grandmother Julia Fields Key, born to ex-slaves in East Texas five years after Emancipation. Julia gave birth to her oldest daughter, Mary, as an eighteen-year-old singlewoman in 1888. Mary was far lighter-skinned than Julia's next two daughters with her husband, and she carried her mother's last name, Fields, rather than any father's. "The white man got her," G. G. Rose would say matter-of-factly about Julia. Even as a child, I knew what she meant. On the 1900 federal census, Mary Jane Fields is twelve years old. Under "father's birthplace" the census taker writes, "don't know."[17] The record appears to give oblique confirmation of this family lore of interracial rape, histories of violation embedded within its dispassionate official language.

---

15. Ahmed, *Living a Feminist Life*, 33.

16. Sumi Cho, Kimberlé Williams Crenshaw, and Leslie McCall, "Toward a Field of Intersectionality Studies: Theory, Applications, and Praxis," *Signs: Journal of Women in Culture and Society* 38, no. 4 (2013); Brittney Cooper, "Intersectionality," in *The Oxford Handbook of Feminist Theory*, ed. Lisa Disch and Mary Hawkesworth (Oxford: Oxford University Press, 2016), 386; Kimberlé Crenshaw, "Mapping the Margins: Intersectionality, Identity Politics, and Violence against Women of Color," *Stanford Law Review* 43, no. 6 (1991): 1245. Valerie Smith discusses how an intersectional framework can be useful for analyzing texts that are not necessarily centered on black women, in *Not Just Race, Not Just Gender: Black Feminist Readings* (New York: Routledge, 1998), xiii–xxiii.

17. 1900 United States Federal Census, Enumeration District 0024, Sheet Number and Letter 12B, Household ID 261, Reference Number 62, GSU Film Number 1241630, Image Number 00132.

My foremothers' bodies were marked for violence because they were black women who lived in Texas during slavery and its aftermath. I seek to honor their experiences by probing the violence that came before and after them and fitting it into a larger context, by dissecting the ideologies that made it possible, and by honoring their survival. I analyze these medieval texts with an acute awareness of how the histories of various inequalities, including race and class, contribute directly to women's contemporary experiences of violence. Ahmed writes, "So much violence does not become visible or knowable or tangible. We have to fight to bring that violence to attention." She insists on the necessity of recognizing "a history that is now, a history that is still."[18] Black feminist activism has historically focused its energies on fighting violence against women made vulnerable by intersecting structural inequalities.[19] It sees speaking against sexual violence as imperative for social change; it emphasizes recognizing past injustices and putting the present into historical context; and it stresses the importance of survival, of resilience, of moving forward. I apply this framework, this project of probing histories of violence and paying special attention to intersecting inequalities, to my study of medieval obscene poetry about bodies and desires, focusing on different kinds of intersectionality throughout the book. I view these common experiences of violence as the basis for transhistorical feminist coalition building, as I show how shared harms and inequalities have the capacity to create affective connections across time among marginalized individuals.[20]

---

18. Ahmed, *Living a Feminist Life*, 210, 160.

19. On the centrality of sexual violence to black women's lives from the Middle Passage onward, see Danielle L. McGuire, *At the Dark End of the Street: Black Women, Rape, and Resistance—a New History of the Civil Rights Movement from Rosa Parks to the Rise of Black Power* (New York: Vintage Books, 2010); Sowande' M. Mustakeem, *Slavery at Sea: Sex, Sickness, and the Middle Passage* (Urbana: University of Illinois Press, 2016), esp. 82–90; Estelle B. Freedman, *Redefining Rape: Sexual Violence in the Era of Suffrage and Segregation* (Cambridge, MA: Harvard University Press, 2013), esp. 73–88, 104–24. Freedman explores how black woman activists like Ida B. Wells, Mary Church Terrell, Anna Julia Cooper, and Pauline Hopkins addressed black women's sexual vulnerability in *Redefining Rape*, 113–19; McGuire examines Rosa Parks's involvement in antirape activism in *At the Dark End of the Street*, 11–47; see also Collins, *Black Feminist Thought*, 29–37.

20. Crenshaw declares that "we [must] first recognize [that] the organized identity groups in which we find ourselves in are in fact coalitions, or at least potential coalitions waiting to be formed," and suggests that shared experiences of violence are one starting point for coalition building ("Mapping the Margins," 1299); similarly, Cathy J. Cohen "envision[s] a politics where one's relation to power, and not some homogenized identity, is privileged in determining one's political comrades," as she outlines "a politics where the *nonnormative* and *marginal* position . . . is the basis for progressive transformative coalition work" (emphasis in original). "Punks, Bulldaggers, and Welfare Queens: The Radical Potential of Queer Politics?" *GLQ: A Journal of Lesbian and Gay Studies* 3 (1997): 438; see also Patricia Hill Collins, "On Violence, Intersectionality and Transversal Politics," *Ethnic and Racial Studies* 40, no. 9 (2017). Dinshaw explores the possibilities of transhistorical queer coalition building and argues that "the medieval . . . becomes itself a resource for subject and community formation and materially engaged coalition building" around shared interests, in *Getting Medieval: Sexualities and*

I link my discussion of medieval texts with my own experience, bringing personal histories into conversation with literary and cultural ones, in line with Collins's assertion that "knowledge for knowledge's sake is not enough," as black feminist scholarship "must both be tied to Black women's lived experiences and aim to better those experiences in some fashion."[21] I have written this book inhabiting a black woman's body that moves through the world, that walks city blocks and sits on crowded buses. I cannot help but see the larger issues I write about—power, inequality, oppression, misogyny—at work in my everyday experiences, just as I cannot help but notice how the quotidian violations of inhabiting this body have structural causes and political import.[22] Lewd words yelled from moving cars. Men's hands brushing deliberately and repeatedly against my ass on a downtown street, grasping me around the rib cage just under my right breast as I sit at a bar, the brazenness of the violation shocking me into speechlessness even though I have tried to condition myself to expect it at any time. A man in a Philadelphia Eagles cap saying, "Holy shit, them titties bounce!" as he passes me on a busy street. Bodies much larger than mine who block my path until the last possible moment, just to show me that they can, before stepping out of the way and letting me pass.[23] I know that the things I write about from the past are not over. I know that with my body. And while fifteenth-century lyrics about fictional British women may not seem directly tied to the lived experience of a twenty-first-century woman of color, I am convinced that, by understanding how gender intersected with class, youth, and single status to render certain bodies inordinately vulnerable to violence, we can better understand how power operates and comprehend the urgent necessity of social change. I cannot read medieval pastourelles without thinking of my own experiences riding public transportation or walking down the street, nor can I read Middle English proverbs commanding young

---

Communities, Pre- and Postmodern (Durham, NC: Duke University Press, 1999), 21; also 181–82. I am grateful to Suzanne Edwards for suggesting the usefulness of feminist coalition building to my analysis.

21. Collins, Black Feminist Thought, 35; also Charlotte Pierce-Baker, Surviving the Silence: Black Women's Stories of Rape (New York: W. W. Norton, 1998), which powerfully combines academic scholarship with the author's personal trauma narrative. Ahmed notes how the "embodied experience of power provides the basis of knowledge" (Living a Feminist Life, 10), and Dinshaw effectively brings medieval scholarship into conversation with her own experience throughout How Soon Is Now? (32–33, 101–3, 123–27, 129–31, 151–52).

22. Renee Heberle, "The Personal Is Political," in Disch and Hawkesworth, Oxford Handbook of Feminist Theory; Patricia Hill Collins, Fighting Words: Black Women and the Search for Justice (Minneapolis: University of Minnesota Press, 1998), 46–76; Audre Lorde, "The Master's Tools Will Never Dismantle the Master's House," in Sister Outsider: Essays and Speeches (Berkeley, CA: Crossing Press, 1984).

23. These are all things that happened to me while I was writing this book in 2014 to 2017, in some cases, as I was walking to or from the coffee shop to write.

women to save their "cunte[s]" for marriage without recalling the evangelical vogue for adolescent virginity pledges at the turn of the twenty-first century.

I have chosen to embrace the immediacy generated by obscenity's potent charge across time, noting as Dinshaw does that "the present is ineluctably linked to other times, people, situations, worlds," while at the same time acknowledging the significant differences between then and now.[24] The resonances between past and present cannot be denied, as Suzanne M. Edwards demonstrates in her reading of rape survivor Emma Sulkowicz's yearlong mattress-carrying campaign at Columbia University in 2014–15 as part of a long history of viewing survival as "a shared experience of suffering," and as Nicole Nolan Sidhu explores in her discussion of the relationship between medieval obscenity and modern pornography.[25] These cross-temporal resonances have important implications for scholars and activists who seek a more sexually ethical future.

We are not accustomed to seeing the Middle Ages as intimately familiar, particularly when it comes to sexual violence, because the term "medieval" is frequently mobilized to signify especially egregious violence or inequality. In pieces such as the *Slate* article titled "North Carolina Fails to Fix Its Horrifying, Medieval Rape Law," decrying a law that prevents individuals from revoking consent to sexual contact once it has begun, "medieval" functions as shorthand for *backwards, other. We are not like that. We are not that bad.*[26]

We are more like that than we want to admit, and our impulse to demarcate present from past, to posit ourselves as "progressive," as *not-that*, has profound implications because it elides the continuities of violence and inequality over time and prevents us from seeing the full scope of the issue.[27] By arguing for the absolute alterity of the past and refusing to name sexual violence both past and present, we remain blind to the resonances between sexual cultures across time. And by refusing to call violence both past and present by its name, as Ahmed contends, "that violence is both concealed and reproduced."[28] We see this willful occlusion of histories of violence in newspaper headlines naming Sally Hemings as Thomas Jefferson's "enslaved mistress," with the fact

---

24. Dinshaw, *How Soon Is Now?*, 36.

25. Suzanne M. Edwards, *The Afterlives of Rape in Medieval English Literature* (New York: Palgrave Macmillan, 2016), 137–42; Nicole Nolan Sidhu, *Indecent Exposure: Gender, Politics, and Obscene Comedy in Middle English Literature* (Philadelphia: University of Pennsylvania Press, 2016), 233–36.

26. Mark Joseph Stern, "North Carolina Fails to Fix Its Horrifying, Medieval Rape Law," *Slate*, June 29, 2017, http://www.slate.com/blogs/outward/2017/06/29/north_carolina_fails_to_outlaw _rape_after_woman_revokes_consent.html. On the function of the medieval in contemporary culture as simultaneously "a period that produces our modernity, and as a period quite separate and different from our own," see Dinshaw, *Getting Medieval*, 200; see also 183–206.

27. Dinshaw, *How Soon Is Now?*, 19–20.

28. Ahmed, *Living a Feminist Life*, 72.

that she was fourteen years old when her forty-four-year-old owner began raping her camouflaged under the guise of illicit interracial romance.[29] We see it
when male comedians defend jokes about violence against women as "free
speech," and when literary critics characterize medieval rape poems as "amorous encounter[s]" and "lover's dialogues."[30] We do not want to believe that
the world is as violent as it is, that awful, inexplicable things can happen to
you even when you are not "asking for it" because we live in a deeply unequal
world. Ahmed writes, "Feminist ideas are what we come up with to make sense
of what persists."[31] *Obscene Pedagogies* is devoted to making sense of what persists, to recognizing how the past's violence lives on in the present.

At the same time that we need to trace the deep roots of violence and misogyny stretching back to the Middle Ages, I do not want to flatten the differences between then and now. I am aware that my search for a usable past in
these texts can be a dangerous endeavor because it risks collapsing the differences not only between past and present but also between fiction and reality.
I do not intend to suggest that the medieval and modern map seamlessly onto
each other, nor do I mean to elide the particularities of each, preferring instead to follow Dinshaw in using Donna Haraway's notion of "partial connection (not a full identification)" to argue for linkages without collapsing
differences.[32] And there are indeed differences. The centuries between the
Middle Ages and now have witnessed significant changes in the recognition
of sexual violence in its many forms. Estelle B. Freedman shows how U.S. activists in the generations after the Civil War successfully raised the age of

---

29. Krissah Thompson, "For Decades They Hid Jefferson's Mistress. Now Monticello Is Making
Room for Sally Hemings," *Washington Post*, February 19, 2017, https://www.washingtonpost.com
/lifestyle/style/for-decades-they-hid-jeffersons-mistress-now-monticello-is-making-room-for
-sally-hemings/2017/02/18/d410d660-f222-11e6-8d72-263470bf0401_story.html?tid= sm_tw&utm_
term=.071ee03b88fd. After public outcry, "Jefferson's Mistress" in the article title was updated to "Jefferson's Relationship with Her," although the original headline is still visible in the URL. See also
Michael Cottman, "Historians Uncover Slave Quarters of Jefferson's Enslaved Mistress Sally Hemings
at Monticello," *NBC News*, July 3, 2017, http://www.nbcnews.com/news/nbcblk/thomas-jefferson-s
-enslaved-mistress-sally-hemings-living-quarters-found-n771261; this title was later revised as "Historians Uncover Slave Quarters of Sally Hemings at Thomas Jefferson's Monticello." For more on Sally
Hemings and slavery's oft-elided legacy of rape, see Mia Bay, "Love, Sex, Slavery, and Sally Hemings,"
and Catherine Clinton, "Breaking the Silence: Sexual Hypocrisies from Thomas Jefferson to Strom
Thurmond," both in *Beyond Slavery: Overcoming Its Religious and Sexual Legacies*, ed. Bernadette J.
Brooten (New York: Palgrave Macmillan, 2010).

30. For a critique of the "free speech" argument applied to rape jokes, see Lindy West, *Shrill:
Memoirs of a Loud Woman* (New York: Hachette Books, 2016), 165–212. For these characterizations of
pastourelles, see *DIMEV* entries for 6851 and 2142.

31. Ahmed, *Living a Feminist Life*, 12.

32. Dinshaw, *Getting Medieval*, 14, 21; Donna Haraway, "Situated Knowledges: The Science Question in Feminism and the Privilege of Partial Perspective," in *The Feminist Standpoint Theory Reader:
Intellectual and Political Controversies*, ed. Sandra Harding (New York: Routledge, 2004), esp. 90.

consent, brought increased awareness to the sexual abuse of boys, and named marital rape as a problem, while Jody Raphael traces a recent growing awareness of the problem of acquaintance rape.[33] Susan Brownmiller's influential book *Against Our Will: Men, Women, and Rape* showed how rape is a widespread, transhistorical structural phenomenon keeping all women in fear of harm and argued that sexual violence is not a runaway expression of desire but is rather spurred by an urge to dominate and disempower.[34] By seeing this violence as systemic terrorism rather than individual trauma, scholars began to analyze the problem of "rape culture," teasing out the erroneous, widely held attitudes that allow sexual violence to continue by blaming victims and failing to hold perpetrators accountable, including seven key components of "rape myths"— "she asked for it," "it wasn't really rape," "he didn't mean to," "she wanted it," "she lied," "rape is a trivial event," and "rape is a deviant event"—and the frequent erasure of cisgender male and transgender victim-survivors from discussions of sexual violence.[35] Conversations about consent have shifted from *no means no* to *yes means yes*, and institutions ranging from colleges and universities to the state of California have adopted affirmative consent policies that define consent as, for example, "the communication of an affirmative, conscious and freely-made decision by each party to engage in agreed upon forms of sexual contact" and predicate it on "the presence of yes" rather than "the absence of no."[36] I am heartened by these changes, but they are not enough, as I show in my linking of rape culture in Chaucer's *Canterbury Tales* to a rape trial involving professional athletes in Wales, and in my analysis of the implications of Donald Trump's famous encouragement to "grab 'em by the pussy."

33. Freedman, *Redefining Rape*, 125–46, 168–90, 226–28. On the history of marital rape, see Rebecca M. Ryan, "The Sex Right: A Legal History of the Marital Rape Exemption," *Law and Social Inquiry* 20, no. 4 (1995); Jill Elaine Hasday, "Contest and Consent: A Legal History of Marital Rape," *California Law Review* 88, no. 5 (2000). On acquaintance rape, see Jody Raphael, *Rape Is Rape: How Denial, Distortion, and Victim-Blaming Are Fueling a Hidden Acquaintance Rape Crisis* (Chicago: Lawrence Hill Books, 2013); Freedman, *Redefining Rape*, 283–85.

34. Susan Brownmiller, *Against Our Will: Men, Women, and Rape* (New York: Fawcett Books, 1975). For a discussion of how Brownmiller's book shaped feminist approaches to rape, see Ann J. Cahill, *Rethinking Rape* (Ithaca, NY: Cornell University Press, 2001), 15–49.

35. Diana L. Payne, Kimberly A. Lonsway, and Louise F. Fitzgerald, "Rape Myth Acceptance: Exploration of Its Structure and Its Measurement Using the *Illinois Rape Myth Acceptance Scale*," *Journal of Research in Personality* 33, no. 1 (1999): esp. 37; Kate Harding, *Asking for It: The Alarming Rise of Rape Culture—and What We Can Do about It* (Boston: Di Capo, 2015), 22–25.

36. Washburn University (Topeka, KS), "Equal Opportunity and Non-Discrimination Policies," September 22, 2016, http://washburn.edu/statements-disclosures/equal-opportunity/Regulation%20and%20Procedure%20Final%20formatted%20BOR%20Approved_2015.pdf. See also Jaclyn Friedman and Jessica Valenti, eds., *Yes Means Yes! Visions of Female Sexual Power and a World without Rape* (Berkeley, CA: Seal Press, 2008).

As part of providing "an account of power" in these texts, I focus on recovering forgotten lyrics in women's voices and bringing them into the scholarly conversation. Since many of the texts I discuss have been overlooked by critics, I provide glossed editions in two appendices so that others can read and write about them. The voices from these pastourelles and "songs of lusty maidens" were sung by living women in alehouses, at village festivals, and among friends, and they have much to tell us about widespread cultural attitudes regarding violence, consent, desire, and pleasure. Noting how marginalized perspectives have been excluded from critical conversations and subsequently forgotten, Alice Walker writes, "It is our duty . . . to collect them again . . . if necessary, bone by bone."[37] While Walker is speaking specifically about African American writers, her sentiments apply to my project of gathering neglected voices from the past and placing them in dialogue with each other as well as with the present. I want to listen to the fictive voice of the rape survivor. I want to hear the tapster, the milkmaid, the servant girl far from home.

Reading the significance of long-ago fictional texts alongside contemporary realities is further complicated by the fact that many texts voiced by women were composed and copied by men. Matilda Tomaryn Bruckner argues that medieval woman's song is encoded with "double voicing," for these lyric voices are simultaneously "locate[d] . . . in the daily work and life cycle of real women who sing about and along with their experience" and "a literary convention written by men."[38] These voices sometimes speak in service of patriarchal interests or embody misogynist stereotypes of feminine duplicity and sexual voracity, like the woman who reminisces regretfully about her days as "a wanton wench / Of twelve yere of age."[39] E. Jane Burns names this "resistant doubled discourse" as "bodytalk" and argues it is "something that we as feminist readers can choose to hear" because "female voices, fashioned by a male author to represent misogynist fantasies of female corporeality, can also be heard to rewrite the tales in which they appear."[40] We hear this resistance when women's literary voices articulate protest against social stigma and vociferously challenge men who assault, mistreat, betray, or harass them.[41]

---

37. Alice Walker, *In Search of Our Mothers' Gardens: Womanist Prose* (New York: Harcourt, 1983), 92.

38. Matilda Tomaryn Bruckner, "Fictions of the Female Voice: The Woman Troubadours," in *Medieval Woman's Song: Cross-Cultural Approaches*, ed. Anne L. Klinck and Ann Marie Rasmussen (Philadelphia: University of Pennsylvania Press, 2002), 133.

39. I discuss these lines from *And I war a maydyn* in chapter 4.

40. E. Jane Burns, *Bodytalk: When Women Speak in Old French Literature* (Philadelphia: University of Pennsylvania Press, 1993), 4–7.

41. Anne L. Klinck notes that "repeatedly the woman's view [in medieval woman's song] is associated with protest against the assumptions and arrangements of men." *An Anthology of Ancient and Medieval Woman's Song* (New York: Palgrave Macmillan, 2004), 12.

"Spekyng Rybawdy": Obscenity in Late Medieval Britain

Due to centuries of scholarly embarrassment, study of medieval obscenity is only in its incipient stages despite the prevalence of obscene words and imagery in medieval culture, and its pedagogical dimensions have gone largely unaddressed.[42] Michael Camille explores how visual artworks like dragons wearing pink penis-hats, naked men exposing their gaping anuses, and nuns selecting plump penises from phallus-laden trees were often relegated to the margins—of manuscript pages, cathedral facades, and choir stalls—where liminality imbued them with a special kind of power even as it reinforced their taboo status.[43] Art historians note the survival of eight sexually explicit metal badges recovered from the banks of London's River Thames, including a fourteenth-century bronze vulva pendant whose labia are inscribed with the words *con por amours* (a pun on "as for love / cunt for love"); a large phallus inside an ornate tasseled purse, giving new meaning to the contemporary slang expression "bag of dicks"; and three ships filled with crews of phalluses.[44] They suggest that these badges functioned apotropaically, to "dispel evil, protect the wearer, bring good luck, and avert misfortune," much like the prominent phallus carvings meant to ward off the "evil eye" that were popular in Roman Britain.[45] In her exploration of obscene gender comedy, a popular discourse that deployed bawdy humor to dramatize domestic power struggles, Sidhu draws links between past and present, arguing that "medieval thinkers, artists,

---

42. Two important collections on the topic include Nicola McDonald, ed., *Medieval Obscenities* (York: York Medieval Press, 2006) and Jan Ziolkowski, ed., *Obscenity: Social Control and Artistic Creation in the European Middle Ages* (Leiden: Brill, 1998).

43. Michael Camille, *Image on the Edge: The Margins of Medieval Art* (London: Reaktion, 1992); see also Paul Hardwick, *English Medieval Misericords: The Margins of Meaning* (Woodbridge, UK: Boydell, 2011), esp. 85–109. Camille examines how obscene images were censored in manuscripts especially during the late fifteenth century, as when readers erased depictions of copulating couples from copies of Aristotle's *De generatione* and *Posterior Analytics*, in "Obscenity under Erasure: Censorship in Medieval Illuminated Manuscripts," in Ziolkowski, *Obscenity*, 151.

44. A. M. Koldeweij, "Lifting the Veil on Pilgrim Badges," in *Pilgrimage Explored*, ed. J. Stopford (York: York Medieval Press, 1999); Malcolm Jones, "Sex, Popular Beliefs, and Culture," in Evans, *Cultural History of Sexuality*, 142. I am grateful to Joseph Derosier for discussing the significance of *con por amours* with me.

45. A. M. Koldeweij, "A Barefaced *Roman de la Rose* (Paris, B.N., ms. fr., 25526) and Some Late Medieval Mass-Produced Badges of a Sexual Nature," in *Flanders in a European Perspective: Manuscript Illumination around 1400 in Flanders and Abroad*, ed. Maurits Smeyers and Bert Cardon (Leuven: Uitgeverij Peeters, 1995), 506. For Roman examples, such as the still visible phalluses carved into Hadrian's Wall at the Chesters Bridge Abutment and set in the courtyard paving of the Chesters Fort headquarters building in the late second century CE, see J. S. Johnson, *Chesters Roman Fort Northumberland* (London: English Heritage, 1990), 23–24, 28–30; Catherine Johns, *Sex or Symbol? Erotic Images of Greece and Rome* (London: Routledge, 1999).

and writers reveal a sense of taboo relating to sexual activity and lower body parts that is remarkably similar to that of the modern West."[46] Sidhu investigates the political implications of obscene gender comedy and explores how obscenity's mixing with laughter enabled "alternative ways of looking at the established order," whereas I examine obscenity's pedagogical currency in fabliaux, erotic songs, alewife poems, pastourelles, and insult battles, showing how it both authorizes and challenges sexual violence.[47]

I use "obscenity" to name "a word or expression that designates explicitly, possibly even with vulgarity, sex or a sexual part of the body, in a way that some at least are likely to find offensive."[48] The *Oxford English Dictionary* notes its etymological links to filth (*caenum*), ill omen, and perversity (*scaevus*) and defines it as "offensively indecent, lewdness," emphasizing its ties to illicit sexuality.[49] I focus on sexual obscenity rather than scatological or religious obscenity, although these categories sometimes overlap with one another.[50] Religious authors repeatedly underscore the distinction between licit and illicit sexual language, attesting to the existence of rules governing bawdy talk. St. Paul repeatedly forbids *turpitudo*, *scurrilitas*, and *turpem sermonem* (offensive, coarse, indecent, and foul speech), sins that medieval translators render in English as "filthe," "harlatrye," and "foul word[s]."[51] In *Handlyng Synne* (c. 1303–17), Robert Mannyng exhorts his readers to "speketh no fylthe oute of skore, / That noun outher synne tharfore" (speak no filth out of limits, / So that no other person sins as a result).[52] This prohibition invokes mutually understood rules for speaking of sex—"skore" means "a limit, boundary"—and cites obscenity's power as social and pedagogical: this forbidden "fylthe" teaches "outher[s]" how to sin.[53] Mannyng and his fellow religious

---

46. Sidhu, *Indecent Exposure*, 15.

47. Ibid., 229.

48. Simon Gaunt, "Obscene Hermeneutics in Troubadour Lyric," in McDonald, *Medieval Obscenities*, 85. John J. Honigmann defines it as "the expression, representation, or display . . . in certain contexts or situations, of something that is culturally regarded as shocking or repugnant," in "A Cultural Theory of Obscenity," *Journal of Criminal Psychopathology* 5 (1944): 716. Henderson defines it as "verbal reference to areas of human activity or parts of the human body that are protected by certain taboos agreed upon by prevailing social custom and subject to emotional aversion or inhibition" (*Maculate Muse*, 2).

49. *OED* s.v. "obscene" (adj.), 1; s.v. "obscenity" (n.), 1.

50. Caputi outlines these categories of sexual, scatological, and eschatological obscenity in *Voluptuous Yearnings*, 5. For a thoughtful discussion of obscenity's various definitions in antiquity and the Middle Ages, see Leslie Dunton-Downer, "Poetic Language and the Obscene," in Ziolkowski, *Obscenity*.

51. Ephesians 5:3–4 and Colossians 3:8; John Wyclif, *The Holy Bible, Containing the Old and New Testaments, with the Apocryphal Books*, ed. Josiah Forshall and Frederic Madden, 4 vols. (Oxford: Oxford University Press, 1850), 4:415, 434.

52. Robert Mannyng, *Robert of Brunne's "Handlyng Synne,"* ed. Frederick J. Furnivall, 2 vols., Early English Text Society, o.s., 119, 123 (London: Early English Text Society, 1901, 1903), 1:126, lines 3679–80.

53. *MED* s.v. "scor" (n.), (d).

authorities repeatedly prohibit verbal obscenity, known as *turpiloquium* (filthy speech) in Latin pastoral discourse and "spekyng rybawdy" in Middle English.[54] Understood as a sin of the tongue *and* the genitals, an act of both gluttony and lechery, "spekyng rybawdy" was believed to be part of the behavioral script leading to intercourse as well as its moral equivalent; thus, sexual words both lead to and substitute for sexual deeds.

In addition to its status as moral transgression, "spekyng rybawdy" was understood as a matter of "curtesie," inflected by social status and gender. In the *Canterbury Tales*, the Chaucer-narrator cautions readers about the bawdy content in the Miller's and Reeve's tales by warning, "The Millere is a cherl; / ye knowe wel this. / So was the Reve eek and othere mo, / And harlotrie they tolden bothe two" (I.3182–84).[55] He characterizes their speech as "harlotrie" and "cherles termes" (I.3917), drawing on the double valence of "cherl" denoting both status and decorum, as it means "any person not belonging to the nobility or clergy" as well as "a person lacking in refinement, learning, or morals."[56] "Harlotrie," derived from "harlot" (a vagabond, beggar), means both "ribald talk, obscenity, a dirty story" and "sexual immorality," blurring the distinction between sexual words and deeds and linking both to the speaker/doer's social status.[57]

Some of the rules governing obscenity are articulated clearly in medieval texts. Commenting on the relationship between gender, language, and taboo, the author of one late fourteenth-century anatomical treatise names the scrotum as "the balloc coddis" and says, "[by] wommen it is ycallid a purs for curtesie."[58] He adds, "men callen [the penis] a ters but for curtesie wymmen callen it a yerde."[59] Men use the explicit terms "ters" and "balloc coddis" for their own genitalia, whereas women are expected to use the multiply signifying "purs" and "yerde," which also meant "pouch" and "pole," out of "curtesie."[60] This expectation portrays genital naming as governed by the rules of gendered etiquette. This rule also reflects the link between language and signification governing the lexicon's politeness spectrum: words with a single, solely sexual meaning—"ters," "pintel," "cunte," "serd," "swyve," and "fuck"—

---

54. *MED* s.v. "ribaudi" (n.), (b): "obscenity, scurrility, bawdry; coarse speech; an obscene story"; *DMLBS* s.v. "*turpiloquium*" (n.): "foul or offensive speech."

55. *The Riverside Chaucer*, 3rd ed., ed. Larry D. Benson et al. (Boston: Houghton Mifflin, 1987). Text references are to fragment and lines in this edition.

56. *MED* s.v. "cherl" (n.), 1(a), 2(a).

57. *MED* s.v. "harlotrie" (n.), 1 and 2; s.v. "harlot" (n.), 1(a).

58. R. N. Mory, "A Medieval English Anatomy: MS Wellcome 564" (PhD diss., University of Michigan, 1977), 168.

59. Ibid., 166.

60. *MED* s.v. "purs" (n.), 1 and 4; s.v. "yerd" (n.[2]), 1–2 and 5; s.v. "courtesie" (n.), 2(a).

are more explicit, and therefore more transgressive, than their multiply signifying synonyms.

While some medieval texts include sexually explicit vocabulary, others
feature obscene metaphor or wordplay, as we see in riddles that describe
everyday objects in suggestive corporeal language and lyrics featuring erotic
wordplay meant to titillate and teach, such as forester songs centered on
the suggestive metaphors of arrows and spears and a marketplace dialogue
about the bawdy possibilities of sausage selling.[61] Gaunt claims that "sexual
metaphor . . . can indeed be as obscene as overt obscene language."[62] He
argues that this "kind of semantic indirection . . . may be more interesting,
perhaps more titillating than outright obscenity," since "obscene metaphors
sometimes seem to enable more outrageously detailed descriptions of sex
than the use of explicit sexual language."[63] Obscene metaphor is deployed for
erotic and misogynist purposes in texts like the pair of fifteenth-century
balades copied by John Shirley that describe men's pursuit of intercourse in detailed metaphorical terms as fishing and plowing, and John Lydgate's *My fayr
lady so fressh of hewe*, which uses the vocabulary of hunting, hawking, and
heraldry to describe his former lover's vulva.[64] I use "obscene" to designate
both explicit terms like "ters" and "swyve" and texts centered on richly suggestive sexual metaphor. In my chapters on pastourelles and "songs of wantonness," I analyze bawdy lyrics such as *My ladye hathe forsaken me, I have ben a
foster*, and *Let be wanton your busynes* alongside songs that are not necessarily
obscene but nonetheless center on sexuality, desire, and embodiment.

Except for those moments when they deploy obscenity deliberately for instructive purposes, religious authors name genitalia with vague, multivalent
terms specific to neither sex such as "privity," "thing," "shap," and "membres,"
with the occasional qualifiers "privy," "shameful," "shamefast," or "secree."
They do not use descriptors like "lang," "best," or "smale" that accompany

---

61. For these riddles, see Thomas G. Duncan, ed., *Medieval English Lyrics and Carols* (Cambridge:
D. S. Brewer, 2013), 286–87; for more on British traditions of obscene riddling stretching back to the
Exeter Book riddles, see Louise O. Vasvari, "Fowl Play in My Lady's Chamber: Textual Harassment of
a Middle English Pornithological Riddle and Visual Pun," in Ziolkowski, *Obscenity*.

62. Gaunt, "Obscene Hermeneutics," 95.

63. Ibid., 94–95.

64. *It is no right all other lustes to lese* (*DIMEV* 2739) and *Of alle the crafftes oute blessed be the ploughe*
(*DIMEV* 4138), in Julia Boffey and A. S. G. Edwards, "'Chaucer's Chronicle,' John Shirley, and the
Canon of Chaucer's Shorter Poems," *Studies in the Age of Chaucer* 20 (1998): 217–18; John Lydgate, *My
fayr lady so fressh of hewe* (*DIMEV* 3594), in *A Selection of the Minor Poems of Dan John Lydgate*, ed. James
Orchard Halliwell (London: C. Richards for the Percy Society, 1840), 199–205. Other lyrics centered
on obscene metaphor include *I have a newe gardyn* (orcharding and grafting), *At the northe ende of selver
whyte* (jousting), *It was a mayde of brenten ars* (milling), *Ther was a frier of order gray* (singing the lit-
urgy), and *We bern abowten no cattes skynnys* (peddling), all in Duncan, *Medieval English Lyrics and Carols*.

these terms in obscene verse. Similarly, they designate intercourse using verbs—"take," "lay by," "dele with," "go to," "know," "do," "meddle with," "have at do with," and "use"—that have a wide range of nonsexual meanings, and whose bawdy significance is secondary or tertiary. These decorous ways of naming sex are often periphrastic, requiring an additional preposition ("by," "with," or "together") plus a gendered pronoun. The more words required to name sexual activity, the greater the distance between the reader's mind and its physical reality, causing these constructions to serve as a linguistic prophylactic. Language functions as a clother and concealer because it renders a term polite by obscuring its bodily significance.

Middle English obscenities appear in texts from a variety of genres: gynecological treatises, proverbs, comic texts, erotic lyrics, and morality plays. Medical texts are the most straightforward, featuring terms like "yerd," "ters," "pintyl," and "cunte."[65] Henry Daniel's *Liber Uricrisiarum* (c. 1375–82) names the clitoris in Latin as *tentigo* before stating, "lewed [lay] folk call [it] the kykyre in the cont."[66] He links obscenity and vernacularity by claiming that the most straightforward terms are the ones used by uneducated layfolk. The verb "fuck" makes its enigmatic first appearance in the form of a man's name, "Roger Fuckebythenavele," in a 1310 Chester court roll.[67] Richard Coates argues that a 1373 Bristol charter referring to a field called "Fockynggrove" constitutes another early sexual usage of the term, suggesting that the location was known as a site for copulation.[68] "Fuck" next appears in macaronic verses in two late fifteenth-century schoolbooks, where both times it is copied with the synonymous "swyve."[69] Writers of antifeminist satires, fabliaux, didactic lyrics, and erotic songs use a range of genital obscenities—"cok" and "pilcok" for the penis, "tikeltaylles" (lascivious vulvas) and "fikel flaptaills" (fickle

---

65. For "yerd," see Mory, "Anatomy," 155, 164, 165, and elsewhere; Alexandra Barratt, ed., *The Knowing of Woman's Kind in Childing* (Turnhout, Belgium: Brepols, 2002), 47, 76; Joanne Jasin, "A Critical Edition of the Middle English *Liber Uricrisiarum* in Wellcome MS 225" (PhD diss., Tulane University, 1983), 75, 159, 292, and elsewhere. For "ters," see Mory, "Anatomy," 166, 167, and elsewhere. For "pintyl," see Jasin, "Liber Uricrisiarum," 48, 49; Barratt, *Knowing*, 46. For "cunte," see Jasin, "Liber Uricrisiarum," 293; Barratt, *Knowing*, 48.

66. Jasin, "Liber Uricrisiarum," 293; *MED* s.v. "kekir" (n.), (a); *DMLBS* s.v. "tentigo" (n.), 1c.

67. This unusual surname was recently discovered by Paul Booth. "An Early Fourteenth-Century Use of the F-Word in Cheshire, 1310–11," *Transactions of the Historic Society of Lancashire and Cheshire* 164 (2015).

68. Richard Coates, "*Fockynggroue* in Bristol," *Notes and Queries* 54, no. 4 (2007).

69. "Fuck" and "swyve" are copied in verses alongside each other in BL MS Harley 3362 (c. 1475), which I discuss below, and in NLW MS Peniarth 356B (1460s–80s), folio 149v, a school notebook owned by Thomas Pennant, who began to copy the manuscript in his grammar school days and later became abbot of Basingwerk Abbey, a Cistercian foundation in North Wales. For an early sixteenth-century occurrence of "fuck," see Edward Wilson, "A 'Damned F . . . in Abbot' in 1528: The Earliest English Example of a Four-Letter Word," *Notes and Queries* 40, no. 1 (1993).

floppy-vulvas) for women—to vilify female desire, mourn lost virility, and teach detailed scripts for sexual conduct.[70] Obscenities were used to amuse and entertain readers, as in one riddle that designates "a pintle of 21 year" as "the best thing in all the land."[71] Speakers deploy obscenity to emphasize their own sexual desirability, as in one lyric whose male speaker boasts that his "tente of xv ynche" (fifteen-inch rod) goes "by-tuynne my lady thyes" (between my lady's thighs) (21, 26).[72] Obscenity could humiliate men for failure to maintain marital dominance, claiming that wives "use wele the lecheres craft / With rubyng of ther toute [ass]" when their spouses are away; it disparaged women, as in a carol claiming they are "of ther ars evyn ryght brytyll" (completely fickle with their vulvas); and it critiqued clerical misconduct, as in one macaronic carol that concludes, "Thus the fryer lyke a pretty man . . . Ofte rokkyd the Nonnys Quoniam [vulva]" (39, 40).[73] Sidhu argues that medieval obscenity differs from contemporary obscenity in the way that it functioned to uphold the established order as well as to challenge it. We see this multivalence when women exclaim, "Now ye speke of a tarse!" and "Here is a pyntell of a fayre lenghte!" to their friends in *A Talk of Ten Wives on Their Husbands' Ware* (c. 1453–1500), an "alewife poem" whose obscenity reinforces misogynous stereotypes of women as inherently foulmouthed and transgressive at the same time that it illuminates the positive possibilities of women gathering for a frank discussion of pleasures.[74]

One way we can understand which Middle English words were viewed as taboo is by seeing what terms are altered, encoded, or replaced in manuscripts, using codicology to shed light on how medieval scribes and readers understood the obscene.[75] The obscenity that scribes most frequently censor is "swyve."

---

70. *I have a gentil cok* (c. 1425), in Duncan, *Medieval English Lyrics and Carols*, 177–78; *Elde makith me geld* (DIMEV 1183), in Thorlac Turville-Petre, ed., *The Texts of BL MS Harley 913, "The Kildare Manuscript"* (Oxford: Oxford University Press for the Early English Text Society, 2015), 74–76; John Lydgate, *Prohemy of a Mariage Betwixt an Olde Man and a Yonge Wife* (c. 1440–60), in Eve Salisbury, ed., *The Trials and Joys of Marriage* (Kalamazoo, MI: Medieval Institute Publications, 2002), 103–9, line 109; *The Tale of Beryn*, in John M. Bowers, ed., *The Canterbury Tales: Fifteenth-Century Continuations and Additions* (Kalamazoo, MI: Medieval Institute Publications, 1992), 55–196, line 1283.

71. CUL MS Dd.5.75, fol. 63r.

72. *May no man slepe in youre halle* (c. 1425), in Duncan, *Medieval English Lyrics and Carols*, 286; DIMEV 3453.

73. *Sir Corneus (DIMEV 382)*, in Melissa M. Furrow, ed., *Ten Bourdes* (Kalamazoo, MI: Medieval Institute Publications, 2013), 118–29, lines 119–20; *Stel is gud, I sey no odur* (DIMEV 5034), in Richard Leighton Greene, ed., *Early English Carols*, 2nd ed. (Oxford: Clarendon Press, 1977), 236, line 13; *Ther was a frier of order gray* (c. 1500, DIMEV 5593), in Duncan, *Medieval English Lyrics and Carols*, 304–5.

74. Sidhu, *Indecent Exposure*, 26–29; *A Talk of Ten Wives on Their Husbands' Ware* (DIMEV 3073), in Salisbury, *Trials and Joys of Marriage*, lines 58, 106.

75. Daniel Wakelin examines scribes' choices to correct as they copy, and Fiona Somerset notes how a copyist or reader may alter a text "to remove something offensive to himself," "whether from affront, disgust, or some other more personal motive." Daniel Wakelin, *Scribal Correction and Literary*

In numerous fifteenth-century manuscripts of the *Canterbury Tales*, copyists replace it with more decorous alternatives like "pleyed," "served," "dight," and "dide."[76] In other cases, readers have scraped the offending word from the parchment page with knives. Some obscenities were written in code, which both confirms their taboo status and restricts their legibility to an educated male audience. In his notebook filled with misogynist proverbs, Latin grammatical exercises, and didactic verses on masculine comportment, one university student copied a macaronic anticlerical poem accusing the Carmelite friars of preying on local wives: they "gxddbov xxkxzt pg imf k" (fuck the wivys of Heli [Ely]) and "txxkxzv nfookt xxzxkt" (swivyt mennis wyvis), he writes.[77] He copies these phrases—and only these—in code, using a popular scholastic system of alphabetic encryption. This use of code to conceal obscenity while still enjoying its transgressive pleasures illuminates obscenity's role as both tantalizing and forbidden. These strategic acts of substitution and encoding illustrate which words were considered to be obscene, and they show how scribes responded to taboo speech.

I focus on obscenity in fourteenth- through late sixteenth-century England and Scotland, reading across periodization boundaries and national borders in order to explore the full breadth of a cultural tradition rich in obscenity, misogyny, and bawdy linguistic innovation. In the generations after the Black Death in 1348–50, women's increased geographical mobility, prominence in the workforce, and earning power was paralleled by a rise in virulent misogyny. We see the literary effects of these historical shifts, for obscenity functioned to assert female desire using the language of the marketplace as well as to authorize violence against young, poor, and working singlewomen.[78]

Craft: English Manuscripts 1375–1510 (Cambridge: Cambridge University Press, 2014), 70; Fiona Somerset, "Censorship" in *The Production of Books in England 1350–1500*, ed. Alexandra Gillespie and Daniel Wakelin (Cambridge: Cambridge University Press, 2011), esp. 257, 255.

76. In BL MS Harley 7333 (c. 1425–75), a manuscript of the *Canterbury Tales* produced by Augustinian canons at St. Mary de Pratis Abbey in Leicester, the monastic scribes have substituted more decorous terms for "swyve."

77. *Flen flyys and freris* (DIMEV 1324), in BL MS Harley 3362 (c. 1450–75), fol. 24r. The first four lines only are copied onto a damaged folio in Oxford, Bodleian Library, MS Digby 196, fol. 196v. The poem is printed, with some errors and omissions, in Thomas Wright and James Orchard Halliwell, eds., *Reliquiae Antiquae: Scraps from Ancient Manuscripts*, 2 vols. (London: William Pickering, 1841–43), 1:91–92. This passage is discussed briefly by Coates, "*Fockynggroue* in Bristol," 374; Mohr, *Holy Shit*, 151–53; and Jesse Sheidlower, *The F-Word*, 3rd ed. (Oxford: Oxford University Press, 2009), 83.

78. I explore these historical changes and their literary implications in chapter 4. In his index of misogynist literature until 1568, Francis Lee Utley notes that 250 of 400 pieces come from 1500–1568, as literary antifeminism gathered steam over the course of the fifteenth century before reaching its zenith at the turn of the sixteenth. Francis Lee Utley, *The Crooked Rib: An Analytical Index to the Argument about Women in English and Scots Literature to the End of the Year 1568* (Columbus: Ohio State University Press, 1944; repr., New York: Octagon Books, 1970), 64.

Many of these late medieval textual trends continued into the sixteenth century, as evidenced by the ongoing popularity of genres like the alewife poem.[79] Manuscript culture's survival in the age of print enabled obscene texts to be circulated far from the printer's censoring eye, and medieval lyrics continued to be copied in sixteenth-century manuscript anthologies and printed in song collections.[80] I read Scottish and English poetry together, since these centuries witnessed both constant border warfare and active literary exchange between the two countries.[81]

Obscene Pedagogies in Late Medieval Britain

I argue that we can find systematic approaches to learning about sexuality in texts associated with medieval academic institutions—poems copied in scholars' notebooks, or verse exchanges that mimic scholarly disputations—as well as in genres and discourses not typically associated with the classroom, such as pastourelles or erotic carols performed by groups of women.[82] I treat violence prevention and sexuality education as two sides of the same coin, following Moira Carmody in analyzing "violence prevention strategies . . . inside

---

79. This genre first appears in the latter half of the fifteenth century with *A Talk of Ten Wives on Their Husbands' Ware* (1453–1500), and it continues into the late seventeenth century with the broadside ballad *The Gossips Meeting, Or The merry Market-Women of Taunton* (London: For F. Coles, T. Vere, J. Wright, and J. Clarke, 1674).

80. The three pastourelles copied into the Welles Anthology (1522–35) likely date from the late fifteenth century, and at least one of the lyrics in Bodleian MS Ashmole 176 (c. 1525–50), *Come over the borne bessye*, first appears in the fifteenth century. Joshua Eckhardt discusses how early modern manuscript culture facilitated the circulation of obscene lyrics in *Manuscript Verse Collectors and the Politics of Anti-Courtly Love Poetry* (Oxford: Oxford University Press, 2009).

81. Priscilla Bawcutt explores the circulation of Scottish texts in England in "Crossing the Border: Scottish Poetry and English Readers in the Sixteenth Century," in *The Rose and the Thistle: Essays on the Culture of Late Medieval and Renaissance Scotland*, ed. Sally Mapstone and Juliette Wood (East Linton, UK: Tuckwell, 1998); Louise O. Fradenburg examines Chaucer's reception in Scotland in "The Scottish Chaucer," in *Writing after Chaucer: Essential Readings in Chaucer and the Fifteenth Century*, ed. Daniel J. Pinti (New York: Garland, 1998); also Julia Boffey and A. S. G. Edwards, "Bodleian MS Arch. Selden.B.24 and the 'Scotticization' of Middle English Verse," in *Rewriting Chaucer: Culture, Authority, and the Idea of the Authentic Text, 1400–1602*, ed. Barbara Kline and Thomas Prendergast (Columbus: Ohio State University Press, 1999). Antony J. Hasler discusses fifteenth- and sixteenth-century English and Scottish court poetry together in *Court Poetry in Late Medieval England and Scotland: Allegories of Authority* (Cambridge: Cambridge University Press, 2011), and Susan E. Phillips analyzes William Dunbar's *Tretis of the Tua Marit Wemen and the Wedo* alongside Chaucer's *Shipman's Tale* and *Wife of Bath's Prologue* in *Transforming Talk: The Problem with Gossip in Late Medieval England* (University Park: Pennsylvania State University Press, 2007), 119–46.

82. I use Rita Copeland's definition of "pedagogy" as "a systematic approach to learning and an understanding of the conditions of learning." Rita Copeland, *Pedagogy, Intellectuals, and Dissent in the Later Middle Ages: Lollardy and Ideas of Learning* (Cambridge: Cambridge University Press, 2001), 8.

a sexual ethics framework that values pleasure at the same time as it acknowledges danger," since many individuals' experiences, in the Middle Ages as well as now, entail intimacy, desire, fulfillment, pleasure, and "varying degrees of pressure, coercion, and sexual assault."[83] Historians have examined systems of sex education both in and out of school, and their work demonstrates how we can look to the past for surprisingly progressive educational paradigms, such as the inclusive, straightforward, accessible sex education programs that Robin E. Jensen traces in the late nineteenth- and early twentieth-century United States.[84]

While they do not discuss sexual education as such, scholars note the pedagogical potential of medieval mother-daughter conduct texts, a popular genre that stages mothers teaching their daughters strategies for avoiding rape and educating them on the importance of maintaining a chaste reputation.[85] These mothers echo some of the lessons that young women are taught in obscene pastourelles and pregnancy laments, and their female-voiced pedagogy is tied to the prominence of the woman counsellor in English poetry during the final decades of the fourteenth century.[86] Other texts stage peer education, a popular model for sexual health pedagogy and antiviolence education in our own time.[87] Kathryn Milburn claims that formalized peer education initiatives

---

83. Moira Carmody, *Sex, Ethics, and Young People* (New York: Palgrave Macmillan, 2015), 5.

84. Robin E. Jensen, *Dirty Words: The Rhetoric of Public Sexual Education, 1870–1924* (Urbana: University of Illinois Press, 2010). Other histories of sexual education include Susan K. Freeman, *Sex Goes to School: Girls and Sexual Education before the 1960s* (Urbana: University of Illinois Press, 2008); Alexandra M. Lord, *Condom Nation: The U.S. Government's Sex Education Campaign from World War I to the Internet* (Baltimore: Johns Hopkins University Press, 2010); Kristin Luker, *When Sex Goes to School: Warring Views on Sex—and Sex Education—since the Sixties* (New York: W. W. Norton, 2006); James Grantham Turner, *Schooling Sex: Libertine Literature and Erotic Education in Italy, France, and England, 1534–1685* (Oxford: Oxford University Press, 2003); Jonathan Zimmerman, *Too Hot to Handle: A Global History of Sexual Education* (Princeton, NJ: Princeton University Press, 2015).

85. Alexandra Barratt, "English Translations of Didactic Literature for Women to 1550," in *What Nature Does Not Teach: Didactic Literature in the Medieval and Early-Modern Periods*, ed. Juanita Feros Ruys (Turnhout, Belgium: Brepols, 2008); Judith M. Bennett, "Ventriloquisms: When Maidens Speak in Middle English Songs, c. 1330–1500," in Klinck and Rasmussen, *Medieval Woman's Song*; Felicity Riddy, "Mother Knows Best: Reading Social Change in a Conduct Text," *Speculum* 71, no. 1 (1996); Myra J. Seaman, "Late Medieval Conduct Literature," in *The History of British Women's Writing, 700–1500*, vol. 1, ed. Liz Herbert McAvoy and Diane Watt (New York: Palgrave Macmillan, 2012).

86. Misty Schieberle, *Feminized Counsel and the Literature of Advice in England, 1380–1500* (Turnhout, Belgium: Brepols, 2014).

87. Louisa Allen, *Young People and Sexuality Education: Key Debates* (New York: Palgrave Macmillan, 2011), 107–31; Claire Maxwell, "The Prevention of Sexual Violence in Schools: Developing Some Theoretical Starting Points," in Henry and Powell, *Preventing Sexual Violence*, 114–17; Gobika Sriranganathan et al., "Peer Sexual Health Education: Interventions for Effective Program Evaluation," *Health Education Journal* 71, no. 1 (2010); Wai Han Sun et al., "Assessing Participation and Effectiveness of the Peer-Led Approach in Youth Sexual Health Education: Systematic Review and Meta-Analysis in More Developed Countries," *Journal of Sex Research* 55, no. 1 (2018). Planned Parenthood NYC has an

build on long-standing informal practices of "same sex peers [serving as] the predominant source of adolescents' information about sexuality," and she argues that this model of reciprocal knowledge transmission increases the persuasiveness of the message.[88] This process of knowledge building among peers is central to texts like *The Incestuous Daughter* (1480–1510), a didactic verse exemplum about a young woman who seduces her father, slits his throat, steals his treasure, and uses the money to open schools for teaching promiscuity to her peers: "All the women that wold be folys, / Fast thei com unto hyr scolys," the narrator says, framing the process of learning transgressive sexuality as a same-sex endeavor.[89]

Medieval texts present obscenity as educational in a variety of ways: preachers use bawdy exempla and tales about illicit sexual speech to dissuade their congregants from sin; the grammar curriculum relies on lurid material to keep schoolboys' attention; and advice poems use explicit genital terminology to teach young men about the dangers of sexual overindulgence. Even obscene comic texts frame themselves as possessing pedagogical import, like *Sir Corneus* (c. 1480–1510), whose narrator addresses "All that wyll of solas lere" (All who want to learn about merry entertainment) with his tale about cuckoldry (1). More recently, scholars have shown how pornography functions as education for young people who seek it out as a source of knowledge.[90] It can be especially instructive for queer youth whose educational needs are not served by many school curriculums, although some note its negative effects on heterosexual young people, particularly men, and warn that it teaches its consumers to "eroticize inequality."[91]

Clerics and church artists used verbal and visual obscenity for instructive purposes to encourage compliance with the Church's sexual prohibitions and to steer men toward clerical occupations by eliciting shame and disgust. Scholars suggest that the carvings that adorned countless churches in the British

award-winning program of teenage peer educators who conduct free interactive workshops in schools and community organizations.

88. Kathryn Milburn, "A Critical Review of Peer Education with Young People with Special Reference to Sexual Health," *Health Education Research* 10, no. 4 (1995): 415, 410.

89. *The Incestuous Daughter*, in George Shuffelton, ed., *Codex Ashmole 61: A Compilation of Popular Middle English Verse* (Kalamazoo, MI: Medieval Institute Publications, 2008), 180–85, lines 157–58. See also the 1395 legal testimony by transgender sex worker Eleanor Rykener, who uses the pedagogical verb *docere* (to teach, instruct) when stating that "Anna, meretrix quondam cuiusdam famuli domini Thome Blount, primo docuit ipsum vitium detestabile modo muliebri exercere" (Anna, a whore to a certain servant in the household of Thomas Blount, first taught them to practice that detestable vice in the manner of a woman). David Lorenzo Boyd and Ruth Mazo Karras, "The Interrogation of a Male Transvestite Prostitute in Fourteenth-Century London," *GLQ* 1, no. 4 (1995): 461.

90. Louisa Allen, "'Looking at the Real Thing': Young Men, Pornography, and Sexuality Education," *Discourse* 27, no. 1 (2006).

91. Kath Albury, "Porn *and* Sex Education, Porn *as* Sex Education," *Porn Studies* 1, nos. 1–2 (2014).

Isles of bald, naked old women exhibiting oversized vulvae served as fertility charms, warnings against sex, or protections against the evil eye, teaching viewers to revere or revile women's genitalia.[92] In instructing their audiences to refrain from "spekyng rybawdy," pastoral writers inadvertently underscore obscenity's social power, as Sidhu notes how preachers used bawdy comic stories to illustrate moral lessons.[93] One exemplum from *An Alphabet of Tales* (c. 1450) features a monk who is incited to masturbate after "privalie" (secretly) devouring a hot fritter as he carries the heaping platter to the refectory. The tale is ostensibly meant to illustrate how gluttony leads to other sins, but it spares no detail in describing the monk's transgression: "he was strekyn with a luste of his flessch, at he laburd hym selfe in such form as he did never befor, unto so muche, at with his awn hand fretyng he had a pollucion of his sede" (he was so stricken with a lust of his flesh that he did something that he never had done before, to such an extent that he made himself ejaculate with the furious rubbing of his own hand).[94] In another popular tale, which appears in *Handlyng Synne* and twice in Geoffroy de La Tour-Landry's *Book of the Knight of the Tower* (trans. 1484), a married couple has sex in a church, only to find themselves joined fast at the genitals as punishment for their sacrilege: "They myghte no more be broghte a-sondre," writes Mannyng, "Than dog and bych that men on wondre."[95] These tales illustrate how obscenity was mobilized in service of the church to dissuade individuals from sin, its vivid detail entertaining audiences while imprinting moral lessons in their minds.

Religious texts teach the destructive effects of "spekyng rybawdy" on the bodies of its speakers and listeners through exempla in which the tellers of obscene tales are punished with dismemberment and damnation. These narratives underscore obscenity's social power by representing it as a tool of peer education. One popular tale from Gregory the Great's *Dialogues* features a

---

92. Juliette Dor, "The Sheela-na-gig: An Incongruous Sign of Sexual Purity?" in *Medieval Virginities*, ed. Anke Bernau, Ruth Evans, and Sarah Salih (Cardiff: University of Wales Press, 2003); Barbara Freitag, *Sheela-na-gigs: Unravelling an Enigma* (New York: Routledge, 2004); Georgia M. Rhoades, "Decoding the Sheela-na-gig," *Feminist Formations* 22, no. 2 (2010).

93. Sidhu, *Indecent Exposure*, 6, 11.

94. Mary Macleod Banks, ed., *An Alphabet of Tales*, pt. 1, 2, Early English Text Society, o.s., 126, 127 (London: Kegan Paul, Trench, Trübner, 1904–1905), 1:238. An unprinted Latin version survives in the *Alphabetum narrationum* in BL MS Harley 268 (1350–1400), fol. 123v.

95. Mannyng, *Handlyng Synne*, 2:281–82, lines 8951–52. In BL MS Harley 1701 (c. 1380), fol. 59v, an offended reader scratched out this couplet so vehemently that they left a hole in the parchment. *The Book of the Knight of the Tower*, translated and printed by William Caxton in 1484, contains two versions of the exemplum. Geoffroy de La Tour-Landry, *The Book of the Knight of the Tower*, ed. M. Y. Offord, Early English Text Society, s.s., 2 (London: Oxford University Press, 1971), 51–52. Dyan Elliott examines the tale's many versions in "Sex in Holy Places: An Exploration of a Medieval Anxiety," *Journal of Women's History* 6, no. 3 (1994).

chaste but foulmouthed nun who corrupts her sisters with her ribald talk.[96] Religious authors emphasize the instructive effect of the nun's speech on her peers, who are named as her "susteres" and "felawys" to highlight their same-sex bond.[97] Mannyng writes, "She made many of here felawys / Thenke on synne for her sawys" (1553–54). Echoing Mankind's assessment of Gluttony's obscene lesson in *The Castle of Perseverance*, Mannyng names the nun's words using the didactic noun "sawys," and he notes that they "made" her companions "thenke" about sex in transgressive ways. After her death, she is punished for her "foule wurdes" (1592) by having her corpse sawn in half by demons who drag her soul to hell. This tale, which also appears in John Mirk's *Festial*, Peter Idley's *Instructions to His Son*, *An Alphabet of Tales*, and *Jacob's Well*, demonstrates acute clerical anxiety over obscenity's instructive potential.

Obscene material occupied a prominent place in pedagogical texts used by medieval schoolboys. Marjorie Curry Woods notes how "sexual imagery is omnipresent in the texts used to teach Latin to medieval boys, and rape is a common narrative vehicle in these texts."[98] She argues that the rape narratives popular in the classroom curriculum required young boys to identify with the perspective of both perpetrator and victim as they underwent the process of learning both Latin and masculinity, and she explores how these texts teach myths like "rape is seduction gone wrong" and "women secretly want to be raped."[99] Mary Carruthers examines the centrality of graphic violent and sexual imagery to medieval memory aids and argues that obscenity's "shock value is useful for the specific mental tasks involved in memory work" because it has the power "to rivet the attention" and imprint information on the mind through its deviation from acceptable norms.[100] But obscene pedagogy was not restricted to sermons or the classroom curriculum, for numerous didactic

---

96. *Gregorii magni dialogi*, ed. Umberto Moricca, 2 vols. (Rome: Forzani e C. Tipografi del Senato, 1924), 1:263.

97. Middle English versions of the tale occur in Banks, *Alphabet of Tales*, 1:304–5; Mannyng, *Handlyng Synne*, 1:56–57, lines 1547–600; John Mirk, *John Mirk's Festial, Edited from British Library MS Cotton Claudius A.II*, ed. Susan Powell, 2 vols., Early English Text Society, o.s., 334, 335 (Oxford: Oxford University Press for Early English Text Society, 2009, 2011), 1:85.

98. Marjorie Curry Woods, "Rape and the Pedagogical Rhetoric of Sexual Violence," in *Criticism and Dissent in the Middle Ages*, ed. Rita Copeland (Cambridge: Cambridge University Press, 1996), 58; also Woods, *Classroom Commentaries: Teaching the "Poetria nova" across Medieval and Renaissance Europe* (Columbus: Ohio State University Press, 2010), 60–65. For more on the role of racy or sexually violent material in the grammar school curriculum, see Derek G. Neal, *The Masculine Self in Late Medieval England* (Chicago: University of Chicago Press, 2008), 158–59; Ruth Mazo Karras, *From Boys to Men: Formations of Masculinity in Late Medieval Europe* (Philadelphia: University of Pennsylvania Press, 2003), 77–78.

99. Woods, "Rape and Pedagogical Rhetoric," 61–62.

100. Mary Carruthers, *The Book of Memory: A Study of Memory in Medieval Culture*, 2nd ed. (Cambridge: Cambridge University Press, 2008), 163–72, esp. 171.

poetic genres—including antimarriage warnings, advice poems, and moral lyrics—deploy it to dissuade men from marriage and to encourage women to be chaste. Obscenity reinforces the misogynous commonplace that women have no control over their appetites in *Al es bot a fantom* (c. 1440–50), whose speaker invokes stereotypes of women's lasciviousness to warn his fellow men against bequeathing their possessions to their wives: he claims that a new widow "wil take hir a yong swayn that wil mai hire swyfe" (will take herself a young manservant who may fuck her well).[101] In another moment of instructive misogyny, the speaker of a fifteenth-century antimarriage carol warns his fellow "man" that "madenys . . . be bothe fals and fekyl, / And under the tayl they ben ful tekyl" (maidens are both deceitful and faithless, / And under the vulva they are very lascivious).[102] He uses "tayl" to impart his lesson that maidens are untrustworthy and incontinent, and he pairs it with the suggestive adjective "tikel" to paint their vulvas as overly sensitive to stimulation and itching for delight.[103] In other lyrics, obscenity teaches that women say "no" to sex when they really mean "yes": according to one fifteenth-century debate poem, "A woman off hauntyng moode, / Blythly sche wyll be swyvyd" (A woman who appears scornful / Will happily be fucked).[104]

I divide my study of medieval obscene pedagogy into five chapters. The first two explore how men in same-sex contexts use obscenity to denigrate women and perpetuate rape culture. Sometimes this paradigm taught men to have as much sex as possible and to ignore women's nonconsent for the purpose of producing narratives for their peer group, as in the code of "felawe masculinity" embraced by a group of pilgrims in Chaucer's *Canterbury Tales* that I discuss in chapter 1. I show how "swyve" creates gendered pedagogical community and teaches men that sexual aggression is both necessary and laudatory. Other times, as I show in chapter 2's discussion of insult poetry in the sixteenth-century Scottish court, men use obscene misogyny to teach one another to refrain from intercourse altogether.

Male-voiced obscenity could be deployed to regulate women's sexual expression, as we see in the thirteenth-century proverb cautioning maidens, "Yeve thi cunte to cunnig and crave affeit wedding, quod Hending" (Give your cunt to the penis and lose out on marriage, said Hending).[105] In contrast, female

---

101. *Al es bot a fantom* (*DIMEV* 339), in Joseph Hall, "Short Pieces from MS Cotton Galba E.ix," *Englische Studien* 21 (1895): 201–4, line 60.

102. *Man bewar of thin wowyng* (*DIMEV* 3172), in Greene, *Early English Carols*, 239–40, lines 1, 15–17.

103. *MED* s.v. "tikel" (adj.).

104. *The Clerk and the Nightingale II* (*DIMEV* 500), in John W. Conlee, ed., *Middle English Debate Poetry: A Critical Anthology* (East Lansing, MI: Colleagues Press, 1991), 272–77, lines 1–2.

105. Hermann Vernhagan, "Zu den sprichwörtern Hending's," *Anglia* 4 (1881): 190.

speakers use obscenity to teach their peers how to navigate the hazards of living as embodied subjects in a patriarchal world. They offer strategies for survival, warnings regarding masculine aggression, models for erotic negotiation, and counsel for obtaining pleasure. In my third chapter, I move from exploring obscenity's role among men to focus on its relationship to sexual violence in pastourelles, as I show how women's obscenity has the potential to disrupt rape narratives and educate audiences about consent and power. I continue this focus on the relationship between obscene pedagogy and women's voices in my fourth and fifth chapters. In chapter 4, I show how alewife poems and singlewomen's erotic songs stage models of peer education in which women teach their peers how to pursue pleasure, minimize risk, and negotiate for satisfaction. Finally, in chapter 5, I explore how scribal practices in sixteenth-century lyric miscellanies can incite audiences' empathy for educational purposes. Overall, I argue that the obscene, through its transgressive power, has the capacity to teach individuals new ways of understanding their own as well as others' embodied subjectivities.

While obscenity can be funny, titillating, scandalous, or upsetting, I remain most compelled by its capacity to rivet in order to educate and to seize listeners' attention through its transgression of the boundaries of acceptable speech. In a world where at least one in five American women and one in seventy-one American men are victims of rape in their lifetimes, and where gender and sexuality are policed through violence and harassment, we need more than ever to recognize, and to harness, the power of obscenity to teach one another different ways of conceptualizing sex and consent and to engender new ways of thinking about violence, desire, power, and pleasure.

CHAPTER 1

"Felawe Masculinity"

Teaching Rape Culture in Chaucer's *Canterbury Tales*

On a warm May night in Rhyl, a run-down seaside town in North Wales, a nineteen-year-old waitress goes out dancing with her friends after her shift is over. In an hour and a half, she drinks two large glasses of wine, four double vodka and lemonades, and a shot of Sambuca. She remembers dancing, then holding a pizza box, then nothing.[1] Surveillance footage shows her staggering into a late-night fast-food takeaway shop called The Godfather after 3:00 a.m. She falls on the floor and has to be helped to her feet, but not before a man walks past her fallen body and points at her. Outside, she sits down in a doorway, stumbles into the side of a building, and wanders with her pizza before trying to get into a taxi without her handbag, which she accidentally left in the shop. A man who had been inside The Godfather with his friends joins her in the taxi. He tells the driver to take them to the budget hotel room that he and a friend have rented for the night. He texts his friend, the man who pointed at the woman when she fell earlier, telling

---

1. Steven Morris, "Ched Evans Trial: Woman Woke Confused in Hotel Room, Court Told," *Guardian*, October 5, 2016, https://www.theguardian.com/uk-news/2016/oct/05/ched-evans-trial-woman-awoke-confused-in-hotel-room-court-told.

him, *I've got a bird*.[2] In court, the taxi driver will describe the woman as "drunk, very docile, and not with it."[3]

The man in the taxi is a six-foot-six professional soccer player named Clayton McDonald. The Premier Inn's security cameras show him walking arm in arm with the woman through the lobby at 4:10 a.m. She is wearing a royal blue sleeveless dress with high tan wedge heels and is leaning heavily on him; she is "out of it," the receptionist on duty will testify.[4] McDonald has sex with her in room 14. His teammate Ched Evans, the friend he texted from the taxi, arrives at the Premier Inn with his younger brother and another male friend. Evans enters the room and watches McDonald having sex for a few moments. He will later testify that he "was being juvenile, having a laugh."[5] In court, he will claim that McDonald asked the woman, "Can my mate join in?" and that she said yes, although he will admit that he never spoke to her before, during, or after the encounter. His brother and friend stand outside watching through the ground-floor window, giggling and using their phones to record the incident for sharing among their peer group. Evans's brother will testify in court, "At the time I thought it was funny."[6] Before he leaves room 14, McDonald opens the curtains so the two men outside can get a better view of Evans's actions.[7] Evans will testify that he used no protection and did not ask the woman if she wanted him to use protection.[8] CCTV shows him leaving the Premier Inn through the fire escape shortly thereafter.

The woman awakes alone in the hotel room the next morning in a panic, having been so intoxicated that she wet the bed. She does not know how she got there or remember anything after holding a pizza box the night before. She is naked and bruised, her right arm in pain, and she is missing her handbag and phone.[9] Later, Evans tells police, "We could have had any girl we wanted. When we go out it's not uncommon to pick up girls. We're footballers.

---

2. Steven Morris, "Ched Evans Trial: Friends Describe Alleged Victim's Distress the Next Day," *Guardian*, October 6, 2016, https://www.theguardian.com/uk-news/2016/oct/06/ched-evans-trial-friends-describe-alleged-victims-distress-next-day.

3. Steven Morris, "Ched Evans Raped Drunk Teenager in Hotel Room, Jury Told," *Guardian*, October 4, 2016, https://www.theguardian.com/uk-news/2016/oct/04/ched-evans-raped-drunk-teenager-hotel-room-retrial-jury-told.

4. Ibid.

5. Steven Morris, "Ched Evans Tells Rape Retrial That Women Consented to Sex," *Guardian*, October 10, 2016, https://www.theguardian.com/uk-news/2016/oct/10/ched-evans-tells-retrial-that-woman-consented-to-sex.

6. Steven Morris, "Ched Evans Admits Not Asking If He Could Have Unprotected Sex with Woman," *Guardian*, October 11, 2016, https://www.theguardian.com/uk-news/2016/oct/11/ched-evans-admits-not-asking-if-he-could-have-unprotected-sex-with-woman.

7. Steven Morris, "Ched Evans Tells Rape Retrial."

8. Steven Morris, "Ched Evans Admits Not Asking."

9. Steven Morris, "Ched Evans Trial: Woman Woke."

Footballers are rich and they have money. That is what girls like."[10] In a 2012 trial, McDonald is acquitted of raping the woman because his interactions with her in the taxi and hotel lobby are interpreted as sufficient evidence of her consent despite her extreme intoxication. Evans, who testifies that he did not speak to the woman, learn her name, or remember what her face looked like, is not so fortunate. His conviction is met with outrage from his supporters, who release the woman's name and address online and bombard her with electronic vitriol. She is forced to change her name twice and move five times in the first three years after the trial.[11]

After serving two and a half years in prison, Evans is released in late 2014. His conviction is quashed shortly thereafter due to the presentation of controversial new evidence, and he is granted an October 2016 retrial. After his friends and family advertise a £50,000 reward for information that would lead to his exoneration, Evans's defense team produces two male witnesses who claim to have had sex with the woman within weeks of that May night at the Premier Inn. This was just one manifestation of the numerous inequalities between Evans, a wealthy professional footballer from Rhyl backed by his girlfriend's millionaire father and legions of fans eager for their hometown hero's return to the sport, and the woman, a waitress who lived at home with her parents and siblings.[12] During the retrial, both of the new witnesses allege that the woman ordered them to "Fuck me harder," a phrase that Evans claims she said to him as well. One man testifies that he was "in shock" due to her assertiveness, while the other says that she "directed" the encounter.[13] In closing arguments, Evans's attorney declares, "Drunken consent is still consent."[14] Swayed by the inclusion of the woman's sexual history, the retrial jury finds

---

10. Steven Morris, "Ched Evans Told Police: 'We Could Have Had Any Girl We Wanted,'" *Guardian*, October 6, 2016, https://www.theguardian.com/uk-news/2016/oct/06/ched-evans-told-police-we-could-have-had-any-girl-we-wanted.

11. Press Association, "Ched Evans's Rape Victim Had to Change Name and Move Five Times, Says Father," *Guardian*, December 28, 2014, https://www.theguardian.com/football/2014/dec/28/ched-evans-rape-victim-change-name-move-house-father.

12. Steven Morris, "The Rich Footballer and the Waitress Living at Home: Ched Evans Trial Profiles," *Guardian*, October 14, 2016, https://www.theguardian.com/football/2016/oct/14/trial-profiles-rich-footballer-waitress-living-home.

13. Steven Morris, "Second Ched Evans Defence Witness Denies £50,000 Reward Motive," *Guardian*, October 12, 2016, https://www.theguardian.com/uk-news/2016/oct/12/second-ched-evans-defence-witness-denies-payment-motive; "Witness in Ched Evans Retrial Accused of Lying to Earn £50000 Reward," *Guardian*, October 11, 2016, https://www.theguardian.com/uk-news/2016/oct/11/witness-in-ched-evans-retrial-accused-of-lying-to-land-50000-reward.

14. Steven Morris, "Ched Evans Accused of 'Callous Indifference' in Rape Trial Closing Speech," *Guardian*, October 13, 2016, https://www.theguardian.com/uk-news/2016/oct/13/ched-evans-accused-of-callous-indifference-in-trial-summing-up.

Evans not guilty. Their verdict is unanimous.[15] Five months after his retrial, Evans re-signs with Sheffield United, his old team.[16]

A striking element in the Evans case is the pivotal role of masculine community among brothers, friends, and teammates in facilitating (alleged) sexual violence. In the taxi, McDonald texts Evans that he "got" a "bird," his language framing the woman as an object he has acquired for the group's enjoyment and demeaning her in gendered terms, as "bird" is a slang term for "a girl, woman" that is "often used familiarly or disparagingly."[17] One man's acquisition of a woman's body belongs to his friends, who soon arrive at the Premier Inn to claim their share of the prize. Evans, who testifies that he previously enjoyed threesomes with McDonald, watches his teammate having sex and becomes aroused at the sight. McDonald deliberately opens the curtains so that Evans's brother and friend can watch and record without the woman's knowledge or consent, allowing them to share in the experience and to capture it for repeated enjoyment. This collective consciousness is underscored by Evans's admission of entitlement articulated in the first-person plural: "*We* could have any girl *we* wanted," he says. For these men, sexuality is a communal enterprise.

Three months before Evans's retrial, I have a conversation with a fellow scholar about rape in Geoffrey Chaucer's *Reeve's Tale*. "I don't think 'rape' is the correct term that applies here," he says.

"How do you read it, then?" I ask.

"I think the Ched Evans case is a useful parallel," he replies.

"Oh," I say. I think about the intoxicated woman falling down in the takeaway shop and waking up alone at the Premier Inn, filled with bewildered horror. And I think of twenty-year-old Malyne in the *Reeve's Tale*, awaking lead-limbed from a drunken slumber to find one of her father's houseguests on top of her, penetrating her before she has a chance to say no or yes.

In the *Canterbury Tales*, Chaucer uses a group of eight male pilgrims from the mercantile-artisan classes to illuminate the workings of a type of masculinity, which I call "felawe masculinity," that is centered on men teaching their peers to perpetuate rape culture, much like the brand of masculinity espoused by Evans, McDonald, and their crew. By "teaching to perpetuate rape culture," I mean that Chaucer's pilgrim faction actively espouses "a complex of beliefs that

---

15. Steven Morris and Alexandra Topping, "Ched Evans: Footballer Found Not Guilty of Rape in Retrial," *Guardian*, October 14, 2016, https://www.theguardian.com/football/2016/oct/14/footballer-ched-evans-cleared-of-in-retrial.

16. Press Association, "Ched Evans 'Delighted' to Seal Sheffield United Return from Chesterfield," *Guardian*, May 8, 2017, https://www.theguardian.com/football/2017/may/08/ched-evans-sheffield-united-return-chesterfield.

17. *OED* s.v. "bird" (n.), 1d.

encourages male sexual aggression and supports violence against women."[18] Anastasia Powell and Nicola Henry define rape culture as "the social, cultural, and structural discourses and practices in which sexual violence is tolerated, accepted, eroticized, minimized, and trivialized. In a rape culture, violence against women is eroticized in literary, cinematic, and media representations; victims are routinely disbelieved or blamed for their own victimization; and perpetrators are rarely held accountable or their behaviours are seen as excusable or understandable."[19] These elements are prominent in the obscene comic tales told by Chaucer's "felawes," who trivialize rape as "pley," name women as "wenches" before they are assaulted in order to blame them for their victimization, and let the perpetrators go unpunished, as when Alisoun "graunt[s]" Nicholas her "love" in the *Miller's Tale* after he assaults her (I.3290), or when the *Reeve's Tale*'s John and Aleyn "gon" "on hir wey" home with their freshly ground flour in hand, eager to share stories with their friends at Soler Hall (I.4310).

Communal obscene storytelling is the group's preferred tool for teaching the lessons of "felawe masculinity." They share bawdy "japes" to dehumanize women, to bond intimately with one another, to compete viciously with one another, and to authorize violence against women and aggression against other men. They present their tales as overtly pedagogical and containing important lessons to be learned. Chaucer's portrayal of the "felawe faction" sheds light on how the telling of violent sexual jokes enacts the violence they ostensibly trivialize, as obscenity creates a gendered social dynamic teaching a set of values and relations among men that results in violence and harm.

This brand of masculinity is prominent in Fragment I of Chaucer's *Canterbury Tales*, where three men tell fabliaux featuring the obscene verb "swyve." The fragment's most comprehensive case study of "felawe masculinity" is the dynamic between the university students John and Aleyn in the *Reeve's Tale*. While Chaucer develops his exploration of this masculinity more fully than most, his representation of sexual storytelling as a tool for teaching collaborative, competitive masculinity can be traced across numerous late medieval texts. Scholars have done much to elucidate the multiple masculinities at work in the *Canterbury Tales*, and I add to this conversation by exploring the relationship between masculinity and obscenity that is central to the teaching of "felawe masculinity."[20] John Stoltenberg argues that "the way to improve

18. Preamble to Emilie Buchwald, Pamela R. Fletcher, and Martha Roth, eds., *Transforming a Rape Culture*, rev. ed. (Minneapolis, MN: Milkweed, 2005), xi.

19. Henry and Powell, "Framing Sexual Violence Prevention," 2. For more on the concept of rape culture, see Nicola Gavey, *Just Sex? The Cultural Scaffolding of Rape* (New York: Routledge, 2005); Harding, *Asking for It*.

20. For more on masculinity in Chaucer's *Canterbury Tales*, see Peter G. Beidler, ed., *Masculinities in Chaucer* (Cambridge: D. S. Brewer, 1998); Holly A. Crocker, *Chaucer's Visions of Manhood* (New

relations between men and women is to expose the codes that control relations among men."[21] This exposure is my chief aim here, as I examine the pedagogical practices of a group of male characters.

The "Joly Felow"

In late medieval England, the term "felawe" carried a web of valences connoting homosociality, shared interests, and sociability. "Felawe" is the word that Chaucer's characters use for one another: the Host refers to his professional rival the Cook as "oure felawe" (IX.7) and responds to the Shipman's fabliau of cuckoldry and economic trickery by exclaiming to his brethren, "A ha! Felawes, beth ware of swich a jape!" (VII.439). Likewise, "felawe" is the term that the *Reeve's Tale*'s John and Aleyn, the most fully fleshed representatives of this type of masculinity, use for one another as well as their peers at Cambridge's Soler Hall.

"Felawe" aptly names this brand of masculinity because it carries an inherent connection to other men and implies a peer relationship of partnership, brotherhood, and sociability. It comes from the Old Icelandic and Old Norse root word *fe-lagi*, meaning "share-holder, partner, mate, comrade," and the *Middle English Dictionary* glosses it as "one of two or more persons in each other's company or society; one of a pair or group of persons associating or acquainted with each other; companion, associate, acquaintance."[22] In addition to denoting community and shared aims, the term signifies intimacy and affection, meaning "a close or intimate companion; a good and loyal friend, comrade."[23] It entails the existence of at least one other "felawe" with a shared interest or experience, and it connotes emotional closeness, loyalty, and friendship. "Felawe" denotes a sociable man who engages in high-spirited homosocial drinking accompanying obscene storytelling because it also means, "one who associates with others in feasting and drinking; drinking companion, boon companion, reveler; hence, a sociable person."[24] Chaucer chooses a term entailing these various social elements—masculine community, intimacy, and

York: Palgrave Macmillan, 2007) and "Affective Politics in Chaucer's *Reeve's Tale*: 'Cherl' Masculinity after 1381," *Studies in the Age of Chaucer* 29 (2007); Carolyn Dinshaw, *Chaucer's Sexual Poetics* (Madison: University of Wisconsin Press, 1989); Elaine Tuttle Hansen, *Chaucer and the Fictions of Gender* (Berkeley: University of California Press, 1992).

21. John Stoltenberg, *The End of Manhood: Parables on Sex and Selfhood*, rev. ed. (London: University College London Press, 2000), 45.

22. *MED* s.v. "felau" (n.), 1(a).

23. *MED* s.v. "felau" (n.), 2(a).

24. *MED* s.v. "felau" (n.), 3.

conviviality—to name his faction of men who organize their group relations and teach their shared code by telling japes to one another.

The interconnected meanings of "felawe" are illuminated in an early sixteenth-century advice carol titled *Joly Felow Joly* (c. 1505–20) that illuminates how "felawe masculinity" was taught among men.[25] Although this song was printed more than a century after the *Canterbury Tales*, it provides useful context for understanding the cultural currency of "felawe" as well as "wenche," another term integral to Chaucer's faction's view of gender relations. In this song for three parts, an experienced male voice shares financial and sexual advice with the unmarried young "joly felow" and instructs him in the tenets of "felawe masculinity." His lesson is encapsulated and repeated in the carol's burden, a refrain sung at the carol's beginning and repeated after each verse:

> Joly felow joly,
> Joly felow joly,
> Yf thou have but lytyll mony
> Spend it not in foly,
> But spend it on a prety wenche,
> And she will help thee at a pinche;
> Hey joly felow joly joly,
> Hey joly felow joly,
> Hey joly. (1–9)

This song sung by at least three men stages men teaching each other how to be "felow[s]," underscoring the masculine communality inherent in the term. The speaker tells the "joly felow" how to conduct his sexual relationships and teaches him what sort of woman he should desire:

> A prety wenche may be plesur,
> In dalyaunce she may endur,
> Yf she be trym, proper and pure . . .
> Lytyll mony doth gret confort,
> Spend on the mynyon sort. (10–12, 15–16)

---

25. *Joly felow joly* (DIMEV 146; TP 41), in *XX Songes* (London, 1530), fol. 1v–3r; Greene, *Early English Carols*, 272–73. Text references are to lines in Greene's edition. For more on *XX Songes*, see David S. Josephson, *John Taverner: Tudor Composer* (Ann Arbor: University of Michigan Press, 1979), 193–94; Corinne Saunders, "A Study of the Book of *XX Songes* (1530)" (M. Music thesis, King's College, University of London, 1985).

In his lesson about the economics of desire, he emphasizes the ideal woman's physical desirability with the descriptors "trym" (comely), "proper" (good-looking), and "prety" (attractive, clever). "Pure" has multiple suggestive possibilities: it can be a slang term signifying "fine, good, excellent"; a sarcastic usage, meaning "sexually undefiled, chaste"; and/or a spelling of "poor" current through the late seventeenth century. If it is the latter, "pure" here could signify material disadvantage compounded by gender, especially since the speaker also uses "wenche" and "mynyon" (a woman kept for sexual favors), two terms of gendered disparagement connoting sexual transgression and subordination.[26] The speaker implies that these women are interchangeable with his command to "Spend on the mynyon sort," drawing on "sort"'s meaning of "a kind or variety of person or animal."[27] In this view, there are certain types of women whose sole purpose is for sexual favors, and the "felow" ought to direct his desires toward someone from this category due to the benefits that she can bring him. The didactic male lyric voice depicts erotic relationships as transactional, an exchange of "money" for "plesur," and he focuses on poor women's utility to men as sexual commodities who can be bought easily for a low price. In return for "but lytyll money," he teaches, these women will "helpe" the young man "at a pinche" (in a crisis) and provide him with "gret confort," "dalyaunce," "dysport," and "plesur." This group of suggestive nouns denotes "amorous talk," "flirting," "gratification," "sexual union," and "sensual pleasure," all provided by the attractive woman for a low price.[28] The speaker deploys the lighthearted, lecherous, and lusty connotations of "joly"—reinforced through its tenfold repetition in the burden—to reinforce what the "felow" is expected to be: "merry," "amorous," "lusty," and sexually "vigorous."[29] He underscores the convivial aspect of "felow" by repeating the cheerful interjection "hey," common in carol burdens and refrains.[30] This repetition reminds us that the song would have been sung by living bodies, staging men singing a didactic carol about masculinity both to and with one another and fostering homosocial community through its performance. This song's various elements—its staging of men teaching one another about desire; its use of "felow" to represent a certain type of masculinity; its misogyny and instrumental view of women as bargain-basement

---

26. *OED* s.v. "poor" (adj.); "pure" (adj.), 8a and 5; *MED* s.v. "wench" (n.); *OED* "minion" (adj. and n.), A.1a and 1b.

27. *MED* s.v. "sort" (n.), 1(b).

28. *MED* s.v. "daliaunce" (n.), 3; s.v. "plesir" (n.), 2(c); s.v. "comfort" (n.), 3(a); s.v. "disport" (n.), 1(b).

29. *MED* s.v. "joli" (adj.), 1(a), 2(a), and 2(c).

30. *MED* s.v. "hei" (interj.), (d).

wenches; its merriment; its all-male three-part performance—shed light on "felawe masculinity" and its pedagogical paradigms.

Equally significant in *Joly Felow Joly* is its repetition of the noun "wenche," functioning here and in the *Canterbury Tales* as the object of the "felow"'s desire and exploitation. The speaker instructs the "joly felow" to spend his money on "a prety wench" and teaches him that "a prety wenche may be plesur." "Wenche" carried a range of meanings: it signified "a girl" or "young woman;—occasionally with disparaging overtones," "a serving maid, a bondwoman," and "a concubine, paramour, mistress; a strumpet, harlot."[31] This multivalence, with its underlying connotations of youth, femininity, lower-class status, servitude, and sexual transgression, invokes multiple grounds of disadvantage. The "wenche" is not only an object or commodity for men; she is also subjugated to other women, and frequently contrasted with the powerful "lady" or the respectable "wyf." She is marked by her class disadvantage, gender, and age, since young women were thought to be especially yielding to sex.[32] This embedded double subordination is illustrated by Chaucer's Manciple, who notes how class inequalities shape the language used to name women's sexuality:

Ther nys no difference, trewely,
Bitwixe a wyf that is of heigh degree,
If of hir body dishonest she bee,
And a povre wenche, oother than this—
If it so be they werke bothe amys—
But that the gentile, in estaat above,
She shal be cleped his lady, as in love;
And for that oother is a povre womman,
She shal be cleped his wenche or his lemman. (IX.212–20)

He claims that language is the only thing that differentiates a respectable lady "of heigh degree" from "a povre wenche": poor women, because of their material disadvantage, bear the brunt of societal judgment against women who are "dishonest" "of hir bod[ies]," and are given the derogatory label of "wenche." Judith Butler states that "injurious names"—like "wenche"—"have a history, one that is invoked and reconsolidated at the moment of utterance, but not explicitly told."[33] She characterizes this linguistic "historicity" as

---

31. *MED* s.v. "wench" (n.), (a), (b), and (d).

32. I discuss this popular rape myth, exemplified by the proverb "Glassis and lassis are brukill wairs" (Glasses and girls are fragile commodities), in chapter 3; similarly, the antimarriage carol *Man bewar of thin wowyng* teaches men that "under the tayl [maidens] ben ful tikel."

33. Judith Butler, *Excitable Speech: A Politics of the Performative* (New York: Routledge, 1997), 36.

"the sedimentation of usages as they have become part of the very name, a sedimentation, a repetition that congeals, that gives the name its force."[34] "Wenche" carries a history of intersecting inequalities, because she is subservient to higher-ranked women as well as to all men and marked by the stain of illicit sexuality. Its usage in Middle English texts illustrates its links to subordination and sexual rule breaking: William Langland's *Piers Plowman* features "wenches of the stewes" (whores from the brothels) at multiple points; *The Book of Vices and Virtues* (c. 1375) decries rebellion by "wenches ayens here ladies"; John Wyclif uses "wenche" derisively six times, in addition to "strumpet" and "yong strumpet," to name the dancing Salome in a sermon about the beheading of John the Baptist; and in the morality play *Wisdom* (c. 1475), the character Wyll expresses his desires by declaring, "Met and drynke and ease, I aske no mare, / Ande a praty wenche, to se here bare," imagining the "praty wenche"'s "bare" body as something to be enjoyed and consumed by men alongside food and drink.[35] More recently, "wench" was a common term for young enslaved black women in the United States, as evidenced by a 1781 advertisement in the *New Jersey Gazette* for the sale of "A Likely Negro Wench, about 17 years of age."[36] "Wenche" is Chaucer's faction's preferred dehumanizing term for a woman, lending additional significance to its usage in *Joly Felow Joly*, where it is repeated four times.[37]

In my discussion of Chaucer's pilgrim band, I use "felawe" to designate a group of laymen from the mercantile-artisan classes—the Host, Miller, Reeve, Cook, Merchant, Manciple, and Shipman—who tell tales from the fabliau genre and use the obscenity "swyve" to establish a close-knit homosocial community of "felawes" based on fraternal craft identity and discursive practice. For these seven characters, manhood is fostered through sharing tales that teach the precepts of "felawe masculinity" and bring laughter and pleasure to the tale teller's comrades. This group's masculinity differs from that of the

---

34. Ibid.

35. William Langland, *The Vision of William Concerning Piers the Plowman*, pt. 2, ed. W. W. Skeat, Early English Text Society 38 (London: Early English Text Society, 1869; repr. 1972), XIX.439, XX.160; W. Nelson Francis, ed., *The Book of Vices and Virtues*, Early English Text Society, o.s., 217 (London: Oxford University Press for Early English Text Society, 1968), 65; *Select English Works of John Wyclif*, ed. Thomas Arnold (Oxford: Clarendon Press, 1869–71), 338–39; *Wisdom*, in Mark Eccles, ed., *The Macro Plays: The Castle of Perseverance, Wisdom, Mankind* (Oxford: Oxford University Press for the Early English Text Society, 1969), 113–52, lines 814–15.

36. "'Negro Wench' to be sold by Thomas Wiggins," *Princeton and Slavery*, https://slavery .princeton.edu/sources/negro-wench-2; see also Dolen Perkins-Valdez's historical novel *Wench* (New York: Harper Collins, 2010) and the racist interracial pornographic trope of the "Negro bed wench."

37. In addition to the examples I discuss from the *Manciple's*, *Miller's*, *Reeve's*, and *Cook's Tales*, "wenche" is used in a derogatory fashion in the *Merchant's Tale* ("I am a gentil woman and no wenche," IX.2202).

aristocratic Knight, Squire, and Franklin; agrarian laborers like the Plowman; and clerics like the Monk, Parson, Summoner, and Friar. It centers not on chivalric code nor physical toil nor religious vocation, but rather on a competitive dynamic of sexual conquest and obscene storytelling. Even though there are three women present on the pilgrimage, the "felawes" see the audience for their bawdy tales as comprising of other men—"Now, sires," says the Reeve at the start of his tale (I.3909), while the Miller addresses his audience as "Now, sire, and eft [again], sire" (I.3271)—which casts their sharing of japes as an all-male enterprise and underscores how obscene storytelling is the medium through which they settle their disputes, build their bonds, and teach their lessons. They trade bawdy barbs suffused with casual misogyny, as when the Manciple mockingly asks the inebriated Cook, "Hastow with som quene al nyght yswonke?" (Have you labored all night with some whore?) (IX.18).

Scholars have shown how the masculinities of certain faction members are rooted in their shared class and gender status, which Holly A. Crocker christens "cherl masculinity." Crocker situates Chaucer's "cherles tales" in their historical moment after the Uprising of 1381 and argues that they "present the exploitation of women that attends the marginalization of men" in order to shed light on how "social oppression fans out to divide members of a community who might otherwise find common ground."[38] Margaret Aziza Pappano argues that the term "leve brother"—which the Host applies to the Miller and the Miller uses to address the Reeve—functions as "a sign of shared class (artisanal) identity" that "implicitly critiques the fraternalism of the rapidly growing urban craft guilds."[39] These "brothers" are part of an urban homosocial world based on pedagogical and quasi-patriarchal as well as fraternal relationships among men.[40]

Masculine Community, Obscenity, and Violence: "Swyve" in Context

Members of the group share lighthearted educational tales, shot through with didactic "sentence" (authoritative teaching) under the cover of "solas" (enter-

---

38. Crocker, "Affective Politics," 229.

39. Margaret Aziza Pappano, "'Leve Brother': Fraternalism and Craft Identity in the *Miller's Prologue* and *Tale*," in *Reading Medieval Culture: Essays in Honor of Robert W. Hanning*, ed. Robert M. Stein and Sandra Pierson Prior (Notre Dame, IN: University of Notre Dame Press, 2005), 249. For more on the fraught nature of guild homosociality, see Christina M. Fitzgerald, *The Drama of Masculinity and Medieval English Guild Culture* (New York: Palgrave Macmillan, 2007), 95–144.

40. Karras, *From Boys to Men*, 109–50; also Lianna Farber, *An Anatomy of Trade in Medieval Writing: Value, Consent, and Community* (Ithaca, NY: Cornell University Press, 2006), esp. 150–79.

tainment), that valorize masculine sexual aggression, including grabbing women by the vulva without their consent, seizing women by their thighs and refusing to let go, and taking advantage of women's intoxication in order to assault them. They teach that sexual violence is a "jape" motivated by the rapist's larger community of "felawes" that strengthens the community by providing them with entertainment and affirmation of their shared values. In "felawe masculinity," competitive virility, misogyny, and obscene speech meld with professional fraternal brotherhood-as-rivalry in a way that anticipates the insult battles I explore in chapter 2. The obscenity "swyve" is the group's shibboleth and trademark articulation, occurring in all the members' tales (other than the *Shipman's Tale*) at climactic moments in the narrative, serving as a pedagogical tool to affix each tale's lesson in its audience's minds.

"Swyve" was the most explicit sexual verb in Middle English, and its illicit status is attested by scribes and readers of the *Canterbury Tales*, who substitute, alter, omit, or erase it in numerous fifteenth-century manuscripts.[41] Its usage is restricted to male authors and speakers in all the surviving Middle English examples except a fifteenth-century version of the *Wife of Bath's Prologue* in which Alisoun articulates "swyve," and it was frequently used to tell explicit sexual narratives in all-male contexts.[42] "Swyve" is associated in the *Tales* with both masculinity and transgression, since the members of the faction present the ability to eschew the rules of courteous diction and utter "swyve" as a marker of aggressive, rule-breaking masculinity. They utter it seven times, giving the *Tales* more "swyves" than any other single Middle English text.[43]

In order to understand why the sevenfold deployment of "swyve" by Chaucer's "felawes" is so significant, it is worth investigating how the term functioned in the later Middle Ages. In the fifteenth-century Paston family correspondence, "swyve" occurs in letters between brothers: Edmond tells his older brother John III how his servant Gregory "ha[d] a knavys loste, in pleyn termes to swhyve a quene" (had a knave's lust, in plain terms to fuck a whore), and John II shares a rape narrative with his younger brother John III about a man who "by force ravysshed and swyvyd an olde jentylwoman, and . . .

---

41. I explore how fifteenth-century scribes and readers encountered Chaucer's obscenity in greater detail in "Inserting 'a Grete Tente, a Thrifty, and a Long': Sexual Obscenity and Scribal Innovation in Fifteenth-Century Manuscripts of the *Canterbury Tales*," *Essays in Medieval Studies* 28 (2012).

42. In the *Wife of Bath's Prologue* in CUL MS Ii.3.26 (1430–50), Alisoun says "swyve" instead of the milder "dighte" on fol. 118r. I discuss this version of the *Prologue* in chapter 4.

43. *Lyarde*, which I discuss in this book's conclusion, is tied with the *Canterbury Tales* with seven iterations of noun, participle, and verb forms of "swyve." Melissa M. Furrow, "Lyarde: A Minor Romance Poem in a Major Romance Manuscript," *Forum for Modern Language Studies* 32, no. 4 (1996), lines 37, 61, 65, 89, 105, 112, 115.

swyvyd hyr oldest dowtre and than wolde have swyvyd the othere sustre."[44]
"Swyve" also survives in two late fifteenth-century anthologies of schoolroom
texts. In his school notebook, one young man writes, "Fratres . . . txxkxzv
nfookt xxzxkt (svvivyt mennis vvyvis)" (friars . . . fucked men's wives), rendering "swivyt" in code as "txxkxzv" to indicate its taboo and restrict its legibility
to a similarly educated group of male readers.[45] Around the same time, a student at Basingwerk Abbey's grammar school, Thomas Pennant, copied and translated a four-line Latin poem about women who "sweryt . . . that thay swylde fuc
ne men" (swore that they should fuck no men).[46] In response to the women's dis-
avowal of intercourse, "men were wys" and changed their behavior "and sowyvyd
ham" (fucked them). In all these cases, "swyve" occurs in all-male contexts—
correspondence between brothers and notebooks copied in universities or grammar schools—and designates intercourse occurring under less-than-consensual
conditions involving trickery or violence. These fraternal and pedagogical associations directly influence the term's use in the *Canterbury Tales* to teach the
lessons of rape culture, rendering it the perfect tool for Chaucer's "felawes."

The Pedagogy of the Jape

"Felawe masculinity" entails complicated bonds with other men and a view
of heterosexual relations in which women are instrumental, useful solely for
the conquests needed to impress one's peers and to manufacture titillating tales
for group bonding and instruction. The preferred tool for teaching "felawe
masculinity" in the *Canterbury Tales* is the jape, a brief, comic, obscene story
that teaches its audience about women and sexuality.[47] Indeed, all of Chaucer's "felawes"—with the exception of the Manciple, who nonetheless tells a
tale of cuckoldry and violence against women featuring "swyve" at its narrative climax—tell stories from the genre of the fabliau, loosely defined as
"short verse tales made for laughter" (*des contes a rire en vers*).[48] Old French

---

44. Norman Davis, ed., *The Paston Letters and Papers of the Fifteenth Century*, pt. 1 (Oxford: Oxford University Press for the Early English Text Society, 2004), 636 and 512.

45. See my discussion of *Flen flyys and freris* in the introduction.

46. This quatrain, *Women were wode and sweryn by the ro[d]e*, does not appear in the *DIMEV* and is printed only in a footnote in *William Dunbar: The Complete Works*, ed. John Conlee (Kalamazoo, MI: Medieval Institute Publications, 2004), 367n13.

47. *MED* s.v. "jape" (n.), 2(a).

48. Joseph Bédier, *Les fabliaux: Études de littérature populaire et d'histoire littéraire du moyen âge* (Paris: Champion, 1893), 30. Sidhu discusses Chaucer's engagement with the genre in *Indecent Exposure*, 84–89; also John Hines, *The Fabliau in English* (New York: Longman, 1993).

fabliaux repeatedly tout their pedagogical currency, since narrators frequently name their tales as *un essample* (an exemplum) and present the genre as useful for both *enseignement* (instruction, learning) and *solas* (pleasure, entertainment, sexual delight).[49] Fabliau narrators punctuate their stories with advice to men about women, rendering the genre a tool that men use to educate each other: one exclaims, "He who trusts in women must be mad!" (Qui fame croit, si est derves), and another concludes, "This fabliau teaches all married men . . ." (Cest dit as mariez pramet).[50] The sharing of japes is associated with obscene speech, imagined as same-sex pedagogy, and perceived as a moral threat by medieval religious writers, who frequently designate the sin of *turpiloquium* (filthy speaking) as "japes." *The Book of Vices and Virtues* condemns "japes and knakkes ful of filthe and lesynges" (jokes and jests full of filth and lies), and Mirk illustrates his prohibition against "spekyng rybawdy" with the exemplum of an Irish priest who is punished for being "lusty to speke of rybawdy and japys that turnyd men to lechery," illustrating the capacity of "japys" to teach one's fellow "men" to have sex according to group norms.[51]

In addition to being a multivalent noun denoting obscene comic narratives and meaning bawdiness, trickery, and "a remark not seriously intended," "jape" was an elastic verb used to designate men's role in intercourse, sometimes involving deception or force.[52] One fifteenth-century poem critiquing corrupt friars warns that one can "sle thi fadre and jape thi modre" (kill your father and fuck your mother) and still gain absolution, while in John Skelton's *Manerly Margery Mylk and Ale* (1490s), a tapster resists her rapist by declaring, "I will

---

49. Numerous fabliau narrators position their tales as pedagogical. A few examples include Jean Bodel's *Gombert*, an analogue of Chaucer's *Reeve's Tale* ("essample," 186), *Le sentier batu* ("un example," 13), Jean le Condé's *Les .II. changeors* ("Par cest fablel prover vous vueil" [I told this tale meaning to prove], 283), *La dame escoilliee* ("une essanple petite," 5), and *Le prestre et la dame* ("Par cest flablel poez savoir" [By this fabliau we may know], 169), all in Nathaniel Dubin, trans. and ed., *The Fabliaux* (New York: W. W. Norton, 2013). The narrator of *Le chevalier qui fist les cons parler* introduces his tale by declaring, "Auentures e enseignement/ Fount solas molt sovent" (Adventures and a lesson / Very often bring pleasure) (1–2), in Susanna Greer Fein, ed., with David Raybin and Jan Ziolkowski, *The Complete Harley 2253 Manuscript*, 3 vols. (Kalamazoo, MI: Medieval Institute Publications, 2015), 3:204–19; *OFED* s.v. "enseignement," "essample," and "solaz." I am grateful to Joseph Derosier for his Old French insights.

50. *La dolente qui fu fotue sur la tonbe*, line 120; *La chevaier a la robe vermeille*, line 313. Dubin, *Fabliaux*, 324–31 and 106–25.

51. Francis, *Book of Vices and Virtues*, 56; *Mirk's 'Festial': A Collection of Homilies, Edited from Bodl. MS. Gough. Top. 4*, ed. Theodore Erbe, pt. 1, Early English Text Society, e.s., 96 (London: Kegan Paul, Trench, Trübner, 1905), 192.

52. *MED* s.v. "jape" (n.), 2(c), 1(a), and 3(a); s.v. "japen" (v.), 3(a).

not be japed bodely."[53] In *A Worlde of Wordes*, Florio glosses *fottere* as "to jape, to sard, to fucke, to swive," reinforcing the term's corporeal currency: men tell one another japes about japing women.[54] The jape—entailing bawdy narrative, sexuality, amusement, and trickery or coercion—is the tool used to teach "felawe masculinity" among peers. Ahmed illuminates the key role of the jape's humor by noting that "humor is such a crucial technique for reproducing inequality and injustice" because it "creates the appearance of distance; by laughing about what they repeat, they repeat what they laugh about."[55] Laughter becomes a litmus test for belonging among the "felawes": if one can laugh at women's sexual subordination and refuse to empathize with their trauma, then he is part of the group.

The utility of sexual storytelling to peer pedagogy is attested by educators and scholars who show how men, particularly young heterosexual men, teach one another about sexuality and influence one another's sexual attitudes and behaviors, with obscene storytelling functioning as an effective method for this type of peer education. Michael Flood argues that "male-male peer relations have a profound influence on some men's heterosexual involvements" and claims that "homosociality shapes the sexual relations in which these men engage, the meanings given to their sexual involvements, and the development of narratives about them."[56] He details how homosociality and sexual storytelling shape some men's heterosexual relations:

> Homosociality organizes the male-female sociosexual relations of some young heterosexual men in at least four ways. First, male-male friendships take priority over male-female relations, and platonic friendships with women are dangerously feminizing and rare, if not impossible. Second, sexual activity is a key path to masculine status, and other men are the audience, always imagined and sometimes real, for one's sexual activities. Third, heterosexual sex itself can be the medium through which male bonding is enacted. Last, men's sexual storytelling is shaped by homosocial masculine cultures.[57]

---

53. *Of thes frere mynours me thenkes moch wonder* (DIMEV 4230), in Rossell Hope Robbins, ed., *Historical Poems of the XIV and XV Centuries* (New York: Columbia University Press, 1959), 163–64, line 42. *Manerly Margery Mylk and Ale* (DIMEV 743), in *The Complete English Poems of John Skelton*, rev. ed., ed. John Scattergood (Liverpool: Liverpool University Press, 2015), 29, line 19.

54. Florio, *Worlde of Wordes*, s.v. "fottere" (137).

55. Ahmed, *Living a Feminist Life*, 261. For more on sexual humor as a tool of power and oppression, see Mary Jane Kehily and Anoop Nayak, "'Lads and Laughter': Humour and the Production of Heterosexual Hierarchies," *Gender and Education* 9, no. 1 (1997).

56. Michael Flood, "Men, Sex, and Homosociality: How Bonds between Men Shape Their Sexual Relations with Women," *Men and Masculinities* 10, no. 3 (2008): 339.

57. Ibid., 342.

Attending to the role of sexual storytelling in maintaining fraternal bonds, Flood states that "boasting and telling stories of one's sexual exploits are an important part of homosocial male banter and represent competition in internal 'pecking orders' among men," noting how "men's telling of sexual stories itself represented a form of homosocial interaction" among his research subjects.[58] Sharon R. Bird discusses "competitive sex talk" in all-male settings, in which men engage in explicit sexual storytelling, objectification of women, and fierce narrative one-upmanship, much like Chaucer's pilgrims. Like Flood, she argues that these "bantering sessions" play an integral role in structuring power hierarchies within groups of men, and this phenomenon is evident in the dynamics between the *Reeve's Tale*'s students and among the members of Chaucer's faction.[59]

The homosocial underpinnings of heterosexual masculinity are central to Fragment I of Chaucer's *Canterbury Tales*, especially the *Reeve's Tale*, where the students' choice to rape is motivated by the imagined response of their peer group.[60] After they are tricked and robbed by Symkyn the miller, John and Aleyn imagine the gendered disparagements that their friends will hurl at them "when this tale is tald another day," and they seek instead to provide their peers with a jape that affirms their status as "felawes" who can dominate other men through heterosexual conquest, violence, and the ability to tell a good story. Flood stresses the importance of obscene storytelling to this type of masculinity: of one interview subject, he writes, "'the boys' are the imagined audience for this man's sexual achievements, their collective male gaze informing the meaning of his sexual relations."[61] In her discussion of friendship groups' influence on young people's sexual choices, Carmody states that "friends become a major source of factual information, advice, and guidelines as to what is acceptable or unacceptable sexual behavior" and are "fundamental to shaping how a young man or woman thinks about and creates the beginning of a sexual life."[62] She highlights the importance of communal sexual storytelling by citing "practices in a residential college where everyone had to weekly recount their sexual experiences and pay a monetary fine if they had failed to

58. Ibid., 353.

59. Sharon R. Bird, "Welcome to the Men's Club: Homosociality and the Maintenance of Hegemonic Masculinity," *Gender and Society* 10, no. 2 (1996): 128–29.

60. P. J. P. Goldberg discusses the paramount importance of homosociality in the lives of single men like Fragment I's Nicholas, John, Aleyn, and Perkyn Revelour in "Desperately Seeking the Single Man in Later Medieval England," in *Single Life and the City 1200–1900*, ed. Julie De Groot, Isabelle Devos, and Ariadne Schmidt (London: Palgrave Macmillan, 2015), esp. 124–27.

61. Flood, "Men, Sex, and Homosociality," 348.

62. Carmody, *Sex, Ethics, and Young People*, 65, also 34, 37.

pick-up."[63] In this example, both having sex and sharing sexual narratives with one's peers cements an individual's place in the community, and failure to do so carries relational and financial consequences. These examples illustrate how medieval ways of thinking about masculine community have significant resonances in contemporary culture, for Ruth Mazo Karras notes that "many features of medieval masculinities are similar to those of today, in particular the desire to dominate other men and the use of real or metaphorical violence."[64]

"When this jape is tald another day": Teaching Rape Culture in Fragment I of the *Canterbury Tales*

It is no coincidence that nearly all of Chaucer's "felawes," save the Host and Manciple, choose to tell fabliaux. In Fragment I, the Miller, Reeve, and Cook exploit the genre's widespread pedagogical currency to teach their brand of masculinity. Angela Jane Weisl observes that Chaucer's "fabliaux turn violence against women—particularly sexual violation—into a slapstick comedy that distracts from its severity through humor."[65] They normalize this violence as both entertaining and acceptable by occluding its harms and denigrating its victims as "wenches" who are "asking for it."

The seeming lightheartedness of this genre is the honeyed shell coating the bitter pill of misogyny, because the "felawes" use humorous tales to teach serious lessons about sex, power, and violence. We see "felawe masculinity" in other parts of the *Tales*, but it emerges most comprehensively in Fragment I, where three "felawes" share their fabliaux in succession and where conflicts and coalitions among the faction's members play out in the connective tissue between the tales, shedding light on how men teach their peers to dehumanize women and perpetuate rape culture. Medieval masculinity necessitated that men prove their power and mastery over other men while still maintaining the homosocial bonds necessary for social status.[66] In Fragment I, "felawes" use obscenity as a trenchant weapon to "quite" (punish, get revenge on) one another and to teach their group's shared values.[67]

---

63. Ibid., 28.

64. Karras analyzes medieval and contemporary masculinities in *From Boys to Men*, 163–67.

65. Angela Jane Weisl, "Violence against Women in the *Canterbury Tales*," in *Violence against Women in Medieval Texts*, ed. Anna Roberts (Gainesville: University Press of Florida, 1998), 117.

66. Karras notes, "In the later Middle Ages the primary way by which a boy established his adult masculinity was by testing himself and proving himself against other men. Women were often tools used in that demonstration," since "women . . . measured men's competition with each other" (*From Boys to Men*, 11). See also Neal, *Masculine Self*, 7.

67. *MED* s.v. "quiten" (v.), 3(a), 3(b), 3(c).

"Queynte" Violations: The *Miller's Prologue and Tale*

In the *Miller's Prologue*, conflicts erupt between the Miller, Host, and Reeve, providing the first glimpse of this gendered dynamic. The Host addresses the drunken Miller as "my leeve brother" in a conciliatory attempt to prevent him from telling a tale (I.3129), and the Miller calls the Reeve "leve brother Osewold" during their disagreement about marriage and cuckoldry (I.3151). This appellation shows up again at the tale's end, when Oxford students address each other as "my leeve brother" as they mock the cuckolded carpenter John (I.3848). This recurring use of the language of brotherhood both within and outside the tale unites the "felawes" and elucidates the violence and internal competition integral to their brand of masculinity.[68]

The Miller introduces his audience to Alisoun, John's eighteen-year-old wife, with a thirty-eight-line description encouraging them to view her through the lens of "felawe masculinity": she is portrayed in insistently corporeal terms and as an object existing solely for men's enjoyment (I.3233–70). He begins by describing "hir body gent and smal (shapely and slender)" (I.3234), and he maintains this sustained focus on "hir body" throughout the passage, his lecherous gaze never wavering. He depicts Alisoun as useful only for sex or marriage, with the rhyming pair "bedde" and "wedde" summing up her utility to men: "She was a prymerole, a piggesnye [a primrose, a daisy] / For any lord to leggen in his bedde, / Or yet for any good yeman to wedde" (I.3268–70). Elaine Tuttle Hansen notes that Alisoun's body facilitates "the possibility of male bonding across class lines," because the Miller characterizes her as "the woman for whom men of different ranks can feel common masculine desire, even as they have sexual relations with her in class-specific ways."[69] The Miller portrays Alisoun as a product of men's mental exertions rather than a subject in her own right: "There nys no man so wys that koude thenche [imagine] / So gay a popelote [pet] or swich a wenche," he says (I.3253–54). He uses "wenche" to fix Alisoun with derogatory class and gender connotations and anticipates the term's dehumanizing usage elsewhere in the fragment.[70] The term "popelote" is likely linked to the French word meaning "a small baby," infantilizing her and casting her as utterly lacking agency.[71]

---

68. *MED* s.v. "brother" (n.), 4(c): "fellow member of a guild"; 4(d): "close friend, comrade, associate, partner." The Manciple addresses his audience as "myn owene deere brother" (IX.221). For a discussion of tensions among members of the same guild, see Farber, *Anatomy of Trade*, 173–74.

69. Hansen, *Chaucer and the Fictions of Gender*, 239.

70. Crocker argues that Chaucer's use of "wenche" in the *Miller's* and *Reeve's Tales* "affectively associates the social and moral status of a woman much in the same fashion that 'cherl' does for a man" ("Affective Politics," 246–47n70).

71. *MED* and *OED* s.v. "popelot" (n.).

After teaching his "felawes" to view Alisoun as a sexual plaything, the Miller continues his lesson in rape culture by staging a sexual assault that is quickly minimized and played for laughs. He addresses his account of the assault specifically to the men in the audience: "Now, sire, and eft, sire," he says as a preface. Nicholas waits until John is out of town, then grabs Alisoun's vulva and physically subdues her by holding tightly to her thighs:

> And prively he caughte hire by the queynte,
> And seyde, "Ywis, but if ich have my wille,
> For deerne love of thee, lemman, I spille."
> And heeld hire harde by the haunchebones. (I.3276–79)

The verb "caughte" carries violent valences, meaning "to seize" and often occurring in martial contexts to characterize the motion of a blade sticking fast in flesh.[72] Through his alliterative yoking of "heeld," "hire," "harde" (violently), and "haunchebones" (hips/thighs), the Miller links aggressive restraint and the sexualized female body, emphasizing the force with which Nicholas overpowers Alisoun. She responds to the assault with verbal and physical resistance:

> And she sproong as a colt dooth in the trave,
> And with hir heed she wryed faste awey,
> And seyde, "I wol nat kisse thee, by my fey!
> Why, lat be!" quod she, "Lat be, Nicholas,
> Or I wol crie 'out, harrow' and 'allas'!
> Do wey youre handes, for youre curteisye!" (I.3282–87)

The Miller compares Alisoun's reaction to that of a colt being shod, her response to Nicholas's assault a visceral animal reaction to bodily pain with nowhere to escape, as "trave" means "an enclosure or a frame for restraining horses while their shoes are nailed onto their feet."[73] Her portrayal as a restrained young farm animal jerking in pain from the piercing nail recalls the Miller's characterization of her as a helpless infant thirty lines previously. She utters specific and unequivocal refusals—"I wol nat," "Do wey [remove] youre handes," and a twofold "lat be" (let go, leave me alone)—and reinforces them by "springing" away from Nicholas and "wry[ing] faste [twisting firmly] awey" from his grip.[74] With her promise to "crie 'out, harrow' and 'allas,'"

---

72. *MED* s.v. "cacchen" (v.), 1(a).
73. *MED* s.v. "trave" (n.), (b).
74. *MED* s.v. "don" (v.[1]), 5b(1); s.v. "leten" (v.), 18b.

she threatens to raise the hue and cry, positing his forceful vulva seizing and hip grabbing as the beginning of a rape. After meeting this resistance, Nicholas's violence is ultimately rewarded with "love" and consensual sex, for Alisoun changes her mind after his threats, restraint, and "queynte" grabbing.[75] This episode teaches the "felawes" not only that it is acceptable to assault women, but also that hurting them and ignoring their refusals are effective tactics for wooing them and winning their affection.

Nicholas's assault is only the beginning of the faction's portrayal of violence against women as trivial, comic, and instructional. After another act of sexualized violence intended for Alisoun's vulva, in which the spurned Absolon attempts to attack her "hole" with a red-hot plough blade, the tale's final instance of aggression occurs with the Miller's utterance of "swyved" at the very moment that he establishes his tale's educational import.[76] He is the first to use the group's trademark obscenity when he concludes, "Thus swyved was this carpenteris wyf" (I.3850), and he casts John's fate as a lesson learned by "every clerk" studying at Oxford, who discuss his humiliation among themselves as "brother[s]": "For every clerk anonright heeld with oother. / They seyde, 'The man is wood, my leeve brother'" (I.3847–48). In using "swyve" to close his tale, the Miller articulates three fundamental components of "felawe masculinity" and its version of rape culture: first, "swyving" is construed as an action that men do *to* women rather than *with* them, positing a masculine agent and a feminine object with no possibility of mutuality between partners. Second, his renaming of Alisoun as "this carpenteris wyf" presents "swyving" as an action men do to one another, with women's nameless bodies as the conduits for settling men's conflicts and determining their alliances.[77] Alisoun is portrayed as sexually and grammatically passive, and the tale's bawdiness functions in service of masculine competition. Hansen suggests that the tale's humor "covers up the will to violence against women that is . . . an effect of male fear and sexual anxiety," a storytelling move characteristic of the faction, just as I argue that the *Reeve's Tale* represents rape as motivated by men's fear of other men's mockery.[78] Third, by identifying his tale's cuckolded husband with his "leve brother Osewold"'s trade of carpentry, the Miller shows how

---

75. Corinne Saunders notes how this scene illustrates the rape myth that "female resistance is feigned," in *Rape and Ravishment in the Literature of Medieval England* (Cambridge: D. S. Brewer, 2001), 298–99.

76. Hansen discusses the implications of Absolon's intended violence against Alisoun in *Chaucer and the Fictions of Gender*, 223–36.

77. Hansen notes that Alisoun "become[s] the grammatical object of the verb and a nameless possession of her husband" in this line, as "she is . . . refixed in a position that is clearly marginal" (ibid., 235).

78. Ibid., 232.

the competitive elements of their brand of masculinity are imagined in terms of professional rivalries, with obscenity as the discourse through which these conflicts are articulated.

In response to the Miller's fabliau with its embedded lessons validating masculine aggression and casting women's resistance as both feigned and futile, the "felawes" respond with raucous laughter: "they loughe and pleyde" (I.3858), the Chaucer-pilgrim says. The tale has done its job, and everyone is laughing merrily. Everyone, that is, except for the Reeve, who experiences the Miller's jape as an impugnment of his masculinity, underscoring the central role of craft identity in shaping homosocial relationships.

Rape as Jape in the *Reeve's Prologue and Tale*

In his impassioned response to the *Miller's Tale*, Oswald the Reeve emerges as the faction's most obscene, violent, and comprehensive proponent of their shared sexual code. The *Reeve's Tale* stages "felawes" teaching one another the tenets of rape culture and sheds light on the process by which men choose to perpetrate sexual violence. Here obscene sexual storytelling is an integral part of rape culture: it fosters masculine community and functions as a means for asserting one's gendered identity within the group; it presents sexual violence as entertaining for men and nontraumatic for women, thus authorizing it and minimizing its harms; and it serves as a social weapon to settle conflicts and establish hierarchies among men. For the Reeve, it is a means of asserting his symbolic virility that enables him to perform vengeful violence. Like many older male speakers in Middle English and Middle Scots lyric, the Reeve laments his diminished potency in his *Prologue*:

> We olde men . . . have an hoor heed and a grene tayl,
> As hath a leek; for thogh oure myght be goon,
> Oure wyl desireth folie evere in oon.
> For whan we may nat doon, than wol we speke. (I.3874, 3878–81)

He claims that the desires ("oure wyl") of his "tayl" are ever "grene" (young, desirous), identifying with the priapic youthful masculinity of his tale's students even though his physical "myght" is gone. He depicts men's "spek[ing]" about sex as a substitute for "do[ing]," and he imagines obscene storytelling as a way for men to perform heterosexual conquest for one another across the lifespan.

In addition to depicting obscene speech as a substitute form of virility, a phenomenon I discuss in relation to the Middle Scots flytings in the next chapter, the Reeve interprets the Miller's tale about the cuckoldry of his "brother-in-trade" as an assault on his masculinity, an act of "force" that necessitates a violent response: "For leveful is with force force of-showve" (It is permissible to repel force with force), he declares before telling his fabliau, appropriating a well-known legal maxim to illustrate his lesson (I.3912).[79] He depicts speaking in the shared language of his "felawe"—the bawdy vocabulary of the fabliau, the "cherles termes" of obscene discourse—as an act of interpersonal violence when he snarls, "Right in his cherles termes wol I speke. / I pray to God his nekke mote to-breke!" (I.3917–18). Here, for a man to "speke" obscenity is to "breke" the neck of his "leve brother." The Reeve utters "swyve" an unprecedented three times in his tale, in contrast to his comrades, who each articulate it no more than once, underscoring the link between obscenity and masculine violence.

Scholars have shown how rape in the *Reeve's Tale* is a means of settling disputes and conflicts among men.[80] Less attention has been paid to the dynamic between the two clerks themselves.[81] Chaucer frames the perpetrators' decision-making process to suggest that John and Aleyn commit rape not simply as an act of economic retribution against the thieving miller but primarily to avoid humiliation by their "felawes alle" (I.4112). He explicitly figures John's assault as an answer to Aleyn's attack and to their peers' imagined derision "whan this jape is told another day." Chaucer alters his source material to introduce rape where there previously was none, as the encounter between the Malyne and Aleyn characters in his Old French sources is portrayed as entirely consensual.[82] It is preceded by mutual flirtation over dinner, and the young woman issues affirmative verbal consent and gives the clerk the key to the locked chest where she sleeps at night. Chaucer's strategic changes to a well-known comic narrative enable him to probe the role of homosocial bonds in perpetrating sexual violence.

In performing their brand of masculinity, the clerks illuminate how men can teach one another about sex and power and inculcate the lessons of rape culture with obscene storytelling. They flood harsh light on the ways that

---

79. This is a translation of "licitum est vim vi repellere" (it is permissible to repel force with force), a "well-known legal maxim" from Justinian's *Digestia* (*Riverside Chaucer*, 849n3912).

80. Christopher Cannon, "Chaucer and Rape: Uncertainty's Certainties," in *Representing Rape in Medieval and Early Modern English Literature*, ed. Elizabeth Robertson and Christine M. Rose (New York: Palgrave Macmillan, 2001), 267–68; Crocker, "Affective Politics," 256–57; Christine M. Rose, "Reading Chaucer Reading Rape," in Robertson and Rose, *Representing Rape*, 39–40; Saunders, *Rape and Ravishment*, 300; Sidhu, *Indecent Exposure*, 79; Weisl, "Violence against Women," 119–20.

81. One exception is Hansen, *Chaucer and the Fictions of Gender*, 241.

82. Sidhu, *Indecent Exposure*, 81, 93. For the *Reeve's Tale*'s analogues, including two versions of the thirteenth-century Old French fabliau *Le meunier et les .ii. clers*, see Peter G. Beidler, "The Reeve's Tale," in *Sources and Analogues of the Canterbury Tales*, ed. Robert M. Correale and Mary Hamel (Woodbridge, UK: Boydell and Brewer, 2002).

young men's developing sexual attitudes and practices are hammered out like sheet metal by the words and deeds of their peers. Medieval English university students were typically aged in the mid-to-late teens, and Karras notes they were seen as "young men at an age to be shaped and influenced by the people and institutions around them."[83] The Reeve introduces his pair of "felawes" as indistinguishable from each other in all but their names, linked by shared natal origin and grammatical interchangeability: "John highte that oon, and Aleyn highte that oother; / Of o toun were they born" (I.4013–14). The clerks' distinctive northern dialect sets them apart from the tale's other characters and underscores their bond, since they speak precisely the same language. They are characterized as "testif" (headstrong) and "lusty for to pleye," in eternal search of "myrthe and revelrye" (I.4004–5). This description of the clerks as perpetually seeking "pleye" implicitly authorizes sexual violence by attributing it to youthful headstrongness and elides any harm that such acts of "myrthe" might cause to those who are not in on the joke. The students reside at Cambridge's Soler Hall, an institution "something like an American dormitory but run by private individuals," which fostered homosocial community through shared living arrangements as well as common pedagogical instruction.[84] Flood has shown how "deeply hierarchical, masculine, and homosocial" environments like military schools have pronounced patterns of "male-male peer relations that structure and give meaning to [young men's] heterosexual relations," and we see this in the all-male world of Soler Hall.[85]

The Reeve introduces Symkyn's twenty-year-old daughter Malyne, one of the tale's two rape victims, through the lens of "felawe masculinity," illustrating how this ideology views women as instrumental to masculine relations rather than as subjects in their own right.[86] Karras notes that university officials "recognized [male students] as sexual beings and called for them to relate to women in that way alone," positing "the instrumental use of women" and "aggressive heterosexuality" as integral to student masculinity, and the Reeve and his two clerks view women in precisely this way.[87] Like Alisoun in the *Miller's Tale*, Malyne is introduced in exclusively corporeal terms: "This

---

83. Karras, *From Boys to Men*, 70.

84. Ibid., 73–74. For links between the historical Cambridge and Chaucer's fictional "Soler Hall," see J. A. W. Bennett, *Chaucer at Oxford and Cambridge* (Toronto: University of Toronto Press, 1974), 93–105.

85. Flood, "Men, Sex, and Homosociality," 342–43. Karras argues that "placed in this all-male environment at a formative time in their lives, [university students] learned a particular type of manhood," and notes that "in . . . university towns . . . a main way in which students interacted with women of the town was through violence" (*From Boys to Men*, 75, 77).

86. Crocker notes that Symkyn and the clerks share a view of women as "passive instruments they may employ for advantage" ("Affective Politics," 243).

87. Karras, *From Boys to Men*, 80–81.

wenche thikke and wel ygrowen was . . . With buttokes brode and brestes rounde and hye," he states (I.3973–75). The Reeve's naming of Malyne as "this wenche" establishes a pattern that persists throughout the tale, as Aleyn later calls her "yon wenche" when he declares his intention to assault her. In total, the term is used five times to name her.[88] The appellation "wenche" represents the faction's view of women as subordinate and useful only for conquest, their voluptuous flesh inescapably feminine and transgressive. The Reeve's narrative gaze lingers lecherously on the contours of Malyne's body, detailing the shape of her "brestes" and "buttokes" and reinforcing this corporealization through the alliteration of "buttokes," "brode," and "brestes."

The *Reeve's Tale* portrays, in methodical and detailed fashion, how the "felawes" decide to commit rape. It represents this decision as driven by the homosocial telling of japes and the judgments of male peers.[89] Two passages— Aleyn's meticulous justification to John of his choice to assault Malyne, and John's own monologue in which he decides to attack Malyne's mother based on his peers' imagined reaction—give valuable insight into how rapists' decision-making processes were imagined during the period. The two rapists carefully plan and rationalize their rapes, arriving at their decisions to commit sexual violence only after much thought and deliberation. Sidhu notes that "the tale is remarkable among fabliaux for the extensive time and trouble Chaucer takes explaining the motivations of his male characters," who are "motivated by an anxiety over their social status and a desire to move up the social hierarchy."[90] They make their choices as if for an audience of their classmates, imagining their actions as japes that they will "t[ell] another day" to their friends at Soler Hall. As the clerks lie in bed together after dinner, Aleyn details his plan to avenge Symkyn's theft of their grain by assaulting his unconscious daughter, articulating the tale's first obscenity to punctuate his intention to rape:

> "For, John," seyde he, "als evere moot I thryve,
> If that I may, yon wenche wil I swyve.
> Som esement has lawe yshapen us,
> For, John, ther is a lawe that says thus:
> That gif a man in a point be agreved,

---

88. See lines 3973, 4167, 4178, 4193, 4194.

89. For more on the role of male peer support in rape perpetration, see Martin D. Schwartz and Walter S. DeKeseredy, *Sexual Assault on the College Campus: The Role of Male Peer Support* (Thousand Oaks, CA: Sage Publications, 1997); Henry and Powell, "Framing Sexual Violence Prevention," 6–7; Antonia Quadara, "The Everydayness of Rape: How Understanding Sexual Assault Perpetration Can Inform Prevention Efforts," in Henry and Powell, *Preventing Sexual Violence.*

90. Sidhu, *Indecent Exposure*, 90.

That in another he sal be releved.
Oure corn is stoln, sothly, it is na nay,
And we han had an il fit al this day;
And syn I sal have neen amendement
Agayn my los, I will have esement." (I.4177–86)

Aleyn's speech contains several important rhetorical moves: he occludes rape's physical and psychic harms by casting it in detached economic terms of "los," "amendement" (reparation), and "esement" (compensation); he presents rape as justifiable by law; he uses "swyve" to articulate his decision; he names his intended victim with the derogatory designation "yon wenche"; and he frames his rape justification as a peer lesson. He argues that sexual violence is a fitting and legal response to theft, representing women's bodies as the terrain on which men settle their economic disputes. He twice characterizes his attack as "esement," using a legal term meaning "the right or privilege of using something not one's own."[91] He uses his knowledge of the law to rationalize rape, illustrating how institutions can be mobilized against victims by claiming that his rape solution is "yshapen [made for] us" by the law.[92] Aleyn portrays the impulse to rape as both bodily urge and economic reparation when he claims he shall "be releved" (satisfied, recompensed) after he assaults Malyne.[93] Before Aleyn makes this speech, John laments to him, "Our corn is stoln; men wil us fooles calle, / Bathe the wardeyn and oure felawes alle" (I.4111–12). This anxiety that they will be ridiculed as "fooles" by their community of fellow "men" underscores the paramount influence of "oure felawes alle" on the two clerks' decisions, with the inclusive adverb "alle" emphasizing the group's gendered collectivity. Here, rape is driven by a fear of other men's derisive words and mocking laughter.

This fear of emasculating insults and the centrality of obscene japes to "felawe masculinity" are nowhere more explicit than in John's subsequent inner monologue, in which he decides to rape the miller's wife after Aleyn has left the bed to assault Malyne. While Aleyn rationalized his choice to rape with legal knowledge and justified it as biological drive and economic reparation, John presents his choice as motivated solely by the expected reaction of his peer group. He voices acute anxiety over what their friends at Soler Hall will say when they hear of Aleyn's "swyving" in contrast to his inaction, and he arrives at his decision to rape as a result of this imagined moment of fraternal storytelling:

---

91. *MED* s.v. "esement" (n.), 2.
92. Jennifer Temkin, *Rape and the Legal Process* (Oxford: Oxford University Press, 2002).
93. *MED* s.v. "releven" (v.), 1(d).

"Allas!" quod he, "this is a wikked jape:
Now may I seyn that I is but an ape.
Yet has my felawe somwhat for his harm;
He has the milleris doghter in his arm.
He auntred hym, and has his nedes sped,
And I lye as a draf-sak in my bed;
And when this jape is tald another day,
I sal ben halde a daf, a cokeney!
I wil arise and auntre it, by my fayth!
'Unhardy is unseely,' thus men sayth." (I.4201–10)

In this moment of perpetrator decision making, John illustrates the effect of his comrades' words on his behavior by articulating the step-by-step thought process that leads him to rape the miller's wife, underscoring the relationship between obscene speech, masculine community, and perpetrating sexual violence. He twice uses the word "jape" to characterize Aleyn's rape as well as its retelling. He imagines heterosexual conquest and sexual storytelling as interchangeable, as equally constitutive of one's masculinity. The Reeve has already characterized the assault as a joke—"Now pley, Aleyn" (I.4198), he urges when Aleyn begins to attack Malyne—and John's twofold characterization of rape as jape further reinforces this.

This moment recalls Ched Evans's brother and friend outside the Premier Inn, laughing while they watch and film him through the first-floor window, their laughter affirming his actions and recasting them as a group joke: according to retrial testimony, "Evans said McDonald opened the curtains of the room and there was laughing and giggling from [the men] outside."[94] The laughter was so loud that eventually "Evans texted his brother to suggest that he leave."[95] Part of "felawe masculinity" is refusing to take rape seriously or to acknowledge its harms, and instead enacting further violence by rendering it both comic and trivial, nothing more than a funny story with which to entertain one's friends and bring "the boys" closer together. Rachel E. Moss notes how Chaucer, who "may not have just been a passive recipient of the values embedded into rape culture but also an active promoter of those values," teaches the readers of the *Reeve's Tale* that "rape is funny," and she reminds us how Chaucer's own life experience as a maybe-rapist has serious implications for how we read his tales making light of sexual violence. If we take Chaucer's 1380 *raptus* case into account, we can read these speeches in the *Reeve's Tale*

---

94. Morris, "Ched Evans Told Police."
95. Ibid.

as a perpetrator teaching his audience how to view rape as humorous, justified, and utterly normal because he depicts assault from the perpetrator's
perspective.[96]

By naming Aleyn as "my felawe" and fashioning his choices in response to
his friend's, John touches on the competition and identification inherent in the
term "felawe." Obscene storytelling is the tool by which men impel their peers
to rape, and it is their chief motivator for sexual activity: a "felawe" copulates
not out of desire for his partner but rather to manufacture a humorous, titillating narrative to share with his friends. John emphasizes the effect of other
men's words on his actions with his use of the phrase "thus men sayth," as he
imagines his fellow "men" urging him to prove his "hardy[ness]" through rape.

This passage sheds light on the words that "felawes" use to police each
other's masculinity because name-calling teaches John when and how he
should have sex. In response to his friend's successful perpetration of a rape,
John labels himself "an ape" (a fool) and "a draf-sak" (a rubbish sack) in an act
of self-regulation: he excoriates himself according to his group's values, voicing the epithets that his comrades will apply to him and demonstrating how
he has internalized their version of masculinity.[97] He chooses insults denoting both mental and physical ineffectualness, depicting himself as "easily out-
witted or duped" and casting his inactive body as a useless bag of garbage.
After berating himself, he imagines how the future moment of communal
storytelling back at Soler Hall will lead his peers to impugn his masculinity.
He is convinced they will mock him for his sexual inaction as "a daf, a cokeney."
"Daf," meaning "fool," echoes "ape" in disparaging the man who fails to rape
as unintelligent and foolish; in this formulation, only a fool would fail to take
what is his due.[98] The epithet "cokeney," meaning "chicken egg," denotes "a
pampered child, an effeminate youth, a weakling."[99] It is linked to immatu-
rity and underdevelopment and laden with connotations of weakness, child-
ishness, pamperedness, and dependence on women. Its links to helplessness
and femininity echo the binary that John establishes between the humiliating
passivity of "ly[ing] as a draf-sak" and the bold chivalric venture of "aris[ing]
and auntr[ing] it." The *Promptorium Parvulorum* (c. 1440) glosses "cokney" as
"carifotus, cucimellus, fotus, delicius; et hec sunt nomina derisorie ficta et
adinventa" (pet, milksop, fetus, petted child; and these are names mockingly

---

96. Rachel E. Moss, "Chaucer's Funny Rape: Addressing a Taboo in Medieval Studies," *Meny
Snoweballes*, September 14, 2014, https://menysnoweballes.wordpress.com/2014/09/11/chaucers
-funny-rape-addressing-a-taboo-in-medieval-studies/. For more on the implications of the Chaump-
aigne case for reading rape in the *Canterbury Tales*, see Cannon, "Chaucer and Rape."

97. *MED* s.v. "ape" (n.), 2b; s.v. "draffe" (n.), 3.

98. *MED* s.v. "daffe" (n.), (a).

99. For the former definition, see *MED* s.v. "coken-ei" (n.[1]); for the latter, s.v. "coken-ei" (n.[2]).

made and devised).[100] Another fifteenth-century dictionary includes the entry, "A Coknay: Ambro, mammotropus, delicius" (glutton, one suckled at the breast [for too long], petted child), and still another defines the term as "Delicius, puer in deliciis matris nutritus" (petted child, a boy who delights in suckling his mother).[101] "Cokeney" contains links to breastfeeding and physical dependence on feminine bodies, placing the "cokeney" in stark opposition to the rapist, who proves his manhood through his subordination of women's bodies. The prevalence of "cokeney" in English-Latin dictionaries attests to its prominence in pedagogical contexts, suggesting that it might have been common in all-male educational settings as a term of derision. John imagines his peers will see his failure to rape as both foolish and feminine, implying that to assert oneself as a mature man—rather than a pampered, dependent "cokeney" clinging helplessly to his mother's breast—is to commit sexual violence.

In casting rape as "auntr[ing] it" (risking it), John imagines his attack on the miller's wife as a laudatory act of chivalric masculinity. He sheds light on how rape culture refashions sexual assault, an act in which one person exploits power inequalities to exert their will on another, into an admirable act of bravery and armed violence.[102] He states that Aleyn "auntred hym" and received a favorable reward, recasting an act that he had formerly deemed too "perilous" (I.4189) as one that he will now boldly attempt, as the verb "auntren" is typically applied to feats of military risk taking in medieval romance.[103] With his twofold casting of rape as a valorous act, he touches on how rape is often "constitutive of knightly identity" in romances including Chaucer's *Wife of Bath's Tale*; as Amy N. Vines has shown, "in many romances, the rapist become[s] the hero" after his attack.[104] John's resolution to "arise and auntre it" puns on the erectile and warlike valences of "arise," casting the attempt to assault a woman as both genitally arousing and militarily valiant.[105] He uses a pedagogical proverb as a self-administered teaching tool and call to action, and

<hr />

100. A. L. Mayhew, ed., *Promptorium Parvulorum* (London: Kegan Paul, Trench, Trübner for the Early English Text Society, 1908), 90. *DMLBS* s.v. "carifotus"; "coconellus"; "fotus," 2; "delicium," 2. I am grateful to Joshua Byron Smith for his Latin insights.

101. *Catholicon Anglicum* and *Medulla Grammatice*, both cited in *MED* s.v. "cokenei" (n.[2]). *DMLBS* s.v. "ambro," a; "mammothreptus," b.

102. *MED* s.v. "auntren" (v.), 2(a).

103. Sidhu claims that the Reeve's "persistent use of chivalric language" and his casting of rape as the proving of manhood connects the male conflicts in the *Reeve's Tale* to those in the *Knight's Tale* (*Indecent Exposure*, 98).

104. Amy N. Vines, "Invisible Woman: Rape as Chivalric Necessity in Medieval Romance," in *Sexual Culture in the Literature of Medieval Britain*, ed. Amanda Hopkins, Robert Allen Rouse, and Cory James Rushton (Woodbridge: Boydell and Brewer, 2014), 167.

105. *MED* s.v. "arisen" (v.), 6(c): "Of parts of the body: to increase in size, swell up"; 9: "Of persons: to rise in hostility, make war."

he again emphasizes the link between rape and chivalric masculinity: his choice not to rape would make him both "unhardy" (not bold or daring, cowardly, afraid)—the opposite of "hardi" (strong in battle), a common term of praise for knights in romance—and "unsely" (luckless, unhappy).[106] Moreover, in portraying rape as having one's "nedes sped," John represents men's perpetration of sexual violence as based in a physical "nede" that must be satisfied by women's bodies, validating the myth that men are incapable of preventing themselves from raping when they are tempted by women's intoxication, revealing clothing, or irresistible beauty.

In a third moment of "felawe masculinity," Aleyn performs obscene sexual storytelling just as John anticipated he would, illuminating how the faction's values are enforced through the telling of japes among peers. At daybreak, Aleyn leaves Malyne's bed to rejoin John (or so he thinks) and names him as "my felawe" (I.4250). The Reeve repeats the term nine lines later when he refers to "his felawe John" (I.4259), and his repetition reinforces its link to practices of homosocial jape sharing. Aleyn delivers his tale in a fashion that is both intimate and violently menacing: he "caught hym by the nekke, and softe he spak" (I.4261), grabbing his listener by the throat and whispering in his ear. He enacts the collaborative, competitive elements of the faction's dynamic in a moment of obscene storytelling:

He seyde, "Thou John, thou swynes-heed, awak,
For Cristes saule, and heer a noble game,
For by that lord that called is Seint Jame,
As I have thries in this shorte nyght
Swyved the milleres doghter bolt upright [lying flat],
Whil thow hast, as a coward, been agast." (I.4262–67)

Just as John predicted, Aleyn's assault of Malyne has become a "jape," "a noble game" to be shared with one's "felawes." Aleyn refashions his rape into a humorous, laudatory story, and he embellishes his account with details like "thries," "shorte," and "bolt upright." Aleyn's retelling of his jape is accompanied by disparagements of John's masculinity, with the two men imagined in competition, linked by the subordinating conjunction "whil" that places their actions in comparison to each other: Aleyn "thries . . . swyve[s]," "whil" John is a "coward," a "swynes-heed" (fool). Aleyn's characterization of rape as "game"

---

106. *MED* s.v. "unhardi" (adj.); "hardi" (adj.), 1(a); "unseli" (adj.), (a). For this proverb, see Bartlett Jere Whiting, *Proverbs, Sentences, and Proverbial Phrases; from English Writings Mainly before 1500* (Cambridge, MA: Belknap Press, 1968), U3. Whiting links this to the more popular "Fortune helps the hardy man" (F519), which explicitly valorizes gendered bravery and risk taking.

(jest) echoes the Reeve's naming of it as "pley" and John's twofold figuration of it as a "jape."[107] Aleyn dehumanizes Malyne by referring to her as "the milleres doghter" instead of by her name even though we have heard him call her "Malyne" to her face (I.4236), indicating that her status as the miller's patriarchal property trumps everything else. His use of "bolt upright" to characterize her supine, unconscious posture underscores her physical incapacitation, emphasizing that he has exploited the effects of her drunkenness to assault her. With his use of the adjective "noble" to characterize his tale, he represents rape as a heroic act of chivalric masculinity. In contrast, he characterizes the nonraping man as "agast" (terrified, frightened), paralyzed with fear, and he represents refraining from rape as being "a coward," with its connotations of wickedness and fright, thus portraying sexual violence as homosocial imperative.[108] His characterization of John as "agast," "coward," and "swynes-heed" represents nonviolence as foolish and unmanly, as an act of fear rather than of human decency or ethical restraint. Aleyn's post-rape jape illustrates precisely what John feared in his pre-rape monologue: he knew that when the "jape [was] tald another day," he would be verbally abused by his peers, his masculinity impugned. Aleyn teaches that "swyv[ing]" an unconscious woman is both humorous and valiant. His rape becomes fodder for a homosocial "game," an obscene lesson about sex, power, and consent.

"So was hir joly whistle wel y-wet": Intoxication and Consent

The clerks' choice to exploit Malyne's and her mother's intoxication is an often-unacknowledged but significant element of the tale's rape script. It is central to "felawe masculinity" in the Middle Ages as well as today, as we see in the Ched Evans case, where Evans and McDonald witnessed the intoxicated woman fall down in the takeaway shop shortly before McDonald took her to the Premier Inn. Evans is shown on surveillance footage "pointing and walking past her," making her incapacitated body a humorous spectacle.[109] One element of this version of masculinity entails drinking communally with one's "felawes" and using alcohol as a tool to facilitate the conquests necessary to bolster one's status within the group. Chaucer's "felawes" are fond of their

---

107. *MED* s.v. "game" (n.), 4(b).
108. *MED* s.v. "couard" (n.), 1(a) and 2; "agasten" (v.), 2.
109. Katie Forster, "Ched Evans: Court Hears What Happened on Night Out as Footballer Cleared of Rape," *Independent*, October 14, 2016, http://www.independent.co.uk/news/uk/home-news/ched-evans-what-happened-latest-really-did-trial-admitted-court-footballer-not-guilty-rape-a7361966.html.

booze, as evidenced by the "dronke Millere," who is so inebriated that he nearly falls off his horse (I.3150), and the heavily intoxicated Cook, whose inability to hold his liquor is roundly mocked by the Manciple and the Host (IX.675). "Felawes" in medieval guild culture as well as in modern fraternities, sports teams, and other all-male communities use alcohol to cement their bonds in hazing initiation rituals and communal events.[110] They use it to take advantage of others and to justify assault: he was too drunk to realize that she didn't want it, she was asking for it by drinking with men.[111] Alcohol is central to "felawe masculinity," a tool of homosocial bonding and a marker of group membership as well as an instrument to facilitate rape that works alongside misogynist double standards governing drinking to displace the culpability for violence entirely onto women.

Skeptics may argue that alcohol-facilitated sexual assault is a modern concept, and that medieval audiences would not have recognized intercourse with an intoxicated individual as a violation. However, legal evidence suggests otherwise. Gwen Seabourne examines a landmark Herefordshire case from 1292 in which a surgeon used a narcotic beverage called "dwoledreng" ("dwale"-drink) to incapacitate and rape Isabella Plomet, one of his patients. She argues that the case is "worth noting as an example of a woman, a jury, and the common lawyers involved agreeing that the law should afford some remedy in a case of drug-facilitated sex contrary to the will of the woman."[112] The jury found in Isabella's favor, demonstrating that medieval society recognized that sexual assault could be facilitated through intoxication. "Dwale," meaning "a narcotic drink, sleeping potion," appears in the *Reeve's Tale* when everyone staggers to bed after their ale-soaked dinner and the Reeve remarks, "hem nedede no dwale," rhyming "dwale" with "ale" to reinforce the link between the two intoxicants and their effects (I.4161–62). Dwale's thirteenth-century use as a rape facilitator renders its mention by the Reeve, shortly before Aleyn rapes the intoxicated Malyne, especially chilling: both ale and dwale are portrayed as substances with comparably stuporific effects, and their similarities extend

---

110. Karras claims that "drinking together was an important way of forming bonds" for urban craft workers in formal guild feasts as well as informal gatherings, with the tavern serving as an important site of masculine identity formation (*From Boys to Men*, 143–44). For drinking as a bonding activity for university students like John and Aleyn, see ibid., 95–97.

111. Maria Testa and Kathleen A. Parks suggest that "men are more likely to display severe sexual aggression against drinking women, whom they view as vulnerable or sexually available due to intoxication" and observe that women's drinking violates misogynist norms, a transgression for which women are "punished" through violence. Testa and Parks, "The Role of Women's Alcohol Consumption in Sexual Victimization," *Aggression and Violent Behavior* 1, no. 3 (1996): 222–23, 227–28.

112. Gwen Seabourne, "Drugs, Deceit, and Damage in Thirteenth-Century Herefordshire: New Perspectives on Medieval Surgery, Sex, and the Law," *Social History of Medicine* 30, no. 2 (2017): 272. *MED* s.v. "dwale" (n.), 4(a).

to their use by rapists to render their victims unable to resist. A popular obscene proverb declares that "A drukin cunt hes na dure bar" (A drunken cunt
has no door bar), and Chaucer's Alisoun of Bath is well aware of men's exploitation of women's vulnerability resulting from intoxication: "In wommen
vinolent [wine-drunk] is no defence [resistance]— / This knowen lecchours
by experience," she declares (III.467–68).[113]

The Reeve repeatedly emphasizes the degree to which Malyne and her
mother are rendered defenseless by the "strong ale" they have consumed,
touching on the misogynist myth that women's choice to drink functions as
preemptive consent to anything that happens to them while they are intoxicated. Emily Finch and Vanessa E. Munro discuss the factors that result in
women being held culpable for their own assaults, which we see in contemporary culture as well as in the *Reeve's Tale*: women's choice to drink is
taken as an indicator of sexual interest, because "women who consume alcohol in the presence of a male drinker [are often] perceived to be more sexually disinhibited and sexually available."[114] Women's drinking to the point of
intoxication violates gender norms for appropriate behavior, since heavy drinking is typically associated with masculine homosociality.[115] The Reeve's references to the women's alcohol consumption authorize their assaults and justify
their victimization. He relates that "the millere into toun his doghter sende /
For ale" (I.4136–37), setting up the link between Malyne and alcohol and displacing onto her the culpability for her intoxication; she buys the ale that is
later used to overpower her. After he relates that they "drynken evere strong
ale atte beste" (I.4147), with the adverb "evere" highlighting the continual nature of their ale consumption and "strong" emphasizing its potent alcohol
content (which one could conceivably blame on Malyne, since she was the one
who purchased it), the Reeve focuses on Malyne's inebriation, stating that
"whan that drunken al was in the crowke, / To bedde wente the doghter right
anon" (I.4158–59). He implies that Malyne has passed out from inebriation,
with the adverbial phrase "right anon" (without delay) highlighting how she
goes to bed immediately after "al" the ale has been drunk; everyone has consumed the alcohol, but only Malyne is singled out as going directly to bed after

---

113. M. L. Anderson, ed., *The James Carmichaell Collection of Proverbs in Scots* (Edinburgh: Edinburgh University Press, 1957), no. 56. Another version claims that "Ane druken cunt had never ane
good dore bar." Erskine Beveridge, ed., *Fergusson's Scottish Proverbs, from the Original Print of 1641,
Together with a Larger Manuscript Collection of About the Same Period Hitherto Unpublished* (Edinburgh:
William Blackwood and Sons for the Scottish Text Society, 1924), 16; Whiting, *Proverbs*, C619.

114. Emily Finch and Vanessa E. Munro, "The Demon Drink and the Demonized Woman:
Socio-Sexual Stereotypes and Responsibility Attribution in Rape Trials Involving Intoxicants," *Social
and Legal Studies* 16, no. 4 (2007): 598–99.

115. Ibid., 594–95.

it is finished. We are encouraged to read her state when Aleyn rapes her not simply as sleep but as alcohol-induced unconsciousness. The Reeve notes the physical effects of her intoxication, signified not only by her unconsciousness but also by her inebriated snoring, when he relates that "the wenche rowteth [snores]" (I.4167). Aleyn is well aware of her snoring because it prevents him from sleeping, and one could argue that this awareness of her deep stupor emboldens him to believe he can get away with assaulting her. Malyne's defenselessness is further highlighted in the Reeve's description of her assault as she lies passed out and snoring, unable to fend off her attacker in her own bed: "This wenche lay uprighte and faste [soundly] slepte" (I.4194), he relates, emphasizing that she is lying flat on her back, completely unconscious. Once again, he uses "wenche" to name her, invoking the term's derogatory sexual connotations to discount her unequivocal nonconsent.

The Reeve similarly emphasizes Symkyn's wife's intoxication and implies her complicity in her assault: "As any jay she light was and jolyf, / So was hir joly whistle wel ywet," he says (I.4154–55).[116] His repetition of "jolyf" and "joly" to characterize the wife's body and demeanor depicts her as "willing victim" due to the terms' implications of lecherousness. His characterization of her as "light" paints her as already consenting to and even actively desiring whatever happens to her while she is drunk, because it contains valences of eagerness, lighthearted merriment, and feminine lewdness.[117] The Reeve prepares his audience to view Symkyn's wife as "asking for it," and he links her imputed willingness and lasciviousness to her intoxication. It is why she has to get up to go "out to pisse" in the dead of night (I.4215), and it is why she is so disoriented on her way back to bed after John's cradle trick. We are reminded of her drunken fatigue when the Reeve says, "[She] lith ful stille, and wolde han caught a sleep" (I.4227). This normalization of men exploiting women's inebriation to excuse assault and facilitate homosocial bonding is one of the tale's most pernicious elements. It is also one of its most historically persistent, as demonstrated by Ched Evans's retrial over six hundred years later, where his defense team used the woman's alcohol consumption and sexual behavior to argue successfully that Evans had not raped her. One defense witness "said they had sex on the weekend of the alleged rape and that she was drunk. 'She started instigating sex. She was coming on to me,' he said."[118]

---

116. Whiting, *Proverbs*, W225; also *MED* s.v. "whistle" (n.), (b): "**weten whistle**, to wet one's whistle, take an alcoholic drink; **hire whistle was wel wet**, her throat was well moistened, she was drunk." It is worth noting that all the examples cited by the *MED* and Whiting refer specifically to women's drunkenness.

117. *MED* s.v. "light" (adj.[2]), 6, 7(a), and 8(c).

118. Morris, "Second Ched Evans Defence Witness."

The Reeve's Lesson

Like many fabliaux, the *Reeve's Tale* ends on a note that is both obscene and educational, illustrating the pedagogical currency of the jape. When the Reeve sums up his lesson, he uses the faction's trademark obscenity along with two proverbs to articulate what his peers should learn from his narrative:

His wyf is swyved, and his doghter als.
Lo, swich it is a millere to be fals!
And therfore this proverbe is seyd ful sooth,
"Hym thar nat wene wel that yvele dooth."
A gylour shal hymself bigyled be . . .
Thus have I quyt the Millere in my tale. (I.4317–21, 4324)

As he did with Aleyn earlier in the tale, here the Reeve excuses the students, casting their rape of the two women as a fitting response to Symkyn's economic treachery. He displaces rape's harms onto Symkyn, casting him as the sole sufferer of the clerks' violence: "*his* wyf," "*hys* doghter," "gylour . . . *hym*self*," "*hym* . . . that yvele dooth" (emphasis mine).[119] He frames his jape as an instructive exemplum illustrating two "proverbe[s]."[120] As always in Chaucer's *Tales*, "swyved" is deployed strategically to imprint the text's lessons on the audiences' minds: rape can be both morally and legally justified, rape makes a jape for group bonding, women's inebriation renders them willing, women are nothing more than "wenches" on whose flesh men can build their bonds and wage their wars. Like vultures, the "felawes" pick away the skin and sinew of women's trauma, leaving only the grinning white skeleton of a story to display as a trophy to their friends.

Through his portrayal of a pair of "felawes," the Reeve underscores the integral role of sexual violence in male bonding and shows how homosocial relations can shape perpetrators' decision making. The men's speeches about their assaults illuminate the relationship between rape and male fear, representing rape as an admirable act of chivalric masculinity and a defiant refusal to fear violence from other men, when in fact their choices are driven by a deep-seated fear of their peers' emasculating words.

---

119. Daniel F. Pigg reads this violence at the tale's close as signifying a "symbolic" "homosexual rape," an act "seen as separating one from community in addition to feminizing the victim" ("Performing the Perverse: The Abuse of Masculine Power in the *Reeve's Tale*," in Beidler, *Masculinities in Chaucer*, 60).

120. For the two proverbs, "He that does evil need not expect well" and "The guiler is beguiled," see Whiting, *Proverbs*, E185, G491.

Responding to Rape: The *Cook's Prologue and Tale*

The *Cook's Prologue* affirms that the *Reeve's Tale* works precisely the way the jape is intended to operate in its homosocial context: it incites mirthful pleasure, fosters same-sex intimacy, and leaves its pedagogical mark on its teller's peers. The Cook, another member of the faction, is overcome with delighted laughter on hearing the tale, and just as the Reeve intends, he interprets the jape as an instructive exemplum illustrating a proverb:

> The Cook of Londoun, whil the Reve spak,
> For joye him thoughte he clawed him on the bak.
> "Ha! ha!" quod he, "For Cristes passion,
> This millere hadde a sharp conclusion
> Upon his argument of herbergage!
> Wel seyde Salomon in his langage,
> 'Ne bryng nat every man into thyn hous,'
> For herberwynge by nyghte is perilous." (I.4325–32)

The Cook imagines the Reeve's storytelling as a form of physical closeness between the two men. As his comrade narrates his tale, the Cook enjoys it so much that he imagines the Reeve, through his fabliau, is providing him with "joye" and corporeal pleasure by scratching him on the back, highlighting how obscene storytelling fosters intimacy between peers.[121] The Cook reads the tale's rapes as a comic jape directed at the miller—"[The miller] hadde a jape of malice in the derk!" (I.4338), he crows; the victims' trauma is occluded entirely. The Cook interprets the tale as instructive and provides a proverb of his own, emphasizing how japes were understood to function pedagogically in spite of their obscenity and levity, as he follows the Reeve in framing his fabliau as an exemplum illustrating a biblical proverb. Editors read the Cook's interpretation of the tale as a "conclusion / Upon [an] argument" as a "joking use of the technical language of the schools," highlighting how the fabliau is received by the "felawes" as pedagogy masquerading as a joke.[122]

The Cook follows his brethren's fabliaux by sharing a jape of his own about another pair of youthful "felawes." By introducing his tale as "a litel jape that fil in oure citee" (I.4343), he follows the Miller and Reeve in aligning himself

---

121. *MED* s.v. "clauen" (v.), 2(a). Hansen states that the Cook's response "acknowledges the bonds of pleasure, mutual irritation, and reciprocal service between male comrades that such tale-telling affords" (*Chaucer and the Fictions of Gender*, 242), and Crocker observes the "frustrating efficacy" of the *Reeve's Tale* on the Cook ("Affective Politics," 256).

122. *Riverside Chaucer*, 852.

with the faction's preferred mode of instruction, recreation, and community bonding. Like the Reeve, he positions his tale as pedagogical by sprinkling it with proverbs: "Of a proverbe that seith this same word: / 'Wel bet is roten appul out of hoord'" (I.4405–6), he proclaims of his unruly apprentice, presenting his jape as a lesson with his use of this "proverbe" and highlighting the faction's practices of peer education because one rotten apple / apprentice indelibly influences its fellows.[123] The Cook's protagonist is "a propre short felawe" named Perkyn Revelour (I.4368), a London food seller's apprentice who loves dancing, partying, sex, and playing dice in the street with his friends. In addition to aligning him with the faction's code of masculinity by introducing him as a "felawe," the Cook emphasizes Perkyn's sexual dealings and close relationships with other men, underscoring the value that "felawe masculinity" places on homosocial conviviality and heterosexual conquest. Using the faction's trademark term for women, he declares, "Wel [blessed] was the wenche with hym myghte meete" (I.4374), imagining his partners as "wenche[s]" who are fortunate to sleep with him. He notes that Perkyn is "free / Of his dispense" with sex workers (I.4387–88). When he is not busy copulating, Perkyn hangs out with a posse of male companions, "a meynee of his sort" (I.4381), a group characterized by collectivity and similarity; "meynee" denotes a community of individuals—a domestic household, a band of retainers, an army, a family—whose individualities are subsumed under the heading of the group.[124] "Sort" indicates a specific variety of people who resemble one another, casting the members of Perkyn's urban peer group as united in their likeness. As a "meynee," they are a tribe of their own, subject to their own rules. After he is ejected from his master's patriarchal authority, Perkyn moves in with "a compeer of his owene sort, / That lovede dys, and revel, and disport" (I.4419–20), and they set up a household of party-loving "felawes." The Cook underscores the inherently relational component of this type of masculinity: "compeer" means "an equal," "a companion, an intimate friend," denoting both intimacy and equality between peers, while "lowke" (I.4415) designates "a friend, an accomplice."[125] Once again, the term "sort" reminds us of the fundamental similarities and shared code of masculinity between Perkyn and his friend.

---

123. Whiting, *Proverbs*, A167. The Cook deploys another proverb about masculine peer relationships for pedagogical purposes ten lines later when he declares, "for ther is no theef withoute a lowke" (4415) (ibid., T73). The Cook also uses multiple proverbs in his *Prologue* (4355, 4357) (ibid., S488, P257).

124. *MED* s.v. "meine" (n.), 1(a), 1(c), 2(a), and 3(a).

125. *MED* s.v. "comper" (n.), (a) and (b); s.v. "louke" (n.[2]).

But something unexpected forces the Cook's merry tale of the two friends' adventures to a screeching halt. This abrupt truncation sheds light on how the structure of "felawe masculinity" depends on the objectification and subordination of women for its very existence. The Cook relates that Perkyn's new roommate "hadde a wyf that heeld for contenance / A shoppe, and swyved for hir sustenance" (I.4221–22), and it seems as though we are in for another leering introductory description like that of Alisoun in the *Miller's Tale* or Malyne in the *Reeve's Tale*. Instead, the tale breaks off at this point, and we hear no more of Perkyn, his friend, or his friend's wife.

Some scholars speculate that the remainder of the tale was too bawdy for an early scribe, who destroyed it; others believe it was lost by an accident of textual transmission; and others argue that the tale is complete as it is.[126] Regardless of the cause, the fact that the tale—and the fragment as a whole— ends here on such an obscene and startling note, and that this ending has been preserved in most manuscripts of the *Canterbury Tales*, carries important implications for the faction's link between masculinity and obscene storytelling. The tale closes with a married woman who sustains herself with sex work and a husband who seems to tolerate it, preferring instead to go dicing and drinking with his "compere" and privileging his male friendships over his marital responsibilities. In contrast to the fragment's previous two fabliaux that represent women as bodies whose exploitation shapes male bonds, here we are confronted with an independent woman who is doubly productive, keeping a shop for social respectability and selling her body for enough cash to survive. And in contrast to popular portrayals of the youthful urban wastrel exploiting his partner, like the character Ryotte in Skelton's *Bowge of Court* (1498) who "lete[s his lover] to hyre that men maye on her ryde" and lives off the profits from "her tayle," here the woman's gain is for "hire" alone.[127] This act of singular agency was revised by some scribes who changed "hire" to "his" so that the wife's work is all for her husband's gain and fits more comfortably into the faction's portrayal of women's subordination.[128]

---

126. Stephen Partridge, "Minding the Gaps: Interpreting the Manuscript Evidence of the *Cook's Tale* and the *Squire's Tale*," in *The English Medieval Book: Studies in Memory of Jeremy Griffiths*, ed. A. S. G. Edwards, Vincent Gillespie, and Ralph Hanna (London: British Library, 2000); M. C. Seymour, "Of This Cokes Tale," *Chaucer Review* 24, no. 3 (1990); Hansen, *Chaucer and the Fictions of Gender*, 243–44. Seymour suggests that Chaucer originally "finished" the *Cook's Tale* but that the leaves were lost before the Hengwrt manuscript was copied in c. 1405, a hypothesis that renders the pivotal position of the tale's final couplet an accident of textual transmission.

127. *Complete English Poems of John Skelton*, 38–51, lines 402, 405.

128. The "his" variant occurs in four manuscripts. A. S. G. Edwards, "Chaucer's *Cook's Tale* 4422," *Notes and Queries* 64, no. 2 (2017). I am grateful to Dr. Edwards for drawing my attention to this variant and discussing its implications with me.

In addition to his portrayal of feminine sexual and economic independence, the Cook's use of "swyve" in his tale's final line is of paramount significance. In all other surviving examples of "swyve" in Middle English, the verb is rendered with a masculine agent and a feminine object: swyving is done grammatically *by* men *to* women, even when the woman initiates the encounter.[129] We can read the final couplet as illustrating the close relationship that the "felawes" posit between masculinity, pedagogy, and obscenity; there is no place for a woman who habitually "swyve[s]" for her own benefit in their script, and the tale, now no longer a jape, ceases to be funny or edifying for the group. The tale's conclusion shows that the Cook, in spite of his best efforts, has failed to absorb the faction's lessons fully: like his "felawes," he stresses the importance of male bonds, presents women as transactional bodies, and articulates "swyve," but he accidentally reverses the gendered power hierarchies that his peers present as inherent in the term and integral to their version of masculinity. He uses the faction's obscene shibboleth and favored pedagogical tool to teach a new lesson about women's sexual agency, and his peers have nothing to say in response.

Revising "Felawe Masculinity"

While I have painted a bleak picture of men teaching their peers the tenets of rape culture through obscene storytelling, I conclude by pointing to two sites where I see potential for challenging this ideology. The first sheds light on the possibility of bystander intervention, of men dissuading their peers from committing assault. When Aleyn declares his intention to "swyve" Malyne, John responds not with affirmation, but rather with horrified discouragement:

> This John answerede, "Alayn, avyse thee!
> The millere is a perilous man," he seyde,
> "And gif that he out of his sleep abreyde,
> He myghte doon us bathe a vileynye." (I.4188–91)

Although John's objection is based in self-preserving fear of Symkyn's violence rather than concern for Malyne or regard for rape's ethical wrongs, it is nonetheless significant that this passage illustrates how men can intervene and

---

129. See all quotations cited under *MED* s.v. "swiven" (v.). Hansen notes that the wife is the subject of the verb here, in contrast to its use in a similar line at the end of the *Miller's Tale*, but she does not probe the implications of this difference, focusing instead on the Cook's echoing of the Miller's diction (*Chaucer and the Fictions of Gender*, 243).

dissuade their "felawes" from sexual violence, as John urges his friend to "avyse thee" (reflect on your decision) and choose a different action.[130]

The second site of resistance to the faction's lessons lies in fifteenth-century manuscripts of the *Canterbury Tales*, where readers' responses to Chaucer's obscenities raise a number of intriguing possibilities for challenging the faction's aggressive version of masculinity. In BL MS Additional 35286 (1430–50), early readers censored the obscenities and explicit details of assault in the *Reeve's Tale* using methods normally used to correct textual errors to revise the tale's graphic violence instead. By handling textual errors and rape's obscenities in similar fashion, the codex's readers mark the obscenities of the *Reeve's Tale* as errors in empathy and sexual ethics.

The manuscript is copied in a single, clear, professional Anglicana hand and consists solely of an incomplete text of the *Canterbury Tales* with numerous leaves missing, including the first part of the *General Prologue*.[131] Its earliest origins are unknown, but Manly and Rickert claim that it was owned by the Agarde family on the Staffordshire–Derbyshire border in the sixteenth century.[132] It contains numerous names, pen trials, annotations, and scribbles in hands from the fifteenth and sixteenth centuries, and it is relatively free of scribal errors, corrections, and erasures.[133] Simon Horobin remarks on the "extremely small number of . . . errors throughout such a large piece of copying," with only two corrected by erasure without overwriting.[134] Unlike many manuscripts of the *Canterbury Tales*, neither the manuscript's scribe nor its readers censor its obscenities by erasure, omission, or substitution of a less obscene term like "served," "pleyed," "dight," or "dide": all the genital terms in the *Wife of Bath's Prologue*, and all the "swyves" in Chaucer's fabliaux, are left untouched—except in the *Reeve's Tale*.[135]

MS Additional 35286's readers show an extraordinary interest, unmatched elsewhere in the codex, in the portion of the manuscript containing the *Reeve's Tale*'s two assaults. This part of the tale, beginning on folio 41r, is first singled

---

130. *MED* s.v. "avisen" (v.), 4(a). For an overview of bystander approaches to sexual violence prevention, see Anastasia Powell, "Shifting Upstream: Bystander Action against Sexism and Discrimination against Women," in Henry and Powell, *Preventing Sexual Violence*.

131. On MS Additional 35286, see Simon Horobin, "A Transcription and Study of British Library Additional MS 35286 of Chaucer's *Canterbury Tales*" (PhD diss., University of Sheffield, 1997) and "Additional 35286 and the Order of the *Canterbury Tales*," *Chaucer Review* 31, no. 3 (1997); John M. Manly and Edith Rickert, *The Text of the Canterbury Tales*, 8 vols. (Chicago: University of Chicago Press, 1940), 1:41–47.

132. Manly and Rickert, *Text of the Canterbury Tales*, 1:45.

133. Ibid., 1:45–47.

134. Horobin, "British Library Additional MS 35286," 99. The two erasures of errors without overwriting occur on folios 60r and 213v.

135. For the uncensored "swyves," see folios 37v, 43r, 121v, 213r, and 215v.

out by a fifteenth-century Anglicana hand different than the main scribe's that has written "nota bene de hac re" (pay attention regarding this thing) in the right margin at the beginning of the double rape scene, calling readers' attention to this moment in the narrative. The first erasure in the *Reeve's Tale* occurs on this same folio, shortly after the note to readers, where "swyve" is scraped from the page.[136] The scribe originally wrote Aleyn's declaration as "yon wenche wol I swyeffe." However, one of the codex's readers scraped "I swyeffe" from the parchment, rendering the first-person declaration of intention to rape as something that does not belong on the page. This is puzzling because the knife-wielding reader left "swyve" untouched at the end of the *Miller's Tale* just four folios earlier. What does this reader find objectionable about Aleyn's "I swyeffe," if not its obscenity?

Folio 41's verso contains more erasures, which proliferate with the second assault, for our reader erases the specific details of John's attack on the miller's wife. The original scribe wrote, "He priketh hard and depe as he were mad," but someone erased "priketh," "hard," "depe," and "as," obliterating the parts of the line that most graphically depict sexual violence—the penetrative adverbs "hard" and "depe" and the suggestive verb "priketh," which denotes both piercing and vigorous riding.[137] Enough remains on the page that readers are aware that the assault has happened, but we are spared the details provided by the Reeve. Further down on the folio, when Aleyn boasts that he has "swyved the milleres doghter bolt upright," someone, either the original scribe or an early reader, scraped out the *w* and wrote *ch* in Anglicana script so that "swyved" became "schyfed." This substitution means "to remove the woody parts of flax by beating" or could be a form of "shiften," whose meanings include "to share in, to strike, to control, to change."[138] The reader trades an obscenity for a similar-sounding alliterating euphemism and once again, with erasure and alteration, registers their disapproval of the explicit depiction of rape.

The erasures on folio 41r–v, in which early readers take knives to parchment to challenge the Reeve's leering, obscene description of sexual violence, call to mind the Reeve's own words in his *Prologue*: "For leveful is with force force of-showve." We cannot know when the erasures happened or who made

---

136. Somerset discusses erasure in medieval manuscripts as a form of reader response and secondary censorship in "Censorship," 255–57.

137. "Priketh" has erotic valences in a *Ladd y the daunce a myssomur day* (*DIMEV* 3044), a carol voiced by a singlewoman who states, "He prikede and he praunsede, nolde he never lynne" (38). *MED* s.v. "priken" (v.), 1(b) and 4b(a); Duncan, *Medieval English Lyrics and Carols*, 281–83.

138. *MED* s.v. "shifen" (v.) and "shiften" (v.). I am grateful to Mary Flannery for helping me think through this term.

them, but we can read them as showing readers repelling the "force" of rape with the equal, opposite "force" of resistance to rape's gratuitously explicit representation for comic purposes. Nor do we know the gender of the resisting reader(s): it could be one of the many men who wrote their names in the manuscript in the sixteenth and seventeenth centuries, or it could be a female reader angry at the Reeve's use of obscenity to make light of women's violation. Either way, MS Additional 35286 provides valuable insight into how sexual violence could be interpreted by the early readers of the *Reeve's Tale*. This reader response, whether it is men challenging the behavior of Chaucer's fictional men or women offended by the Reeve's joking, graphic rape narratives, poses a direct challenge to the masculinity that we see in the *Reeve's Tale*, in which "felawes" spur one another to violence and brag about their exploits with obscene storytelling, and where the Reeve portrays rape as "pley." Because it is only the obscenities during the rape scenes in the *Reeve's Tale* on folio 41r–v, along with details of John's assault of Symkyn's wife, that are erased and overwritten, it is not *all* obscenities that are objectionable, only those that are deployed when narrating sexual violence.[139] We can see a small, localized challenge to the explicit representation of rape in the *Reeve's Tale* when readers treat Chaucer's obscenities and bodily details as a form of error, which is especially visible in a manuscript containing so few errors. They suggest the possibility of men challenging cultures of obscene storytelling and teaching their peers that using japes to condone women's victimization is unacceptable. As Flood states, "We will only make progress in preventing violence against women if we can change the attitudes, identities, and relations among some men, which sustain violence."[140] Only by laying bare those relations, probing how they are taught, and understanding obscenity's integral role as a teaching tool, can we fully understand the homosocial underpinnings of sexual education.

---

139. It is important to note that the "queynt"-grabbing in the *Miller's Tale* remains untouched on fol. 30v.

140. Flood, "Involving Men in Efforts to End Violence against Women," *Men and Masculinities* 14, no. 3 (2011): 372.

CHAPTER 2

"With a cunt"

Obscene Misogyny and Masculine Pedagogical Community in the Middle Scots Flyting

Like Chaucer's "felawes," poets at the sixteenth-century Scottish court use obscene misogyny to foster homosocial community and teach one another codes of masculine sexuality.[1] But while Chaucer's men use it to instruct their peers to have sex with as many "wenches" as possible, the Scottish poets use it for a different purpose. Through composing literary insult battles known as "flytings," in which two men take turns attacking each other with scurrilous anecdotes and alliterating torrents of insults, they harness obscenity's capacity for same-sex pedagogy to teach one another to eschew contact with women and focus their libidinal energies on writing obscene poetry with other men. These exchanges dislodge the primacy of copulating with women from models of exemplary masculinity. In the code espoused by Chaucer's faction, *not* having sex is unmanly, while for the flyters over a century later, intercourse imperils one's masculinity and bodily sovereignty.

---

1. Priscilla Bawcutt notes that Older Scots literature contains "a surprisingly large quantity of crudely antifeminist verse and prose" in "Images of Women in the Poems of Dunbar," *Études Écossaises* 1 (1992): 50. Evelyn S. Newlyn discusses the rampant misogyny in sixteenth-century Scottish verse in "Of 'Vertew Nobillest' and 'Serpent Wrinkis': Taxonomy of the Female in the Bannatyne Manuscript," *Scotia* 14 (1990) and in "Images of Women in Sixteenth-Century Scottish Literary Manuscripts," in *Women in Scotland, c. 1100–c. 1750*, ed. Elizabeth Ewan and Maureen Meikle (East Linton, UK: Tuckwell Press, 1999).

In *The Flyting betwixt Montgomerie and Polwart* (c. 1582), two members of James VI's court trade verses full of epithets like "tuirdfacit" (turd-faced) (IX.27), "foul ers" (IX.4), and "dryd sting" (dried-out penis) (IX.70) to disparage each other and assert their poetic primacy.[2] Sir Patrick Hume of Polwarth levels twin insults against Alexander Montgomerie's genitalia when he jeers, "With a cunt, deid runt" (dead stump) (IX.63). Linking his epithets with internal rhyme, he insists that Montgomerie possesses a vulva, derisively invoking women's genitalia to feminize his opponent. At the same time, he accuses Montgomerie of impotence by alleging that his penis is "deid" like a dried-up and decayed tree stump.[3] The phrase "with a cunt" was too much for Edinburgh printer Andrew Hart, who replaced it with "Jock blunt," a slang term for a henpecked husband, in his 1621 edition of the flyting, removing the insult's obscenity but retaining its misogynist overtones: instead of claiming that Montgomerie has a vulva, Hart's censored version accuses him of failing to exercise control over his domineering wife.[4] In 1584, James VI praised his courtiers' poem as a shining exemplar of Scots verse, demonstrating that it found royal approval in spite of, or perhaps even due to, its obscenity.[5] Montgomerie and Polwarth's duel, marked by its conflation of physical virility with poetic prowess and its deployment of obscene misogyny by each poet to attack the other, is part of a larger literary phenomenon of obscenity's mobilization for the purposes of sexual education among men of the Stewart court.

Flyting's Gendered Contexts: Criminal Speech, Antifeminist Satire, and Scholastic Disputation

Flyters draw their vocabulary of insult from the feminized discourse of speech crime in sixteenth-century Scotland, refashioning a discourse associated with disorderly women into a tool for proving masculinity. They draw their obscene same-sex pedagogical function from the popular Middle Scots genre of didac-

---

2. *The Flyting betwixt Montgomerie and Polwart*, in *Alexander Montgomerie: Poems*, ed. David J. Parkinson, 2 vols. (Edinburgh: Scottish Text Society, 2000), 1:139–75.

3. *DOST*, s.v. "runt" (n.), (a) and (c).

4. Alexander Montgomerie and Sir Patrick Hume of Polwarth, *The Flyting betwixt Montgomerie and Polwart* (Edinburgh: Andrew Hart, 1621). Roderick J. Lyall notes that "there is a good deal of Anglicization in the work of Hart and his successors, combined with the elimination . . . of the more obviously obscene terms." Lyall, *Alexander Montgomerie: Poetry, Politics, and Cultural Change in Jacobean Scotland* (Tempe: Arizona Center for Medieval and Renaissance Studies, 2005), 77.

5. Lyall, *Alexander Montgomerie*, 102–3; David J. Parkinson, "Alexander Montgomerie, James VI, and 'Tumbling Verse,'" in *Loyal Letters: Studies in Mediaeval Alliterative Poetry and Prose*, ed. L. A. J. R. Houwen and A. A. MacDonald (Groningen: Egbert Forsten, 1994).

tic antiwoman poems about penile governance addressed by older men to younger men. They base their exchanges on the highly structured rhetorical form and masculinity-asserting function of scholastic disputation, which comes from the all-male world of the university and is linked to discourses of clerical misogyny that urged men to forgo marriage altogether. In stressing the genre's links to these three discourses, I show how flyters draw on three separate but overlapping misogynist cultural traditions to teach their lessons about sexuality: the internalized misogyny in women's criminal quarrels that accuses women of breaking patriarchal rules governing sexual conduct; the literary misogyny articulated by aged male lyric voices that views women's bodies as devouring men's virility; and the clerical misogyny that encourages men to eschew matrimony by invoking women's inherent lasciviousness and moral depravity.[6]

Priscilla Bawcutt suggests that flytings were performed orally as court entertainment in addition to being circulated in manuscript among court coteries and printed for the enjoyment of the reading public.[7] The earliest surviving literary flyting is *The Flyting of Dunbar and Kennedy* (c. 1505), an exchange between William Dunbar, the foremost poet of James IV's court, and Walter Kennedy.[8] A generation later, Sir David Lyndsay participated in a flyting exchange with James V, of which Lyndsay's *Answer to the Kingis Flyting* (c. 1535–36) survives. Alexander Montgomerie and Patrick Hume of Polwarth jointly composed *The Flyting betwixt Montgomerie and Polwart* (c. 1582) for James VI's court.[9] Montgomerie exchanged flyting verses with his kinsman and political coconspirator Hugh Barclay of Ladyland in 1585, demonstrating flyting's

---

6. For more on medieval misogyny, see Anke Bernau, "Medieval Antifeminism," in *The History of British Women's Writing, 700–1500*, ed. Liz Herbert McAvoy and Diane Watt (New York: Palgrave Macmillan, 2012); Alcuin Blamires, ed., *Woman Defamed and Women Defended: An Anthology of Medieval Texts* (Oxford: Clarendon Press, 1992); Kathleen Forni, "The Antifeminist Tradition: Introduction," in *The Chaucerian Apocrypha: A Selection* (Kalamazoo, MI: Medieval Institute Publications, 2005); Utley, *Crooked Rib*.

7. Priscilla Bawcutt, *Dunbar the Makar* (Oxford: Clarendon Press, 1992), 233. Hasler examines courtly poetic rivalries and genital discourse in Dunbar's poetry in *Court Poetry*, 63–86.

8. For more on *The Flyting of Dunbar and Kennedy*, see Ian MacLeod Higgins, "Tit for Tat: The *Canterbury Tales* and *The Flyting of Dunbar and Kennedy*," *Exemplaria* 16, no. 1 (2004); Nicole Meier, "*The Flyting of Dunbar and Kennedy* in Context," in *Language Cleir Illumynate: Scottish Poetry from Barbour to Drummond, 1375–1630*, ed. Nicola Royan (Amsterdam: Rodopi, 2007); Christine M. Robinson, "More than One Meaning in *The Flyting of Dunbar and Kennedy*," *Neuphilologische Mitteilungen* 99, no. 3 (1998); Jacquelyn Hendricks, "The Battle of 'Trechour Tung[s]': Gaelic, Middle Sots, and the Question of Ethnicity in the Scottish Flyting," *Fifteenth Century Studies* 37 (2012).

9. For more on *The Flyting betwixt Montgomerie and Polwart*, see Sally Mapstone, "Invective as Poetic: The Cultural Contexts of Polwarth and Montgomerie's *Flyting*," *Scottish Literary Journal* 26, no. 2 (1999).

social capacity to perform bonds of brotherhood and political solidarity in spite of its seeming antagonism.[10]

The flyters reject models of masculinity that entail heterosexual conquest, and the lessons they teach are especially intriguing in light of the social contexts that produced them. The courts of James IV (1473–1513) and his son James V (1512–42) were heavily male and notoriously licentious, as illustrated in poems by Dunbar, Lyndsay, and others.[11] Both kings were renowned for their prodigious sexual appetites, open affairs with unmarried and married women alike, numerous bastards, and use of royal funds to support their mistresses and out-of-wedlock children. James IV kept a woman listed as "Janet bair ars" on his payroll from 1508 to 1512, and his favorite mistress, Janet Kennedy (a different Janet), was niece to the flyter Walter Kennedy.[12] James V spent his teens and early twenties fathering illegitimate children with nine different women, who were "almost all the daughters of nobles or lairds in the king's service and so, presumably, were present at least on the periphery of the court before they became mothers of royal bastards."[13] The flyting's procontinence pedagogy is especially striking in its cultural context because it instructs men to follow a paradigm of sexual conduct different from the one embraced by the king and much of his court.

In addition to naming a popular literary genre, "flyting" referred to the crime of obscene verbal wrangling associated with unruly women.[14] Bawcutt observes how poets make use of "the non-literary world of actual street-

10. For more on the Montgomerie-Ladyland relationship, see *Alexander Montgomerie: Poems*, 2:14; for the flyting, see ibid., 1:133–34.

11. Lyrics about the lasciviousness of James IV and James V's courts include Lyndsay, *The Compleynt of Schir David Lyndsay* (c. 1530), lines 186–254, in *Sir David Lyndsay: Selected Poems*, ed. Janet Hadley Williams (Glasgow: Association for Scottish Literary Studies, 2000), 41–57; Dunbar, *Doverit with dreme devysing in my slummer, Madam your men said thai wald ryd, Sir Thomas Norny, Thir ladies fair that maks repair*, and *This hinder nycht in Dumfermeling*, in *The Poems of William Dunbar*, ed. Priscilla Bawcutt, 2 vols. (Glasgow: Association for Scottish Literary Studies, 1998), 1:71–74, 116–17, 133–34, 238–39, 245–47; *The use of court richt weill I knaw*, in *The Bannatyne Manuscript*, ed. W. Tod Ritchie, 4 vols. (Edinburgh: Scottish Text Society, 1928), 4:31–32. Ishbel C. M. Barnes characterizes James IV's court as "a very masculine group" in *Janet Kennedy, Royal Mistress: Marriage and Divorce in the Courts of James IV and V* (Edinburgh: John Donald, 2007), 19.

12. Norman Macdougall, *James IV* (Edinburgh: John Donald, 1989), 286; Barnes, *Janet Kennedy*, 48 and 38.

13. Andrea Thomas, "'Dragonis Baith and Dowes ay in Double Forme': Women at the Court of James V, 1513–1532," in Ewan and Meikle, *Women in Scotland*, 86–87.

14. Sandy Bardsley, *Venomous Tongues: Speech and Gender in Late Medieval England* (Philadelphia: University of Pennsylvania Press, 2006); Elizabeth Ewan, "'Many Injurious Words': Defamation and Gender in Late Medieval Scotland," in *History, Literature, and Music in Scotland, 700–1560*, ed. R. Andrew McDonald (Toronto: University of Toronto Press, 2002); Laura Gowing, *Domestic Dangers: Women, Words, and Sex in Early Modern London* (Oxford: Oxford University Press, 1996); Kirilka Stavreva, *Words Like Daggers: Violent Female Speech in Early Modern England* (Lincoln: University of Nebraska Press, 2015).

quarrels" when crafting their insults, bringing the abusive feminized language of the streets to the court's all-male literary coterie.[15] Literary flyters draw heavily on the colloquial vocabulary of criminal flyting, repurposing an oral discourse recoverable from legal records. In Elgin in 1542, Megot Stewart attacked Ellen Ternway and her sister Margaret as "shabbit, clangorit carlis birdis" (scabbed, syphilitic churl's women).[16] Not to be outdone, Ellen disparaged Megot as "schabit, blerit, clangorit carling" (scabbed, bleary-eyed, syphilitic old woman). Both women were convicted of flyting and fined as punishment. Sometimes flytings were accompanied by physical violence, as in another case from the same court three weeks earlier, when Christian Varden was convicted of calling Margarat Froster "vild meir, comond huyr, and theif" (vile mare, common whore, and thief).[17] Margarat responded by hitting Christian on the head with a pan and pulling a "greit quantate" of hair "out of hir heid," and both women were convicted of flyting. In another Elgin case from that spring, Janet Anderson and Marion Pakman insulted Muriel Caldour as "commownd hwir, pintill in pintill out hyr and ane horne at thair taill, freris hewir, and prestis hewir, and monkis hewir" (common whore, penis in penis out whore with a horn at her backside [e.g., an outlaw], friar's whore, priest's whore, and monk's whore).[18] Some flytings took place episodically over time, like the ongoing feud between Agnes Henderson and Marion Ray in Stirling during the 1540s, whose back-and-forth vitriol resembles that of a literary flyting. In August 1546, Marion was convicted of "calland [Agnes] commoun huir and that scho wist hir xx tymes swifit, and that scho saw Wille Cuninggame swiff her vj tymes" (calling Agnes common whore and saying that she knew her to be fucked twenty times and that she saw Will Cunningham fuck her six times).[19] Marion said to Agnes's husband, "Sclaverand Henry, wer you worthie to swiff thi wiff thi self you wald nocht lat otheris swiff hir" (Slobbering Henry, if you were worthy to fuck your wife yourself you would not let others fuck her), and she attacked William Cunningham, Agnes's reputed lover, with "trublus

15. *Poems of William Dunbar*, 2:429. This connection between literary and criminal flyting is also explored in Bawcutt, *Dunbar the Makar*, 222–24; *The Poems of Walter Kennedy*, ed. Nicole Meier (Edinburgh: Scottish Text Society, 2008), cix–xi; and Ewan, "'Many Injurious Words,'" 169–70.

16. William Cramond, ed., *The Records of Elgin, 1234–1800*, 2 vols. (Aberdeen: New Spalding Club, 1903, 1908), 1:72.

17. Ibid. For the role of physical violence in flyting cases like these, see Elizabeth Ewan, "Disorderly Damsels? Women and Interpersonal Violence in Pre-Reformation Scotland," *Scottish Historical Review* 89, no. 2 (2010).

18. Cramond, *Records of Elgin*, 1:69.

19. Robert Renwick, ed., *Extracts from the Records of the Royal Burgh of Stirling AD 1519–1666*, 2 vols. (Glasgow: Glasgow Stirlingshire and Sons of the Rock Society, 1887–89), 1:43. Agnes's sharp tongue got her into legal trouble one year earlier, when she called Annabel Grahame "ane freris get and freris yawde" (a friar's bastard and friar's whore), 1:40–41.

[bothersome] wordis." In response, Agnes called Marion "huir and breikar of spousage" (whore and homewrecker). Their conflict continued the next year, when Marion called Agnes "huir and theiff, landlowper, breikar of spousage" (whore and thief, vagabond, homewrecker).[20] As these cases show, Scotswomen used flyting's creative obscenity and internalized misogyny to articulate interpersonal conflicts and to accuse one another of sexual transgression.

Criminal flyting's same-sex verbal violence was particularly powerful in the context of stringent social, religious, and legal codes restricting women's sexuality. In hurling epithets like "huir," "meir," "loune," "jade," and "quene," which all mean "whore," flyting women attacked one another with terms of criminal transgression that carried meaningful weight in a culture where women were punished publicly for fornication or adultery and where a woman's social and economic credit rested on her good reputation.[21] Legal statutes outlawing flyting target women specifically, prescribing punishment for "wemen [and] menis wiffis . . . found flytand on the Hie Gait" (women and men's wives found flyting in the main road) and "women at flytis . . . [and] skanderis ony gud menis wyfis" (women that flyte and slander any good men's wives).[22] This feminization of criminal flyting is not restricted to legal codes but also occurs in literary discourse. Dunbar underscores this link between unruly femininity and obscene insult in multiple poems: the crowded streets of Edinburgh, he claims, resound with "feusum flyttinis of defame" (foul, slanderous quarrels) and "cryis of carlingis and debaittis" (old women's cries and debates).[23] Many of the insults in literary flytings such as "glengoir" (syphilitic), "quene," "loun" (lecher, whore), and "sow" recur as prosecuted speech in conflicts between women, who sling epithets like "glangoir, myssaell, lypper carles geit" (syphilitic, diseased, leprous churl's brat), "skowkand sow" (deceitful sow), "English jade landlooper queane" (English prostitute vagabond whore), and "drunken harlot and lowne" at one another.[24] While poetic

---

20. Ibid., 1:48.

21. The Scots proverb "The may that winnis ane ill renome sits lang at hame" (The maiden who wins a bad reputation sits long at home [e.g., unmarried]) illustrates how flyting's public slander could affect young women's marital options (Anderson, *James Carmichaell Collection*, no. 1457).

22. W. Chambers, ed., *Charters and Documents Relating to the Burgh of Peebles with Extracts from the Records of the Burgh AD 1165–1710*, 2 vols. (Edinburgh: Burgh Records Society, 1872, 1909), 1:325, and 167. The punishments that these statutes specify for flyting women include being put "sax houris in the linkis without favouris" (six hours in fetters without exceptions) and being led to the town gate carrying stones hung by heavy iron chains on their shoulders.

23. *Quhy will ye, merchantis of renoun*, lines 10–11; similarly, in *This nycht I my slep I wes agast*, hell is filled with the din of "fische wyffis [who] flett and swoir with granis" (fishwives who quarreled and swore with groans) (76). *Poems of William Dunbar*, 1:250–57 and 174–76.

24. William MacKay, Herbert Cameron Boyd, and George Smith Laing, eds., *Records of Inverness*, 3 vols. (Aberdeen: New Spalding Club, 1911, 1924), 1:243; Cramond, *Records of Elgin*, 1:180; John

flytings draw on other traditions of literary invective, they are primarily derived from the obscene, antagonistic words between women in the streets and marketplaces.[25] But whereas women's flyting is something for which women are maligned collectively, as poets and lawmakers exploit the misogynous stereotype of the unruly scold in order to justify tighter controls on feminine behavior, male poets are able to use those same insults to assert their virility and teach a code of masculine sexuality based in a deep-seated contempt for women.

In addition to repurposing the colorful insult vocabulary of women's criminal flyting, the flyters draw on the obscenity, virulent misogyny, and samesex educational function of the antifeminist satirical verse that was wildly popular in sixteenth-century Scotland.[26] This didactic lyric genre features an older man addressing younger men with sexual counsel and disparaging women as greedy, duplicitous, unfaithful, and insatiate. He urges his youthful peers to limit their amorous contact with women and seek out the company of other men instead. To teach their lessons about continence, the speakers rely on obscenities like "mouth thankles" (ungrateful mouth), "cuntlairdis" (vulva-dominated men), and "pen and purs" (penis and scrotum), which are also used by the flyters. Examples of this genre, many of which are copied in the section titled "ballatis of luve—aganis evill women" alongside *The Flyting of Dunbar and Kennedy* in the massive Older Scots verse anthology known as the Bannatyne Manuscript (c. 1565–68), include *Be mirry bretherene ane and all* (attributed to an otherwise unknown "Flemyng"), Kennedy's *An aigit man, twyis forty yeiris*, John Balnavis's *O gallandis all I cry and call*, Alexander Scott's *May is the moneth maist amene*, and Dunbar's *Madam, your men said thai wald ryd*.[27] Scott's speaker exhorts, "Heirfoir, ye wantoun men in yowth, / For helth of

---

Stuart, ed., *Extracts from the Presbytery Book of Strathbogie, 1631–54* (Aberdeen: Spalding Club, 1843), 231; *Cramond Kirk Session*, MS NAS CH2/426/1–4, cited under *DOST* s.v. "loun" (n.), 2.

25. Meier links the flyting to Provencal debate poetry, Celtic satire and elegy, and Latin legal formulae in "Flyting of Dunbar and Kennedy" in Context," 63–64; Paul Robichaud reads it as shaped by Scots Gaelic oral culture in "'To Heir Quhat I Sould Wryt': The Flyting of Dunbar and Kennedy and Scots Oral Culture," *Scottish Literary Journal* 25, no. 2 (1998); and Bawcutt links it to Middle English invectives, including Lawrence Minot's protonationalist political poems, in *Dunbar the Makar*, 237.

26. Evelyn S. Newlyn, "Luve, Lichery, and Ewill Women: The Satirical Tradition in the Bannatyne Manuscript," *Studies in Scottish Literature* 26 (1991); "The Function of the Female Monster in Middle Scots Poetry: Misogyny, Patriarchy, and the Satiric Myth," in *Misogyny in Literature*, ed. Katherine Ackley (New York: Garland, 1992); "The Political Dimensions of Desire and Sexuality in the Poems of the Bannatyne Manuscript," in *Selected Essays on Scottish Language and Literature*, ed. Steven D. McKenna (Lewiston, NY: Edwin Mellen, 1992).

27. Meier links these lyrics to a tradition of literary antifeminism that includes Ovid's *Amores* and *Ars amatoria*, Juvenal's sixth satire, Proverbs 5–7, Jerome's *Adversus Jovinianum*, Andreas Capellanus's *De amore*, and the anonymous antimarriage poem *De coniuge non ducenda* (*Poems of Walter Kennedy*, xcvi).

body now haif e / Not oft till mell with thankless mowth" (Herefore, you wanton men in youth / For your body's health take care right now / Not often to
mingle with that ungrateful mouth).[28] Dunbar's speaker instructs "all young
men" to "Keip you fra harlottis nycht and day" to avoid sexually transmitted
infection.[29] Kennedy's protagonist teaches that military service under other
men is preferable to toiling for women's pleasure in the bedroom, much as
Kennedy and his fellow flyters present flyting with other men as a favorable
alternative to intercourse: "Bettir it wer ane man to serfe, / With worship and
honour undir a scheild, / Than hir to pleis" (It were better to serve a man /
With worship and honor under a shield / Than to please her), he says (25–
27).[30] Here, subordinating oneself to another man entails honor, dignity, and
renown and is "bettir" than attempting to "pleis" the vulva. Kennedy's speaker
warns "all men" away from contact with women's genitals: "Now god help
and the haly rude, / To keip all men fra mouth thankles" (Now may God and
the holy cross help / To keep all men from that ungrateful mouth), he declares
(39–40).[31] In this view, it is more "manly" to exercise restraint and retain one's
erectile capacities than to put them into physical practice and risk losing them.

Middle Scots literary flytings are intimately linked to educational practices
from the all-male world of the university because the flyting's highly formalized, back-and-forth rhetorical structure and role in publicly asserting the
speaker's masculinity through linguistic mastery share strong affinities with
scholastic disputation, the preferred pedagogical technique in university education.[32] Walter Ong states that "the entire academic curriculum [was] pro-
grammed as a form of ritual male combat centered on disputation," as "boys

---

28. *May is the moneth maist amene,* in *Bannatyne Manuscript,* 3:67–70, lines 63–65.

29. *Madam, your men said thai wald ryd,* lines 31–32. On syphilis in Scotland, see *Poems of William Dunbar,* 2:257n24.

30. *An aigit man twyis fourty yeiris* (DIMEV 468), in *Poems of Walter Kennedy,* 2–5. Text references are to lines in this edition. Additional obscene man-to-man advice poems include Richard Maitland's *Thocht that this warld be verie strange,* in W. A. Craigie, ed., *The Maitland Folio Manuscript,* 2 vols. (Edinburgh: William Blackwood and Sons for the Scottish Text Society, 1919), 1:329–30 and *My hart is quhyt and no delyte I haif of ladeis fair,* in *Bannatyne Manuscript,* 4:18–19.

31. This view of masculine self-control and sublimation of sexual energies can be traced back to Paul and the Church Fathers. See *Poems of Walter Kennedy,* xciv–vi; Newlyn, "Luve, Lichery, and Ewill Women," 292.

32. Karras, *From Boys to Men,* 89. For more on disputation as masculinity-building rhetorical vio-lence, see ibid., 83–96; Jody Enders, *Rhetoric and the Origins of Medieval Drama* (Ithaca, NY: Cornell University Press, 1992), 89–98; Andrew Taylor, "A Second Ajax: Peter Abelard and the Violence of Dialectic," in *The Tongue of the Fathers: Gender and Ideology in Twelfth-Century Latin,* ed. David Townsend and Andrew Taylor (Philadelphia: University of Pennsylvania Press, 1998). For a cultural history of disputation from the classical era to the thirteenth century, see Alex J. Novikoff, *The Medi-eval Culture of Disputation: Pedagogy, Practice, and Performance* (Philadelphia: University of Pennsylvania Press, 2013).

went to school to war ceremonially with each other (and with the teacher)."[33] Disputation, a mutually antagonistic practice in which young men took turns using language to assert their manhood in the presence of their peers, was a form of "ceremonial combat" by which men proved their superior rationality, knowledge, and verbal facility over one another.[34] Many of the flyters had formal academic backgrounds and received extensive training in disputation: Kennedy earned multiple degrees from the University of Glasgow and served as an examiner there, while Dunbar is thought to have attended St. Andrews University, and Lyndsay received at least a Latin grammar school education.[35] The flyters draw on disputation's linking of homosociality and pedagogical debate, because flyting's generic rules and the university curriculum both present verbal dueling as central to proving manhood. Karras notes that "the university had adopted the notion of masculinity as violent domination of other men, but the violence was metaphorical, using words as weapons," and the flyters embrace disputation's capacity for asserting masculinity among a group of elite men who speak the same highly specialized language.[36]

The version of *The Flyting of Dunbar and Kennedy* copied by George Bannatyne in the Bannatyne Manuscript highlights flyting's close ties to disputation because Bannatyne adds instructional rubrics inviting his readers to interpret the poem as a formal dispute between two combatants and to understand flyting as a competitive homosocial knowledge-producing practice. He introduces it on folio 147r as "The flyting of Dunbar and Kennedie," establishing it as a collaborative work, and he formats the warring invectives as a structured debate, making sure to specify the author of each portion. After the first round of insults has been exchanged on each side, Bannatyne introduces the second bout by using a rhyming couplet to encourage readers to think of the verbal duel in terms of violence and loss in battle: "Quod Kennedy to Dumbar / Juge in the nixt quha gat the war" (judge in the next part who received the more painful outcome), he writes on folio 148r, invoking "war"'s associations with harm and defeat in armed combat.[37] At the flyting's close, he again portrays it as a violent conflict between two combatants: "Juge ye now heir quha gat the war," he commands readers on folio 154r. In framing the flyting as a formal dispute between two combatants, Bannatyne

---

33. Walter Ong, *Rhetoric, Romance, and Technology: Studies in the Interaction of Expression and Culture* (Ithaca, NY: Cornell University Press, 1971), 17–18.

34. Karras, *From Boys to Men*, 90.

35. *Poems of Walter Kennedy*, xv; Bawcutt, *Dunbar the Makar*, 6; *Sir David Lyndsay: Selected Poems*, vii.

36. Karras, *From Boys to Men*, 91.

37. *DOST* s.v. "war" (adj.), 2.

reinforces the genre's links to the masculinity-proving educational practices of the university.

Flyting's academic ties illuminate how the genre could be understood pedagogically and provide an additional valence to flyting's misogyny. Along with invoking disputation's structure and masculinity-proving power, the flyters echo the clerical antifeminism that inflected scholastic texts by clergymen warning against the evils of women in general and wives in particular.[38] Unlike Chaucer's "felawes," the flyters do not deploy obscene misogyny to authorize violence against women or to spur one another to engage in sexual conquest. Rather, the flyters, some of whom were clerics themselves, deploy it in the vein of writers like the monk Lydgate who seek to dissuade men from the shackles of marriage and encourage them to join the clergy by portraying wives as incorrigible shrews and all women as malicious agents of impotence and disease.[39] Instead of urging their peers to copulate with as many women as possible, as we see in the teachings of Chaucer's "felawes," the flyters echo clerical antifeminism in instructing their fellow men to view contact with women as emasculating and disempowering, and they portray wives as duplicitous and domineering.

In using obscenity to teach their peers about sexuality, flyters draw on women's criminal insult speech, antifeminist satire's man-to-man sexual pedagogy, and university disputation's educational antagonism. Flyting's links to these discourses, with their three strands of antifeminism and connections to educational practice, illuminate how poets deployed obscene misogyny to foster gendered community, prove masculinity, encourage collaborative literary creation, and teach their younger peers to limit their carnal engagement with women.

The Pedagogy of Obscene Insult in Middle Scots Flytings

The flyters present their exchanges as entailing learning for their literary opponents and fashion their verses as collaborative peer education. They use misogyny to instruct one another to avoid contact with women and embrace

---

38. Karras examines clerical misogyny's centrality to university education in *From Boys to Men*, 79. For more on the centrality of misogyny to clerical superiority, see Dyan Elliott, *Spiritual Marriage: Sexual Abstinence in Medieval Wedlock* (Princeton, NJ: Princeton University Press, 1993), 132–52.

39. Kennedy might have been in minor orders and was styled parson in 1510, while Dunbar was a chaplain. *Poems of Walter Kennedy*, xvi; Bawcutt, *Dunbar the Makar*, 6–7. For more on Lydgate's especially virulent clerical misogyny, see Sidhu, *Indecent Exposure*, 113–48.

the literary company of men instead, portraying women's bodies as agents of impotence and infection. Instead of asserting their masculinity through feats of copulation, as their monarchs James IV and James V were so fond of doing, the flyters offer a noncorporeal form of proving potency by presenting flyting as a manhood act analogous to "fukki[ng]" with one's virile "pen."

In addition to being shaped by disputational practices in form and function, the flytings are fraught with pedagogical rhetoric, lending further instructive dimension to their torrents of abuse. "Go sey thy science [knowledge]," Montgomerie orders Polwarth, using a term for book learning to demand that Polwarth share whatever knowledge he has gleaned from private study or formal education.[40] Polwarth replies, "Learne, scybald knave, to knaue thy sell" (learn, roguish scoundrel, to know yourself) (IV.2), insisting that Montgomerie "learne" and "knaue" as a result of their exchange and portraying flyting as a process with the capacity to produce self-knowledge.[41] He declares, "Quhairfoir, loun . . . . I bothe command and counsall the" (Wherefore, lecher, I both command and advise you) (IV.9–10), fashioning his invective as "command" and "counsall," advice and instruction, to his peer. By framing their insults in pedagogical terms, the flyters emphasize the genre's social purpose of providing sexual knowledge for its participants as well as its listeners.

The flyters use the obscenity "fuck" to posit parallels between flyting and fucking, between copulating vigorously with women and composing insult poetry with other men, and they represent flyting as more "manly" than intercourse. In one of the earliest uses of "fuck," Kennedy calls Dunbar "wan fukkit funling, that natour maid an yrle" ("ill-fucked" foundling, that nature made a dwarf).[42] In drawing on the negative prefix *wan-*'s meanings of "badly, wrongly" to insult Dunbar's body as "poorly fucked" at his conception, he disparages Dunbar's father's coital prowess and suggests that this propensity for sexual feebleness is hereditary, passed down from father to son. Montgomerie attacks Polwarth's literary skills using the same slur on men's performance: "your flirdome wanfuckit, ye tersell of ane taid" (your ill-fucked poetic mockery, you toad's pizzle), he scoffs (I.22).[43] Rather than maligning his opponent's body as "wanfuckit," Montgomerie applies the insult to Polwarth's poetry, presenting verse as originating in an act of copulation. He attacks Polwarth's invective as "flirdome" (mockery, scorn) that is "wanfuckit," accusing him of

---

40. *DOST* s.v. "science" (n.), 2.

41. *DOST* s.v. "knaw" (v.[1]).

42. *The Flyting of Dunbar and Kennedy*, in *Poems of Walter Kennedy*, 88–179, line 38. Text references are to lines in this edition.

43. "Pizzle" is Parkinson's gloss (*Alexander Montgomerie: Poems*, 2:128n22), although this does not capture the obscenity of "ters" in the original.

badly fucking his verses into existence. In calling Polwarth "ye tersell of ane taid," he adds the diminutive -*ell* suffix to the genital obscenity "ters" (penis) to claim that Polwarth's poetry is poorly fucked because he does not possess the proper rhetorical-genital equipment.[44] He attacks Polwarth by linking literary composition and intercourse: he is a pint-sized toad's penis, a miniature "tersell" incapable of properly "fucki[ng]" powerful invective into existence.

The flyters reinforce their links between virility and poetic potency by using the richly multivalent terms "mell" and "pen" to characterize their exchanges. The verb "mell" could signify intimate fellowship between friends or lovers as well as fierce fighting in battle, as its valences include "to engage in fighting," "to engage in flyting," "to associate with," and "to copulate with."[45] The flyters repeatedly use "mell" to name the act of flyting, and they exploit its range of meanings to emphasize flyting's links to sexual activity and violent conflict. Montgomerie declares that his words will "teiche [Polwarth] to think with thy maister to mel" (I.50), presenting obscene insult poetry as a "teich[ing]" tool and portraying himself as Polwarth's "maister" (teacher, schoolmaster) in the exchange.[46] He tells Polwarth, "Mischevous mischant, we sall mell / In landward language loud and large" (Mischievous evildoer, we shall fight / Loudly and liberally in crude language) (IV.7–8). Elsewhere in Middle Scots poetry, "mell" names men's coital performance, as in John Maxwell's commonplace book (compiled c. 1584–89), which contains the line, "Ye tyne yowr sell . . . with quenes to mel" (You allow yourself to have sex with whores), and in Scott's obscene antifeminist lyric instructing young men, "I counsale yow to mel with mesure."[47]

In addition to exploiting the multivalence of "mell," at once signifying flyting, fighting, and fucking, flyters highlight the twin meanings of "pen" as writing instrument and penis, since to "mell" with one's "pen" could mean to have sex with women or to flyte with one's fellow man.[48] The conflation of pen and penis stretches back to antiquity, rendering literary creation as an act of procreative copulation.[49] The flyters take up this convention by referring

---

44. *DOST* s.v. "ters" (n.).

45. *DOST* s.v. "mell" (v.[1]), 2, 5, and 6.

46. *DOST* s.v. "maister" (n.[1]), 16.

47. *John Maxwall's Commonplace Book* (Edinburgh, Edinburgh University Library, MS EUL La. III.467), fol. 2a, cited in *DOST* s.v. "quene" (n.[1]), 2(a); Scott, *May is the moneth maist amene*, line 67.

48. *DOST* s.v. "pen" (n.), 3 and 6. In addition to the examples I discuss here, the flyters use "pen" in *Dunbar and Kennedy*, lines 12, 85; *Montgomerie and Polwart*, III.20.

49. J. N. Adams, *The Latin Sexual Vocabulary* (Baltimore: Johns Hopkins University Press, 1982), 38–40. Gaunt discusses how troubadour Guilhem IX similarly deploys "terms that would more normally be associated with rhetoric and poetics, but which here are clearly used to describe the poet's sexual prowess" ("Obscene Hermeneutics," 95).

suggestively to their own "pens" as well as those of their opponents. Montgomerie attacks Polwarth's "poysonit . . . pen" not thirty lines after he has called Polwarth's poetry "wanfuckit" (I.54). Polwarth retorts that his "pen" is a potent source of knowledge: "Provok my pen profundlie to distell" (Provoke my pen to distill with intellectual insight), he dares Montgomerie (VI.4). Elsewhere in their poetry, Kennedy and Dunbar both use "pen" to name the penis.[50] Two of the sixteenth-century manuscripts containing *The Flyting of Dunbar and Kennedy* include another didactic poem instructing young men to copulate less by warning them of the despair they will feel "quhen pithless is thy pen" (when your penis is impotent) from youthful overindulgence.[51] By drawing on the multivalence of "pen" and "mell," the flyters blur the distinctions between verbal jousting, intercourse, violent combat, and homosocial fellowship.

Misogyny is central to the flyters' pedagogy because they teach one another to eschew sexual congress with women in favor of textual congress with other men by mobilizing obscenity's capacity to engender revulsion and disgust attached to women's bodies, slinging epithets like "fals harlott hursone" (deceitful fornicating son of a whore), "yadswyvar" (old mare fucker), and "fornicatour by natour" (natural fornicator).[52] They appropriate the vocabulary of women's criminal flyting to create a men-only literary game in which elite, powerful men prove their masculinity by maligning women. They leave fully intact criminal flyting's ingrained misogyny, with its vocabulary of sexual insult, slander, and shame, and they populate their verses with derogatory stereotypes of witches ("wirdsisteris"), foul old women ("decrepit karlingis . . . cryis owt"), and shrieking "fische wyves."[53] They insist on poetic mastery as a form of virility, using the erectile body as a paradigm for literary prowess. They mobilize the disgust for wives from scholastic antifeminism and the mingled contempt and fear associated with women's genitalia from didactic misogynous verse to teach their peers that sex with women breeds disease and impotence, while marriage results in a humiliating loss of power. Sidhu argues that clerical writers like Lydgate use misogyny to "establish a cross-rank

50. "Pen" names the penis in Kennedy's *An aigit man twyiss fourty yeiris*, line 31 and Dunbar's *Tretis of the Tua Mariit Wemen and the Wedo*, line 135.

51. Balnavis's *O gallandis all, I cry and call*, in *Bannatyne Manuscript*, 3:18–22, line 36; this poem and *Dunbar and Kennedy* are both copied in the Bannatyne Manuscript as well as the Maitland Folio.

52. For "hurson," see *Dunbar and Kennedy*, line 359 and *Montgomerie and Polwart*, I.53; for "yadswyvar," see *Dunbar and Kennedy*, line 246; for "fornicatour," see *Montgomerie and Polwart*, IX.60.

53. Montgomerie tells a story of Polwarth's conception by three witches in Part II of their flyting; for the other examples, see *Dunbar and Kennedy*, lines 136, 231, 221–24. Bawcutt discusses the negative stereotypes associated with fishwives in "Images of Women," 49–50.

homosocial community based on the shared problem of women"; similarly, misogyny unites the flyters even as they use it to attack one another.[54]

Kennedy was married and Dunbar was not, and Dunbar's attacks on Kennedy emphasize the ravages wrought by marital sex on his opponent's body, as he insults Kennedy as physically exhausted and disparages Kennedy's wife using gendered terms of insult from criminal flyting discourse.[55] He maligns Kennedy as "glengoir loun" (syphilitic lecher) (83), "ane forlane loun" (a sexually exhausted lecher) (132), "lowsy, loun of lownis aw" (lice-ridden lecher of all lechers) (178), and "lene, larbar loungeour, baith lowsy in lisk and lonye" (lean, impotent idler, lousy in both groin and loin) (121).[56] Both "glengoir" and "loun" recur in criminal flyting cases; "loun" meant "a lewd rascal, a lecher, whoremonger" when applied to a man and "strumpet, harlot, whore" when naming a woman, and "glengoir" referred to syphilis, which arrived in Scotland in 1497.[57] Women were punished for calling each other "raistit huir and glengoir huir" (shriveled whore and syphilitic whore) and "glengorie bitch," while Marjorie Cassin was put in the stocks for calling Jonet Broomside "comon theef, common whoore, and that she was a loun to 7 or 8 men."[58] Polwarth follows a similar strategy when attacking Montgomerie, whom he accuses of "hurdome . . . baidrie and bordaling" (whoredom, lewdness, and brothel going) (VII.28, 32). He portrays Montgomerie's body as impotent and disease-ravaged from his excesses, describing him as "in the stewis brunt" (infected with syphilis in the brothels) (VI.36), "beistlie begger impotent" (impotent, beastly beggar) (VI.16), and "gum gait" (IX.7), an epithet meaning "gum-galled, with sores on the gums, a symptom of gonorrhea."[59] He disparages Montgomerie as "licherous lowne" (lecherous lecher) (VII.54) and "over laidnit loune with lang taillit lyse" (over-exhausted lecher with long-tailed lice) (IV.99), and he emphasizes his exhaustion from coital activity.[60] The flyters use obscene insult to teach that *all* sexual contact with women, even within

---

54. Sidhu, *Indecent Exposure*, 116.

55. Kennedy was married to Christian Hynd and had at least two sons (*Poems of Walter Kennedy*, xvin10). In response, Kennedy repeatedly accuses Dunbar of sodomy, calling him "sodomyt" (253), "bugrist abhominable" (526), and "sodomit unsaciable" (527).

56. "Loune" is one of the flyters' favorite epithets, and Dunbar and Kennedy use it elsewhere in lines 203, 233, and 484. Montgomerie wishes "the glengoir" on Polwarth in *Montgomerie and Polwart*, II.37.

57. *DOST* s.v. "loun" (n.), 1d and 2; s.v. "glengoir" (n.).

58. Renwick, *Extracts from the Records of the Royal Burgh of Stirling*, 1:47; E. Henderson, ed., *Extracts from the Kirk-Session Records of Dunfermline from AD 1640 to 1689* (Edinburgh: Fullarton and Mac, 1865), 58, 10. Ewan discusses the popularity of the insult "glengoir" in slander cases in '"Many Injurious Words,"' 169–70.

59. *Alexander Montgomerie: Poems*, 2:151n7.

60. "Loune" appears elsewhere in *Montgomerie and Polwart*, II.129 ("lowsie lowne"), III.319, IV.9, IX.40.

marriage, irrevocably emasculates and exhausts men's bodies, invoking the louse-ridden, diseased masculine body as a cautionary example.

The unmarried Dunbar directs his venom at Kennedy's wife, Christian Hynd, hurling slanderous epithets at her in his literary battle with her husband. In accusing Kennedy and Hynd of being homeless hen stealers and squatting in a "laithly luge that wes the leppir menis" (foul lodge that belonged to the leper men) (154), Dunbar invokes the links between leprosy and sexual transgression that were common during the period.[61] He claims the couple roams the countryside like penniless scavengers: "Thow and thy quene as gredy gleddis ye gang" (You and your whore go about like greedy kites), he says (146). In calling Hynd "thy quene," Dunbar echoes criminal cases like Margaret Duffe's complaint against Isobell Thaine "for calling her drunken jade, filthie queen and loussie hussie," and when Margaret Gray attacked Issobell Greige, "calling her Jad and queyn and offering to strik her with stones."[62] Refusing to acknowledge Hynd's status as Kennedy's wife, Dunbar disparages her as "this dowsy" (harlot) (158) and "thy bryd" (your woman) (189). He calls Hynd "ane sowtaris wyfe" (a shoemaker's wife) (155), an insult that associates her with the oft-reviled craft of shoemakers and accuses her of the crime of adultery.[63] In flyting, women's bodies are the ground on which men wage their homosocial conflicts, as Hynd's reputation becomes collateral damage in Dunbar's attack on Kennedy. By linking profession, illicit sexuality, and gender in the insults he hurls at Hynd, Dunbar invokes intersectional disadvantage to reduce her to a misogynist stereotype of lower-status female sexuality.

In contrast to Dunbar's slandering of Kennedy's wife and Polwarth's attacks on Montgomerie's brothel frequenting, Montgomerie deploys misogyny for a different purpose, as he invokes the popular trope of the domineering, abusive shrew and accuses Polwarth of embodying the submissive henpecked husband from obscene gender comedy.[64] Once again, flyting's insults reflect biographical fact: Polwarth was married to Julian Ker of Ferniehirst, while

---

61. Meier notes that "leprosy was regarded as a divine punishment for sin, particularly for sexual immorality or lechery" (*Poems of Walter Kennedy*, 194n68).

62. William Cramond, ed., *The Church and Churchyard of Cullen* (Aberdeen: G. Cornwall and Sons, 1883), 130; William Cramond, ed., *The Annals of Banff*, 2 vols. (Aberdeen: New Spalding Club, 1891–93), 1:145.

63. In *Quhy will ye, merchantis of renoun*, Dunbar derides "Tailyouris, soutteris and craftis vyll" (tailors, shoemakers, and [other such] filthy crafts), line 36. As Meier notes, "Cobblers did not enjoy much esteem" (*Poems of Walter Kennedy*, 236n155). For more on the term's derogatory connotations, see Keely Fisher, "The Contemporary Humour in William Stewart's *The Flytting betuix the Sowtar and the Tailyour*," in *Literature, Letters, and the Canonical in Early Modern Scotland*, ed. Nicola Royan and Theo van Heijnsbergen (East Linton, UK: Tuckwell, 2002).

64. Sidhu discusses these popular fifteenth- and sixteenth-century literary tropes in *Indecent Exposure*, 122.

Montgomerie, whom Polwarth attacks for his whoremongering, seems never to have married.[65] Using the literary figure of the angry shrew to emasculate his married opponent, Montgomerie mocks Polwarth for desiring to be dominated by his wife: "Thow grenis to gaip upon the grey meir" (You long to dote on a domineering wife), he declares (I.26).[66] He applies to Polwarth two alliterating verbs of earnest longing, "grene" and "gaip," accusing him of yearning ardently to be overpowered by his spouse. "Meir," a gendered animal insult akin to "bitch," "jade," and "sow," was used between women in flyting cases, as when Elspet Patersone called Elspet Mill "whore and fals theiff swollin meir" (whore and false thief distended mare) and "mismaid meir" (deformed mare).[67] Montgomerie again invokes the figure of the shrew when he disparages his foe as "Jok Blunt," a nickname for a henpecked husband (IX.58), as he continues to insist that Polwarth's wife holds the upper hand in domestic and sexual matters.[68]

The flyters use female genital obscenity to reinforce their lessons about masculine sexuality by invoking disgust, which Miller defines as "a strong sense of aversion to something perceived as dangerous because of its powers to contaminate, infect, or pollute by proximity, contact, or ingestion."[69] This use of obscenity for instructive purposes by generating shame and disgust is central to proverbs like "He that dies for ane cunt causs burie him in the ars" (He who dies for a woman-related cause, bury him with his ass facing upward) and "Ther was never a slut but sho had a slit" (There was never a disreputable woman without a slit).[70] In these examples, women's vulvas are the sole attribute that defines them, and they contribute directly to men's humiliation through their polluting power.[71] The "cunt" is a malignant agent in poems like *Be mirry bretherene ane and all*, which features "cuntlairdis and cukkaldis all togidder" (cunt lords and cuckolds all together) whose "wyfis hes maistery" (wives have mastery).[72] "Cuntlairdis" are married men dominated by the "cunt," whose very existence poses a threat to masculine power. As I note at this chapter's outset, Polwarth attacks Montgomerie with the descriptive epithet "with a cunt" and orders him to "kis the cunt of ane kow" (kiss the cunt of a cow)

---

65. Michael R. G. Spiller, "Hume, Sir Patrick, of Polwarth (c.1550–1609)," *ODNB*.

66. *Alexander Montgomerie: Poems*, 2:128n26.

67. *DOST* s.v. "mare" (n.[1]), 1c. This 1628 selection from the unpublished Fraserburgh Kirk Session, 2 vols., MS NAS CH2/11142, is cited under this entry.

68. Dunbar uses this term in *The Tretis of the Tua Mariit Wemen and the Wedo*, line 142.

69. Miller, *Anatomy of Disgust*, 2.

70. Beveridge, *Fergusson's Scottish Proverbs*, 61, 104; also "Many fair face hes a foul taill," 81.

71. Miller links the association between disgust and female genitalia to misogyny, male anxieties about ejaculation and vulnerability, and fears over the polluting power of semen, which was called "pollucioun" in Middle English (*Anatomy of Disgust*, 101–5); *MED* s.v. "pollucioun" (n.), (c).

72. Flemyng, *Be mirry bretherene ane and all*, in *Bannatyne Manuscript*, 3:76–79, lines 47, 49.

(IX.58), claiming that his opponent possesses this disgust-inducing body part and demanding that Montgomerie engage in bestial cunnilingus. The flyters harness the revulsion generated by female genital obscenity to reinforce their lessons about sexuality and poetic practice: by tapping into widespread cultural misogyny, they depict bodies possessing or coming into contact with "cunts" as weakened and penetrable, as sources of infection and humiliation.[73] This pedagogical mobilization of disgust teaches listeners to turn away from "the cunt" and focus instead on the "pens" of their peers.

Dunbar draws on this linking of female genital obscenity with disgust when he impugns his foe as "cuntbittin crawdoun, Kennedy, coward of kynd" (impotent coward, Kennedy, coward by nature) in his opening salvo of their battle (50). He uses "cuntbittin," literally "bitten by the cunt," to signify Kennedy's impotence.[74] In doing so, he represents the "cunt" as the vicious wounding agent behind Kennedy's lack of virility, and he depicts Kennedy as dominated and victimized by it. He addresses his opponent by his illustrious family surname, linking the K of "Kennedy" to the hard c of "cunt" through alliteration to reinforce the link between impotence and the Kennedy clan, which was one of the most powerful families in Scotland at the time.[75] He uses two different synonyms for "coward" to underscore Kennedy's emasculation. Due to the strong association between individual and family honor in Scottish culture, this insult would have been particularly scathing because Dunbar implies that all men bearing the Kennedy surname are "cuntbittin." The "cunt" is the sexual-grammatical agent here: figured as a vengeful mouth equipped with grisly teeth, it "bit[es]" Kennedy's penis and renders it unusable.[76] Dunbar deploys the insult again when he maligns Kennedy in a barrage of epithets as "forflittin, countbittin, beschittin" (outdone in flyting, impotent, filthy) (239). By linking "forflittin" and "countbittin" using juxtaposition and internal rhyme, Dunbar suggests that being out-flyted and being impotent are analogous. The flyters present the lack of virility that results from excessive contact with women's genitalia as comparable to losing a literary battle, just as they liken corporeal "wan-fucki[ng]" to composing subpar invective. Dunbar's linking of the two

---

73. Miller, *Anatomy of Disgust*, 104.

74. Bawcutt glosses "cuntbittin" as "impotent," linking it to a similar Middle English compound used to signify impotence in *Lyarde*, where every "counte betyn man" in England is relegated to a park for the impotent (*Poems of William Dunbar*, 2:432n50, 2:438n239; *Lyarde*, line 60). For more on "cuntbittin," see Robinson, "More than One Meaning," 279–80; Priscilla Bawcutt, "Dunbar: New Light on Some Old Words," in *The Nuttis Schell: Essays on the Scots Language Presented to A. J. Aitken,* ed. C. Macafee and Isobeal Macleod (Aberdeen: Aberdeen University Press, 1987), 84–85.

75. The Gaelic-speaking Kennedy clan was one of the most prominent in late medieval Scotland. Hector L. MacQueen, "Kennedy family (*per. c.*1350–1513)," *ODNB*.

76. For more on the trope of the "biting cunt," see Burns, *Bodytalk*, 57–58.

insults implies that the opposite can also be true: if men can flyte vigorously and obscenely enough to avoid being "forflittin," they can signify their symbolic potency and teach each other new paradigms of virility.

No More "fukkand lyke ane furious fornicatour": Lyndsay's *Answer to the Kingis Flyting*

Having shown how the flyters use obscene misogyny within their homosocial literary circle for pedagogical purposes, I now turn to the most provocative and politically significant flyting, Lyndsay's *Answer to the Kingis Flyting* (c. 1535–36). This poem was addressed to the twenty-four-year-old James V on the eve of his marriage to Madeleine de Valois, the teenage daughter of King Francis I of France. Lyndsay mobilizes flyting's same-sex pedagogy and obscene insult to teach James that his pursuit of sexual conquest is draining, degrading, and likely to result in impotence and venereal disease. Lyndsay's flyting illustrates the inescapable political stakes and power dynamics of sexual education and underscores the ends to which it can be put, as he illuminates the destructive consequences of the faulty pedagogy that James received in his youth and seeks to instruct the king in a different path. Reading Lyndsay's *Answer* in light of James's sexual biography and educational history, I explore how Lyndsay mobilizes flyting's obscene misogyny to teach the king a new lesson about masculine sexuality.

James V (1512–42) inherited the crown when he was only seventeen months old, after his father, James IV, was killed in the Battle of Flodden in 1513, and his biography sheds light on the powerful role of sexual pedagogy in the power struggles of 1520s Scotland. During his long minority rule, James was at the center of violent conflicts among Scotland's nobles. Sexual education was one tool with which the kingdom's factions sought to control the young king and exert political influence. James's ruthless stepfather, Archibald Douglas, sixth earl of Angus, had physical custody of him from 1525 to 1528, when he was aged thirteen to sixteen.[77] Douglas refused to give up custody in spite of a parliamentary declaration ordering him to do so in 1526, and instead kept James as a virtual prisoner until he escaped at age sixteen.[78] To keep the heavily guarded monarch distracted from the fact of his captivity, Douglas and his relatives sought to divert him with sex. This instruction that James received as a

---

77. Andrea Thomas, *Princelie Majestie: The Court of James V of Scotland, 1528–1542* (Edinburgh: John Donald, 2005), 7–8.

78. Jamie Cameron, *James V: The Personal Rule, 1528–1542*, ed. Norman Macdougall (East Linton, UK: Tuckwell, 1998), 9–30.

teenager had far-reaching political and dynastic implications. As Andrea Thomas relates, "James V's amorous career really was quite spectacular," since "as a fourteen or fifteen year old he was deliberately encouraged into promiscuity by the Angus regime in order to distract him from wanting to exercise political power."[79] Historian Robert Lyndsay of Pitscottie, writing a generation after James's death, alleges that religious officials from the king's advisory council instructed him that "he might tak his plesour throw all Scottland and . . . cheise any of quhat gentillwoman he pleissit, quhither they war marieit or unmarieit," promising to make "sic spetiall paperis for him that god sould nocht be movit witht him" (he might take his pleasure through all Scotland and choose whatever gentlewoman he pleased, whether they were married or unmarried, [promising to make] such special papers for him so that God would not be angry with him).[80] James fathered nine known illegitimate children with nine different women—many of them wives or daughters of Scottish noblemen—beginning when he was seventeen until his death at age thirty, and his mistresses and out-of-wedlock children are so numerous that they have their own entry in the *Oxford Dictionary of National Biography*.[81] In another poem written around 1530, Lyndsay dramatizes the corruption of the teenage king by unscrupulous councilors and presents this process in same-sex pedagogical terms: one of James's advisors instructs him, "Schir . . . tak my counsall, / And go, all, to the hie boirdall. / Thare may we lope at lybertie!" (Sir, take my counsel, / And let's all go to the Edinburgh brothel. / There we may freely leap [on women]!).[82] The advisor frames his sexual instruction as "counsall" and imagines a group of men "all" copulating together, teaching each other how to have sex by example. In a society where youthful excess was thought to cause impotence, and where fear of venereal disease had reached the court during his father's reign, James's unabated wantonness struck terror into the hearts of those who had survived his turbulent minority rule and feared further upheavals if he were to die without a legitimate heir.[83] In

---

79. Thomas, *Princelie Majestie*, 41.

80. Ibid., 40–44; Robert Lyndsay, *The Historie and Cronicles of Scotland*, ed. Æ. J. G. Mackay, 2 vols. (Edinburgh: William Blackwood and Sons for the Scottish Text Society, 1899–1911), 1:408–9, also 1:383; George Buchanan, *The History of Scotland*, trans. James Aikman, 4 vols. (Edinburgh: Archibald Fullarton and Blackie, Fullarton, 1827–29), 2:324.

81. On James's mistresses and illegitimate children, see Cameron, *James V*, 134, 160n253, 189n212, 261–62, 276, 281n54–58; Peter D. Anderson, "James V, mistresses and children of (*act. c.*1529–1592)," *ODNB*.

82. *The Complaynt of Schir David Lyndsay*, lines 249–51.

83. For more on the perceived causal relationship between youthful excess and later impotence, see Joan Cadden, *Meanings of Sex Difference in the Middle Ages* (Cambridge: Cambridge University Press, 1995), 273–76; Neal, *Masculine Self*, 138; and numerous Middle English and Middle Scots poems from the fifteenth and sixteenth centuries, including Dunbar's *Tretis of the Tua Mariit Wemen and the*

his *Answer*, Lyndsay condemns the instruction given to the young king by his self-serving "counsale" (council of advisors) on behalf of his violent, power-hungry stepfather (43).[84] He details how the behavior resulting from this education is unwise and inimical to James's long-term health and future virility.

The close relationship between Lyndsay and James began in the king's infancy and lasted throughout his short lifetime.[85] Lyndsay (c. 1486–1555) joined James IV's court as a teenager, then served as a surrogate father figure to James V and traveled to France on his behalf several times between 1531 and 1536 to negotiate the Franco-Scots marital alliance.[86] Lyndsay's wife, Janet Douglas, was James's longtime seamstress.[87] Lyndsay was not alone in addressing pedagogical poetry to his monarch, who attracted an unusually large number of advice poems, as James "increasingly became the focus of literary offerings by Scottish scholars and writers hoping . . . to influence his beliefs and attitudes."[88] Lyndsay addressed several advice poems to James during the king's teens and early twenties. Williams argues that Lyndsay uses the structural cover of the flyting genre in his *Answer* to offer "a piece of pointed advice" regarding James's wanton behavior, and she links the poem to the popular "mirror for princes" genre, typically written to mark a monarch's coronation and instruct him in good governance as a Christian king.[89] But whereas other poets advised James more generally against indulging his "lust," Lyndsay delivers explicit instructions to the king regarding his past, present, and future sexual behavior.[90]

Wedo, lines 168–238. Dunbar's *Madam, your men seyd that thai wald ryde*, dating from James IV's reign, features a refrain warning young men of "the pockis" (syphilis) (5, 10, 15, 20, 25, 30, 35).

84. *The Answer to the Kingis Flyting*, in Williams, ed., *Sir David Lyndsay*, 98–100. Text references are to lines from this edition.

85. For more on this close relationship, see Janet Hadley Williams, "David Lyndsay and the Making of King James V," in *Stewart Style 1513–1542: Essays on the Court of James V*, ed. Janet Hadley Williams (East Linton, UK: Tuckwell, 1996); Janet Hadley Williams, "James V, David Lyndsay, and the Bannatyne Manuscript Poem of the Gyre Carling," *Studies in Scottish Literature* 26 (1991); Cameron, *James V*, 263–65; Carol Edington, *Court and Culture in Renaissance Scotland: Sir David Lindsay of the Mount* (Amherst: University of Massachusetts Press, 1994), 14–56.

86. Edington, *Court and Culture*; Janet Hadley Williams, "Sir David Lyndsay," in *A Companion to Medieval Scottish Poetry*, ed. Priscilla Bawcutt and Janet Hadley Williams (Cambridge: D. S. Brewer, 2006).

87. Douglas served as royal seamstress in 1522–40 (Thomas, "'Dragons Baith and Dowes ay,'" 85).

88. Thomas, *Princelie Majestie*, 153. See also R. James Goldstein, "Normative Heterosexuality in History and Theory: The Case of Sir David Lindsay of the Mount," in *Becoming Male in the Middle Ages*, ed. Jeffrey Jerome Cohen and Bonnie Wheeler (New York: Garland, 2000); A. A. MacDonald, "William Stewart and the Court Poetry of James V," in Williams, *Stewart Style*; Thomas, *Princelie Majestie*, 124–54; Williams, "David Lyndsay and the Making of James V," 208–11.

89. Williams, "David Lyndsay and the Making of James V," 217–18.

90. William Stewart, *O man remember*, in *Bannatyne Manuscript*, 2:90–95, line 108: "Thow lykis in lust and ryalte to ring" (You prefer to persist in lust and magnificent pomp). See also Thomas, *Princelie Majestie*, 139.

R. James Goldstein, Janet Hadley Williams, and Antony J. Hasler emphasize the *Answer*'s didacticism regarding James's sexual behavior, arguing that
Lyndsay uses the poem to teach his monarch about normative heterosexuality.[91]
I extend their work to probe Lyndsay's pedagogical techniques and to explore how his pedagogy depends on obscene misogyny. Here, flyting's obscenities carry political weight, because Lyndsay deploys them to instruct his
monarch to forsake his unrestrained rampages for marital continence.
Lyndsay's *Answer* is centrally concerned with James's sexual education, as he
focuses on the negative effects of the instruction the teenage king received
from his guardians and teaches him a new behavioral regime so that he
can father a legitimate heir and avoid future dynastic instabilities like those
that marred his own minority rule. In order to convince James to modify his
behavior, Lyndsay encourages him to reflect critically on his past choices and
use that knowledge to change his future actions. He uses flyting's misogynist
obscenity to encourage James to feel disgust and revulsion regarding his previous partners, whom Lyndsay mocks as "ladronis" (loose women) from
the lower classes. Unlike his fellow flyters, who represent *all* carnal contact
with women as emasculating, Lyndsay teaches a more nuanced lesson by exploiting the intersecting inequalities of class, gender, and profession to make
his point. He separates women into two categories—the "ladyeis" of the court
and the "ladronis" of the kitchen quarters—differentiated by social status, using
flyting's gender- and class-inflected lexicon of abuse to teach James whom
he should and should not copulate with. As in Fragment I of the *Canterbury
Tales*, where the term "wenche" marks women as vulnerable to violence, with
overlapping derogatory connotations of femininity, lower social status, and
sexual transgression, here James's assault of a female brewhouse worker is
played for laughs, as Lyndsay blames her for her own victimization and uses
obscenity to portray her body as both polluting agent and punch line.

Lyndsay frames his instructional invective as an "answer" to a "flyting" (3,
18) allegedly written by James that does not survive. James's poem had accused
the married, fifty-year-old Lyndsay of impotence. In response to this charge,
Lyndsay exclaims, "Apon your pen, I cry ane loud vengeance!" (14), invoking
"pen"'s multivalence as signifying the penis as well as the writing instrument
that differentiates literary flyting from the feminized criminal street quarrels
of the same name.[92] In his instructional attack on James's "pen," Lyndsay em-
ploys four pedagogical strategies: he points to his own purportedly impotent

---

91. Hasler, *Court Poetry*, 171–73. Hasler discusses the figure of the impotent poet in Dunbar's
court poetry at 75–77.

92. Lyndsay refers to James's "prunyeand [sharp-pointed] pen" in line 6, and to "my pen" in line 15.

penis as a bodily exemplum illustrating the consequences of single-mindedly "persew[ing]" sex; he deploys the obscenity "fukkand" to educate James about his behavior; he uses bawdy storytelling, the technique favored by Chaucer's "felawes," to instruct James to view his lower-status partners with misogynist disgust; and he uses obscene metaphor to teach James how to copulate in the future.

Lyndsay confirms James's accusations of impotence, and he turns the insult into a lesson about the dangers of unrestrained masculine sexuality, lecturing James that he will be similarly impotent if he continues his current pattern of behavior.[93] In admitting his loss of virility and pointing to youthful excess as its source, Lyndsay uses his own genital capacities, past choices, and personal experiences as tools to instruct his fellow man:

> Quhat can ye say forther, bot I am failyeit
> In Venus werkis? I grant, schir, that is trew.
> The tyme hes bene, I wes better artailyeit
> Nor I am now. Bot yit full sair I rew
> That ever I did mouth thankles so persew.
> Quharefor, tak tent, and your fyne powder spair,
> And waist it nocht, bot gyf ye wit wel quhair. (29–35)
> [What more can you say, except that I am impaired
> In Venus's works? I grant, sir, that is true.
> The time has been, that I was better provided with "artillery"
> Than I am now. But yet I regret full bitterly
> That I ever so pursued that thankless mouth.
> Wherefore, take heed, and spare your fine gunpowder
> And do not waste it, unless you know well where (you are spending it).]

Lyndsay claims to have followed the code of Chaucer's "felawes," with their singular focus on "swyving" women, and he draws on his experiences to teach James an alternate model of sexual conduct. Drawing on pedagogical rhetoric, he uses the didactic phrase "tak tent" (take heed, pay attention) to instruct the king to exercise care regarding his precious royal semen. As he does throughout the *Answer*, Lyndsay deploys martial-sexual metaphor to portray his past body as "better artailyeit" (furnished with large guns) than his present one.

In this moment of instructive impotence, Lyndsay aligns his flyting with other antifeminist didactic poems that use obscenity to teach young men to

---

93. Hasler notes how "the poet's impotence allows him to speak from a position of authority" here (*Court Poetry*, 172).

preserve their virility by exercising self-restraint. These lyrics include Balnavis's *O gallandis all I cry and call*, whose speaker counsels his peers to "Keip strenth quhill that ye haif it" (Keep strength while you have it) and "cast not our oft / Your speir in to the reist" (do not thrust your spear too often / into its resting place), and John Moffat's *Bruthir be wyiss I reid yow now*, whose speaker warns his "bruthir" to "preif nevir thy pith so far in play / That thow forthink [it]" (never prove your potency in sex / so much that you regret it).[94] In his warning that James's penis will become "failyeit" if he continues to use it in this fashion, Lyndsay reduces women to their genitalia ("mouth thankles"), which he names with a popular derogatory phrase that characterizes vulvas as ungrateful and insatiate. Lyndsay turns his own impotence resulting from youthful overindulgence into a lesson for younger men: he claims it is the result of "persew[ing]" "mouth thankles," and he confesses that he "ful sair . . . rew[s]" his single-minded youthful pursuit of sex.

Lyndsay chooses Older Scots' most sexually explicit verb to teach James how his behavior is perceived by others, invoking obscenity's shock value and shame-generating capacity to add didactic heft to his rebuke of the king's wantonness. He accuses James of wasting his time and embarrassing himself by "ay fukkand lyke ane furious fornicatour" (constantly fucking like a raging fornicator) (49). Lyndsay uses "fukkand" to seize the king's attention and force him to recognize how unwise, unbecoming, and self-destructive his behavior is. He emphasizes the unremitting nature of James's copulation with the adverb "ay." He links "fukkand" through alliteration with derogatory terms signifying criminal sexual transgression and legal insanity, as "fornicatour" occurs chiefly in the context of legal punishment for fornication and "furious" was used to designate individuals as legally insane.[95] With the attention-grabbing charge of the obscene word, Lyndsay teaches James that his pattern of unremitting coitus is both senseless and transgressive. Lyndsay uses "fuk" only twice in his literary corpus—here and in the bawdy play *Ane Satyre of the Thrie Estaitis* (1552), where he notes that "Bischops . . . may fuck thair fill and be unmaryit [unmarried]"—and each time it serves as a stinging rebuke of men who abuse their positions of power to satisfy their carnal appetites.[96]

---

94. *O gallandis all I cry and call*, lines 2, 13–14; *Bruthir be wyiss I reid yow now*, in *Bannatyne Manuscript*, 4:26–28, lines 22–23.

95. *DOST* s.v. "furious" (adj.), 2; the term also appears as an insult ("Infortunate, fals, and furius") in *Dunbar and Kennedy*, line 492. In the four quotations cited under *DOST* s.v. "fornicator" (n.), three are from legal records and refer to "dowkeing" (ducking), "penalties," and "paynis" as punishment for fornicators; the term also occurs as an insult in *Montgomerie and Polwart*, IX.60.

96. David Lyndsay, *Ane Satyre of the Thrie Estaitis*, ed. Roderick Lyall (Edinburgh: Canongate, 1989), I.1370–71.

Lyndsay follows Chaucer's "felawes" in sharing bawdy narratives to teach carnal values. He relates a violent, messy encounter between James and an unnamed woman, presumably a kitchen worker, in the palace brewhouse:

> On ladronis for to loip ye wyll nocht lat,
> Howbeit the caribaldis cry the corinoch.
> Remember how, besyde the masking fat,
> Ye caist ane quene overthort ane stinking troch?
> That feynd, with fuffilling of hir roistit hoch,
> Caist doun the fat; quharthrow, drink, draf, and juggis
> Come rudely rinnand doun about your luggis.
>
> Wald God the lady that luffit yow best
> Had sene yow thair, ly swetterand lyke twa swyne!
> Bot to indyte how that duddroun wes drest
> (Drowkit with dreggis, quhimperand with mony quhryne),
> That proces to report it wer ane pyne.
> On your behalf, I thank God tymes ten score
> That yow preservit from gut and frome grandgore. (50–63)

[You will not refrain from copulating with loose women,
No matter how often the monsters make a loud outcry.
Remember how, beside the malt-mashing vat,
You threw a whore across a stinking trough?
That fiend, with jerking of her overheated haunch,
Knocked over the vat; as a result, drink, dregs, and liquid refuse
Came crudely flowing down around your ears.

I wish to God that the lady who loved you best
Had seen you there, lying wallowing like two swine!
But to describe the condition of that slovenly slut,
(Drenched with lees, whimpering with many squeals),
The process of reporting it would be a great effort.
On your behalf, I thank God two hundred times
That you were protected from gout and from venereal infection.]

Lyndsay claims that James aggressively mounts his partners in spite of their vocally resisting by "cry[ing] the corinoch," using a Gaelic term for a legal outcry for help or a funeral lament.[97] In alluding to the women's loud cries arising from sorrow or criminal harm, he implies that James's promiscuity has

---

97. *DOST* s.v. "corenoch" (n.), 1 and 2.

crossed the line into assault, but he forecloses empathy for the women by dehumanizing them as "ladronis" and "caribaldis": they are monsters, filthy drabs, marked by class disadvantage.[98] His use of "ladron" draws on the intersections between gender and class inequality to depict lower-status rape victims as culpable for their own assaults: this "term of derogation," which likely comes from "lad," with its connotations of "low rank," "menial" labor, and servitude, means "a base person, a low rascal" when applied to men; however, when used to name women, it acquires negative sexual connotations, meaning "a drab, a lowwoman."[99]

Lyndsay follows this with an exemplum to teach James to change his behavior by invoking misogynist disgust at the body of the debased and dehumanized "ladron." With his use of the familiar phrase "Remember how . . ." to introduce his narrative, Lyndsay presents his tale as fond reminiscence, a story that has been shared many times between close comrades, and he highlights how obscene storytelling can foster homosocial bonds. Lyndsay emphasizes the king's use of sexual force with the violent verbs "loip" (leap) and "caist" (throw), which entails "forcible or sudden movement."[100] Thomas reads Lyndsay's tale as a rape narrative that erases the woman's humanity and presents her violation as comic, in the vein of the "funny rapes" in the *Reeve's Tale*.[101] By noting the episode's location in the brewhouse and naming the trappings and foul byproducts of brewing—"ane stinking troch," "the masking fat," "the fat," "drink, draf, and juggis," "dreggis"—Lyndsay invokes common associations between women, drink work, and sexual transgression.[102] He links the filth of brewing byproducts with feminine sexuality, depicting James as physically defiled by his contact with the woman and portraying her as a source of sexually transmitted infection. Marjorie Keniston McIntosh notes how drink work rendered women "vulnerable to sexual advances and social disapproval," and here the woman's profession both exposes her to workplace assault and serves as a means of eliding her victimization and denying her suffering.[103] Lyndsay draws on popular misogyny against drink workers to blame her for the attack, to portray James as the victim of her befoulment, and to incite

---

98. Dunbar calls Kennedy "fowll carrybald" (184), and Polwarth applies the term to Montgomerie (VI.3).

99. *DOST* s.v. "lad" (n.[1]), 1 and 2; "ladron" (n.).

100. *DOST* s.v. "cast" (v.), 2; s.v. "lope" (v.).

101. Thomas, *Princelie Majestie*, 43.

102. For historical connections between women and brewing in Scotland, see Elizabeth Ewan, "'For Whatever Ales Ye': Women as Producers and Consumers in Late Medieval Scottish Towns," in Ewan and Meikle, *Women in Scotland*.

103. Marjorie Keniston McIntosh, *Working Women in English Society 1300–1620* (Cambridge: Cambridge University Press, 2005), 253.

visceral, gut-churning disgust at lower-class female sexuality, a point ham-mered home by his inclusion of the olfactory detail "stinking."

Lyndsay invokes derogatory stereotypes of lower-status femininity, begrimed with sexual stigma and literal dirt, and he draws on "a sexual hierarchy in operation that holds certain female bodies in higher regard than others" in order to make his point.[104] He dehumanizes James's partners by naming them with a range of abusive terms—"ladronis" (loose women), "caribaldis" (monsters), "ane quene" (a whore), "feynd" (fiend), "swyn" (swine), and "dud-droun" (slovenly slut)—to teach James to eschew sex with working-class women by painting them as wicked, disgusting, malicious, inhuman, and sex-ually transgressive.[105] Unlike the other flyters with their blanket proscriptions of all heterosexual contact, Lyndsay does not teach James to reject relations with *all* women, just with certain *kinds* of women. He illustrates how the brew-house worker's gender, social status, and profession intersect to render her vulnerable to assault, to blame her for her rape by insisting that "she wanted it," to portray her as the punch line to a bawdy joke between men, and to cast her as a dangerous agent of pollution and sexually transmitted infection.

Lyndsay uses his tale to teach James that intercourse with "quene[s]" is hu-miliating and degrading, literally covering both partners in filth. He claims that the wriggling woman overturns the malt-mashing vat filled with fer-mented barley and liquid, drenching both partners in stinking refuse.[106] In light of Lyndsay's use of the verbs "caist" and "loip" to name James's coital actions, it seems likely that what he jokingly paints as the woman's overwhelm-ing desire, the uncontrollable movements of her ravenous hindquarters, is in fact her desperate attempt to wrench free from the king's grasp. By blaming the foul swill-shower on the woman's "roistit hoch" (sexually overheated haunch), Lyndsay insists that she is "asking for it." Her trauma is recast as plea-

---

104. Crenshaw notes how sexual hierarchies among women work to erase violence against black women, similarly to how Lyndsay invokes hierarchies to erase violence against poor working women ("Mapping the Margins," 1269). She writes, "Black women are essentially prepackaged as bad women within cultural narratives about good women who can be raped and bad women who cannot" (ibid., 1271). Here, the brewhouse worker is prepackaged as a source of disease and disgust by Lyndsay's introduction of the encounter as "besyde the masking fat."

105. *DOST* s.v. "ladron" (n.), "caribald" (n.), and "duddroun" (n.). For another misogynous self-identified "flyting" (line 152) addressed to James in which Lyndsay links lower-class femininity with sexual insult and physical dirt, see *Ane Supplicatioun, Directed . . . to the Kingis Grace, in Contemptioun of Syde Taillis*, in *The Works of Sir David Lindsay of the Mount, 1490–1555*, ed. Douglas Hamer, 4 vols. (Edinburgh: Scottish Text Society, 1931–36), 1:117–22; C. Marie Harker, "Skirting the Issue: Misogyny and Gender in Lyndsay's *Ane Supplicatioun Directit . . . to the Kingis Grace, in Contemptioun of Syde Taillis*," in *Older Scots Literature*, ed. Sally Mapstone (Edinburgh: John Donald, 2005).

106. The insult "swine" also occurs in criminal flytings, as when an Elgin brewster called a male ale-taster "a fool swoyne carl." *Transactions of the Buchan Field Club*, 13 vols. (Peterhead, UK: P. Scrogie, 1913), 11:34.

sure for the enjoyment of the aristocratic men giggling at her degradation, much as Malyne's and her mother's confusion and fear is played for laughs by Chaucer's "felawes." Even though James "caist" the woman across the brewing trough, Lyndsay places the blame for overturning the vat solely on "hir" bodily movements. He mocks her bewildered surprise and compares her to farm livestock, laughing at "that duddroun"'s degradation. He dehumanizes her with his characterization of her reaction as "quhryne," a term typically used to name the squeals voiced by pigs, along with his rhyming use of "swyne" two lines earlier.[107] Lyndsay concludes his anecdote with a reminder to James that his actions could result in gout and syphilis, lecturing him about venereal disease in the vein of contemporary educators who emphasize the risks of sexually transmitted infections as their chief means of teaching young people about sexuality, instead of focusing on consent or pleasure.[108] Lyndsay locates these ailments squarely in the body of the "duddroun," teaching James that her vulva—the despised "mouth thankles" that contaminates and consumes all it touches—is a source of infection.

Lyndsay uses obscene storytelling to encourage James to have less sex, and he teaches the king a new system of values. He instructs James to abandon his excesses and restrict his energies to two partners: Lady Margaret Erskine (d. 1572), his favorite mistress, and his soon-to-be bride, Madeleine de Valois. Lyndsay teaches James to engage in critical reflection on his past, present, and future coital behavior by inciting the king's misogynous revulsion in order to dissuade him from that behavior.[109] He twice instructs James to "be war" (well-informed, cautious with regard to his actions) about how he uses his penis (39, 67).[110] By warning James about the adverse physical effects of his behavior, including gout, syphilis, impotence, and exhaustion, Lyndsay teaches James to consider the consequences of his actions and to care for his own body, warning the king that he is "waistand [his] corps [and] lettand the tyme overslyde" (wasting his body and frittering time away) (46) by following the values he was taught as a teenager.

As part of instructing James to reflect critically on his actions, Lyndsay teaches him to consider the effect of his "furious fukking" on those who care

---

107. *DOST* s.v. "quhryne" (v.), a.

108. Allen notes that the chief aim of sexuality education in countries like New Zealand, Australia, England, and the United States has traditionally been to reduce rates of unintended pregnancies and sexually transmissible infections, and she discusses alternatives to this approach in *Young People and Sexuality Education*, 132–53.

109. Carmody discusses the importance of critical reflection to ethical sex in *Sex, Ethics, and Young People*, 115–16.

110. *DOST* s.v. "war" (adj.), 1 and 2.

about him, namely Erskine, "the lady that luffit [him] best."[111] Erskine was the mother of James Stewart, Earl of Moray (1531–70), who became the most powerful of the king's seven illegitimate sons and served as regent of Scotland after the abdication of his half sister, Mary Queen of Scots, from 1567 until his assassination in 1570.[112] In June 1536, around the time the *Answer* was written, James attempted to divorce Erskine from her husband so he could marry her himself, but Pope Paul III refused to grant the annulment, and James gifted her 500 merks a year as compensation.[113] Lyndsay encourages James to consider the effect of his choices on Erskine by imagining her response to his swill-soaked assault in the palace's kitchen quarters, although it is unclear whether Lyndsay thinks her reaction would be one of humiliation, shock, disgust, horror, or disappointment. Part of instructing young people in ethical critical reflection regarding their sexual behavior entails asking them how they would feel if the people they most admired knew about their choices, and this is precisely what Lyndsay does here with James.[114] However, Lyndsay privileges the king's consideration for one aristocratic partner at the expense of others, using intersectional misogyny to exclude "ladronis" from the category of women deserving care.

In the *Answer*'s closing lines, Lyndsay uses obscene metaphor to offer a final lesson to the king by looking ahead to his coming union with Madeleine, who was sixteen when James married her at Notre Dame in Paris in January 1537. He instructs James to reserve his energies for vigorous, heir-producing matrimonial sex with his new bride:

Bot yit be war with lawbouring of your lance:
Sum sayis thare cummis ane bukler furth of France
Quhilk wyll indure your dintis, thocht thay be dour. (67–69)

[But still be careful with laboring your lance:
Some say there comes a small shield out of France
That will withstand your blows, though they are fierce.]

---

111. Thomas, *Princelie Majestie*, 42.

112. John Guy, *Queen of Scots: The True Life of Mary Stuart* (New York: Mariner Books, 2005), esp. 373–83.

113. Cameron, *James V*, 160n253, 188n176, 206–8; Anderson, "James V, mistresses and children of."

114. Carmody, *Sex, Ethics, and Young People*, 116. Williams discusses how Lyndsay portrays Erskine, Madeleine, and the unnamed woman in the brewhouse as "symbols rather than three-dimensional relationships." Janet Hadley Williams, "Women Fictional and Historic in Lyndsay's Poetry," in *Women and the Feminine in Medieval and Early Modern Scottish Writing*, ed. Sarah M. Dunnigan, C. Marie Harker, and Evelyn S. Newlyn (New York: Palgrave Macmillan, 2004), 55.

Lyndsay concludes his lesson with a didactic warning—"Bot yit be war"—that James exercise discretion with his genital weaponry. He appropriates the language of chivalric masculinity—"lance," "bukler," "dintis . . . dour"—from battle-filled epics like Gavin Douglas's *Eneados*, John Barbour's *Wallace*, and Blind Hary's *The Bruce*. He transforms this violent discourse into erotic meta-phor for instructive purposes, teaching James that marital intercourse is an ex-emplary act of military prowess, a one-sided jousting match between shield and lance.[115] Lyndsay deploys martial-sexual rhetoric throughout his *Answer*—accusing James of "Schutand your bolt at mony sindrie schellis" (Shooting your arrow at many sundry targets) (37), urging James to "spair" his "fyne" semen-gunpowder (34), and lamenting James's advisory council "tholand yow rin schutand frome schell to schell" (allowing you to run shooting from tar-get to target) (45)—but here he replaces metaphors of target practice and gun firing with single combat.[116] To flatter the king, Lyndsay characterizes his co-ital style as "dintis . . . dour," a popular alliterative phrase that he uses else-where to praise the military might of James's father, James IV, and "his dyntis dour" in battle.[117] "Dint" signifies "a severe blow or heavy stroke, especially one given with a weapon in fighting," underscoring the wounding power of James's penile lance strokes, and its descriptor "dour" means "hard, severe, harsh."[118] Lyndsay's use of "dintis . . . dour" to teach James how to copulate serves as an implicit authorization of sexual force, because he assures the king that Madeleine will withstand his aggressive thrusts and fulfill his notoriously capacious appetites in spite of her tender age and fragile health.

Lyndsay depicts Madeleine as "ane bukler furth of France" who "will in-dure" James's mighty lance blows. In portraying her vagina as a small, round shield, a defensive object meant to absorb violent blows and protect its bearer

---

115. "Bukler" and "lance" name genitalia elsewhere in Middle Scots poetry, and in both cases they are used by male speakers to denigrate women's sexuality: in *This use of court richt weill I knaw*, a lady returns home with "hir buclar bord and all backwart borne" (her vulva pierced-through and car-ried backward [because its front is so damaged from combat]) after settling her husband's legal cases with sexual favors, line 25; and in *To ane unthankfull friend*, the speaker tells his former lover, "He tuik the onlye for thy gear / And thou chust hym for lance and speir," in Joanna M. Martin, ed., *The Mait-land Quarto: A New Edition of Cambridge, Magdalene College, Pepys Library MS 1408* (Edinburgh: Scottish Text Society, 2015), 258–60, lines 53–54, also 60.

116. The euphemism "bolt" (short, heavy arrow) for the penis and "schell" (target) for the vulva is popular in Middle Scots poetry, and the phrase "schutand at the schell" is deployed didactically by male speakers to dissuade their younger peers from excessive sexual activity in *O gallandis all I cry and call*, line 58; *My hart is quhyt and no delyte I haif of ladeis fair*, line 26.

117. *The Testament of the Papyngo* (1530), in *Sir David Lyndsay: Selected Poems*, 58–97, line 496. For more on James IV as a powerful military commander who won multiple victories in the Anglo-Scottish border wars until his recklessness led to his death at the Battle of Flodden, see MacDougall, *James IV*, 264–76.

118. *DOST* s.v. "dint" (n.), 1; s.v. "dour" (adj./adv.), 3.

from harm, Lyndsay teaches the king about his queen's limited sexual agency within the marriage.[119] Lyndsay's leering reference to Madeleine's "bukler" in this moment of homosocial familiarity is laden with gross presumption: what can a fifty-year-old Scottish courtier possibly know about the sixteen-year-old French princess's genitalia and what it can "indure"? Lyndsay invokes Madeleine's private body for instructional purposes in a poem circulated at the same predominantly male court where she will soon be queen, claiming her "bukler" as an object of prurient public conversation. Lyndsay's use of "indure" normalizes women's bodies as objects of violence: it means "to endure, suffer, sustain, bear," none of which sound enjoyable from Madeleine's perspective.[120] In his claim to possess intimate knowledge of Madeleine's body, his insistence on her ability to withstand aggressive coitus, and his application of obscene metaphor to her genitalia as a teaching tool, Lyndsay underscores the centrality of misogyny to his pedagogy. Earlier in the *Answer* he incites contemptuous disgust for lower-status female sexuality in order to teach the king to change his behavior, and here he exhibits the entrenched refusal to acknowledge women's subjectivity that underpins his educational regime. Lyndsay's boasts notwithstanding, Madeleine was unable to "indure" much of anything, as she died of tuberculosis seven months after her wedding.[121]

The flyters demonstrate how, by centering their pedagogy on misogyny and viewing women as polluting bodies rather than erotic subjects, their exclusionary all-male community perpetuates inequalities and portrays them as unquestionable truth. In all the surviving flytings, poets deploy obscene insult to teach their peers to limit their sexual engagement with women, adopting the vocabulary of feminized criminal flyting and drawing on the masculinity-proving capacity of university disputation. Dunbar, Kennedy, Montgomerie, and Polwarth teach one another that *all* sex with women is antithetical to exemplary masculinity; Lyndsay, in contrast, instructs his monarch to change the behavior that he was taught as a youth, advocating marital monogamy to preserve the Stewart line. Flytings, particularly Lyndsay's *Answer*, show how obscene same-sex pedagogy was imagined as having the transformative potential to teach men to evaluate and change their sexual values.[122]

---

119. *DOST* s.v. "buklar" (n.), 1.

120. *DOST* s.v. "indure" (v.[1]), 2.

121. For more on James and Madeleine's marriage, see Cameron, *James V*, 133; Thomas, *Princelie Majestie*, 184–89. Lyndsay wrote a formal lament commemorating her death, *The Deploratioun of the Deith of Quene Magdalene*, in *Sir David Lyndsay: Selected Poems*, 101–8.

122. For an overview of the challenges and benefits of male peer delivery of sexual health programming, see Jacqueline B. Cupples, Ann P. Zukoski, and Tatiana Dierwechter, "Reaching Young Men: Lessons Learned in the Recruitment, Training, and Utilization of Male Peer Sexual Health Educators," *Health Promotion Practice* 11, supplement 1 (2010).

After Flyting: Playing the Dozens, Cyphering, and Angel Haze

The pedagogy of misogynist insult central to flyting shares affinities with later African American literary-cultural practices such as playing the dozens, a competitive pastime in which men trade obscene insults about each other's female relatives, and cyphering, which is "a public gathering where MCs 'freestyle'—produce unscripted spontaneous rhymes—to sharpen their technique and build community."[123] These overlapping practices, both foundational elements of contemporary hip-hop culture, enable individuals to prove masculinity by trading misogynist insults, making heterosexual boasts, and showcasing their verbal dexterity in fierce competition with one another.[124] Obscenity, with its "tremendous emotive power," is as central to playing the dozens and cyphering as it is to flyting.[125] These resonances across time and culture shed light on how obscene all-male discourses can teach misogyny and mold masculinity, and they also show how misogyny can be challenged to pave the way for more ethical sexual paradigms.[126] I focus on the work of Detroit-born MC Angel Haze, whose forceful challenges to hip-hop's misogyny and rigid gender politics are a fitting pivot between the pedagogical model I outline in this chapter, in which men use obscenity to instruct one another about virility through misogynist insult, and the pastourelle lyrics I discuss in the next chapter, where women teach audiences of all genders about rape and consent.

Recent scholarship on playing the dozens provides a useful lens for understanding how flyting, with its similar combination of ritualized insult, homosocial community, verbal creativity, and implicit violence, shapes masculine identity and educates its participants about sexuality. Both the dozens and flyting can be understood as same-sex peer education, and both practices are

---

123. Rashad Shabazz, "Masculinity and the Mic: The Uneven Geography of Hip-Hop," *Gender, Place, and Culture* 21, no. 3 (2014): 383n11.

124. While these discourses are not exclusively male, they are predominantly male and typically privilege a masculine subject position. For women's restricted participation in the dozens, see Elijah Wald, *The Dozens: A History of Rap's Mama* (Oxford: Oxford University Press, 2012), 198; for the masculinization of hip-hop, see Miles White, *From Jim Crow to Jay-Z: Race, Rap, and the Performance of Masculinity* (Urbana: University of Illinois Press, 2011); for women's resistance to this masculinization, see Gwendolyn D. Pough, *Check It While I Wreck It: Black Womanhood, Hip-Hop, and the Public Sphere* (Boston: Northeastern University Press, 2004).

125. White, *From Jim Crow to Jay-Z*, 57. White discusses the role of obscenity in hip-hop at 55–58; also Kimberlé Williams Crenshaw, "The 2 Live Crew Controversy," in *Feminism and Pornography*, ed. Drucilla Cornell (Oxford: Oxford University Press, 2000), 219–22.

126. I do not mean to suggest that flyting, playing the dozens, and cyphering are the same, as misogynist insult competitions among sixteenth-century Scottish court elites are quite different from those among marginalized African Americans in the United States, but I believe that they nonetheless resonate with one another in edifying ways.

centered on men asserting their virility through insulting women. Elijah Wald and Simon Frith explicitly link sixteenth-century Scottish flyting with playing the dozens by noting that both are competitive practices of building masculinity through creative, stylized exchanges of obscene misogynist insults.[127] The dozens' ritualized verbal dueling serves as both a pedagogical exercise and an adolescent male rite of passage. Alan Dundes argues that, in trading insults as part of a "battle to express masculinity," each speaker "tries to assert his virility by attacking his opponent or his opponent's female relatives. He can do so *positively* by asserting that he has had sexual liaisons with his antagonist's mother or sister; or he can proceed in *negative* fashion by denying his opponent's virility or that of his opponent's male relatives."[128] In addition to functioning as a social ritual for proving masculinity, playing the dozens can be understood as an educational process for its participants in the vein of medieval scholastic disputation, as Laurence Levine suggests that it constitutes "training in verbal facility and . . . self-discipline."[129]

Dozens players exchange insults about one another's mothers and sisters, much as the flyters trade obscene barbs about each other's intimate partners. "I fucked your mother on a red-hot heater / Missed that pussy and burned my peter," goes one old dozens rhyme.[130] Another declares, "I remember one time your mama was sitting on a fence, / Selling her pussy for fifteen cents."[131] Many others feature "insults about mothers or sisters having sex with dogs."[132] Some scholars view the dozens as inculcating young men with misogynist hate speech, since its maligning of women's sexuality, coupled with women's frequent exclusion from participating in the game, both reflects and perpetuates real-life violence and inequality.[133] Addressing the problem of misogyny in hip-hop, which frequently features the dozens' discourse of sexual insult, Crenshaw declares that "sexual humor in which women are objectified as packages of body parts to serve whatever male-bonding/male competition needs men please subordinates women in much the same way that racist humor subor-

---

127. Wald, *The Dozens*, 122; Simon Frith, *Performing Rites: On the Value of Popular Music* (Oxford: Oxford University Press, 1996), 318–19n44.

128. Alan Dundes, *Mother Wit from the Laughing Barrel: Readings in the Interpretation of Afro-American Folklore* (Englewood Cliffs, NJ: Prentice-Hall, 1973), 297; also Wald, *The Dozens*, 171–72.

129. Lawrence W. Levine, "The Ritual of Insult," in *Black Culture and Black Consciousness: Afro-American Folk Thought from Slavery to Freedom* (Oxford: Oxford University Press, 1977), 357; also Wald, *The Dozens*, 173.

130. Wald, *The Dozens*, 188.

131. Ibid., 106.

132. Ibid., 32.

133. Ibid., 198.

dinates African-Americans."[134] In the dozens as well as in flyting, men disparage their opponents' female partners and relatives even though their conflicts have nothing to do with women. They use insults about women's bodies as verbal weapons to play vicious homosocial games, sacrificing women's humanity to the needs of the male collective.

Cyphering, which typically stages a group of male voices in competition with one another, overlaps with playing the dozens, as both foster same-sex community, privilege verbal dexterity as a tool for proving one's status within the group, and teach a model of aggressive heterosexual masculinity. Like flyting, the cypher is a useful teaching tool because of its collectivity, competitiveness, violent misogyny as a means of both bonding and attack, and emphasis on obscene insult. The BET (Black Entertainment Television) Hip-Hop Awards has featured an ever-growing number of cyphers annually since 2006, underscoring cyphering's entertainment value, influence, and social power.[135] Rashad Shabazz shows how the creative space of the cypher is gendered masculine through misogyny, exclusion, and a linking of verbal prowess to a specific brand of masculinity. He explores the persistent connections between masculinity and the mic in hip-hop, a relationship strikingly similar to that between manhood and the "pen" in the flytings, and he observes that "masculinity and the mic are often seen as synonymous. And not just any masculinity; the male figure that dominates in this scenario embodies a hyper-sexualized, hyper-aggressive, heterosexual masculinity."[136] Shabazz argues that this connection, coupled with the curtailment of women's access to the mic, "normalizes misogyny, homophobia, and narrow forms of masculinity within hip-hop, all of which undermines the revolutionary potential of hip-hop space."[137]

Angel Haze embodies this "revolutionary potential." Haze, who identifies as agender and uses both feminine and masculine pronouns, shows how the

---

134. Crenshaw, "2 Live Crew Controversy," 226. For more on misogyny in hip-hop, see Michael P. Jeffries, *Thug Life: Race, Gender, and the Meaning of Hip-Hop* (Chicago: University of Chicago Press, 2011), 154–63; Shabazz, "Masculinity and the Mic," 276–79; Guillermo Rebollo-Gil and Amanda Moras, "Black Women and Black Men in Hip Hop Music: Misogyny, Violence and the Negotiation of (White-Owned) Space," *Journal of Popular Culture* 45, no. 1 (2012). Pough explores how black female artists challenge misogyny in *Check It While I Wreck It*, 97–101.

135. The BET Hip-Hop Awards featured two cyphers in its inaugural ceremony in 2006, and this number has increased over time to six cyphers—including Eminem's headline-making solo cypher attacking Donald Trump—in 2017's show.

136. Shabazz, "Masculinity and the Mic," 378. For more on the vexed role of gender in the cypher, see Imani Kai Johnson, "Dark Matter in B-Boying Cyphers: Race and Global Connection in Hip Hop" (PhD diss., University of Southern California, 2012), 9–10. I am grateful to Dr. Johnson for generously sharing her unpublished work with me.

137. Shabazz, "Masculinity and the Mic," 377. Shabazz shows how, despite the instrumental role of female MCs like Salt N Pepa, Queen Latifah, MC Lyte, and Missy Elliott in shaping hip-hop, "Black men never challenged the masculinization of hip-hop's geography; instead, they naturalized it" (ibid., 376).

connections between masculinity and the mic, between penis and pen, can be disrupted. In October 2012, Haze participated in "The Man with the Iron Fists," one of the cyphers staged at that year's BET Hip-Hop Awards. The cypher's very name focuses on the violent masculine body, and Haze's five fellow MCs are all men who boast about their heterosexual prowess, demonstrating how the cypher functions to exert male supremacy and teach masculine sexuality. Haze's performance in the cypher illustrates how this normalization of masculinity as erotic conquest can be challenged. Rejecting her competitors' sexual bluster, Haze argues that her verbal dexterity and rhetorical violence give her primacy over her peers. Like literary flyting, the cypher is a discursive space within which men prove their symbolic virility. By refusing to engage in obscene verbal competition over women's bodies, Haze disrupts the cypher's status as a closed pedagogical circle of men insulting, competing with, and teaching one another, and she illuminates its potential for creating new knowledge.

Haze commits an even more radical revision of hip-hop's sexual politics in "Cleaning Out My Closet," a song that she self-released online in late 2012 as part of her *Classick* mixtape. In it, Haze repurposes the beat and title from fellow Detroit MC Eminem's 2002 song of the same name to share a graphic autobiographical narrative of childhood sexual abuse. Haze positions herself in a virtual cypher with Eminem and illustrates how cyphers, like flytings, can take place in installments over time. In disrupting an exclusionary obscene discourse that typically functions to shore up male supremacy, Haze shines the floodlights back on misogyny, exposes it as far more than a literary game, protests its ineluctable violence, and testifies to its lived effects on individual bodies. Haze's song illustrates how, as noted by Linda Alcoff and Laura Gray, "survivor speech has great transgressive potential to disrupt the maintenance and reproduction of dominant discourses as well as to curtail their sphere of influence."[138] In this context dominated by misogynist hate speech as "the instrument through which power is exercised," Haze's appropriation of Eminem's song to articulate the wounds of misogyny functions as what Butler calls "a reverse citation in the scene of trauma," "a reworking [of injurious terms] that . . . shift[s] their context and purpose."[139] Haze shows how, through interruption and resignification, the lessons that men teach one another about

---

138. Linda Alcoff and Laura Gray, "Survivor Discourse: Transgression or Recuperation?" *Signs* 18, no. 2 (1993): 270.

139. Toni Morrison, *Lecture and Speech of Acceptance, upon the Award of the Nobel Prize for Literature, Delivered in Stockholm on the Seventh of December, Nineteen Hundred and Ninety-Three* (New York: Alfred A. Knopf, 1995), 12; Butler, *Excitable Speech*, 38. Butler discusses Morrison's formulation of language as violence at 6–10 and explores the risks and possibilities of resignification at 36–38.

sexuality can be challenged, and she illuminates how marginalized individuals can use obscenity to shed light on the harms resulting from injustice.

In adapting the beat and song title from Eminem—an artist known for his violent misogyny, homophobia, and rape threats, especially during his early career—to tell a searing personal narrative about childhood assault, Haze presents her obscene testimony as cathartic for herself and edifying for her listeners.[140] She draws attention to a violation that occurs with unacknowledged frequency due to the intersecting inequalities of race, age, class, and gender, because African American women are both more likely than white women to suffer childhood sexual abuse and less likely to disclose their experiences.[141] Haze breaks the "uncanny silence surrounding the trauma of black rape" by voicing her experience of violation in a discursive space typically characterized by virulent misogyny.[142]

Haze signals her song's obscenity in the intro when she cautions, "Parental discretion is advised." She describes her first assault, at the age of seven, in vivid detail: "He took me to the basement and after the lights had been cut / He whipped it out and sodomized and forced his cock through my gut." In her trademark relentless staccato intonation, Haze encourages her audience to imagine themselves in her position and to feel visceral disgust at the details of her violation: "Imagine being seven, seeing cum in your underwear / I know it's nasty but sometimes I'd even bleed from my butt / Disgusting, right? Now let that feeling ring through your guts." In her exhortation that her listeners let the feelings of "disgust" generated by her testimony's explicit obscenity "ring through [their] guts," Haze presents her narrative as having the power to elicit a physical reaction from those who hear it, demanding that audiences feel the anguish of rape in their very viscera. Mobilizing obscenity's power to invoke disgust, "a feeling about something and in response to something" entailing bodily sensations of "nausea or queasiness" and "an urge to recoil and shudder," Haze uses obscenity to marshal her listeners' deep, embodied

---

140. Eminem's extreme misogyny is well documented—in "My Name Is," he boasts of raping lesbians, while in "'97 Bonnie and Clyde," he fantasizes in graphic detail about murdering his estranged wife and disposing of her body—and this makes Haze's choice to use his beat and song title particularly significant. White discusses Eminem's lyrics' "vile misogyny" in *From Jim Crow to Jay-Z*, 110.

141. Jody Miller, *Getting Played: African American Girls, Urban Inequality, and Gendered Violence* (New York: New York University Press, 2010), 114–50; Shaquita Tillman et al., "Shattering Silence: Exploring Barriers to Disclosure for African-American Sexual Assault Survivors," *Trauma, Violence, and Abuse* 11, no. 2 (2010); Patricia A. Washington, "Disclosure Patterns of Black Female Sexual Assault Survivors," *Violence against Women* 7, no. 11 (2001). Crenshaw explores how women of color are both more likely to suffer violence and less likely to have those sufferings recognized in "Mapping the Margins."

142. Pierce-Baker, *Surviving the Silence*, 18.

revulsion at the harms of sexual violence.[143] In contrast to invoking disgust at the exposed, humiliated body of the victim-survivor, as we saw in Lyndsay's *Answer*, here disgust's emotional heft is leveraged against perpetrators and their actions.

In addition to using obscenity to articulate the gut-wrenching details of her violation, Haze mobilizes it to express unbridled rage at her victimization: "[I] wanted to take a fucking brick and push they teeth through they liver / Wanted to smash the fucking world and burn its leftover parts / Wanted to rip it out and just fucking step on my heart," she declares. She adopts the violent rhetoric of hip-hip masculinity, which male artists typically use to assert their primacy over women as well as other men, to voice her righteous anger at being habitually violated. With her ferocious rapid-fire delivery like a hail of bullets from an AK-47, Haze uses obscenity to transform blind howls of rage into searing pedagogical testimony regarding the lived effects of the misogyny that is so central to playing the dozens, cyphering, and flyting. In contrast to Lyndsay's and Chaucer's use of rape narratives for instructional purposes by eliciting laughter and disgust, Haze exposes sexual violence as the logical end point of misogyny. She uses her narrative of suffering and survival to teach her audience and empower herself: "I'm just saying this to tell you there's a way from the ground," she explains at her song's end, offering her story as solace for other survivors. In repurposing the work of Eminem, whose lyrics advocate rape and intimate partner violence, Haze illustrates how the destructive same-sex pedagogy of the cypher, the flyting, and the dozens can be blown wide open by including marginalized voices and perspectives. We cannot know what Madeleine de Valois thought about her vagina being discussed openly at the Scottish court in Lyndsay's *Answer to the Kingis Flyting*, or what the unnamed "duddroun" might have said about being mocked as a punch line among the men responsible for her victimization. Nor can we know how Christian Hynd felt about being sexually slandered by her husband's literary rival in *The Flyting of Dunbar and Kennedy*. But through the words of Angel Haze, we can see possibilities for disrupting these harmful narratives by co-opting the generic form of homosocial misogynist insult and sharing individual experiences of violence with ferocity, candor, and obscene potency.

---

143. Miller, *Anatomy of Disgust*, 8, 2.

CHAPTER 3

Pastourelle Encounters
Rape, Consent, and Sexual Negotiation

This book's first two chapters have focused on obscenity's role in perpetuating rape culture and educating men about gendered embodiment. But obscenity served a host of other purposes in late medieval England and Scotland, including to articulate female desire, to shed light on inequality, and to teach audiences about rape's harms, particularly in lyrics known as pastourelles. *All to lufe and not to fenyie*, copied by Edinburgh merchant George Bannatyne in the Bannatyne Manuscript (1565–68) along with *The Flyting of Dunbar and Kennedy*, invites readers to eavesdrop on a rape in progress. In this debate between victim and perpetrator, the woman begs the man to leave her alone and protests that he is tearing her clothing. He dismisses her cries and insists, "ye sall not be the war" (you shall not be any worse [for this]).[1] She says, "Ye hurt me with your quhinyear heft [dagger handle]" (19), using double entendre to voice her resistance to the assault and emphasize the physical pain he inflicts on her. With her characterization of her rapist's penis as "your quhinyear heft," the woman uses martial-sexual metaphor to highlight the violence in his actions. She repeats the verb "hurt" a total of three times (9, 19, 33), and she narrates her assault in excruciating detail, crying out, "Allace allace ye thrist me throw!" (Alas, alas, you thrust

---

1. *All to lufe and not to fenyie*, in *Bannatyne Manuscript*, 3:6–8, line 26. Also Newlyn, "Political Dimensions," 77–80.

through me!) (36). Although she is unable to stop her assailant, she hits him on the cheek, curses him repeatedly, and scratches him until he bleeds, registering her resistance with words and fists even as she acknowledges that there will be "no help" to rescue her (37). He orders her to be quiet, and he rapes her before kissing her goodbye. After the attack, she vows to run home and spread the word about what has been done to her, and she insistently repeats the verb "tell" to emphasize her commitment to speaking publicly about her assault (58, 60).

Chaucer's Wife of Bath opens her tale with a similar narrative about a "lusty bacheler," a strapping young knight in King Arthur's court who attacks a maiden on his way home from hunting waterfowl:

> On a day [he] cam ridynge from ryver,
> And happed that, allone as he was born,
> He saugh a mayde walkynge hym biforn,
> Of which mayde anon, maugree hir heed,
> By verray force, he rafte hire maydenhed. (III.883–88)

Unlike the victim in *All to lufe and not to fenyie*, who has more lines than the perpetrator does, Chaucer's "mayde" never speaks.[2] Instead, we are reminded of her status as a virgin, a point hammered home by the repetition of "mayde," "mayde," and "maydenhed" in three consecutive lines; we are told that the knight uses "verray force" (brute strength) to attack her; we learn that she is traveling alone and on foot; and we are informed that the attack is "maugree hir heed" (against her will). She disappears from the tale entirely after these lines.[3] Chaucer elides her assault, refusing to give voice to her experience and focusing instead on the rehabilitation of her rapist.[4] We saw this occlusion of victims' perspectives in the *Reeve's Tale*, which closes with the two rapists merrily "go[ing]" "on hir wey" to their friends at Soler Hall (I.4310).

These two poems, with their two nameless maidens—one vocal, one silent—illustrate two ways that Middle English and Middle Scots literary texts engage with rape.[5] In some texts, women's experiences of violation are not

---

2. For a genealogy of the literary trope of the silenced rape survivor, see Mark Amsler, "Rape and Silence: Ovid's Mythography and Medieval Readers," in Robertson and Rose, *Representing Rape*.

3. Edwards explores the implications of the maiden's disappearance from the tale in *Afterlives of Rape*, 98–99.

4. Rose, "Reading Chaucer Reading Rape," 36–39; Saunders, *Rape and Ravishment*, 300–301.

5. I am using she/her pronouns to refer to rape survivors unless specified otherwise, since the victims of violence in these texts are portrayed as overwhelmingly female, with a few exceptions. Dyan Elliott explores medieval representations of male victims in "Sexual Scandal and the Clergy: A Medieval Blueprint for Disaster," in *Why the Middle Ages Matter: Medieval Light on Modern Injustice*, ed.

the chief focus, and we rarely hear from the victim herself.[6] Instead, rape functions as a literary trope.[7] As Christine M. Rose observes, "rape acts as a figure for agendas other than sexual: property crimes, homosocial interaction, acts of war, or religious evil."[8] This is the case in the *Reeve's Tale*, where rape is portrayed as a means of settling economic disputes and performing masculinity for one's peers. In contrast, pastourelles are centrally concerned with women's experiences of the threat of sexual violence, and their female speakers articulate resistance, fear, anguish, and anger in response to that threat.[9] They emphasize the intersectional violence faced by young, unmarried peasant women who are multiply disadvantaged by gender, age, class, and single status, like the "wenches" in Chaucer's *Canterbury Tales* and the "quenes" in Scottish flytings. They use female-voiced obscenity to illuminate how *all* heterosexual encounters in a rape culture—even encounters that are consensual and pleasurable—are inflected by the ineluctable threat of violence. They feature a rich diversity of narratives about sexual violence, teaching audiences that neither rape nor consensual sex follows a single paradigm. Echoing the rape prevention strategies of female-voiced conduct texts, they show how fictive female voices were imagined as educating young women about how best

Celia Chazelle et al. (New York: Routledge, 2012). In the anticlerical fifteenth-century macaronic lyric *Freers, freers, wo ye be!* (*DIMEV* 1456), male householders are warned about the perils of letting Franciscan friars stay overnight in their homes, as the friars might assault their sons, daughters, or wives: "Odur thi wyf or thi doughtour / hic vult violare / Or thi sun he weyl prefur" (Either thy wife or thy daughter / This man will seek to violate / Or he will prefer your son) (Duncan, *Medieval English Lyrics and Carols*, 303–4, lines 23–25).

6. See the Duchess of Brittany's rape by the Giant of Mont St. Michel in Thomas Malory's *Le Morte D'Arthur*, the *Alliterative Morte D'Arthur*, and related texts. In these narratives, the duchess's rape and murder are the impetus for Arthur to slay the giant and build his chivalric reputation. Saunders argues that "the protection of women from rape and abduction functions as a leitmotif in the exploration of male chivalry and villainy" in medieval romance (*Rape and Ravishment*, 243), and Vines analyzes assaults by heroic characters themselves ("Invisible Woman"); also Laurie Finke and Martin Shichtman, "The Mont St. Michel Giant: Sexual Violence and Imperialism in the Chronicles of Wace and Laʒaman," in Roberts, *Violence against Women in Medieval Texts*.

7. For more on rape as a medieval literary trope, see Caroline Dunn, *Stolen Women in Medieval England: Rape, Abduction, and Adultery, 1100–1500* (Cambridge: Cambridge University Press, 2013), 53; Kathryn Gravdal, *Ravishing Maidens: Writing Rape in Medieval French Literature and Law* (Philadelphia: University of Pennsylvania Press, 1991), 42–71.

8. Rose, "Reading Chaucer Reading Rape," 35.

9. In addition to the pastourelles, female-voiced lyrics featuring sexual violence from the survivor's perspective include the pregnancy lament *The last tyme I the wel woke* (*DIMEV* 5369), in Duncan, *Medieval English Lyrics and Carols*, 283–84; *I can be wanton and yf I wyl*, which I discuss in chapter 5; and clerk-and-serving-maid ballads like *Be pes, ye make me spille my ale* and Skelton's *Manerly Margery Mylk and Ale*, which I also discuss in chapter 5. The popularity of female-voiced rape songs persisted throughout the sixteenth century, as evidenced by *Naye phewe nay pishe*, which survives in at least thirty-eight manuscripts, and *Susanna fayre sometime assaulted was*, printed with music in William Byrd's oft-reprinted *Songs of Sundrie Natures* (London: Thomas East for William Byrd, 1589), no. 8. I am grateful to Dianne Mitchell and Christopher Shirley for directing my attention to these later texts.

to navigate life as embodied subjects in a world where assault is an ever-present possibility.

The British Pastourelle in Context

The pastourelle flourished in Western Europe during the twelfth through fourteenth centuries, and William Paden has shown how hundreds of pastourelles were written in many European languages, including Old French, Occitan, Latin, German, Italian, Galician-Portuguese, Spanish, and Welsh.[10] The typical pastourelle is a debate poem, a confrontation between a man and a woman who give alternating speeches. The man is first to speak, narrates all nonverbal action, and frequently has the last word in the exchange, inviting readers to view the encounter from his perspective. These poems center on a social and sexual clash: a knight or cleric encounters a young peasant woman in a rustic, secluded setting and engages in dialogue with her, attempting to seduce her with sweet words of courtly love, promises of marriage, and gifts of clothing or jewelry. She initially resists, often rebuffing him with harsh language. Sometimes she is won over by his promises or gifts, but many times she continues to refuse him.[11] Kathryn Gravdal explores the assault that sometimes follows the maiden's rejection, noting that in 18 percent (or 38 of 160 extant Old French pastourelles), the knight rapes her after she resists his advances.[12] These poems' tone is lighthearted and cynical despite their violent content, and brutal attacks are often followed by the maiden consenting afterward, smiling and laughing, and requesting more, as in *Quant fuelle chiet et flor fault*, where "she sighed, / Wrung her hands, pulled her hair, / And tried to get away" (ains sospire, / ces poins tort, ces chavols tire / et quiert son eschaipement) before "laugh[ing] aloud" (bien rire) and urging her assaulter to "come back this way often" (per si reveneis sovent).[13] These lyrics' refusal to acknowledge victims' suffering, coupled with the woman's subsequent expressions of pleasure or her thanks and request for more, discourages empathy

---

10. William D. Paden, trans. and ed., *The Medieval Pastourelle*, 2 vols. (New York: Garland, 1987).

11. The shepherdess is persuaded by gifts in *Belle Aëlis, une jone pucelle, Ou pertir de la froidure*, and Castra of Florence's *Una fermana iscoppai da Cascioli*, and relents after being promised marriage in *Qant pert la froidure* (ibid., 1:222–25, 234–37, 194–97, 110–15).

12. Gravdal, *Ravishing Maidens*, 105. For more on rape in the pastourelle, see Geri L. Smith, *The Medieval French Pastourelle Tradition: Poetic Motivations and Generic Transformations* (Gainesville: University Press of Florida, 2009), 31–38.

13. *Quant fuelle chiet et flor fault*, lines 40–42, 43, 46, in Paden, *Medieval Pastourelle*, 1:236–39.

and downplays rape's seriousness, implying that assault is a trivial event and that women's refusals are always open to reversal even after the fact.[14] British pastourelles similarly portray violence as an ever-present threat in their encounters, but they differ by focusing on the female speaker's subjectivity. Anne L. Klinck claims that British pastourelles demonstrate a keen awareness of genre conventions coupled with a flexibility that allows for new interpretive possibilities. She observes that, in contrast to their Old French counterparts, English and Scots pastourelles feature a more vocal, vividly characterized, and sympathetic maiden who often has the last word in the exchange.[15] Just as the British poets' pattern of representing the maiden as outspoken and sympathetic enables the genre to represent resistance and survival and to generate empathy, their emphasis on the pastourelles' class- and gender-inflected conflict underscores the genre's willingness to represent violence and its aftermath in unflinching terms and highlights its links to anti-rape education.[16] I categorize nine Middle English and ten Middle Scots poems as pastourelles, although as Klinck notes, the genre conventions for the pastourelle in Britain are more relaxed than in other countries.[17] Ann J. Cahill

---

14. Gravdal notes that this occurs "in no fewer than twelve pastourelles" (*Ravishing Maidens*, 111). The myths embedded in this pastourelle scenario—"she wanted it," "rape is a trivial event," "it wasn't really rape"—are three of the seven key rape myths, defined as "attitudes and beliefs that are generally false but are widely and persistently held, and that serve to deny and justify male sexual aggression against women" (Payne, Lonsway, and Fitzgerald, "Rape Myth Acceptance," 29, 59).

15. Anne L. Klinck, "Thinking outside the Box: Pastourelle Encounters in Middle English and Middle Scots," paper delivered at the 47th International Congress on Medieval Studies, May 2012, 3. I am grateful to Dr. Klinck for sending me a typescript of this paper. Klinck explores the pastourelle in the context of medieval woman's song in "The Oldest Folk Poetry? Medieval Woman's Song as Popular Lyric," in *From Arabye to Engelond: Medieval Studies in Honour of Mahmoud Manzalaoui on His 75th Birthday*, ed. A. E. Christa Canitz and Gernot R. Wieland (Ottawa: University of Ottawa Press, 1999), 239–40. Conlee similarly notes that "the English poets tend to place a greater emphasis on the psychological and verbal struggle" between the two speakers (*Middle English Debate Poetry*, xxxv).

16. For more on the pastourelle in Britain, see Keely Fisher, "Comic Verse in Older Scots Literature" (PhD diss., Oxford University, 1999), 15–64; Karl Reichl, "Popular Poetry and Courtly Lyric: The Middle English Pastourelle," *Yearbook of Research in English and American Literature* 5 (1987); Helen Estabrook Sandison, *The "Chanson d'Aventure" in Middle English* (Bryn Mawr, PA: Bryn Mawr College, 1913), 61–67; John Scattergood, "The Love Lyric before Chaucer," in *A Companion to the Middle English Lyric*, ed. Thomas Duncan (Cambridge: D. S. Brewer, 2005), 60–64; Scattergood, "Courtliness in Some Fourteenth-Century English Pastourelles," in *Reading the Past: Essays in Medieval and Renaissance Literature* (Dublin: Four Courts Press, 1996); Theo van Heijnsbergen, "The Bannatyne Manuscript Lyrics: Literary Convention and Authorial Voice," in *The European Sun, Proceedings of the Seventh International Congress on Medieval and Renaissance Scottish Language and Literature*, ed. Graham Caie et al. (East Linton, UK: Tuckwell Press, 2001).

17. Klinck, "Thinking outside the Box," 2, 3, 8. I count the following nineteen lyrics as pastourelles: *All to lufe and not to fenyie, Ane fair sweit may of mony one, As I me rode this endre dai, As I stod on a day, Beware my lytyll fynger, Come over the woodes fair and grene, Commonyng betuix the Mester and the Heure (Lord god my hairt is in distres), Hey troly loly lo, I met my lady weil arrayit, I saw me thocht this hindir nycht, In a fryht as Y con fare fremede, William Dunbar's In secreit place this hyndir nycht, In somer quhen flouris*

observes that one of rape's great wrongs is its denial of subjectivity: "In the act of rape, the assailant reduces the victim to a non-person . . . [and] denies the victim the specificity of [her or his] own being."[18] English pastourelles can be read as responding directly to this denial of selfhood by representing women as embodied subjects who articulate the fear and anger engendered by living under constant threat of violence. Scottish pastourelles go even further: by portraying maidens who resist, who are assaulted, who negotiate the terms of their erotic encounters, and who voice pleasure using the bawdiest of obscenities, they illuminate the degree to which even consensual sex occurs within a larger context of violence, and they depict women using obscenity to challenge that violence.

The pastourelles depict powerful, well-off men targeting women who are young, poor, single, and alone, leveraging the women's multiple disadvantages to coerce them and illustrating how perpetrators can exploit structural inequalities so that they do not need to use physical force.[19] The men in these lyrics use their economic advantage by attempting to entice peasant women into sex by offering lavish gifts the women could never afford. Other times, they exploit women's work responsibilities as milkmaids or tapsters to assault them. This habitual, widespread sexual exploitation of peasant women is attested in legal records. Jeremy Goldberg has collected numerous cases of female servants impregnated by their masters or sons of their masters, including a case from 1505 of a husband and wife who force their female servant to sleep in their son's bed, resulting in her pregnancy; a case from 1482 of a married couple pimping out their servant girl to a Venetian galley captain; and a case from 1381 of a male servant who rapes a twelve-year-old servant girl and cuts her with a knife.[20] Peasant women's gender and class identities interlock to put them in harm's way, and these pastourelles vividly illustrate the workings of these intersecting inequalities.[21]

---

will smell, *My deth Y love my lyfe ich hate*, *Quhy so strat strang go we by youe*, Robert Henryson's *Robene and Makyne*, *Still undir the levis grene*, *Throughe a forest as I can ryde*, and *When that byrdes be brought to rest*. Although I do not discuss them here, multiple pastourelles survive in Welsh, including Dafydd ap Gwilym's *Fal yr oeddwn yn myned* and Pseudo-Dafydd ap Gwilym's *A mi ar deg foregwaith* from the middle of the fourteenth century and Tudur Penllyn's mid-fifteenth-century macaronic Welsh-English *Ymddiddan Rhwng Cymro a Saesnes*.

18. Cahill, *Rethinking Rape*, 192.

19. Dunn notes that "if the parties involved in the rape allegation were of disparate status, the case was more likely to involve a higher-status rapist ravishing a lower-status victim" and discusses the difficulties faced by lower-status rape victims in *Stolen Women*, 62.

20. P. J. P. Goldberg, trans. and ed., *Women in England, c. 1275–1525: Documentary Sources* (Manchester: Manchester University Press, 1995), 96, 120, 123, 253.

21. For a thorough discussion of the rape and murder of a young servant woman in London in 1385, see Wendy J. Turner, "The Leper and the Prostitute: Forensic Examination of Rape in Medieval England," in *Trauma in Medieval Society*, ed. Wendy J. Turner and Christina Lee (Leiden: Brill, 2018).

British pastourelles contain a variety of narratives about women's experiences of the threat of sexual violence. Some maidens resist their aggressors with witty comebacks, repeated refusals, or stinging insults until the men leave them alone; some eventually articulate their consent but protest the degree to which their choices are constrained; and others are assaulted, then loudly decry their violation. This diversity is valuable because it allows readers to see rape not as following a single narrative, a predictable script that can be avoided if one "does the right things," but rather as a power relationship taking a variety of forms, with one individual's refusal of another's subjectivity and bodily autonomy as the common denominator among them. Nicola Gavey argues that one prevention strategy is "to incorporate the heterogeneity of rape" into our cultural narratives and acknowledge that "not all rapes are the same," since recognizing only a narrow paradigm for rape allows other assaults to go unaddressed.[22]

Three Middle English pastourelles illustrate this narrative diversity, because they stage divergent outcomes to the encounter between aggressive man and resisting maiden and highlight the intersectional nature of the man's coercion. In *Hey troly loly lo* (c. 1510–13), a carol for three voices copied with music, a man confronts a milkmaid walking to the meadow to milk her cow, highlighting her disadvantages of youth, gender, and profession.[23] McIntosh notes that dairy work was a "key area of economic activity for women" that was also feminized within the domestic economy.[24] The man interrupts the milkmaid as she is on her way to work in a gendered profession, asking her where she is going. She tells him, "I go to the medowe to mylke my cow" (3), illustrating that it is her need to perform her job by walking alone to and from the meadow that puts her in harm's way and renders her vulnerable to assault. He responds, "Than at the medow I wyll you mete / To gather the flowres both fayer and swete" (4–5). He insists he will follow her to work and uses obscene flower-gathering metaphors that are common in the pastourelles. She vocalizes her opposition in two different refrains opening with the negative assertion "Nay," highlighting her unbending resistance. The first refrain, "Nay, God forbede! That may not be— / I wysse my mother then shall us se!" (7–8), is repeated twice. The second, "Nay, in good feyth, I wyll not melle [copulate] with you; / I pray you, sir, let me go mylke my cow" (12–13), repeats four times and serves as the final words of the exchange, ending the song on a

22. Gavey, *Just Sex?*, 229.

23. *Hey troly loly lo* (*DIMEV* 3324), in Raymond G. Siemens, ed., *The Lyrics of the Henry VIII Manuscript* (Grand Rapids, MI: English Renaissance Text Society, 2013), 61–62. Text references are to lines in this edition.

24. McIntosh, *Working Women*, 196–98.

note of staunch refusal. This second refrain is significant because of its direct sexual rejection and its speaker's request that the man allow her to perform her job. By insisting that she "wyll not melle with" the man, the milkmaid issues an unequivocal sexual refusal and makes a declaration of agency: "melle" typically takes a masculine gendered agent and a feminine object when used in a sexual sense, but here she reverses that formulation to depict herself as the agent capable of declaring she "wyll not" have sex with her aggressor, and she insists on her right to return to work and "mylke" her cow instead. In response, he demands, "graunte me here your maydynhed, your maydynhed" (26), his repetition of the object of his desire underscoring his entitlement. He finally agrees to release her, but he follows his capitulation by threatening future violence, reminding her that she will never be safe: "Then for this onse I shal you spare, / But the nexte tyme ye must beware / How in the medow ye mylke your cow," he says menacingly (28–30). With his use of the warning verb "beware" reinforced by the didactic "must," he demands that she fear assault. He ties her vulnerability directly to her job as a dairy worker; the next time she goes to work, she must fear his attack. She can protect herself by refusing to perform her job and thus lose her means of economic survival, or she can go to work and expect that she will be raped. In this way, her identities as female, as single, and as a dairy worker interlock to put her at risk of violence, and she has no choice but to deal with that risk in order to survive. She refuses to be cowed by his threat, and she rejects his request for a parting kiss in the exchange's final lines.

Hey troly loly lo is the final item in a large, lavishly decorated songbook associated with Henry VIII's court.[25] It is copied by a later hand than the manuscript's other contents, and its depiction of a privileged man's victimization of a peasant girl, coming after the book's numerous courtly songs—some polite supplications to the beloved, others bawdy "forester lyrics" imagining masculine sexuality in terms of predation, hunting, and fatal violence—issues an implicit rebuke to their valorization of aristocratic masculine aggression by giving voice to a peasant woman targeted by its violence. Dietrich Helms argues that the songbook was used to teach music to royal children and suggests that its audience may have been a young Mary I, pointing to the possibility of young women learning about victimization and resistance from fictive

---

25. BL MS Additional 31922, fol. 124v–128r. For a facsimile of the manuscript, see David Fallows, ed., *The Henry VIII Book (British Library, MS Add. 31922)* (Chicago: University of Chicago Press for the Renaissance Society of America, 2014); for more on the manuscript's provenance, see Siemens, *Lyrics of the Henry VIII Manuscript*, 13–14.

women's voices, since the milkmaid's words of unbending refusal are the final ones in the codex.[26]

In *In a fryht as Y con fare fremede* (c. 1331–41), the maiden resists the man's advances with witty retorts, rebuffing his offers of costly clothing and pledges of eternal devotion.[27] The poem vividly depicts her internal struggle—will she be better off if she acquiesces, or if she continues to resist?—and closes with her seemingly on the verge of capitulation, decrying her lack of options due to her status as "a maide" (47). She despairs that she cannot escape her embodied femininity "mid shupping" (with shape-shifting/altering her genitals) (45–46), using a punning phrase indicating that she sees her "shap"—which could denote one's body, gender, or genitals—as limiting her choices and rendering her vulnerable.[28] She protests the man's "gyle" (treachery) (48), implying that she feels her choices are constrained by manipulation or trickery, and she voices her dissatisfaction with the inequalities in the sexual status quo.[29] She has the last word in the exchange, vociferously challenging the larger power disparities that shape the genre's sexual politics. In BL MS Harley 2253, *In a fryht* is sandwiched between *Most I ryden by Rybbesdale* and *A wayle whyt ase whalles bon*, two male-voiced secular love lyrics that feature a sustained focus on women's sexualized bodies; the former praises her "Body ant brest wel mad al" (Body and breast all well designed), while the latter voices a refrain expressing the speaker's wish to hide himself "Bituene hire curtel ant hire smoke" (Between her skirt and her undergarment).[30] The lyrics surrounding *In a fryht* guide readers to view women as corporeal objects, as perpetually available for men to look at, touch, and proposition at will. Carter Revard shows that these lyrics were copied by a professional legal scribe from Ludlow into a trilingual household book possibly belonging to the Ludlow family of Stokesay Castle in Shropshire, and Susanna Fein suggests that the manuscript was compiled for "the inculcation of manners and learning for a

---

26. Dietrich Helms, "Henry VIII's Book: Teaching Music to Royal Children," *Music Quarterly* 92 (2009).

27. *In a fryht as Y con fare fremede* (DIMEV 2246), in Fein, *Complete Harley 2253 Manuscript*, 2:148–52. Text references are to lines in this edition. For more on this poem, which has generated the most critical conversation of the British pastourelles, see J. J. Anderson, "Two Difficulties in *The Meeting in the Wood*," *Medium Ævum* 49 (1980): 258–59; Reichl, "Popular Poetry," 44–50, and "Debate Verse," in *Studies in the Harley Manuscript: The Scribes, Contents, and Social Contexts of British Library MS Harley 2253*, ed. Susanna Fein (Kalamazoo, MI: Medieval Institute Publications, 2000); Rosemary Woolf, "The Construction of *In a fryht as I con fare fremede*," *Medium Ævum* 38 (1969).

28. *MED* s.v. "shap" (n.), 2(b), 6(a), and 6(b).

29. *MED* s.v. "gile" (n.[3]), 1(b) and 2.

30. *Most I ryden by Rybbesdale* (DIMEV 3550) and *A wayle whyt ase whales bon* (DIMEV 183), in Fein, *Complete Harley 2253 Manuscript*, 2:144–49 and 150–57, lines 74 and 10–11.

male heir or heirs in a well-bred, perhaps aristocratic setting."[31] In this context, *In a fryht* could have taught higher-status young men how to use their privilege to exploit structural inequalities for their own sexual gratification, and its placement between two bawdy songs from amorous men's perspectives serves to normalize and eroticize the aggression in the pastourelle.

The third pastourelle, *As I stod on a day* (c. 1325), portrays the female speaker's fear of assault and fierce resistance in spite of her fear, as she is able to thwart a man's persistent efforts to "tast" "hir wil" (test her will) (22).[32] The knight encounters "a may in a medewe" (2) who reacts to his presence with terror: "With a cri gan sche me sey; / Sche wold a-wrenchin awey but for I was so neye" (She cried out when she saw me; / She would have run away had I not been so near) (10–11). Her fear indicates that she anticipates the encounter may turn violent. Despite her terror, she issues a series of scathing rebuttals, demonstrating levelheadedness and sharply articulated anger in response to the threat of rape. Unable to escape, she must listen to the man's entreaties, to which she reacts with scorn and derisive laughter. "Ye an sayd inowe" (You have said enough) (25), she declares. This exchange, like the previous two, closes with the woman having the last word, as she instructs the man to leave her alone and find a consenting partner instead: "wet ye wat I rede / Wend fort ther ye wenin bett for to spede" (learn what I teach / Move on to where you may expect better to succeed) (30–31). In her command that he follow "wat I rede," the maiden deploys a verb with strong pedagogical valences—meaning "to teach, instruct, advise"—to educate the man about consent, and he obeys her instructions, proving her teaching to be effective.[33] Her strategy of resistance combines scornful laughter, outright dismissal, witty retort, and didactic instruction. *As I stod on a day* illuminates the role of women's economic status in these encounters: unlike the peasant women in other pastourelles, this maiden is richly dressed in furred clothing and reading a book when the man interrupts her, and her success at dismissing him can be read as a function of her class advantage. *As I stod on a day* is written at the end of the Anglo-Norman romance *Gui de Warewic* in the hand of an early owner, John de Haukeham, who identifies himself on a flyleaf as "rector of the church

---

31. Carter Revard, "Scribe and Provenance," in Fein, *Studies in the Harley Manuscript*, 21–110; Fein, *Complete Harley 2253 Manuscript*, 1:10–11.

32. *As I stod on a day* (DIMEV 628), line 22, in Conlee, *Middle English Debate Poetry*, 301–2. Text references are to lines in this edition. For this poem's manuscript context and early origins, see Karl Reichl, "The Beginnings of the Middle English Secular Lyric: Texts, Music, Manuscript Context," in *The Genesis of Books: Studies in the Scribal Culture of Medieval England in Honour of A. N. Doane*, ed. Matthew T. Hussey and John D. Niles (Turnhout, Belgium: Brepols, 2011), 231; Reichl, "Popular Poetry," 41–44.

33. *MED* s.v. "reden" (v.[1]), 4(a) and 8a.

at Fleet" (*rector ecclesie de Flet*).[34] Its copying by a London cleric has intriguing implications due to the genre's emphasis on clerical predation, which is thwarted here because the aggressor chooses a higher-status target instead of a peasant maiden. In these three pastourelles alone, we see how English poets use the genre to explore a variety of different outcomes to the encounter, to highlight the workings of intersectional disadvantage, and to give voice to the particularities of women's experiences as embodied subjects. In one, the maiden is able to negotiate her escape but is threatened with future violence; in another, she decries the manifold ways that her choices are constrained by larger inequalities; and in the third, she wins the debate and sends the man on his way.

Like the English pastourelles, the ten surviving Middle Scots pastourelles portray a range of narratives regarding violence and consent. In some, the male speaker either threatens or carries out a brutal assault on the maiden; in others, the maiden, not the man, initiates the exchange; and in others, she voices her agreement to his overtures before witheringly denigrating his subsequent sexual failure. The most striking aspect of these lyrics is their depiction of young peasant women using obscenity to teach their partners and articulate their desires. This further expands the genre's possibilities from giving voice to the full range of women's experiences of the threat of violence, as we see in the English pastourelles, to staging new gendered pedagogical models and exploring how women navigate hostile conditions in spite of their class and gender disadvantage. The Scots pastourelles emphasize the maiden's speech, which is characterized by her outspoken obscenity and unflinching appraisal of her partner's sexual capacities. In eight of the ten poems—incidentally, the ones that do *not* feature masculine violence or threats thereof—the woman is the one who speaks last.[35] These lyrics illustrate that even consensual sex takes place under the larger shadow of culturally sanctioned masculine aggression. They remind us that we cannot consider women's pleasure without acknowledging the larger circumstances under which it occurs, and they illuminate the tight web of intersecting inequalities that undergirds all heterosexual erotic relations in a patriarchal culture.

Pastourelle speakers deploy obscenity for a variety of purposes, including to articulate desire, to inflict violence, and to express resistance. Both men and women use it during the genre's fraught encounters, although the maidens

---

34. London, College of Arms, MS Arundel 27; Reichl, "Beginnings," 231.

35. In some of these lyrics, including *In somer quhen flouris will smell, I saw me thocht this hinder nyght,* and *The Commownyng betuix the Mester and the Heure,* the male *chanson d'aventure* narrator speaks the final lines, but only after the debate is over and the maiden has departed. In each of the conversations featured in these eight pastourelles, the woman is the last to speak.

resisting or negotiating sex do so far more frequently than do the men who proposition them. When the genre's men speak obscenity, it typically functions as an act of sexual aggression. One rapist taunts his victim by boasting, "Now the pye hath pecked yow," using bawdy metaphor to inflict further violence. Numerous other men use obscene flower-gathering metaphors in their coercive attempts. When pastourelle women voice obscenity, they articulate resistance to unwanted advances and testify about rape's harms: one insists, "Your bryde shall never hoppe yn my cage," while another decries the pain her assailant inflicts with his "quhinyear heft" (dagger handle). Other times, women deploy obscenity to voice ardent desire, like the maiden who praises her partner's "courtly fukking" and issues instructions regarding his "taikill" (sexual equipment). While the pastourelles portray male-voiced obscenity as a tool of domination, they imagine women's obscenity as expressing resistance or desire and depict it as integral to sexual negotiation, echoing singlewomen's erotic lyrics, another genre that stages young women obscenely teaching one another about reciprocity and pleasure.

These lyrics' generic flexibility, obscenity, narrative diversity, and emphasis on women's intersectional disadvantage, along with their articulations of women's fear, anger, sorrow, and desire, reflect a larger trend of featuring maidens who vociferously protest both threatened and actual violence and depicting strategies for coping with as well as challenging it. We can read these pastourelles as fictive testimonies in the empowering, pedagogical vein of the "survivor speech" theorized by Alcoff and Gray, who argue that "speaking out serves to educate the society at large about the dimensions of sexual violence and misogyny, to reposition the problem from the individual psyche to the social sphere where it rightfully belongs, and to empower victims to act constructively on our own behalf."[36] This enables contemporary readers to trace over time the continuity of women's voices sharing experiences of violence. We see that many facets of rape culture—victim blaming, treating silence as consent, refusing to heed women's refusals, trivializing rape's impact on survivors, and assuming that unaccompanied women are legitimate targets of men's sexual attention—remain largely unchanged. These lyrics enable us to identify histories of representing survivor speech, teaching negotiation, and viewing female alliances as a tool for challenging sexual violence.

---

36. Alcoff and Gray, "Survivor Discourse," 261. For more on the importance of sharing individual first-person rape narratives, particularly by those afflicted by structural disadvantage, see Pierce-Baker, *Surviving the Silence*. On the role of rape speak-outs in addressing the "collective harms" of sexual violence during feminism's second wave, see Heberle, "Personal Is Political," 598. Survivor speak-outs continue to be a central feature of the annual international Take Back the Night march against sexual violence.

In order to understand these poems' grappling with sexual ethics, we must take their representations of rape seriously. Bennett notes that critics and editors have traditionally refused to recognize certain pastourelles as "rape songs," choosing instead to characterize them as "amorous dialogues" or "love adventures."[37] One critic refers to *Hey troly loly lo*, with its repeated rape threats, as "a delightful Tudor song."[38] When scholars elide these texts' depictions of violence to read assault as nothing more than a game or a friendly verbal sparring match, they enact the very rape myths that these lyrics challenge. The survivors and resistors of sexual violence in those lyrics, such as the woman in *All to lufe and not to fenyie* determined to "tell" the world about her assault, are still speaking to us many centuries later in spite of this critical silencing. In light of the vast and ongoing problem of sexual violence in our own culture, it is imperative that we listen to them.

Pastourelle Pedagogies

The pastourelle enacts three different levels of pedagogy that operate simultaneously. The first is pedagogy performed within the poems, as when maidens address men with explicitly instructional speech. Also embedded within many pastourelles are popular discourses of medieval antirape education, most notably risk-avoidance methods from didactic mother-to-daughter conduct texts. The second level of pedagogy is between pastourelle texts and medieval readers, for these lyrics both confirm and challenge rape myths, teaching their audiences about violence and consent. The pastourelles spoke to different audiences in different ways. The seven pastourelles copied by Edinburgh merchant George Bannatyne in the Bannatyne Manuscript would have been read in the context of acute public misogyny, expressed in the form of ribald verses and pornographic placards, directed at Mary Queen of Scots after her estranged husband's murder and her hasty remarriage in 1567. Pastourelles copied in manuscripts owned by royal or gentry families, such as *Hey troly loly lo* in the Henry VIII Manuscript and the three lyrics in the Welles Anthology, could have taught aristocratic women that rape happens only to young, poor "wenche[s]" alone in the wilderness; their economic dissimilarity allowed the higher-status women to think that they were safe from such a fate. This is challenged by one pastourelle maiden's educational address to "all medons" among her readership, as she collapses the class differences reinforced by terms

---

37. See *DIMEV* entries for 6851 and 5908. Bennett, "Ventriloquisms," 198.
38. Reichl, "Popular Poetry," 36.

like "gyll" and "wenche" by calling on "all" her peers to learn from her narrative.[39] The third level of pastourelle pedagogy is between medieval texts and contemporary readers, for these lyrics teach us about past views of rape and consent and shed important light on histories of antirape education, suffering, and survival.

Pastourelles both reinforce and challenge numerous rape myths, the sturdy pillars upholding rape culture that taught medieval audiences about violence and consent. Many of these myths are familiar to modern audiences, enabling us to see continuities over time. Amy Grubb and Emily Turner note that rape myths vary across time and culture but "consistently follow a pattern whereby they blame the victim for their rape, express a disbelief in claims of rape, exonerate the perpetrator, and allude that only certain types of women are raped."[40] One of the genre's central rape myths is its location of sexual violence: its confrontations always occur in idyllic, secluded natural settings such as meadows, forests, or fields of wildflowers, a convention reflecting the myth that an assault only qualifies as such if it happens in an isolated rural space. According to a Middle English translation of Deuteronomy 22:23–27's victim-blaming law, a maiden assaulted "in the cytee" must die along with her assailant due to her perceived failure to raise sufficient outcry, while an attack "in the feeld" qualifies as legally recognized "suffr[ing]":

> If a womman [is a] mayden . . . and eny man in the cytee fynde hir, and lye with hir, thow shalt lede either to the yate of that cytee, and thei shulen be throwun doun with stonus; the maydyn, for she cryed not, whanne she was in the cytee. . . . Forsothe if in the feeld a man fynde a woman . . . and takynge ligge with hir, he shal dye alone; the womman no thing shal suffre, ne is gilti of deeth . . . so and the womman hath suffred; aloone she was in the feeld, and criede, and no man was nigh that myght delyver hyr.[41]

The text vividly portrays the woman "aloone . . . in the feeld," attempting to raise the hue and cry to no avail, and it imagines that rape can be stopped only

---

39. Amy Grubb and Emily Turner discuss how victim blaming often results from "defensive attribution," "whereby observers do not want to believe that a similar fate could befall them and therefore distance themselves from this possibility by blaming the victim and concluding that they would never [be] in the same situation." Grubb and Turner, "Attribution of Blame in Rape Cases: A Review of the Impact of Rape Myth Acceptance, Gender Role Conformity, and Substance Abuse on Victim Blaming," *Aggression and Violent Behavior* 17, no. 5 (2012): 450, also 444–45; Finch and Munro, "Demon Drink."

40. Grubb and Turner, "Attribution of Blame," 445; for more on rape myths, see Gavey, *Just Sex?*, 35–38; Payne, Lonsway, and Fitzgerald, "Rape Myth Acceptance."

41. Wyclif, *Holy Bible*, 1:519.

by other men. By representing a natural setting and feminine solitude as preconditions for rape, the pastourelles suggest that no other acts qualify as assaults, and they implicitly blame the victims of urban rapes for their own violation. Numerous medieval romances follow this rape script: in *Le Bone Florence of Rome* (c. 1400), Florence, "a maydyn yyng," is attacked "in a wode thyck" by the treacherous Myles, who twice attempts to rape her and is thwarted only when the Virgin Mary afflicts him with miraculous impotence; and in *Sir Gowther* (c. 1400), a demon rapes the hero's mother "in hur orchard . . . undur a tre."[42] In reality, according to legal records, "rapes occurred indoors and outdoors, in manor houses and crofts, in fields and forests."[43] The pastourelle's staging of its fraught encounters in verdant outdoor settings serves to naturalize sexual violence because it enacts the myth that men's aggression is an instinctive, expected response to encountering an attractive young woman alone and teaches that it is natural to violate a woman's boundaries when no other men are around to "delyver hyr."[44]

About a quarter of British pastourelles feature resistant women later changing their minds and voicing their consent to sex, although it is important to note that this reversal only happens *before* the act, not after.[45] These lyrics perpetuate the myth that women's "no" eventually becomes "yes," as illustrated by popular proverbs and carol refrains like "Maidens move [change] their minds," "Winters nicht and womans thocht and lords purpose changes oft," "Women are oft unstable," and "[Women] love to raunge, ther myndes doth chaunge."[46] Helen Solterer explores how Ovid and his medieval successors deploy this stereotype to justify rape, noting that "both female 'No!' and

---

42. Jonathan Stavsky, ed. and trans., *Le Bone Florence of Rome: A Critical Edition and Facing Translation of a Middle English Romance* (Cardiff: University of Wales Press, 2017), lines 1396–500; *Sir Gowther*, in Anne Laskaya and Eve Salisbury, eds., *The Middle English Breton Lays* (Kalamazoo, MI: Medieval Institute Publications, 1995), 263–307, lines 67–71; Saunders, *Rape and Ravishment*, 202–5; Edwards, *Afterlives of Rape*, 120–21.

43. Dunn, *Stolen Women*, 64–66; also Barbara A. Hanawalt, "Medieval English Women in Rural and Urban Domestic Space," *Dumbarton Oaks Papers* 52 (1998): 21–22.

44. Vanessa E. Munro observes that "male sexuality is depicted as uncontrollably natural, consisting of overwhelming urges and desires, which leaves the male sexual imperative and its utilization of coercive strategies of sexual persuasion . . . unchecked." Munro, "Constructing Consent: Legislating Freedom and Legitimating Constraint in the Expression of Sexual Autonomy," *Akron Law Review* 41 (2008): 936. For more on this popular myth, see Gavey, *Just Sex?*, 19–20; Grubb and Turner, "Attribution of Blame," 446–47.

45. This happens in *When that byrdes be brought to rest, In somer quhen flouris will smell, In secreit place this hyndir nycht, My deth I love my lyf Ich hate,* and *Quhy so strat strang go we by youe.*

46. Whiting, *Proverbs*, M17, W526; Anderson, *James Carmichaell Collection*, no. 1701; *These women all* (*DIMEV* 5621), in E. K. Chambers, ed., *The Oxford Book of Sixteenth Century Verse* (Oxford: Clarendon, 1932), 39–40, lines 7–8. For more on this myth, see Gavey, *Just Sex?*, 20–22, 38, 68–69.

female 'Yes!' are read to mean much the same thing."[47] These pastourelles can be read as teaching men to ignore women's refusals because they imply that women's rejection of sexual advances is a "cultural requirement" and insist that they will change their minds if they are subjected to sufficient pressure.[48]

Pastourelle men share an unwavering faith in the popular myth that women, especially young, economically disadvantaged ones, are weaker and more exploitable than men. This is illustrated by the proverb "Glassis and lassis are brukill wairs" (Glasses and girls are fragile commodities), which insists that young women are physically fragile (and thus easily overpowered) as well as "morally frail or weak" and "readily yielding" to temptation.[49] "Lass" connotes class disadvantage, youth, and femininity because it meant "a girl, a young woman" and "a maid-servant, servant-girl."[50] This myth renders young lower-status women especially vulnerable to coercion by men who view them as easy targets, and it enables violence against them to be blamed on their inherent susceptibility to carnal transgression. However, many pastourelle maidens challenge these myths about women's inconstancy by being anything but "brukill," remaining steadfast in their refusals, resisting with words as well as fists, demanding restitution for their assaults, and proclaiming the wrongs that have been done to them. This emphasis on resistance is reflected in an intriguing legal case: in Shropshire in 1405, Isabella Gronowessone and her daughters Johanna and Petronilla waylaid Roger de Pulesdon in a field, tied a cord around his neck, cut off his testicles, and stole his horse, only to be pardoned shortly thereafter.[51] Goldberg suggests that the women were exacting a brutal form of extralegal justice for rape.[52] If so, this case shows women uniting to execute physical punishment on a rapist *in campo* (in a field, meadow), an isolated natural setting much like the pastourelles', and it implicitly authorizes castration and women's retaliatory violence as a fitting response

47. Helen Solterer, *The Master and Minerva: Disputing Women in French Medieval Culture* (Berkeley: University of California Press, 1995), 46.

48. Louise M. Sylvester, *Medieval Romance and the Construction of Heterosexuality* (New York: Palgrave Macmillan, 2008), 38; Shannon McSheffrey and Julia Pope, "Ravishment, Legal Narratives, and Chivalric Culture in Fifteenth-Century England," *Journal of British Studies* 48 (2009): 835–36.

49. *DOST* s.v. "brukill" (adj.), 1 and 2; Anderson, *James Carmichaell Collection*, no. 569.

50. *DOST* s.v. "las" (n.), 1 and 3. Kim M. Phillips notes the term's "negative overtones" and discusses a 1453 Yorkshire case in which Agnes Cosyn objected to marrying Robert Chew because "his relatives called and named her 'lass'" in Phillips, *Medieval Maidens: Young Women and Gender in England, 1270–1540* (Manchester: Manchester University Press, 2003), 194–95.

51. Elisabeth G. Kimball, ed., *The Shropshire Peace Roll, 1400–1414* (Shrewsbury, UK: Printed for the Salop County Council, 1959), 75.

52. P. J. P. Goldberg, "Women in Later Medieval English Archives," *Journal of the Society of Archivists* 15 (1994): 70n26; Dunn, *Stolen Women*, 79.

to rape.[53] In addition to repudiating the fiction of women's pliability, British pastourelles challenge the myth that rape is a trivial event for its victims, because none portray women who consent after their assaults.[54] Instead, they attack their attackers with full-throated curses and later share wrenching accounts of their suffering.

The pastourelles echo the same-sex antirape education in fourteenth- and fifteenth-century conduct texts addressed to young women, demonstrating the prevalence of pedagogical paradigms across genres.[55] These poems, which shed further light on medieval ideas about violence prevention, depict mothers instructing their daughters to protect themselves from assault using risk-avoidance discourse, a popular but flawed antiviolence strategy that puts the responsibility on individual women to manage risk and avoid victimization by traveling in groups, limiting their alcohol consumption, not staying out too late, and assessing every man as a potential threat.[56] The mother in *The Good Wyfe Wold a Pylgremage* (c. 1475) cautions, "Syt not witt no man aloune, for oft in trust ys tressoun. / Thow thou thenk no thenke amyse, yett feyr wordys be gayssoun" (Do not sit alone with any man, for often in trust is treachery. / Even though you think nothing amiss, fair words are empty), dismissing men's speech as "barren, empty, vain."[57] *The Good Wiif Taughte Hir Doughtir*'s maternal speaker warns that "all men ben nought trewe / That kunne fair her wordis schewe, / Mi leve child."[58] Another mother urges young women to remain at home to avoid being coerced "agane thair will," reasoning that this "savis thame mony a tym fra ill" (saves them many times from harm).[59] The pastourelles illustrate these warnings against "feyr wordys" and serve as cautionary exempla teaching women to be wary of well-spoken men because they feature courteous suitors whose honeyed speech disguises their violent entitlement. Both pastourelles and conduct texts depict female fellowship and

---

53. *DMLBS* s.v. *"campus"* (n.). For more on authorizing women's physical strength and bodily know-how in combating sexual violence, see Gavey, *Just Sex?*, 220–21, and Martha McCaughey, *Real Knockouts: The Physical Feminism of Women's Self-Defense* (New York: New York University Press, 1997).

54. The myth that rape is a trivial event is cited in Grubb and Turner, "Attribution of Blame," 445.

55. Milburn, "Critical Review of Peer Education," 415, 410. For a fuller discussion of contemporary perspectives on same-sex peer education, see my introduction to this book.

56. Carmody, *Sex, Ethics, and Young People*, 88–90; Rachel Hall, "It Can Happen to You: Rape Prevention in the Age of Risk Management," *Hypatia* 19, no. 3 (2004).

57. *The Good Wyfe Wold a Pylgremage*, lines 38–39, in Tauno F. Mustanoja, ed., *"The Good Wife Taught Her Daughter," "The Good Wyfe Wold a Pylgremage," "The Thewis of Gud Women"* (Helsinki: Suomalaisen Kirjallisuuden Scuran, 1948), 173–75; *MED* s.v. "gesoun" (adj. and n.), b.

58. *The Good Wiif Taughte Hir Doughtir*, lines 82–84, in Mustanoja, *Good Wife*, 197–203. Riddy analyzes these poems in "Mother Knows Best." For more on medieval maidens' education, see Phillips, *Medieval Maidens*, 61–107.

59. *Incipiunt Documenta Matris Ad Filiam* (*DIMEV* 5303), lines 225–26, in Mustanoja, *Good Wife*, 177–96.

solidarity as one key site of rape prevention; the maiden's appeal to her absent mother for protection is a commonplace in the pastourelle script, and one pastourelle portrays female peers as protective allies against men's violence.[60]

The pastourelles shed light on medieval conceptions of antiviolence education and teach young women strategies for resisting unwanted advances. They present obscenity, especially when voiced by women, as integral to sexual negotiation. Most importantly, by giving voice to fictional rape survivors and allowing them to speak back eloquently to their rapists as well as to address living readers, they portray women performing survival and peer pedagogy.

Divergent Narratives: The Pastourelles of the Welles Anthology

The largest extant collection of English pastourelles in the same manuscript—a group of three—survives in Bodleian MS Rawlinson C.813, known as the Welles Anthology.[61] This manuscript was owned and possibly compiled by Humphrey Welles (c. 1502–65), a London-educated lawyer and Staffordshire member of the House of Commons who had numerous connections with the Tudor court and whose name is written in cipher on folio 98v.[62] In addition to the pastourelles, this verse miscellany contains courtly love lyrics, vicious attacks on women, excerpts from Stephen Hawes's *The Pastime of Pleasure*, erotic dream visions, didactic poems, and political prophecies. It is organized into coherent sections, with the lyrics followed by the prophecies. It was copied between 1522 and 1534 or 1535, although editors argue that many of its lyrics, including the pastourelles, date from the late fifteenth century.[63] The manuscript contains references to a "Coffyn" (on folio 98v), whom editors identify as the courtier and MP William Coffin, and to various Welles family

---

60. The girl calls on "my dame" (21) in *Throughe a forest as I can ryde*, "my mother" (25) in *Come over the woodes fair and grene*, and "my moder" (11) and "my deme" (60) in *All to lufe and not to fenyie*. See *Throughe a forest as I can ryde* (DIMEV 5908), in Sharon L. Jansen and Kathleen H. Jordan, eds., *The Welles Anthology: MS Rawlinson C.813, A Critical Edition* (Binghamton, NY: Medieval and Renaissance Texts and Studies, 1991), 216–19; *Come over the woodes fair and grene* (DIMEV 1052), ibid., 223–26. For the importance of female companionship, see my discussion of *Come over the woodes* below.

61. MS Rawlinson C.813 was originally two separate codices, and the Welles Anthology comprises folios 1–98 of the manuscript.

62. Jansen and Jordan, *Welles Anthology*, 1–7. For further background on the manuscript's provenance, see Edward Wilson, "Local Habitations and Names in MS Rawlinson C.813 in the Bodleian Library, Oxford," *Review of English Studies* 41, no. 161 (1990); on Welles's life, see N. M. Fuidge, s.v. "Welles, Humphrey," in *The History of Parliament: The House of Commons 1509–1558*, ed. S. T. Bindoff (London: Secker and Warburg for the History of Parliament Trust, 1982), iii (Members N–Z), 573–74.

63. Jansen and Jordan, *Welles Anthology*, 7–9.

connections from Staffordshire, suggesting possible coterie circulation, either among London civil servants or the Staffordshire gentry.[64] The Welles Anthology could have served important social purposes of entertainment, recreation, and community building, like the Findern Manuscript, a late fifteenth- and early sixteenth-century lyric anthology copied by a network of country gentry families and friends, which was used in convivial settings, as evidenced by drippings of candle wax, food, and drink on its pages, and whose texts "predominately ask their readers to consider the status of women in a sympathetic light."[65] The Welles Anthology's context has important implications for how we read pedagogy in its three pastourelles. If the manuscript first circulated within an all-male coterie of urban civil servants, which seems likely since the dates of its copying coincide with Welles's time at the Inner Temple and as a London administrator, then we can read it as having the potential to teach male readers about consent through its narrative diversity and emphasis on women's lyric subjectivity, or we can read its pastourelles' embedded rape myths—that peasant girls are acceptable targets of aristocratic male aggression, and that some women eventually reverse their refusals—as reinforced by the anthology's misogynist pieces, which insist on women's inherent lust and inconstancy. And during its later life circulating among Welles, his wife, and his in-laws in Staffordshire during his career as a local public servant in the 1540s and 1550s, as evidenced by a reference to his brother-in-law Anthony Chatwyn on folio 7v, then its mix of gendered lyric subject positions and courtly emphasis might have appealed to its mixed-gender provincial gentry audience, while the pastourelles' class politics could have taught well-born female readers that peasant women are "asking for it" and discouraged them from identifying with lower-status rape survivors.[66]

The manuscript contains lyrics voiced by and addressed to both women and men, providing a diversity of gendered voices and audience possibilities as well as important context for reading the pastourelles' portrayals of gender and

---

64. Ibid., 3–7. Boffey proposes that "the physical appearance of the collection—small, informal, probably copied by amateur, if practiced, scribes—suggests a collective commonplace book," speculating that it may have circulated among London civil servants as an all-male urban coterie manuscript. Julia Boffey, ed., *Manuscripts of English Courtly Love Lyrics in the Later Middle Ages* (Cambridge: D. S. Brewer, 1985), 27, 127. Wilson disagrees with this, and cites M. B. Parkes in his assertion that "there can be no doubt that one hand only is responsible for all the items" in the anthology ("Local Habitations and Names," 13).

65. Cynthia A. Rogers, "'Make Thereof a Game': The Interplay of Texts in the Findern Manuscript and Its Late Medieval Textual Community" (PhD diss., Indiana University, 2015), 19, 253–72. I am grateful to Dr. Rogers for sharing her work with me.

66. Welles had married Mary Chatwyn, the daughter of a prominent local family, by 1532–33, and folios 8r–9r of the manuscript contain a humorous verse epistle (*Right wel-beloved prentise*, DIMEV 4504) addressed to her brother Anthony (Wilson, "Local Habitations and Names," 26–28).

power. Male-voiced courtly lyrics pledging eternal devotion, praising the lady's beauty, and bemoaning love's suffering constitute the bulk of the miscellany's contents. Yet only pages later, the language of polite supplication and courteous flattery reappears verbatim in the mouths of pastourelle rapists.[67] The anthology's self-consciously pedagogical antifeminist pieces also provide important context for reading the pastourelles because they profess to educate men about women's inherent deceitfulness and sexual voracity, reflecting many of the attitudes that wreak violence in the pastourelles. The speaker of *She that hathe a wantan eye* uses obscene wordplay to teach his fellow men about female sexuality by asserting, "Thys case wolde have a cover pounte" (Her vulva requires a "sword-scabbard"), "Hur tayll shulde be lyght of the stere" (Her vulva will be easily controlled), and "A lyttle thyng wolde hur nought" (A little penis cannot satisfy her).[68] Another misogynous poem, which addresses a male audience ("O man") in its first line, warns, "Womans words thei be but as wynde," denying women's legitimacy as speaking subjects and echoing one pastourelle rapist's dismissive declaration to his distraught victim that "The wynde ys wast that thow doyst blowe" (Your words are but meaningless wind).[69] The anthology's inclusion of courtly lyrics worshipping women alongside antifeminist texts denigrating them as faithless, insatiate liars highlights the aggression undergirding courtly discourse, exposing the assumption that women owe men their attention, time, and bodies. Despite their pleas for mercy and rhetoric of humble service, the Welles Anthology's male speakers believe they are owed a "yes." When rejected, they become enraged at being denied what they see as their due, and the violence resulting from that anger is most visible in the pastourelles.

In addition to its courtly and antifeminist pieces, the Welles Anthology contains seven female-voiced lyrics expressing unabashed desire and featuring women in a range of roles—as lovers of men, as writers of amorous epistles, and as friends to other women.[70] These poems affirm women's erotic subjectivity and echo the outspoken female voices in the pastourelles who excoriate their rapists, negotiate for their safety using sophisticated legal language, and

---

67. Kathleen Andersen-Wyman examines the use of courtly flattery in love lyrics as well as pastourelles in *Andreas Capellanus on Love? Desire, Seduction, and Subversion in a Twelfth-Century Latin Text* (New York: Palgrave Macmillan, 2007), 84–85. Also see Roberta L. Krueger, "Misogyny, Manipulation, and the Female Reader in Hue de Rotelande's *Ipomédon*," in *Courtly Literature: Culture and Context*, ed. Keith Busby and Erik Kooper (Amsterdam: Benjamins, 1990).

68. *She that hathe a wantan eye* (DIMEV 4827), lines 32, 48, 4, in Jansen and Jordan, *Welles Anthology*, 155–58.

69. *O man more then madde what ys thi mynde* (DIMEV 3979), lines 36, 46, in Jansen and Jordan, *Welles Anthology*, 247–50; Whiting, *Proverbs*, W515.

70. These include DIMEV 3639, 4039, 1668, 1210, 2218, 5067, and 4494. See also Holly Barbaccia, "Remembrance in an Early Modern Woman's Seduction Lyric," *Early Modern Women* 6 (2011).

engage in obscene wordplay. *My loving frende amorous bune*, laced with bawdy humor and scatological vulgarity, is a verse epistle addressed from "on yonge woman to a noder" (one young woman to another), according to its title in the manuscript.[71] Other female-voiced lyrics in the collection express ardent longing and frustration over lack of marital choice. One woman declares, "I love so sore" (fervently), while another asserts, "Swete harte, I love you more fervent then my fader," representing women as enthusiastically voicing their desires.[72] Another female speaker relates how she loves one man even though she is betrothed to another, and she emphasizes her lack of erotic volition by lamenting, "ytt ys nott as I wolde" and "I have nott all my wyll."[73] These lyrics, which represent a range of feminine subject positions, suggest how we can read the women's voices in the anthology's pastourelles. The pastourelle *When that byrdes be brought to rest* reflects assertions about female sexuality in the manuscript's antifeminist lyrics, namely that women change their minds capriciously and say "no" when they really mean "yes." At the same time, the pastourelles and the codex's courtly lyrics share language such as the epithets "mastres" (mistress) and "swete harte" and pleas to "rewe on me" uttered by suppliant lovers and rapists alike. This imbrication of linguistic registers exposes the violent denial of women's subjectivity inherent in courtly ideology, while the pastourelles' placement alongside female-voiced love lyrics acknowledges women as erotic subjects.

The anthology's three pastourelles—*Throughe a forest as I can ryde, Come over the woodes fair and grene,* and *When that byrdes be brought to rest*—are remarkably similar in language, form, and content, and are written in cross-rhymed quatrains in folios 56v–60v.[74] The proximity of these lyrics in the manuscript points to the educational value of reading them alongside one another, and their varied narratives of violence, coercion, consent, and resistance are valuable because they teach readers that neither rape nor consensual sex follows a single narrative paradigm. In the first pastourelle, *Throughe a forest as I can ryde,* a nobleman riding through the forest spots "a fair mayde" (5) and attempts to woo her with flattery and gifts before tiring of her refusals and raping her.[75] He initially addresses her as "damesell" (9), "my dere swetyng" (19), and

---

71. Wilson discusses this piece at length and provides glosses and notes in "Local Habitations and Names," 23–25, 43–44.

72. *I love so sore I wolde fayne descerne,* line 1, and *Swete harte, I love you more fervent then my fader,* line 1, in Jansen and Jordan, *Welles Anthology,* 228–30 and 233–34.

73. *Evyn as mery as I make myght* (*DIMEV* 1210), lines 38 and 52, ibid., 221–22.

74. For a brief discussion of the three poems, see ibid., 30–31.

75. This has received the most critical attention of the three Welles pastourelles. Conlee, *Middle English Debate Poetry,* 303–7; Scattergood, "Courtliness," 65. Text references to this poem are from the edition in Jansen and Jordan, *Welles Anthology,* 116–19.

"lemman myn" (20), using language identical to that of the supplicatory lovers in the codex's courtly lyrics.[76] In choosing the possessive pronouns "my" and "myn," he assumes she is already his, betraying his sense of entitlement. He frames his desire as a humble plea rather than the demand that it really is by entreating, "I pray yow" (9), and using the same verb again nineteen lines later. She remains staunch in her refusal, "answer[ing] . . . all yn scornyng" (7) and insisting, "Nay, for God, sir, that I nyll!" (13). Her alliterating juxtaposition of "nay" and "nyll" in the same line reinforces her rejection. She declares, "Thow shalt nott fynde me such a gyll [hussy]" (15), using a nickname for Gillian that was sometimes "used contemptuously," functioned as "a name for a mare," and carried lower-status connotations.[77] She maintains that she will not behave according to his self-serving class-based expectations of peasant women's sexual availability.

Exasperated by the maiden's refusals, the knight seizes her by the waist and forcefully kisses her cheek. She "scorn[s] hym and call[s] hym hew" (29), insulting him in class-inflected terms as "a person of low degree."[78] He responds by raping her:

> He toke hur abowte the myddell small
> And layd hur downe upon the grene.
> Twys or thrys he served hur soo withall
> He wolde nott stynt tyet [stop quickly], as I wene. (33–36)

This use of "served" to name rape inverts the courtly rhetoric of service to the lady.[79] The knight's violence is emphasized by the fact that he is the sole agent of each verb in the stanza: he "toke," "layd," "served," "wolde not stynt." Their difference in size and strength is highlighted by the repeated designation of her waist as "myddell small," underscoring her physical disadvantage and using the descriptive terms of courtly discourse to do so (25, 33).[80]

---

76. The speaker of the love lyric I recommende me to yow with harte and mynde (DIMEV 2253) addresses "my dere swetyng" (41) (Jansen and Jordan, Welles Anthology, 88–91).

77. MED s.v. "gil(le" (n.[2]). Gyll is the name of the "fowll dowse" (filthy harlot) married to the peasant Mak in the Wakefield Second Shepherd's Play, in G. England and A. Pollard, eds., The Towneley Plays, Early English Text Society, e.s., 71 (London: Oxford University Press for Early English Text Society, 1897; repr., 1973), 116–40, line 246. It also names a servant girl in Chaucer's Miller's Tale ("thy mayde Gille," I.3556), pointing to its class associations.

78. MED s.v. "heue" (n.[1]), 1(b).

79. Many of the anthology's courtly lyrics feature this rhetoric, such as Entierly belovyd and most yn my mynde (DIMEV 1199), whose speaker calls himself "Your fethfull servant as ye shall well fynde / Yf ytt wyll please yow to accepte my service" (3–4) (Jansen and Jordan, Welles Anthology, 205–6).

80. For "middel smal" as a conventional feminine descriptor in courtly lyric and romance, see the quotations listed under MED s.v. "middel" (n.), 2(a).

The maiden protests the injury done to her and demands that the knight make amends. She ferociously castigates him, declaring, "ye have . . . brought my body unto shame" (41–42). She first demands that he marry her; next she asks him for "some of your good" (43); and finally she requests his name and dwelling place in case she is pregnant from the assault. She references extralegal forms of rape reparation common during the period, including out-of-court monetary settlement and marriage between rapist and victim.[81] Her assailant refuses all three requests for restitution and rides off, shouting, "For now the pye hathe peckyd yow!" (40, 48, 56). He uses this refrain to punctuate each of his three stanzas that follow his attack, deploying obscenity to taunt his victim. He brags of his assault, emphasizing its violence with the verb "pekken," meaning to peck or strike repeatedly with a sharp object.[82] He exploits the valences of "pye" as signifying not only a magpie, a bird associated with transgressive speech, but also someone who is untrustworthy.[83] He addresses her as "gyll" (39), invoking the term's intersecting valences of femininity, lower status, and overall disparagement to dismiss her suffering.

The woman is left alone in the forest and uses the poem's final three quatrains to excoriate her rapist and address her fellow maidens, underscoring the genre's links to antiviolence education by positing a model of peer pedagogy. She has the last word and declares,

> But all medons be ware, be rewe,
> And lett no man downe yow throwe,
> For and yow doo ye wyll ytt rewe,
> For then the pye wyll pecke yow. (57–60)

These lines are troubling because she appears to take responsibility for her assault by implying that she "lett" her assailant overpower her, an interpretation at odds with the third-person narrator's statement that the armed knight forcibly "layd hur downe" after seizing her by the waist. Her exhortation to "all medons" is also illustrative of medieval ideas regarding antirape education, because it stages a peer model using risk-avoidance discourse. Her use of the inclusive term "all" to designate her audience of singlewomen casts the threat of attack as a shared experience for herself and her fellow maidens, testifying to its pervasiveness and imagining women as sources of information

81. Dunn, *Stolen Women*, 76–77.

82. *MED* s.v. "pekken" (v.), (a). "Pecker," a chiefly American slang term for "penis," comes from the same root, although the *OED* claims it did not acquire bawdy significance until the early twentieth century (*OED* s.v. "pecker" [n.], 5).

83. *MED* s.v. "pi(e)" (n.[1]), (b).

for one another. Positioning herself as a peer educator, the woman represents her testimony as engendering knowledge, vigilance, and sorrow. By instructing her fellow maidens to "be ware," she draws on the valences of "ware" indicating wisdom, shrewdness, caution, and awareness of potential harm.[84] She demands that they be informed through hearing her account, and she urges them to be aware of their potential for similar victimization, drawing attention to systemic conditions that render *all* women vulnerable to violence at the same time that she collapses the differences that single out peasant women like her for greater violence. Her pedagogy operates in a fashion similar to that traced by Edwards in devotional texts such as *Hali Meiðhad* and *Ancrene Wisse*, which invoke women's "shared vulnerability to the threat of sexual violence" to imagine didactic communities of female readers constituted "through an imagined experience of sexual violence that unites widows, wives, and virgins across the experiences that would otherwise distinguish them."[85] With the command to "be rewe" (sorrowful), the maiden instructs her peers to empathize with her and feel sadness on her behalf, imagining "all medons" as an affective community.[86] She warns that they will share her grief if they are similarly attacked, presenting her testimony as an instructive exemplum illustrating the trauma of rape and advocating a risk-management model of combating assault. Carmody critiques this paradigm as "fostering fear in women," but when the maiden instructs her peers to share her anguish and learn from her story, she introduces the possibility of agency despite injury, representing herself as an eloquent survivor and showing how the pastourelle can give voice to women's anger over assault.[87] In advising her peers in this way, she blames herself and takes undue responsibility for her assault—demonstrating the impact on survivors of living in a victim-blaming culture—at the same time that she performs antiviolence pedagogy.

The woman concludes *Throughe a forest as I can ryde* by speaking back to her rapist with rage and resilience, as she berates him and sends him on his way:

> Fare well, corteor, over the medoo,
> Pluke up your helys, I beshrew [curse] yow,
> Your trace [path] wher so ever ye ryde or goo,
> Crystes curse goo wythe yow /
> Thoughe a knave hathe by me leyne,

---

84. *MED* s.v. "ware" (adj.), 1(a), 2(a), 2b(a), 3(a), 3(b).
85. Edwards, *Afterlives of Rape*, 55.
86. *MED* s.v. "reu" (adj.), (a).
87. Carmody, *Sex, Ethics, and Young People*, 89.

Yet am I noder dede nor sleyne.

I trust to recover my harte agayne,

And Crystes curse goo wythe yow / (61–68)

She curses her assailant, using the verb "beshrew" to articulate her contempt and anger.[88] She orders him to leave her presence as quickly as possible. Her curse will remain with him for the rest of his life, following his path wherever he goes in the future. She seeks to cope with the assault, reminding us that there is life beyond rape. At the same time, she acknowledges the reality that some women were "sleyne" after their assaults, as in the 1363 case of Ellen Katemayden, whose rapist "lay with her against her will and assaulted her and so battered her that she died within the next three days."[89] Other women were killed for resisting rape, such as Christina de Menstre, who in 1301 was accosted in a London churchyard at twilight by a man who propositioned her and stabbed her to death with a dagger after "she refused and endeavoured to escape from his hands."[90] The pastourelle's maiden represents her assault as physical and emotional injury, claiming it not only harms her "body" but also damages her "harte." She articulates her unbridled fury at her rapist, twice repeating the impassioned refrain "Crystes curse goo wythe yow." This line is highlighted in both instances by a *virgula suspensiva* in the manuscript, denoting a pause; these are the only *virgulae* in the poem, lending visual prominence to the maiden's curse. In repeating this rapist-cursing refrain, which is further emphasized by the scribe, she indicates that Christ is on her side and shares her righteous anger. "Crystes curse" could name excommunication, and its usage here prescribes excommunication and eternal damnation as fitting punishment for rapists.[91] Speaking the decisive final words in the exchange, the maiden provides her imagined audience of "all medons" with a compelling lesson in survival, as she looks forward to a future of "recover[y]" and articulates an unwavering faith in her own resilience while still acknowledging the grave harm that her attacker has inflicted on her "harte."

In the anthology's next pastourelle, *Come over the woodes fair and grene*, a smooth-talking aristocrat uses deception and threats to extort sex from a penniless peasant girl, illustrating how her gender and economic disadvantages render her so vulnerable to his coercion that he does not need to use force. In this way, her status as young, peasant, and female occludes his violence and

---

88. *MED* s.v. "bishreuen" (v.), 1(a).

89. Goldberg, *Women in England*, 254.

90. Reginald R. Sharpe, ed., *Calendar of Coroners Rolls of the City of London A.D. 1300–1378* (London: R. Clay and Sons, 1913), 7–8.

91. *MED* s.v. "Crist" (n.), (b).

makes it invisible to the naked eye. This narrative, particularly when read alongside the previous lyric's portrayal of physical force, demonstrates that coercion takes many forms, and it represents the girl speaking in legal language to defend herself in response to the man's invoking of the law.[92]

When the man spots the maiden gathering flowers alone in the forest, he praises her beauty and invites her to sit with him under a greenwood tree.[93] He hails her as "that goodly mayde, that lustye wenche" (2), his use of apposition illustrating how he views her as both "goodly" (beautiful) and "lustye," meaning "attractive" or "fine" but also "tempting, willing, desirous, eager, amorous, pleasure-loving, lecherous."[94] He identifies her as a young singlewoman—a "mayde"—and a "wenche," naming her in terms of lower-status femininity and sexual transgression and using intersectional misogyny to frame her as "asking for it." She reacts by begging him not to assault her, indicating that his flattery fails to mask his aggression:

> Sir, I pray yow, doo none offence
> To me, a mayde, thys I make my mone;
> But as I came, lett me goo hens
> For I am here my selfe alone. (5–8)

She frames her request to leave in legal terms as a "mone," a formal charge or grievance, and she names the man's anticipated actions toward her as an "offence," a violation of the law.[95] She articulates fear that he will hurt her, grounding it in her gendered embodiment as "a mayde." For the maiden, the state of being "my selfe alone" renders her vulnerable and exposes her to danger, and she punctuates her appeals for release by repeating that she is "all alone" (24, 40). She acknowledges her physical disadvantage, pleading, "Now, for thys tyme, let me goo quyte [completely]; / Yow to wythstande, strengthe have I non" (37–38). Her use of the verb "wythstande," meaning "to offer resistance" and "to keep someone from doing something," coupled with her reference to her relative lack of "strengthe," indicates her awareness of rape as a potential outcome, as she imagines herself needing to fight against the man and lacking the bodily power to do so.[96] Her use of "quyte" to modify her request betrays her fear of harm and her desire to be as far away from

---

92. I am grateful to Kathleen Kennedy for drawing my attention to the legal valences of the maiden's speech.

93. The multivalent "flower-gathering" motif also appears in *Hey troly loly lo.*

94. *Come over the woodes fair and grene (DIMEV* 1052), in Jansen and Jordan, *Welles Anthology*, 222–26. Text references are to lines from this edition. *MED* s.v. "godli" (adj.[2]), 1(b) and "lusti" (adj.).

95. *MED* s.v. "mon" (n.[1]), 3; "offens" (n.), 2.

96. *MED* s.v. "withstonden" (v.), 1(a) and 3(a).

him as possible, for she begs him to release her "without legal impediment, undisputedly."[97]

The maiden's use of legal terminology to negotiate her escape renders her the man's rhetorical equal, as he claims that all maidens caught gathering flowers "here" must "pay a trepytt [tribute, tax] or they passe" (17, 20), using legal language to argue that she owes him sex since she cannot pay the fine with money. He puts a monetary price on her safety, a price that both of them know she is unable to pay. She responds with refusals grounded in her legal claim to corporeal safety from harm, calling on the law to protect her from rape just as he invokes it to justify rape. She attempts to bargain her way out of the situation, underscoring her poverty and her awareness that the man views her body as a commodity, saying, "Then of my mouth come take a basse [kiss], / For oder goodes have I non" (21–22). Her use of "take" highlights the predatory nature of his request—she does not offer the kiss freely, but instead highlights the inequality undergirding the encounter and reminds him that she is offering it only because she has "non" "oder goodes." She reiterates her desire to leave, emphasizing that her offer of the kiss was solely due to her material disadvantage: "Lett me departe, I yow requere" (28), she says. In using "requere" to characterize her plea for release, the maiden chooses a term frequently used to name formal requests in legal documents such as wills.[98] He responds with an explicit threat, invoking the law on *his* side, not hers: "I must observe the courte lawe / By courtes maner or by myght [in a courteous fashion or with force]," he insists (33–34). In his eyes, polite manners and brute force have the same result, confirming her fears that he intends to "doo . . . offence / To" her. Despairing that "ther be non other wey" (41), the girl offers him the flowers she has gathered, protesting that she has nothing of any value and underlining the economic disadvantage that prevents her from negotiating effectively and renders her vulnerable to his aggression. He insists, "Anoder floure is bettur for my purpoose" (61). Drawing on the double meaning of "floure" as also signifying virginity, the man uses the term's multivalence as a tool of coercion, deploying it to claim her body instead of her flowers.[99] Taking his payment, he declares, "I call ytt myne owne as my very [lawful, legally entitled] dett" (68), underscoring his manipulation of the law to exploit the numerous inequalities between him and the maiden.[100] She never articulates her consent, and the assault is not described but rather referred to after the fact; it occurs in the gap between stanzas. The man's entitled

---

97. *MED* s.v. "quit" (adv.), (a).
98. *MED* s.v. "requeren" (v.), 1(a)–(e).
99. *MED* s.v. "flour" (n.[1]), 2(d).
100. *MED* s.v. "verrei" (adj.), 2(b) and 2(c).

claiming of the peasant girl's body as "my very dett" because she is too poor to pay a fictive toll aligns with his initial view of her as a "lustye wenche" and highlights how he views her as a commodity that he deserves to consume because of her youth, gender, and economic disadvantage.

In her final speech in the exchange, the maiden vows never to gather wild-flowers alone again, offering an enigmatic promise to the man who has co-erced her:

> I wyll no more gader the vyolett,
> Under thys woode my selfe alone.
> But shall I gether the floures here
> Nay, never more, I make a vowe;
> And yff I doo with owten a fere [companion],
> Doo to me then as ye dyd now. (71–76)

We could read this, as it has previously been read, as the woman's tongue-in-cheek acknowledgment that she has enjoyed being threatened and duped, since she tells the man to repeat his actions if he ever finds her gathering flowers alone in the future.[101] However, we can also read it as a renunciation of the circumstances of her assault and an articulated desire to avoid another such encounter. She makes a solemn promise ("vowe"), using the alliterating re-fusals "nay" and "never more" to punctuate her claim. She vows to avoid that location, "here," with its laws that demand such severe penalties from maid-ens caught unawares. She promises never to travel again without a "fere" (com-panion, helper, or advocate), implying that there is empowering safety in numbers for young women, who can help protect and support one another.[102] Her stipulation that she will no longer gather violets is especially poignant because the violet symbolized chastity and virginity, which the man has forc-ibly taken from her.[103] *Come over the woodes fair and grene* shows the manifold ways that sexual coercion operates—through deception, threats, economic in-equality, and the law itself. The man's use of courtly rhetoric after the assault emphasizes the link between violence and courteous speech: in his final lines, he addresses his victim as "fair maydon" and "swete lady" (77), echoing the

---

101. The editors read this as evidence that the two have "reach[ed] a mutually satisfactory con-clusion" (Jansen and Jordan, *Welles Anthology*, 30).

102. *MED* s.v. "fere" (n.[1]), 1(a). I am grateful to Sarah Baechle for discussing the implications of this line with me.

103. *MED* s.v. "violet" (n.), (c).

appellations "swete ladye" and "fair lady" spoken by a languishing lover in one of the anthology's love complaints.[104]

In the third Welles pastourelle, *When that byrdes be brought to rest*, the female speaker uses obscenity to signal her consent in an exchange that can be read either as highlighting the possibilities of women's affirmative consent and bawdy wordplay or as reinforcing the rape myths that women say "no" when they really mean "yes" and that all women eventually consent when faced with enough persistence.[105] After seeing how vocal resistance can be overcome through violence and how economic disadvantage can be exploited through coercion, readers of the Welles Anthology finally have a model, albeit vexed, for sexual negotiation. This debate, which is both shorter and more lighthearted than the previous two, features a hapless courtly lover and a witty, confident female speaker. He trots out an arsenal of tired tropes, addressing her as "My ladye as freshe as floures yn May" (9), claiming to suffer lovesickness, threatening to drown himself, and bemoaning her hard-heartedness. But whereas the men in the previous pastourelles praise the maidens' physical attractiveness and emphasize their class disadvantage, this man praises her personality, declaring, "I love hur person and goodly haveour [behavior]" (4). He voices his appreciation of her overall being and actions rather than her beauty, and he refrains from resorting to violence and threats.

The woman stubbornly refuses the man's overtures with self-possessed humor and obscene metaphor. She ends most of her stanzas with an unequivocal rejection: "Your bryde shall never hoppe yn my cage," she declares (8, 16, 24), recalling the use of avian terminology for male genitalia in the erotic lyric *I have a gentil cok*. Her refrain stands in stark contrast to the rapist's repeated taunt in the first pastourelle, "For now the pye hathe peckyd yow," because her use of "hoppe" instead of "peck" to characterize sexual penetration invokes joyful, nimble movement—dancing, leaping, bounding, and bouncing—rather than wounding violence.[106] In a series of spirited comebacks, she insults the man's "feble corage" (weak virility) (14), assesses his body as "full weyke" (very weak) (14), mocks his slender calves (15), and orders him away with the dismissal "Good sir, owt of my syght!" (7). She repeatedly states that he will never have sex with her and dismisses him with gusto, providing a model of how to respond to unwanted advances with eloquence and wit.

---

104. *O love most dere O love most nere my harte* (DIMEV 3973), lines 29, 70, 111, 146, in Jansen and Jordan, *Welles Anthology*, 136–42.

105. *When that byrdes be brought to rest* (DIMEV 6417), in Jansen and Jordan, *Welles Anthology*, 226–28. Text references are to lines in this edition.

106. *MED* s.v. "hoppen" (v.), 1(a)–(b).

The woman has the last word and makes a complete about-face in the exchange's final stanza, articulating enthusiastic consent through obscene metaphor while simultaneously implying that women's refusals are always open to reversal. Instead of sending the man on his way, she alters her refrain to signify her consent: "And yn a place of privyte, / Your bryde shall hoppe yn my cage," she declares (31–32). With the same self-assurance she expressed earlier to reject his propositions, she now sets the time, place, and terms of their future tryst, and she uses the playful verb "hoppe" to characterize it as pleasurable rather than violent. "Cage" carries connotations of domestication and confinement for birds, animals, or prisoners, and she exploits its multivalence to invite the man to submit to her vaginal dominion.[107]

This pastourelle can be read multiple ways which underscore the genre's utility as a tool for grappling with sexual ethics. Its implicit "no-means-yes" script—of staunch rejection followed by last-minute acquiescence—could encourage male readers to disregard women's refusals and persist in making unwanted advances. It could indicate the efficacy of courtly rhetoric as a tactic for getting women into bed, a motif we see in multiple Old French pastourelles, because the man's suicide threat is what ultimately convinces the woman to sleep with him. We could read her affirmative declaration as a woman wearily capitulating, worn down by a persistent man's entreaties and recognizing that she has little power in the situation.

We can also read the woman's obscene declaration as another strategy of resistance. In one Old French pastourelle, the maiden first attempts to flee and then voices her acquiescence, a tactic that causes her would-be rapist to let go of her skirt; she is then able to escape into the woods, taunting him in the exchange's closing lines as she runs free.[108] Or we can read it as an example of enthusiastic consent, especially since it is compelled by neither threats nor force and she has expressed no fear of the man, unlike the maidens in the previous two lyrics. Some critics have interpreted women's obscenity in the pastourelle as an indicator of class difference, describing their speech as "coarser, more demotic . . . more sensible, down to earth, practical" than the courtly language of the aristocratic knight or educated cleric.[109] But I am certain that there is something more at stake in this poem and others like it, because the speaker's use of obscenity connects her to female-voiced erotic lyrics that advocate for women's desires and make a case for their pleasures, as I show in the next chapter. This voicing of desire copied after two rape narratives shows

---

107. *MED* s.v. "cage" (n.), 1(a) and 2(a).

108. *Or voi yver defenir*, in Paden, *Medieval Pastourelle*, 1:232–35.

109. Scattergood, "Love Lyric before Chaucer," 60.

that there is desire after assault, that women are still erotic subjects after vio-lation.[110] We can also read this as an example of erotic negotiation. Carmody encourages antiviolence educators to "shift focus from teaching refusal skills and awareness-raising to a focus on promoting and developing ethical non-violent relating" and teaching "the dynamic nature of negotiating desire and pleasure," and we can interpret this poem as an imperfect example of this dynamic negotiation even as it enacts the "no-becomes-yes" myth.[111]

Read together, as we are invited to do by the scribe's choice to copy them in a cluster, the three Welles pastourelles underline the importance of listening to many different narratives of rape and resistance. They tell us that rape is devastating, rape is not always physically violent, rape can be survived with anger and resilience, and violence is not the only outcome in a pastourelle en-counter. With its multiple audience possibilities and competing portrayals of female desire, victimization, and demonization, the Welles Anthology likely taught a diverse range of lessons. *Come over the woodes fair and grene*'s focus on the law's relationship to sexual power would have especially resonated among Humphrey Welles's London coterie of civil servants educated at the Inns of Court, as it could have taught them how to abuse their legal knowledge and multiple grounds of social privilege, or it might have shown them the harm-ful effects of this privilege on those over whom it is wielded. The anthology's female-voiced lyrics about ardent desire and bawdy humor could have taught readers like Mary Chatwyn Welles about erotic agency and boldness, while *Throughe a forest as I can ryde*'s invocation of "all medons" invites female read-ers to join cross-class coalitions united by their shared vulnerability to violence.

"Courtly Fukking": Disrupting the Rape Script in the Middle Scots Pastourelle

Like *When that byrdes be brought to rest*, the ten surviving Middle Scots pastourel-les highlight female-voiced obscenity's usefulness in teaching and negotiating sex. The genre's popularity continued unabated into the late sixteenth century in Scotland, where numerous pastourelles survive in verse anthologies such as Stewart courtier Sir Richard Maitland of Lethington's Maitland Folio (1570–86) and the Bannatyne Manuscript.[112] I close this chapter by examining

---

110. I am grateful to Lucy Allen for this insight.

111. Moira Carmody, "Ethical Erotics: Reconceptualizing Anti-Rape Education," *Sexualities* 8, no. 4 (2005): 478.

112. Seven pastourelles and pastourelle-esque dialogues are copied in the Bannatyne Manuscript, including Henryson's *Robene and Makyne*, Dunbar's *In secret place this hyndir nycht* (c. 1505), and the

four Scottish pastourelles—*Quhy so strat strang go we by youe, Ane fair sweit may of mony one*, Robert Henryson's *Robene and Makyne*, and *In somer quhen flouris will smell*—in which women articulate sexual consent, as they most clearly exemplify the genre's possibilities for teaching audiences about negotiation. Two lyrics explore men's bodily responses to women's vocalized consent, while the other two portray maidens as their partners' instructors, providing alternate paradigms for thinking about gender and pedagogy. All four stage maidens speaking obscenity to articulate knowledge and express refusal, demonstrating the disruptive potential of women's transgressive speech to rewrite pastourelle narratives of coercion. In the first two pastourelles, men follow the genre's script of courtly flattery and unflagging persistence in the face of women's rejection. Both maidens assent to sex after some initial resistance, only for the men to fall victim to impotence or premature ejaculation so that the encounter goes unconsummated. *Quhy so strat strang go we by youe* is copied, along with an incomplete courtly farewell lyric titled *Adoue deir hart of Aberdene*, on a heavily worn and damaged blank page at the end of a legal record book for the burgh of Aberdeen covering the years 1502–7.[113] It is copied in the same hand as some of the records, pointing to the pastourelle's circulation among Aberdeen legal scribes.[114] Editors speculate that it "is probably an over-writing of an obscene poem," and it was first printed in an expurgated Victorian version due to its graphic climax.[115] *Quhy so strat strang go we by youe* exploits the multiple meanings of its title refrain to underscore the ambiguity and multivalence of the language of consent, desire, and refusal.

Early one morning, the man encounters "ane wenkollet clad in ploue" (a young woman dressed in blue) (3); "wenkollet" signifies "a young woman, a wench."[116] The color of her clothing aligns her with artistic representations of the Virgin Mary and underscores her virginal status. He hails her with the courtly commonplace "my fair and fresche of houe" (my fair and beautiful maiden) (4), and she immediately rebuts his advances:

---

anonymous *In somer quhen flouris will smell, I saw me thocht this hindir nycht, All to lufe and not to fenyie, I met my lady weil arrayit*, and *Commonyng betuix the Mester and the Heure. Still undir the levis grene* and *Ane fair sweit may of mony one* survive in the Maitland Folio (Cambridge, Magdalene College Library, MS Pepys 2553).

113. Aberdeen, Aberdeen City Records Office, Aberdeen Sasines Register, vol. 2, on the recto of the second-to-last page; Helena M. Shire and Alexander Fenton, "'The Sweepings of Parnassus': Four Poems Transcribed from the Record Books of the Burgh Sasines of Aberdeen," *Aberdeen University Review* 36 (1955–56): 47.

114. Ibid., 43.

115. Ibid., 46.

116. *DOST* s.v. "winklot" (n.). Shire and Fenton, "'The Sweepings of Parnassus,'" 47. Text references are to lines from this edition.

Away, uncoucht man, lat be
And ye foluene I wele flee
Be gode man I defy youe. (9–11)

[Away, vile man, stop it now;
If you follow me, I will flee.
By God, man, I defy you.]

With her invocation of God on her side, use of insults, and declaration of "defy[ance]," she registers her unequivocal resistance. He responds with more flattery, coupled with a warning that she will likely be raped by a forest incubus ("sum uncoucht spret") after nightfall. In response to his persistence and threats, she reconsiders her options and reverses her choice in the final stanza: "Scho wnbechot hir at the last / Ande traistit that scho had traispast" (She relaxed her decision after some thought / And trusted that she had erred) (19–20). Munro warns that it is important to view moments of consent in their larger context and to acknowledge the possibility that "the reality is one of 'submit to survive' rather than a reflection of genuine autonomy. The alternatives are too unpleasant, too draining, or too dangerous to be meaningful, and compliance . . . emerges as the inevitable conclusion."[117] The maiden abandons her resistance only after she is threatened. The pastourelle vividly illustrates how the man's persistence and threats constrain her choices, for he posits rape as the unavoidable outcome of failing to comply with his demands. His use of "traispast" to characterize her rejection, with its connotations of wrongdoing and legal offense, implies that he sees her refusal as a crime and believes she owes him an affirmative response; this is a still-current tenet of rape culture that authorizes violence against women who reject unwanted overtures.[118]

The tables are turned in the final lines when the man reacts to the maiden's acquiescence by involuntarily ejaculating all over himself, an action narrated by her pragmatic appraisal:

Scho saide, "Suet hart, ye ryve ourfast;
It semis me ye ar agast.
Cum tak my curche and dry youe." (21–23)

---

117. Munro, "Constructing Consent," 931.

118. *DOST* s.v. "trespass" (v.), 1a and 1b. The case of Cristina de Menstre that I cite above, which involved a woman who was stabbed to death for resisting a stranger's advances, makes clear this myth's devastating real-life consequences. Similar contemporary murder cases indicate that this view of women's sexual refusal as an offense that deserves to be met with violence is an ongoing problem particularly affecting women of color, as discussed in Robin R. Means Coleman and Douglas-Wade Brunton, "'You Might Not Know Her, but You Know Her Brother': Surveillance Technology, Respectability Policing, and the Murder of Janese Talton Jackson," *Souls* 18, no. 2 (2016).

[She said, "Sweetheart, you arrive too quickly;
It seems to me you are filled with fright.
Come take my kerchief and dry yourself."]

Her blunt assessment was censored by a Victorian-era editor due to its graphic nature.[119] With practical savvy rather than naïveté, she instructs the man to use her "curche" (kerchief), a gendered article of clothing, to mop up his semen.[120] Her characterization of the ejaculating man as "agast," an adjective meaning "filled with fright or terror" used frequently to name the fear of overmatched men in battle, represents a power shift in the encounter: whereas she was previously propositioned and threatened with rape, now she has rendered him the weaker combatant.[121] Her use of "agast" portrays his ejaculation as an expression of fear, which has important implications for how this poem invites us to interpret her vocalized consent. This seminal moment implies that sex was never the point for the man, as he derives his enjoyment from the verbal combat of cornering the maiden into compliance; once that has been accomplished, he is finished. It paints her consent as having the capacity to frighten and disempower her would-be assailant, because his involuntary "arrival" emphasizes his lack of sexual control.

The pastourelle's title, *Quhy so strat strang go we by youe*, is written in large textura letters embellished with intricate decorative penwork, and it functions as the lyric's refrain by punctuating each of its four stanzas (6, 12, 18, 24). The title refrain's significance hinges on its ambiguity, which renders its meaning flexible enough to be spoken by persistent man and resistant, then consenting, maiden. Its editors state that the refrain "retain[s] . . . an implicit sexual reference," although they do not elaborate on this.[122] "Quhy so strat strang" can mean "Why so immediately unfriendly?" or "Why so unwaveringly resistant?" when it is spoken by the man as he attempts to cajole the maiden into sex in the first and third stanzas.[123] In contrast, it can also mean "Why so strongly aroused?" or "Why so erect, stranger?" when spoken by the defiant maiden in the second stanza, with "strat" referring to the man's erection, or it

---

119. The expurgated version was edited by William Dauney, who describes the poem as a "rude specimen . . . of Scotish song" and omits line 23, in *Ancient Scotish Melodies* (Edinburgh: The Maitland Club, 1838), 49.

120. *DOST* s.v. "curche" (n.[1]).

121. *DOST* s.v. "agast" (adj.). Fisher reads the final stanza's "assertive female voice" as suggesting that the maiden "is, ultimately, the sexual conqueror of the male" ("Comic Verse," 24).

122. Fenton and Shire, "'Sweepings of Parnassus,'" 46.

123. *DOST* s.v. "strang(e" (adj.), 6: "Unfriendly, cold, distant"; "strang" (adj.), 3: "Firm of purpose; bold, resolute" and 7: "Of a castle, fortification, etc.: Capable of offering strong resistance; difficult to capture; impregnable. Also, in fig. context, of a person"; "strait" (adv.), 3: "Strictly; rigorously"; "straucht" (adv.), 2: "Immediately, without delay; straightaway."

could mean "Why so immediately forceful?"[124] Finally, it can mean, "Why so quickly cold?" when she voices it after the man "ryve[s]" all over himself. "Go we by youe" likewise carries a range of meanings: "Let us proceed according to your wishes," "We will proceed against your wishes," "I will follow you," or "I act in opposition to you."[125] The refrain's imprecision and staggering range of possible interpretations emphasizes the pastourelle's larger points about multivalence and sexual negotiation. It depicts the language of refusal, consent, and seduction as identical, its meanings dependent on speaker and context.

Ane fair sweit may of mony one features a similar script, in which a maiden refuses a man's courtly overtures before voicing her firm consent, only to be met with a flaccid response.[126] It opens with a "gymp" (handsome) man named John encountering "ane fair sweit may" (1–3) as she gathers flowers alone in a field. He tells her, "This hart of myn is youris" (5). She dismisses him, then changes her mind and orders him to return the next day: "Sche sayis, 'Cum meit me heir to morne. / Paradventure ye may sum freyndschip fang'" (She says, "Come meet me here tomorrow morning. / Perchance you may obtain some friendship") (11–12). Like the woman in *When that byrdes be brought to rest*, she sets the time, place, and terms for the encounter. He follows her instructions and meets her "at hir tryst" (18), a term indicating "an arrangement to meet at a set time and place" that emphasizes her agency.[127] At first he performs the role of amorous lover: he whispers "fair sweit wourdis" in her ear, "grapit her out throw the gowne" (groped her through her gown), and declares, "I mon ryd yow" (I must ride you) (19–22). Their rendezvous hits a snag when he has difficulty unlacing his trousers and finds himself limp. The dialogue concludes with the woman dismissing the man in disgust: "'For schame,' quod scho, 'for schame go hyd yow, / I feill your lang thing standis nocht'" ("For shame," she said, "for shame go hide yourself, / I feel your 'long thing' is not erect") (30–31). Her blunt assessment of his genital state points to her sexual knowledgeability, while her use of the experiential statement "I feill" to announce his lack of erection emphasizes her active role in the encounter. *Ane fair sweit may of mony one* is copied in the Maitland Folio, which Boffey argues ought to be read "firstly as a 'family book'" because it

---

124. *DOST* s.v. "straucht" (adv.), 3: "Erect, upright"; "strang(e" (adj.), 3: "Unknown, unfamiliar; not met with before" and also 1(a), which cites an instance of "strangeris" shortened to "strang" in Blind Hary's *Wallace*; "strang" (adv.), 1: "powerfully, violently"; "strang" (adj.), 4: "Forceful, assertive."

125. *DOST* s.v. "be" (prep.), 1: "By the action or agency of (a person)"; 4: "On or upon, beside, along, by (a way, etc.)"; "by" (prep.), 2(c): "Without; at variance with; contrary or in opposition to, against."

126. *Ane fair sweit may of mony one*, in Craigie, *Maitland Folio Manuscript*, 1:194. Text references are to lines in this edition.

127. *DOST* s.v. "trist" (n.[1]), 1.

was compiled at the Maitland family's regional country estate in East Lothian and contains names of both male and female family members, including Sir Richard Maitland's daughter Helen, whose name appears in a marginal annotation that scholars read as a mark of ownership.[128] The Maitland Folio's mixed-gender aristocratic context, with women active as readers, annotators, and owners, furnishes provocative possibilities for how this poem about women's bawdy wordplay and outspoken sexual disappointment might have been read by other women.

Both *Quhy so strat strang go we by youe* and *Ane fair sweit may of mony one* revise pastourelle paradigms of masculine aggression and feminine resistance, providing insights into how women's consent could function socially. Once the woman gives her explicit verbal agreement, which is ostensibly the man's goal, he becomes unable to perform sexually. These two lyrics imply that women's enthusiastic participation was never the point. Rather, their refusal is eroticized, and when they voice consent to what is asked of them, the game is over.

Robene and Makyne and *In somer quhen flouris will smell*, known as "comic pastourelles" because they are relatively devoid of masculine aggression, survive in unique copies in the Bannatyne Manuscript, and both represent women educating their partners. They are two of the eight pastourelles and pastourelle-like dialogues that Bannatyne copied into his massive verse anthology in 1565–68 while Edinburgh roiled with scandalized outrage over Mary Queen of Scots's unconventional behavior and colorful marital career, which featured domestic violence, an estrangement, allegations of adultery and murder, a hasty remarriage, and an episode of ravishment involving kidnapping and claims of rape.[129] Scholars argue that the manuscript is a "Marian anthology," its virulently antifeminist lyrics copied in a political climate in which pornographic placards and verses comparing the queen to a "harlot" were posted anonymously in public places, Captain Richard Hepburn presented her with four ribald ballads decorated with drawings of "the secret members both of men and of women," and an anonymous 1567 broadside ballad attacked her

---

128. Julia Boffey, "The Maitland Folio Manuscript as a Verse Anthology," in *William Dunbar, "The Nobill Poyet": Essays in Honour of Priscilla Bawcutt*, ed. Sally Mapstone (East Linton, UK: Tuckwell, 2001), 40; also Sebastiaan Verweij, *The Literary Culture of Early Modern Scotland: Manuscript Production and Transmission, 1560–1625* (Oxford: Oxford University Press, 2016), 191–206. This note referring to "helyne m" appears on page 256 of the manuscript.

129. For more on Mary's turbulent erotic life and its role in Edinburgh culture during the 1560s, see Sarah M. Dunnigan, *Eros and Poetry at the Courts of Mary Queen of Scots and James VI* (New York: Palgrave Macmillan, 2002), 15–45; Guy, *Queen of Scots*; Jenny Wormald, *Mary Queen of Scots: A Study in Failure* (London: George Philip, 1988). I am grateful to Lucy Hinnie for discussing Mary's role in the Bannatyne and sharing sources with me.

as "Clitemnestra fell [ruthless]" and "the cruell Jesabell."[130] The Bannatyne's pastourelles about outspoken female desire would have been read in this context of misogynist furor over a powerful woman's alleged sexual insatiability and the murder of her husband. The public discourse surrounding Mary's personal history of violence further complicates how we read these lyrics. In his scurrilous *Ane Detectioun of the duinges of Marie Quene of Scotts* (printed in 1571 but written earlier), George Buchanan alleges that on the night of Mary's second husband Darnley's murder in February 1567, her lover "Bothwel was . . . brought into the Quenis chamber, and there forced hir agaynst hir will forsothe. But how much agaynst hir will . . . tyme the mother of truth hath disclosed."[131] He depicts Mary as an unequivocal victim "forced . . . agaynst hir will," then immediately questions her nonconsent and accuses her of orchestrating a revenge ravishment. He claims that "within few dayes efter, the Quene intending as I suppose to reaquite force with force and to ravish hym agayne [in return]," Mary sent a burly bawd named Dame Rerese to kidnap Bothwell from his marital bed: "out of his bed, even out of his wives armes, halfe aslepe, halfe naked, sche forceably bringes the man to the Quene."[132] These two Bannatyne lyrics about women's obscenely expressed desire are copied in a cultural context in which women are both dangerous sexual aggressors and "willing victims" who are victimized, blamed for their victimization, and able to "ravish" their rapists "agayne."

Robene and Makyne and *In somer quhen flouris will smell* reverse the Continental pastourelle motif of the experienced man teaching the naïve girl about sex, and this reversal carries important implications for maidens' erotic knowledge and pedagogical capabilities.[133] The trope of the experienced widow as teacher is common in medieval literature, embodied by Chaucer's Alisoun of

---

130. For more on the relationship between Mary and the Bannatyne Manuscript, see Dunnigan, *Eros and Poetry*, 46–73; Carolyn Ives and David Parkinson, "Scottish Chaucer, Misogynist Chaucer," in Kline and Prendergast, *Rewriting Chaucer*; A. A. MacDonald, "The Bannatyne Manuscript—A Marian Anthology," *Innes Review* 37 (1986); David Parkinson, "'A Lamentable Storie': Mary Queen of Scots and the Inescapable *Querelle des Femmes*," in *A Palace in the Wild: Essays on Vernacular Culture and Humanism in Late-Medieval and Renaissance Scotland*, ed. L. A. J. R. Houwen, A. A. MacDonald, and S. L. Mapstone (Leuven: Peeters, 2000). For these public, often obscene attacks, see Guy, *Queen of Scots*, 309, 323; Wormald, *Mary Queen of Scots*, 136–45; *Ane Ballat Declaring the Nobill and Gude Inclination of Our King*, in James Cranstoun, ed., *Satirical Poems of the Time of the Reformation*, 4 vols. (Edinburgh: William Blackwood and Sons, 1890–93), 1:31–38, lines 99, 143.

131. George Buchanan, *Ane Detectioun of the duinges of Marie Quene of Scotts, touchand the murder of her Husband, and hir Conspiracie, Adulterie, and pretensit Mariage with the Erle Bothwell. Translatit out of the latine, quhilk was written be G. B.* (London: John Day, 1571), sig. Bijr–v; Dunnigan, *Eros and Poetry*, 24–31.

132. Buchanan, *Ane Detectioun*, sig. Bijv.

133. In *Quant pré reverdoient, que chantent oisel*, the rapist states, "I taught her my game" (mon jeu li apris) (Paden, *Medieval Pastourelle*, 1:304–5, line 42).

Bath and *The Roman de la Rose*'s La Vieille.[134] However, these lyrics stand apart because they feature *young* women teaching their male partners about sexuality. Robert Henryson's *Robene and Makyne* (c. 1470) is the earliest of the Scottish pastourelles, and the fact that it was copied a century after its composition attests to its enduring popularity.[135] Robin is a stock class-inflected name for the maiden's shepherd lover in numerous Old French pastourelles, while Makyne, a diminutive of Matilda, recurs "proverbially, as a typical girl's name," often with pejorative sexual and class connotations.[136] The name carries additional valences that lend significance to its use here. In multiple poems by Lyndsay as well as the popular fabliau *The Freiris of Berwik* (c. 1461–82), "makine" names the vulva, allowing us to read Makyne in the vein of the "talking cunts" from fabliaux tradition that eschew propriety to speak bluntly about their erotic experiences.[137] Makyne's role as educator is made all the more meaningful by the fact that she is framed as both an ordinary peasant girl and a wise embodied vulva teaching lessons about mutuality and negotiation to young men.

Makyne first encounters Robene sitting with his flock "on a gud grene hill" (1). This is one of the rare pastourelles in which the maiden initiates the conversation, and she is also the last to speak.[138] She vocalizes her desire in courtly

134. For this trope, see Dunbar's *Tretis of the Tua Mariit Wemen and the Wedo* and Chaucer's *Wife of Bath's Prologue*. Parkinson notes how "hostile depictions of . . . Mary draw upon the [literary] type of the vigorous, appetitive widow" ("'Lamentable Storie,'" 148).

135. *Robene and Makyne* (DIMEV 4510), in *Robert Henryson: The Complete Works*, ed. David J. Parkinson (Kalamazoo, MI: Medieval Institute Publications, 2010), 143–46. Text references are to lines in this edition. Rosemary Greentree discusses the poem's links to courtly love poetry and the pastourelle, which she views as unrelated genres, arguing that "Henryson allows us to look and laugh at both of these traditions." Alessandra Petrina links the poem to the Occitan pastourelle tradition, which typically features a more outspoken, assertive maiden than her Old French counterparts. Greentree, "Literate in Love: Makyne's Lesson for Robene," in Mapstone, *Older Scots Literature*, 64; Petrina, "Deviations from Genre in Robert Henryson's 'Robene and Makyne,'" *Studies in Scottish Literature* 31, no. 1 (1999): 113–15.

136. *DOST* s.v. "Makine" (n.), a. The shepherdess has a lover named Robin in Old French pastourelles like Jean Bodel's *L'autrier quant chevauchoie*, Richard de Semilly's *Je chevauchai l'autrier la matinee*, and Bestourné's *An mai a douls tens novel*, to name only a few (Paden, *Medieval Pastourelle*, 1:70–73, 80–83, 104–7). For further discussion of the characters' names, see Greentree, "Literate in Love," 65; Petrina, "Deviations from Genre," 116.

137. *DOST* s.v. "Makine" (n.), b. Lyndsay, *Syde Taillis*, lines 90, 91; *Ane Satyre of the Thrie Estaitis*, line 1920. In the version of *The Freiris of Berwik* printed in 1622, the female protagonist "pulde her Makin, gave it buffets tway" (pulled her vulva, gave it two smacks) (139). In the other two surviving versions in the Maitland Folio and Bannatyne Manuscript, "makin" is replaced with the more straightforward "cunt." *The Mirrie Historie of the Thrie Friers of Berwicke* (Aberdeen: Edward Raban for David Melvill, 1622). For more on the "talking cunts" motif, prominent in fabliaux like the popular *Le chevalier qui fist les cons parler*, see Burns, *Bodytalk*, 54–65.

138. The only other British pastourelle in which the woman speaks first is the sixteenth-century English song *Beware my lytyll fynger* (DIMEV 6851), which opens mid-assault with the woman crying out, "Ye wryng my hand to sore" (*XX Songes*, item 4).

terms, claiming to be dying of lovesickness and pleading, "Robene, thou rew on me!" (5). In adopting this discourse, Makyne performs the role of the genre's aristocratic or clerical aggressor.[139] This generic reversal, with the maiden making overtures to a reluctant partner, enables Henryson to explore the workings of men's consent and refusal.

Makyne further revises pastourelle convention by performing the role of educator. Robene claims to know nothing of love and requests a lesson: "Makyne, to me thou shaw . . . Fane wald I leir that law" (Makyne, show it to me . . . Gladly would I learn that law) (15, 17). He portrays himself as a student eager to "leir" from her. She teaches him using the language of schoolroom instruction, the peasant girl appropriating the authority of the erudite schoolmaster: "At luvis lair gife thow will leir, / Tak thair ane A B C" (Of love's teaching if you will learn, / Take there an A B C) (18–19). In characterizing her speech as "lair" (teaching) meant to "leir" (teach) her audience, she underscores the genre's capacity to educate young men about sexuality.[140] By using the verb and noun forms of the pedagogical term "leir" in the same line, she imagines a reciprocal model of education in which teaching and learning are mutual. She paints sexual negotiation as an educational process when she offers Robene sex if he follows her lesson:

> Robene, tak tent unto my taill
> And wirk all as I reid
> And thow sall haif my hairt all haill,
> Eik and my madinheid . . .
> I dern with thee bot gif I daill
> Doutles I am bot deid. (34–37, 40–41)

> [Robin, pay attention to my tale/vulva
> And do everything as I instruct
> And you shall have my entire heart,
> And also my virginity . . .
> Unless I have sex with you in a secret place
> Undoubtedly I shall die.]

Makyne's use of "taill" contains multiple valences emphasizing her role as teacher, as she exploits the homophony between "tail" (the sexual parts of a

---

139. Greentree, "Literate in Love," 66. The maiden initiates the conversation and propositions the man in Occitan pastourelles including Giraut de Bornelh's *L'autrier le primier jorn d'aost* and Gui d'Ussel's *L'autrier cavalgava* (Paden, *Medieval Pastourelle*, 1:44–57 and 62–67).

140. *DOST* s.v. "lare" (n.), 2; "lere" (v.), 1.

woman) and "tale" (statement) to instruct Robene to pay careful attention to her verbal instruction as well as her vulva.[141] She introduces her lecture with the didactic formula "tak tent," and she reinforces her role as pedagogue by using the verb "rede" (advise) to characterize her speech.[142] She portrays education as a dynamic process involving both knowledge and action, as she expects Robene to "wirk" (perform actions) according to her teaching.[143] He responds with a litany of excuses for why he cannot follow her instructions, and he asks her to return the next day. His repeated refusals of enthusiastically offered sex have important implications for understanding the poem's sexual politics. While scholars have read Robene's rejection of Makyne's advances as comic, painting him as a fainthearted coward in a humorous inversion of the pastourelle aggressor, I am interested in the pedagogical implications of Henryson's portrayal of a youth rejecting sex from a "fair" (82) and willing maiden.[144] By depicting a young man who refuses sex when it is available, Henryson provides new ways of reading gendered desire in the pastourelle, and he challenges the myth of "natural" masculine aggression. This is especially significant given the poem's context in the Bannatyne Manuscript, which was copied by a male scribe and circulated among an Edinburgh coterie of legal and administrative elites.[145]

After mulling over Makyne's lesson, Robene professes his reciprocal desire, only to be met with an unexpected refusal. "Robene with thee I will nocht deill" (120), she declares, using the same multivalent sexual verb, "deill," that she used earlier to voice her desire. The poem closes with her triumphant laughter:

Malkyne went hame blyth anneuche
Attour the holttis hair.
Robene murnit and Malkyne lewche,
Scho sang, he sichit sair. (122–25)

141. *DOST* s.v. "tail" (n.), 5; "tale" (n.), 1b. Burns notes a similar "Old French homophony between *con* (cunt) and *conter* (to tell a tale) [that] reinforces linguistically the bond between the woman's lips and labia" (*Bodytalk*, 55).

142. *DOST* s.v. "red(e" (v.[1]), 1.

143. *DOST* s.v. "wirk" (v.), 1.

144. Michael G. Cornelius, "Robert Henryson's Pastoral Burlesque *Robene and Makyne* (c. 1470)," *Fifteenth-Century Studies* 28 (2003): 84; Greentree, "Literate in Love," 66.

145. For the manuscript's readership, see Theo van Heijnsbergen, "The Interaction between Literature and History in Queen Mary's Edinburgh: The Bannatyne Manuscript and its Prosopographical Context," in *The Renaissance in Scotland: Studies in Literature, Religion, History, and Culture Offered to John Durkan*, ed. A. A. MacDonald, Michael Lynch, and Ian B. Cowan (Leiden: Brill, 1994); also Verweij, *Literary Culture*, 134–43.

[Malkyne went home full of joy
Over the woodland gray.
Robene mourned and Malkyne laughed,
She sang, he sighed sadly.]

Makyne's jubilation points to the disruptive potential attached to women's laughter. Lisa Perfetti observes that "controlling women's laughter is . . . related to the control of their sexuality" in conduct manuals and literary texts, arguing that "women's laughter could rewrite medieval narratives that victimize women."[146] This is the case in *As I stod on a day*, another pastourelle where the maiden's dismissive laughter in response to her aggressor's advances prompts him to leave her alone.[147] Makyne's laughter after teaching her lesson, articulating her refusal, and leaving unscathed shows how women's laughter was imagined as having the capacity "to turn upside down the positions of power in the pastourelle encounter."[148] *Robene and Makyne* explores the possibilities of women's refusal, suggesting that it can be both effective and empowering. Robene does not become angry or violent in response to Makyne's rejection, nor does he curse her or attempt to change her mind. The pastourelle closes with him sitting alone in the forest with his herd of sheep, "in dolour and in cair" (in sadness and in sorrow) (127). Because "Makyne" can name a stereotypical peasant girl as well as the vulva, her status as educational authority is significant: Henryson portrays Robene, like the male readers of the Bannatyne Manuscript, as having something to learn from lower-status women's genitalia.

In somer quhen flouris will smell likewise features a woman voicing bold desire and speaking in traditionally masculine discourse, although the speech she adopts is not that of the courtly lover but the most obscene verb in Middle Scots.[149] It is the only British pastourelle that portrays a consummated consensual encounter. It contains "features of traditional medieval misogyny and of male fantasy" in its depiction of a peasant girl who voices sassy refusal before she is overcome by lust and issues explicit sexual instructions to the man. It also stages young women as erotic pedagogues, revising the pastourelle stereotype

---

146. Lisa Perfetti, *Women and Laughter in Medieval Comic Literature* (Ann Arbor: University of Michigan Press, 2003), 9, 136.

147. Here the maiden "lowe" (laughed) at her suitor before sending him on his way (23).

148. Perfetti, *Women and Laughter*, 137.

149. *In somer quhen flouris will smell* (*DIMEV* 2584), in Conlee, *Middle English Debate Poetry*, 309–12; van Heijnsbergen, "Bannatyne Manuscript Lyrics," 442–44. While Conlee's edition is useful for its explanatory notes, he has omitted one of the poem's more explicit stanzas from his edition without acknowledgement or explanation, so all quotations and line references in text are from van Heijnsbergen's edition.

of the naïve, exploitable peasant girl, and the maiden uses obscenity to articulate her pleasure.[150]

The poem opens with the male *chanson d'aventure* narrator encountering "a weilfaird may" (an attractive maiden) as he wanders alone "ouir fair feildis and fell" (over fair fields and hills) (6, 2). He calls her "a[ne] cleir undir kell" (fair lady appareled as a virgin), emphasizing her unmarried status with "kell," a close-fitting cap "recognized as a distinctive headdress of young unmarried women" (5).[151] He initiates the conversation in typically courtly fashion, but she cuts his salutation short:

> I halsit hir with hairt maist fre:
> "I luve yow leill, and nocht to le,
> Wald ye me lane—"
> "Out, hay!" quod scho, "My joy, latt be;
> Ye speik in vane.
> Quhat is the thing that ye wald haif?" (20–25)

> [I greeted her most courteously:
> "I love you loyally, I do not lie,
> Would you lend me—"
> "Be quiet, now!" said she, "My joy, stop it!
> You speak in vain.
> What is the thing that you would have?"]

Her interruption is the only time in a British pastourelle that the maiden interrupts the man. She takes the reins in the conversation, dismissing his blandishments with the interjections "Out hay!" and "latt be!" and asking him what he wants from her. "Hay," "a call to attract attention," was used to raise the hue and cry, reminding audiences of the violence undergirding every pastourelle encounter.[152] The man replies that he seeks "na thing bot a kiss" (26). She grants permission and orders him, "Cum tak it now" (30). After the kiss, she is overcome by passion; he relates, "Than kissit I hir anis or twyiss, / And scho to gruntill as a gryiss" (Then I kissed her once or twice, / And she began to grunt like a suckling pig) (31–32). She articulates her enjoyment in terms of eating and consumption when she marvels, "Itss lyk that ye had eitin pyiss

---

150. Van Heijnsbergen, "Bannatyne Manuscript Lyrics," 429. Newlyn argues that the maiden exemplifies "the myth of the lustful woman" and claims that "the poem is indeed a male fantasy, describing a sexual victory over an eager partner, in a situation with no social constraints and no possibilities of guilt for rape" ("Political Dimensions," 81, 83).

151. *DOST* s.v. "kell" (n.[1]), 1.

152. *DOST* s.v. "hay" (interj.).

[pies], / Ye are so sweitt" (35–36). The dialogue emphasizes the dynamic, on-going process of sexual negotiation: he hails her in courtly terms, she asks him what he wants; he declares he wants a kiss, and she grants it to him with an imperative statement of assent. They kiss, and she voices her pleasure, gifts him her flower-bedecked hat in a gendered reversal of the pastourelle gift-giving motif, and notes the physical effects of her arousal: "Ye gar me swett" (You make me sweat) (41), she says.[153]

The maiden's about-face, affirmatively consenting to a kiss after she has interrupted the man's seduction pitch and voiced her unequivocal disdain, could be interpreted as rendering her resistance nothing more than a cursory gesture, another example of the "no-becomes-yes" trope that we saw in *Quhy so strat strang go we by youe, Ane fair sweit may of mony one,* and *When that byrdes be brought to rest.* The man's comparison of her sounds of enjoyment to the grunting of a young suckling pig dehumanizes her as farm livestock and re-calls the stereotype of peasants' sexuality as animalistic and perpetually avail-able, a myth arising from the intersections of gender and class inequality that undergird the genre's sexual politics.[154]

In somer quhen flouris will smell illuminates how even consensual, pleasur-able sex is shaped by larger power imbalances. The maiden does not rush heed-lessly into sex without considering the consequences; rather, she voices acute awareness of the danger of her actions and acknowledges the potential costs of her pleasure. She states, "Yit I feir I sall by full deir / Your sweit kissing" (Yet I fear I shall pay most dearly for / Your sweet kissing) (47–48). She laments, "Allace . . . that I come heir" (44) and exclaims, "Allace . . . I am unwyiss [unwise]" (33) after voicing her enjoyment of the kiss. While we could read these artic-ulations as illustrating women's stereotypical capriciousness, we can also read them as a self-aware acknowledgement of the risks unmarried women face in breaking the rules constraining their sexual conduct. She is cognizant of the dangers associated with erotic expression—including pregnancy, legal penal-ties, damaged reputation, and loss of marital opportunities—and chooses to proceed in spite of those risks, a move that can be read as brave defiance or foolish insatiability.

The maiden takes the reins in the encounter, portraying herself as the man's educator. She tells him, "I trow this labour I may yow leir, / Thocht I be ying" (I suppose I may teach you this labor, / Though I am young) (45–46). Her dec-laration of pedagogical authority in her claim to "leir" him about sexuality

---

153. Fisher discusses the implications of the maiden's gift giving in "Comic Verse," 34–35.

154. *DOST* s.v. "grys" (n.). Andreas Capellanus claims that peasants are inclined to sex "naturally as is a horse or a mule" (naturaliter sicut equus et mulus) (Paden, *Medieval Pastourelle,* 1:54–55).

echoes Makyne's claim to "leir" Robene. She uses obscenity to articulate her lessons, yoking transgressive talk and instruction together in service of female pleasure. She expresses her active participation with words and movements, as she "thraw[s]" (writhes) (40) and voices urgent arousal. Her voice is the one we hear most, as she speaks twenty-six of the forty lines after the kiss. In keeping with her promise to "leir" her partner about erotic "labour," she issues detailed instructions for how he should please her. She orders, "Sen ye stummer nocht for my skippis, / Bot hald your taikill by my hippis" (See that you don't become weary from my jerking movements, / But hold your equipment by my hips) (61–62). She teaches him what to do with his "taikill," using a bawdy term for "men's sexual equipment" to emphasize its usefulness for "labour," and she includes precise bodily coordinates ("by my hippis") in her lecture.[155]

The maiden uses Middle Scots' most explicit sexual verb to voice enthusiastic pleasure when she exclaims, "Your courtly fukking garis me fling" (Your courtly fucking causes me to dance) (57). This is the earliest attested Scottish instance of a woman articulating "fuck," a word otherwise reserved for male speakers.[156] Her application of "courtly," with its valences of elegance and refinement, to her partner's manner of "fukking" recalls his courteous speech at the dialogue's beginning and exposes the carnality underlying his performance of courtliness.[157] She characterizes her enjoyment as "fling," using a term of exuberant physical movement meaning "to spring or dance, to move quickly and with vigour."[158] In vocalizing her pleasure, she does not speak in euphemism; rather, she is blunt and savvy.

The Middle Scots pastourelles feature well-informed virgins, armed with knowledge and equipped with the vocabulary to articulate their desires, who negotiate their erotic encounters as best they can. At the same time, the lyrics highlight the conditions governing consent, portraying maidens who consent only after being threatened with rape, or abandon their refusals after men have made it clear that they will not honor their "no." As Munro notes, we must

---

155. *DOST* s.v. "takil" (n.), d.

156. "Fuk" is articulated by men in Scott's *Ye lusty ladyes, luke* (1560s), Lyndsay's *Ane Satyre of the Thrie Estaitis*, the anonymous *A Lewd Ballet (First quhen the newis begouthe to ryse)* (1571), and the three flytings I discuss in chapter 2. According to the *DOST*, this is the only example before 1700 of a woman voicing the word.

157. *DOST* s.v. "courtly" (adj.), 1. Van Heijnsbergen reads this as a moment of courtly critique, arguing that "the ridicule in this poem is aimed at the act of courtly love itself as much as at the protagonists' clumsy, 'townish' imitation of it" ("Bannatyne Manuscript Lyrics," 431).

158. *DOST* s.v. "fling" (v.), 3. The term was sometimes derogatorily applied by male speakers to women's sexual activity, as in Scott's bitter breakup poem *Returne the hairt hamewart agane*, whose speaker resolves to "lat fillok ga fling hir fill" (let that wanton hussy go copulate to her heart's content) (*Bannatyne Manuscript*, 4:8–9, line 15).

acknowledge that "the construction and constraint imposed on women's (sexual) agency—by a complex network of socio-economic inequality, cultural expectations and relational obligations that encourage submissive femininity and controlled (but available) sexual access—make it likely that there will be many situations in which a woman will engage in sexual exchanges in pursuit of a benefit that, on closer inspection, she does not endorse."[159] These pastourelles remind us of the constraints placed on women's sexual agency, and they illustrate the double bind in which these maidens find themselves. On one hand, their capacity to avoid unwanted sex is inhibited by differences in physical strength, cultural attitudes that invalidate their refusals and insist on their exploitability, and socioeconomic inequalities that impede peasant women from successfully prosecuting their rapes.[160] On the other hand, as the maiden in *In somer quhen flouris will smell* acknowledges, women are penalized for erotic expression in a society that seeks to regulate their sexuality at every turn and views economically disadvantaged women as sexually transgressive in ways that negate their capacity for meaningful consent.

By focusing on women's experiences of the threat of sexual violence, pastourelles can educate male audiences about the pervasiveness and harms of rape, as scholars note that "there is some promising research suggesting the effectiveness of prevention programs that increase men's empathy toward rape survivors."[161] They depict men as having the capacity to learn from women and be enlightened by their experiences. Pastourelles debunk some rape myths while at the same time perpetuating others, and their diverse readerships—of London clerics, Anglo-Norman gentry schoolboys, coteries of young urban men at the Inns of Court, well-connected merchants in Queen Mary's scandal-roiled Edinburgh, mixed-gender households in Staffordshire and East Lothian—illuminate the diversity of lessons they must have taught in their own time. They emphasize women's sexual subjectivity, illuminate the deeply unequal conditions of consent, emphasize the importance of verbal communication in negotiating ethical sex, and shed light on how gender, youth, and economic disadvantage intersect to render peasant women vulnerable to violence. The genre has much to teach contemporary audiences about consent,

---

159. Munro, "Constructing Consent," 931.

160. Dunn discussed the difficulties peasant women faced in prosecuting their rapes in *Stolen Women*, 53.

161. Antonia Abbey and Angela J. Jacques-Tiura, "Sexual Assault Perpetrators' Tactics: Associations with Their Personal Characteristics and Aspects of the Incident," *Journal of Interpersonal Violence* 26, no. 14 (2011): 2884; also John Foubert and Johnathan T. Newberry, "Effects of Two Versions of an Empathy-Based Rape Prevention Program on Fraternity Men's Survivor Empathy, Attitudes, and Behavioral Intent to Commit Rape or Sexual Assault," *Journal of College Student Development* 47, no. 2 (2006). I discuss the educational possibilities of cultivating audiences' empathy in chapter 5.

power, the persistence of rape myths, and the unbroken trajectory of women's stiff-necked resistance, for these pastourelles' depictions of male aggression and entitlement are chillingly familiar to women who experience street harassment today.

I have had too many pastourelle encounters to count. They happen on public transit, on crowded or deserted streets, walking home alone late at night or in broad daylight, in Cleveland, St. Louis, Chicago, London, Philadelphia. The issues that I highlight in medieval pastourelles—rape myths that insist that any woman who travels alone is a legitimate target of sexual attention, misogyny that treats women's refusals as empty "wynde," a culture of entitlement telling men that women are obligated to engage with them, the myth that women's "no" eventually turns to "yes"—are conditions that have shaped my daily life since I was a teenager. They are part of my walks to and from the coffee shop to write this very book. Street harassment disproportionately affects young black women and other women of color, who experience it with greater violence and frequency and less bystander or police intervention.[162] When police officers, armed with guns and the brutal privilege of their position, sometimes harass us, the inequalities in these encounters echo those between penniless peasant girl and armed knight.[163] The problem is severest in economically disadvantaged neighborhoods, illustrating how the intersections of youth, gender, race, and class directly shape women's lives.[164]

These encounters take a toll. They engender anger, anxiety, an infuriating sense of powerlessness, and a fear so sharp that it leaves me breathless like a stab wound to the lung. I never know when they will happen or how they will unfold. The beginning of the script is always the same—a greeting, a shouted "Hey," a comment about my body—but I never know how it will end, whether the men will respect my bodily autonomy or act on their thwarted sense of

---

162. For more on street harassment, see Fiona Vera-Gray, *Men's Intrusion, Women's Embodiment: A Critical Analysis of Street Harassment* (New York: Routledge, 2016) and Laura Bates, *Everyday Sexism* (New York: St. Martin's, 2016), 158–87. For its disproportionate targeting of women of color, see Deirdre Davis, "'The Harm That Has No Name': Street Harassment, Embodiment, and African American Women," in *Gender Struggles: Practical Approaches to Contemporary Feminism*, ed. Constance L. Mui and Julien S. Murphy (Oxford: Rowman and Littlefield, 2002); Holly Kearl, *Stop Street Harassment: Making Public Spaces Safe and Welcoming for Women* (Santa Barbara, CA: ABC-CLIO, 2010), 45–54. Freedman discusses anti–street harassment activism in the United States during the early twentieth century and notes the invisibility of black women's harassment by black men in this discourse in *Redefining Rape*, 191–209.

163. Andrea J. Ritchie examines police sexual misconduct against women of color in *Invisible No More: Police Violence against Black Women and Women of Color* (Boston: Beacon Press, 2017), 104–26. I have experienced police sexual harassment, most notably from members of the Chicago Police Department and Evanston Police Department, on numerous occasions.

164. Miller, *Getting Played*, 48–66.

entitlement, whether I will walk away unscathed or need to run for my life. I have been grabbed. I have been groped. I have had my skirt pulled up by strangers in the street. I have been followed and chased by men, singly and in groups, in cars and on foot. I have had to sprint, to kick, to curse, to use a swift forearm block to stop a man from kissing me after he grabbed me on the street. It is immeasurably important that pastourelles represent these vexed encounters in all their complexity and diversity, because the thing that renders them so terrifying in real life is their unpredictability and refusal to follow a set script. I never know if the man will get angry, if he will leave me alone, if he will follow me for blocks, if he will call me a bitch, if he will grab me or assault me or try to kill me, as my experiences tell me that any of these are possible outcomes of modern-day pastourelle encounters.

The pastourelles teach both medieval and contemporary audiences that sexual violence does not follow a single script or paradigm. They provide possibilities for using literary representations of violence and resistance as tools to understand rape culture and to imagine new models of education and prevention. They furnish us with knowledge about what it is like to live in a culture where one's existence is inflected by the threat of violence and where a web of preexisting disadvantages—gender, class, race, age—function to mark some women as targets. If we listen carefully to the continuities between then and now, we can acquire knowledge with the capacity to generate empathy, to foster understanding, to empower individuals to act, to resonate in our guts and call us to action to incite long-overdue change.

CHAPTER 4

Pedagogies of Pleasure

Peer Education in Medieval Women's Songs

Pastourelles illuminate the violent conditions governing women's sexuality, and they represent women speaking about pleasure and desire with obscene wordplay in the vein of Chaucer's Alisoun of Bath, the most prominent embodiment of "lusty womanhood" in the medieval literary imagination. Alisoun boasts of her vulva's supremacy by declaring, "I hadde the beste quoniam myghte be" (III.608), and she voices her pursuit of carnal satisfaction when she proclaims, "I . . . evere folwede myn appetit" (622–23). Her autobiographical *Prologue* is both obscene and pedagogical, making it a useful starting point for my discussion of lusty women's lyric voices.[1] She addresses her lessons to her fellow wives as well as to men using rhetorical moves lifted from preachers; she shares personal narratives as didactic exempla; and she names her vulva using a dazzling multilingual array of terms—"bele chose" (III.510), "quoniam," "instrument" (132, 149), "queynte" (444, 332), "tayl" (466), "chambre of Venus" (618) and, in one fifteenth-century manuscript, "conte"—to teach about gender, power, and pleasure.[2] Numerous

---

1. Dinshaw examines the clerical and pedagogical dimensions of Alisoun's *Prologue* in *Chaucer's Sexual Poetics*, 113–31.

2. The scribe who copied the *Prologue* in CUL MS Ii.3.26 (c. 1430–50) substituted "conte" for "queynte" at III.444, fol. 114v. In the same manuscript, Alisoun uses "swyve" twice instead of the milder "dighte," making her case for inclusion in the obscene discursive brotherhood of the pilgrimage's "felawes" that I discussed in chapter 1.

scholars have discussed her deployment of bawdiness for instructive purposes.[3] But Alisoun does not stand alone; her use of obscene wordplay to teach a pleasure-focused, assertive brand of female sexuality is part of a larger late medieval discourse of women's peer pedagogy.

Like the pastourelle *Throughe a forest as I can ryde*, with its lesson about sexual violence addressed by a rape survivor to "all" her fellow "medons," English songs from the fifteenth and sixteenth centuries enact common models of same-sex performative pedagogy. They stage women teaching each other about sexuality in communal settings and adopting didactic rhetoric to emphasize collective gendered knowledge, awareness of widespread inequalities, and the pursuit of pleasure. Just as pastourelles teach audiences about the harms of rape and the possibilities of resistance even as they reinforce certain rape myths, these understudied lyrics reveal a paramount focus on pleasure in women's sexual education even as they traffic in misogynist stereotypes of the "lusty maiden"—young, single, often lower-status—who is always ready for sex. In their emphasis on maidens' self-assured pursuit of pleasure, these lyrics contrast sharply with popular discourses that portray young women's erotic expression as engendering shame, regret, and self-inflicted social and spiritual ruin.[4] These fictive women's voices posit themselves as teaching other women how to obtain enjoyment and navigate the hazards of a treacherous world. They do not teach how to please men; rather, they educate women about how to identify, pursue, and reflect on their desires, and they provide scripts to negotiate for pleasure. They acknowledge the risks of violence, unwanted pregnancy, disappointment, and social censure that accompany singlewomen's sexuality, and they show that sex education was imagined as an ongoing process beginning in adolescence and lasting throughout an individual's life. Most importantly, these lyrics represent same-sex peer pedagogy as having the potential to engender changes in sexual culture that are as necessary today as they were in the Middle Ages.

---

3. For more on Alisoun's obscenity, see Alastair Minnis, "From *Coilles* to *Bel Chose*: Discourses of Obscenity in Jean de Meun and Chaucer," in McDonald, *Medieval Obscenities*; Larry D. Benson, "The 'Queynte' Punnings of Chaucer's Critics," in *Studies in the Age of Chaucer, Proceedings 1 (1984): Reconstructing Chaucer*, ed. Paul Strohm and Thomas J. Heffernan (Knoxville: University of Tennessee Press, 1985); Sheila Delany, "Anatomy of the Resisting Reader: Some Implications of Resistance to Sexual Wordplay in Medieval Literature," *Exemplaria* 4 (1992); James W. Marchand, "*Quoniam, Wife of Bath's Prologue* D.608," *Neuphilologiche Mitteilungen* 100, no. 1 (1999).

4. For examples of this discourse, see *Kytt she wept I axyde why soo* (DIMEV 3005); *The maid that yevit hir silf alle*, which urges "maid[s]" to save their "cunte[s]" for marriage; *Wake wel Anot* (DIMEV 6150), which warns a woman to guard her "mayden bour" from "lichure[s]" (2, 4); and John Audelay's *Cantilena de virginibus* (DIMEV 2672), which admonishes, "Your maydynhede defoule ye noght" (4). In Greene, *Early English Carols*, 279 and 235; Rossell Hope Robbins, ed., *Secular Lyrics of the XIVth and XVth Centuries*, 2nd ed. (Oxford: Clarendon, 1961), xxxix.

Medieval Singlewomen and the Turn to Pleasure

Singlewomen's erotic songs depict obscenity as integral to their pedagogy, because their speakers use transgressive talk to address their peers and arm them with knowledge. Women's voices in some pastourelles use obscenity to challenge rape, and in these lyrics, women mobilize it to make a case for their pleasures, showing how it can teach lessons about sexual negotiation. Nicola F. McDonald has found evidence of aristocratic women's obscene conversations in fifteenth-century social games "that [are] productive of women talking, amongst themselves about their bodies and desires, in a sexually suggestive and often plainly indecorous fashion."[5] This playful polyvalence that McDonald identifies, like Alisoun's bawdy talk, is linked to the discourse of female desire in erotic songs, which feature women's voices asserting their value, voicing their desires, negotiating with their partners to ensure a mutually satisfying outcome, and reflecting on their experiences.

These lyrics' emphasis on women's pleasure is rooted in historical changes in England after the Black Death in 1350. With the rise in wages and increased demand for workers due to population shortages, adolescent girls left their families in the countryside to find work as servants or tapsters in the rapidly growing towns.[6] This meant that they could not follow models of mother-daughter instruction central to conduct texts, where mothers frame sex education in terms of risk avoidance. These mothers warn their daughters to wear modest apparel to shield their bodies from men's lecherous eyes: "Doghttor . . . hyde thy legys whyte, / And schew not forth thy stret hossyn [tight-fitting stockings], to make men have delytt" (25–26), instructs the speaker in *The Good Wyfe Wold a Pylgremage*. Another admonishes, "Ne fare not as thou a gyglot were" (Do not behave like a whore), ordering her daughter not to act "as . . . a strumpet other a gyglote" (a harlot or a whore).[7] As Bennett and Riddy remind us, multiple interests speak through these songs, which often deploy women's voices to ventriloquize the interests of male householders or clerics.[8]

---

5. Nicola F. McDonald, "Games Medieval Women Play," in *Chaucer's Legend of Good Women: Context and Reception*, ed. Carolyn P. Collette (Cambridge: Cambridge University Press, 2006), 188. McDonald discusses these games' dependence on "somatic logic" and sexual metaphor at 183–86.

6. For more on singlewomen during the period, see Cordelia Beattie, *Medieval Single Women: The Politics of Social Classification in Late Medieval England* (Oxford: Oxford University Press, 2007); Judith M. Bennett and Amy M. Froide, "A Singular Past," in *Singlewomen in the European Past 1250–1800*, ed. Bennett and Froide (Philadelphia: University of Pennsylvania Press, 1999); Froide, *Never Married: Singlewomen in Early Modern England* (Oxford: Oxford University Press, 2007); Maryanne Kowaleski, "Singlewomen in Medieval and Early Modern Europe: The Demographic Perspective," in Bennett and Froide, *Singlewomen in the European Past*; McIntosh, *Working Women*, 45–84, 156–63.

7. *Lyst and lythe a lytell space* (*DIMEV* 3067), in Mustanoja, *Good Wife*, 216–21, lines 49, 75.

8. Riddy, "Mother Knows Best"; Bennett, "Ventriloquisms."

The many young women who lived in urban areas far from their mothers would have likely turned to their peers for knowledge, since they lived and worked alongside one another in various service professions.[9] These erotic lyrics reflect this shift, for they depict singlewomen addressing their fellow maidens with instruction emphasizing both pleasure and risk.

The rising prominence of erotic songs voiced by savvy, assertive unmarried women points to the emergence of the singlewoman as a legal and social category in the fifteenth century. In a demographic movement comparable to what Rebecca Traister traces in twentieth- and twenty-first-century U.S. history, unmarried women became a political and economic force in the later Middle Ages.[10] This identity is reflected in the rise of a new legal designation, "singlewoman" or *sola* (unmarried woman), alongside the traditional feminine identities of "maiden" (a term typically reserved for a young woman who still lived at home), "wife," and "widow."[11] Women's marital age rose after the Black Death, and they often lived apart from their families for up to a decade before marrying, in their mid-twenties, men of a similar age.[12] One in ten singlewomen in fifteenth-century England never married.[13] This extended and sometimes lifelong state of singlewomanhood, coupled with a lack of surveillance from protective relatives, meant that many young women enjoyed a significant period of sexual exploration and relative erotic and economic autonomy, because the later age of marriage meant that they could accrue their own money and make their own financial decisions. As these songs acknowledge, working singlewomen were still subject to numerous disadvantages arising from their status as single, working, and female, including wages lower than men's, social and legal double standards that punished them more harshly than their male partners for premarital sexual activity, and the threat of violence from employers and fellow servants.[14] In her analysis of medieval

---

9. Many female servants lived with their employers and shared lodgings with fellow singlewomen. Bennett and Froide note how many "singlewomen lived together—in beguinages, spinster clusters, and other such arrangements—in order to support themselves better both materially and emotionally," and Goldberg discusses how singlewomen often lived together in late medieval York. Bennett and Froide, "A Singular Past," 8–10 and 26; Goldberg, *Women, Work, and Life Cycle in a Medieval Economy: Women in York and Yorkshire c.1300–1520* (Oxford: Oxford University Press, 1992), 314–18.

10. Rebecca Traister, *All the Single Ladies: Unmarried Women and the Rise of an Independent Nation* (New York: Simon and Schuster, 2016).

11. Beattie, *Medieval Single Women*, 124–43; *DMLBS* s.v. "*solus*" (n.), 2(b).

12. Bennett, "Ventriloquisms," 191–92; Kowaleski, "Demographic Perspective," 57–58.

13. Bennett, "Ventriloquisms," 191.

14. For cases illustrating the sexual assault or exploitation of female servants by their employers or their sons, see Goldberg, *Women in England*, 95, 121, 123. The Salisbury visitation register features a staggering number of men accused of fornication with their female servants. T. C. B. Timmins, ed., *The Register of John Chandler Dean of Salisbury 1404–17* (Devizes, UK: Alan Sutton Publishing for the Wiltshire Record Society, 1984).

adolescent female skeletons, Mary Lewis notes the unusually high level of back and spinal injuries in the skeletons of young urban women and concludes that they also "carried the burden of respiratory and infectious diseases, suggesting they may have been the most vulnerable group in medieval society."[15] Some servant women faced the forceful restriction of their sexuality by employers, reflected in one pregnancy lament whose speaker comes home the morning after a sexual encounter to face the wrath of her "dame," who hits her and demands, "Sey, thou stronge strumpet, / whare hastu bene?" (Tell me, you vile whore, where have you been?).[16] Laments voiced by pregnant, abandoned singlewomen warn of the risks of this newfound autonomy by bewailing the hazards of maidens' naïveté, men's coercion, and unwanted pregnancy.[17] In contrast, singlewoman's erotic songs celebrate the pleasures and freedoms made possible by living in bustling towns far from parental control.

The late medieval rise of mercantilism and rapid growth of urban trading centers led to increased opportunities for singlewomen and provided new paradigms for sexual negotiation. McIntosh notes that "because prices were not fixed, bargaining took place between seller and prospective buyer about what was to be bought, how much was to be paid, and when. This included an evaluation of the economic honesty and creditworthiness of both parties as well as an assessment of the quality of the wares."[18] Furthermore, "since all sales were accompanied by bargaining or haggling, shopping offered an element of sport" and "provided an opportunity to visit with friends among the sellers and other buyers and catch up on the latest news."[19] This emerging mercantilism lent its logic to a code of masculinity that viewed women's bodies as commodities to be traded among men, but it also gave women a model for erotic negotiation and enabled them to construe their desires in economic terms. Lianna Farber has shown how "consent was . . . considered a necessary element of trade by medieval writers."[20] She argues that the economic consent model of trade shaped the legal consent model of marriage, as the rise of the

---

15. Mary Lewis, "Work and the Adolescent in Medieval England AD 900–1550: The Osteological Evidence," *Medieval Archaeology* 60, no. 1 (2016): 162.

16. *Ladd y the daunce a myssomur day*, lines 48–51. Goldberg cites cases of a chaplain beating his relative Isold with small rods because she "desired to spend her time among boys and company improper to her rank and not to conform with honest behavior" and of a married woman striking her single maidservant Denise Bray on the jaw after she stayed out all night without permission (*Women in England*, 84, 94–95).

17. For more on pregnancy laments, see my discussion of *Up I arose in verno tempore* and *In wyldernes* in chapter 5.

18. McIntosh, *Working Women*, 240.

19. Ibid., 241.

20. Farber, *Anatomy of Trade*, 93–149.

markets reconfigured heterosexual relations. This image of women as sexual and economic agents is reflected in numerous erotic lyrics. In one, a traveling salesman entreats, "Damsele, bye sum ware of me" and encourages his customer to "assay" (try out) his genital merchandise.[21] Another man uses forestalling or "lurch[ing]," a practice of market manipulation that deeply worried civic officials and was associated with women, as a metaphor for his ex-lover's carnal greed: "Her appetyte ys suche, marke who so Lust to trye / A springing founteyne she wyll lurch and clearlye drawe hym drye," he relates.[22] To "lurch" means "to be beforehand in securing (something); to consume (food) hastily so that others cannot have their share; to engross, monopolize (commodities)."[23] This woman devours men's bodies before they reach the marketplace only to discard them once they can no longer satisfy, permanently sapping their virility and denying other women their share of the penis pie. The speaker imagines competition among women for men's bodies, with some greedily buying up all the commodities before their peers can bargain for them. This fierce contest reflects demographic gender imbalances, as women significantly outnumbered men in English market towns and urban centers.[24] Women's capacity in these lyrics to negotiate on their own behalf for both mercantile goods and erotic satisfaction reflects the rise in workers' wages in general, and urban singlewomen's earning power in particular, during the decades after the plague decimated the English workforce.[25] It also reflects the fact that many singlewomen in service industries made sales and deliveries and purchased goods for their employers as part of their work responsibilities.[26]

As with the pastourelles, the gendered voices in these songs are literary creations, fictive constructions that speak in service of certain interests while ignoring others.[27] Some lyrics, such as John Taverner's *The bella*, were written by men, but most are anonymous. Many were copied by male scribes, like the copyist who writes "Bryan hys my name yet" (Brian is still my name) at the

---

21. *We bern aboute no cattes skynnes* (*DIMEV* 6163), in Duncan, *Medieval English Lyrics and Carols*, 182, lines 6, 9. *Sir Corneus* says of cuckolds, "Ther wyves hath be merchandabull, / And of ther ware compenabull" (Their wives have been enjoyed cheaply, / And generous with their wares) (109–10).

22. *My ladye hathe forsaken me* (*DIMEV* 3618.5). I discuss this lyric's portrayal of female desire in chapter 5. For more on the oft-gendered practice of forestalling, which Goldberg defines as "persons going out to buy goods from country producers before they reach the market in order to resell them at a profit," see *Women, Work, and Life Cycle*, 106–8.

23. *OED* s.v. "lurch" (v.[1]), 3(a).

24. Kowaleski notes "the lower sex ratios (that is, more women than men) common in many large medieval towns of northwestern Europe" ("Demographic Perspective," 57).

25. Ibid., 40. Bennett and Froide note that "singlewomen and widows were often poorer than wives, but they were able to use their meager resources—cash, goods, credit, property—with fewer restrictions" ("A Singular Past," 14).

26. McIntosh, *Working Women*, 51–53.

27. Bennett, "Ventriloquisms."

end of a pregnant singlewoman's lament in CUL MS Ff.5.48 (c. 1450), and John Gysborn, a Yorkshire Premonstratensian canon who copied the celebratory lusty maiden's carol *Off servyng men I wyll begyne* in his pastoral commonplace book.[28] Others were used by clerics in sermons to illustrate scripture or to teach lessons about sex and sin. These lyrics' circumstances of copying and transmission highlight how their celebrations of singlewomens' erotic agency teach different lessons in different contexts; in the wrong hands, they can become tools of oppression by perpetuating stereotypes of young working women's lasciviousness and reinforcing rape myths like "she asked for it" and "she liked it."[29] And even though their speakers identify themselves as members of the urban working classes—one praises servant men as lovers, another calls herself a "wanton wench," and others speak as sellers or buyers in the marketplace—they do not highlight fully how age, gender, socioeconomic status, and profession intersect to disadvantage women in the erotic marketplace. This elision of inequality creates the fiction of equal exchange between buyer and seller.

In acknowledging these songs' potential for misogynist misappropriation while focusing on their emancipatory potential, I follow Burns in tracing "how the fictive women's body that conditions a possible misogynous reading on the one hand, also opens the possibility for constructing female subjectivity on other terms" and "stages key moments of resistance to that stereotype."[30] Even though these songs were copied or composed by men, we cannot forget that they were frequently performed by women, who could alter and interpret them as they chose, at dances, banquets, and parish festivals.[31] Moreover, because of their oral origin as carols, many were performed for generations before being written down. Susan Boynton argues that "the 'authorship' of much medieval song can be seen as at least partly collective," while Ingrid Nelson states that "practices of lyric composition . . . meant that it was often meaningless to speak of a single lyric author."[32] These songs' multivocality

28. *The last tyme I the wel woke*, in Cambridge, Cambridge University Library, MS Ff.5.48, fol. 114v. For more on Gysborn and his book, BL MS Sloane 1584, see John B. Friedman, *Northern English Books, Owners, and Makers in the Late Middle Ages* (Syracuse, NY: Syracuse University Press, 1995), 152–53, 325–26.

29. Payne, Lonsway, and Fitzgerald, "Rape Myth Acceptance," 63.

30. Burns, *Bodytalk*, 243, 19n19.

31. Bennett notes that "it was in the vibrant social world of late medieval parishes that these songs were most often performed" and claims that these songs would have been sung at parish festivals, including "at May Day games, at Robin Hood plays, and at church-ales on Whitsun or midsummer or the saint's day of the parish . . . perhaps sometimes at parish festivals hosted by singlewomen themselves" ("Ventriloquisms," 187–88, 198–99).

32. Bennett, "Ventriloquisms," 190–91; Susan Boynton, "Women's Performance of the Lyric before 1500," in Klinck and Rasmussen, *Medieval Woman's Song*, 61; Ingrid Nelson, *Lyric Tactics: Poetry, Genre, and Practice in Late Medieval England* (Philadelphia: University of Pennsylvania Press, 2017), 11.

and performative collectivity enable them to speak about sexuality with the seeming authority of maidens as a community while also highlighting the multiple messages that they contain.

These songs encode a performative peer education grounded in obscenity and the rhetoric of the marketplace, and they would have been enlivened by the bodies and voices of the women who performed them. Their same-sex pedagogy operates on three levels. The first is embedded within the songs, when fictive women's voices address other fictional women with lessons and bawdy advice.[33] The second is when the songs' voices directly speak to and identify with female audiences outside the song, as one speaker addresses "madyn[s] . . . moni here" (many maidens here). The third type of education takes place in performance, when medieval women sang these didactic songs about desire both to and with other living women as they performed them together at social gatherings.[34]

These lyrics reflect feminist scholars' contention that sexual education must take women's pleasure into account, and they are part of a long, understudied pedagogical history that includes nineteenth-century American sex radicals' focus on women's active desire and "insistence upon a women's right . . . to freely discuss such critical issues as contraception, marital sexual abuse (which they defined as emotional as well as physical mistreatment), and sex education."[35] Michelle Fine argues that "the capacity of young women to be sexually educated—to engage, negotiate, or resist—was hobbled by schools' refusal to deliver comprehensive sexuality education" and by the curriculum's focus on pregnancy and disease.[36] Carmody contends that sexuality education must include "the desire for and the negotiating of pleasures" at the same time that it acknowledges the "pressure, coercion, and sexual assault" that is too often part of young people's experiences.[37] She declares that effective pedagogy cannot operate on "an account where women are doomed to potential

---

33. This occurs in *Kytt she wept I axyde why soo*, *The bella*, and *I pray yow maydens every chone*.

34. For more on performance, see Nelson, *Lyric Tactics*, 10.

35. Allen, *Young People and Sexuality Education*; Louisa Allen and Moira Carmody, "'Pleasure Has No Passport': Re-visiting the Potential of Pleasure in Sexuality Education," *Sex Education* 12, no. 4 (2012); Louisa Allen, Mary Lou Rasmussen, and Kathleen Quinlivan, eds., *The Politics of Pleasure in Sexuality Education: Pleasure Bound* (New York: Routledge, 2014); Carmody, *Sex, Ethics, and Young People*, esp. 111–13; Sharon Lamb, "Feminist Ideals for a Healthy Adolescent Female Sexuality: A Critique," *Sex Roles* 62 (2010); Mary Louise Rasmussen, "Pleasure/Desire, Sexularism, and Sexuality Education," *Sex Education* 12, no. 4 (2012). For more on the sex radical movement, which was part of feminism's first wave and flourished between 1853 and 1910, see Joanne E. Passet, *Sex Radicals and the Quest for Women's Equality* (Urbana: University of Illinois Press, 2003), 1, 74–77.

36. Michelle Fine, "Sexuality, Schooling, and Adolescent Females: The Missing Discourse of Desire," *Harvard Educational Review* 58, no. 1 (1988): 29; also Fine and Sara I. McClelland, "Sexuality Education and Desire: Still Missing after All These Years," *Harvard Educational Review* 76, no. 3 (2006).

37. Carmody, *Sex, Ethics, and Young People*, 5.

victimhood and men to be inherently exploitative"; rather, we need "recognition of the diverse ways in which women and men negotiate sexual intimacy based on mutuality and ethics."[38] Singlewomen's erotic songs show that this emphasis on fostering negotiation and seeking mutual pleasure has a far longer history than previously acknowledged.

In these lyrics, singlewomen use obscenity to give full-throated voice to their passions. Bennett calls this genre "songs of lusty maidens," noting that they "emphasize sexual playfulness" and "imagine women . . . as energetic and delighted lovers."[39] While the category is an elastic one, I designate twelve lyrics as singlewomen's erotic songs, since all give voice to female desire outside an explicitly marital context.[40] They feature singlewomen's voices teaching their peers a range of lessons about sexuality while vocalizing a robust sense of their own worth in the sexual marketplace and articulating their wishes with boldness and specificity. Some ventriloquize parental interests or in women's voices depict misogynist stereotypes about women's wantonness, competition with one another, and exploitability, manipulating the fiction of the female voice to grant authenticity to these stereotypes.[41] At the same time, we can hear resistance to patriarchal power when we listen carefully to these voices, for they insist on their right to "be wanton" and bargain for pleasure in the erotic marketplace while protesting sexual double standards. The social disruptiveness of women speaking candidly about illicit sexual experiences is exemplified by the 1405 Wiltshire case of Joan Grokles, who was sentenced to a triple beating for a litany of offences including "adultery with John Lucas as she once told many," "customarily leav[ing] her husband for long periods," "adultery with strangers," and being "a scold causing quarrels amongst her neighbors."[42] Grokles's obscene openness in "t[elling] many" about her adultery illustrates the transgressive power of women's bawdy

---

38. Ibid., 7.

39. Bennett, "Ventriloquisms," 195–96.

40. The lyrics I count as singlewoman's erotic songs, defined as songs voiced partially or entirely by unmarried women on the subject of sexuality or desire, are *And I war a maydyn*; *At the northe ende of selver whyte* (DIMEV 719); *Ate ston-casting my lemman I ches*; *I can be wanton and yf I wyll* (see chapter 5); *If I be wanton I wott well why*; *In an arber of honor, set full quadrant*, attributed to John Walles, in Thomas Wright, ed., *Songs and Ballads with Other Short Poems Chiefly of the Reign of Philip and Mary* (London: Nichols and Sons, 1860), 136–39; *It was a mayde of brenten ars* (DIMEV 2759); *Let be wanton your busynes* (DIMEV 3052; see chapter 5); *O lord so swett Ser John doth kys* (DIMEV 3971); *Off servyng men I wyll begyne*; *I pray yow maydens every chone*; and *The bella*. In her list of "songs of lusty maidens" in "Ventriloquisms," 256n20, Bennett adds to these *Kytt she wept I axyde why soo*, a song about a regretful "lusty maiden" that seems to be voiced by one of her judgmental female friends.

41. Bennett, "Ventriloquisms," 199–200; Riddy argues that the mother's voices in conduct texts articulate the interests of bourgeois urban householders in "Mother Knows Best."

42. Timmins, *Register of John Chandler*, 4. I am grateful to Taylor Sims for drawing my attention to this case.

talk, exemplifying the interplay between sexual rule breaking, obscene story-telling, self-disclosure, and verbal unruliness.

Desire and Danger: *The bella* and *And I war a maydyn*

And I war a maydyn (c. 1500) is a three-quatrain erotic lyric voiced by a woman who narrates her adolescent sexual experiences to educate her less-experienced peers.[43] This bawdy, didactic song survives in multiple manuscripts, including the Henry VIII Manuscript, where it is copied along with the pastourelle *Hey troly loly lo*. It opens with the woman articulating her lesson:

> And I war a maydyn
> As many one ys,
> For all the golde in Englond
> I wold not do amysse. (1–4)

By introducing her account with the conditional conjunction "and" (if), she shares that she is *not* a "maydyn," invoking the term's valences of virginity rather than its broader meaning of youthful unmarried womanhood.[44] She imagines a gendered community of maidens "many one," and she depicts her sexual status as separating her from that collective. She uses her experience to claim that if she could redo her actions, she "wold not do amysse" (do wrong, sin sexually).[45]

The woman contrasts her sexual history ("When I was . . .") with what she claims she "wold" do differently if she could, underscoring the song's instructive import. In the next two stanzas, she details her "wanton" adolescence as an exemplum to illustrate her lesson that maidens ought to follow rules curtailing their erotic expression:

> When I was a wanton wench
> Of twelve yere of age,

---

43. *And I war a maydyn* (DIMEV 520); this version, the only one copied with music, is in BL MS Additional 31922, fol. 106v–107r; Siemens, *Lyrics of the Henry VIII Manuscript*, 56. Text references are to lines in this edition. The other two surviving versions in BL MSS Harley 1317 and Egerton 3537 are even more fragmentary. The song is performed by soprano Emily Van Evera as the opening track of classical ensemble Circa 1500's album *The Flower of All Ships: Tudor Court Music from the Time of the Mary Rose* (2009).

44. *MED* s.v. "maiden" (n.), 1(a) and 2(a); s.v. "and" (adv. and conj.), 5(a).

45. *MED* s.v. "amis" (adv.), 3.

These cowrtyers with ther amorus
They kyndyld my corage.
When I was come to
The age of fifteen yere,
In all this lond, nowther fre nor bond,
Methought I had no pere. (5–12)

She depicts a model of desire that is first "kyndyld" (incited) at the age of twelve, which was women's earliest possible age of marriage according to medieval canon law, even though archaeological evidence shows that they did not typically have their first period until around age fourteen or fifteen.[46] She names her desire as "my corage," taking first-person possession of a word typically assigned to men when used, as it is here, to denote "sexual desire, lust."[47] Her "corage" emerges at the threshold of adolescence, sparked by urbane courtiers who use their "amorus" (amorous affections) to inflame it. The depiction of courtiers as activators of girls' sexuality is reinforced by the Henry VIII Manuscript's status as a Tudor court songbook possibly used to teach music to a young Mary I.[48] Here the song's ventriloquism of exploitative fantasies is especially transparent, for the speaker embodies the enduring stereotype of the precocious twelve-year-old "wanton wench" far more mature than her age.[49] With this portrayal of her as "wanton" and eager for

---

46. Chaucer's Alisoun of Bath first married at "twelve yeer . . . of age," and her autobiographical narrative reinforces this stereotype of the "lusty maiden" as sexually precocious from an early age (III.4). According to medieval canon law, twelve was the minimum age of marriage for girls, as it was thought to signify "incomplete puberty," although some canonists argued that it be moved later to "full puberty," and Cadden notes how "the beginning of sexual maturity" was imagined "as a moment, usually at the age of fourteen (or sometimes twelve for girls . . .)." James A. Brundage, *Law, Sex, and Christian Society in Medieval Europe* (Chicago: University of Chicago Press, 1987), 357; Cadden, *Meanings of Sex Difference*, 145. For the archaeological evidence, see Lewis, "Work and the Adolescent," 142.

47. *MED* s.v. "corage" (n.), 1(b). All the quotations cited in the *MED* entry attribute sexual "corage" to men. One exception not cited by the *MED* is in Peter Idley's *Instructions to His Son*, where the narrator says of the notoriously lustful Queen Semiramis, "Hir corage was to have adoo with all" (Her desire was to have sex with every man) (II.A.1816). Idley, *Peter Idley's Instructions to his Son*, ed. Charlotte D'Evelyn (Boston: Heath for the Modern Language Association, 1935).

48. For more on the manuscript, see my discussion of *Hey troly loly lo* in chapter 3.

49. For more on this long-lived stereotype's contemporary implications, see Annette Lynch, *Porn Chic: Exploring the Contours of Raunch Eroticism* (London: Berg, 2012), 55–75; Kathleen Sweeney, *Maiden USA: Girl Icons Come of Age* (New York: Peter Lang, 2008), 45–66. In Montana in 2013, a judge sentenced a white fifty-four-year-old teacher to only thirty days in jail for raping a fourteen-year-old Latina student, claiming that she was "older than her chronological age." The young woman, Cherice Moralez, committed suicide weeks before her seventeenth birthday. Tom Lutey, "Judge's Remarks about Teenage Rape Victim Spark Outrage," *Billings Gazette*, August 28, 2013, http://billingsgazette .com/news/local/judge-s-remarks-about-teenage-rape-victim-spark-outrage/article_07466a01-c9c1 -5538-a9e0-41f296074b27.html.

her desire to be "kyndyld" by older men, the twelve-year-old girl can be read according to the rules of rape culture as "asking for it." This self-proclaimed, extremely youthful wantonness serves implicitly to justify socially privileged men's exploitation of girls who are multiply disadvantaged by age, gender, and class.[50] Her self-characterization as "wench," with its connotations of lower status and transgressive sexuality, contrasts with "cowrtyers" to emphasize the power imbalances between them.

In claiming that "In all this lond . . . Methought I had no pere," the speaker vocalizes the self-confidence that characterizes the desiring maiden's voices in many of these songs. While she imagines herself vying with other women for supremacy in accordance with misogynist assumptions about women's same-sex competitiveness and clerical stereotypes of feminine pride, she nonetheless voices a strong sense of her own value, which is important in a culture where women are taught from birth that they are less than men.[51] The song's peer-to-peer didactic potential is highlighted in the fragmentary version in BL MS Egerton 3537, which begins, "And I war a madyn as moni *here* is" (emphasis mine), pointing to the presence of "moni" maidens gathered "here" with the female speaker. In the next line, she declares, "for all the gold *in this toune* I wold not don a mise," anchoring her song in a local urban context and underscoring that she is speaking directly to a group of maidens who are physically present to hear her song.[52] She invokes a pedagogical community of young women "here" "in this toune," gathered to hear her lesson about the perils of wantonness and "do[ing] amysse." In performance contexts, this could have been sung by women one to another in the gathering of "moni" "madyn[s]" that the speaker imagines. In spite of its brevity and seeming incompleteness—we never learn *why* she is instructing maidens "not [to] do amysse"—*And I war a maydyn* speaks to the complicated interests that shape these songs. The woman teaches her peers using her experiences and articulates confident self-regard. At the same time, she embodies harmful fantasies of precocious female sexuality and eroticized inequality that authorize young girls' exploitation by older, privileged men.

---

50. Catherine Howard (1518×24–1542), fifth wife of Henry VIII, was sexually exploited by her music teacher, Henry Manox, when she was a young teenager and punished by her grandmother, even though Manox had taken advantage of his position and bragged to his fellow servants, "I have had her by the cunt." Gareth Russell, *Young and Damned and Fair: The Life of Catherine Howard, Fifth Wife of Henry VIII* (New York: Simon and Schuster, 2017), 55, 358–59.

51. This stereotype of female competition and same-sex discord is illustrated by a popular verse aphorism (*DIMEV* 6095): "Two wymen in one howse, / Two cattes and one mowce, / Two dogges and one bone, / Maye never accorde in one." Wright and Halliwell, *Reliquiae Antiquae*, 1:233; Whiting, *Proverbs*, W500.

52. BL MS Egerton 3537, fol. 59r. For more on the manuscript, see Greene, *Early English Carols*, 302.

The bella (c. 1510s), a didactic carol for four voices, similarly echoes misogynous stereotypes, gives voice to young women's ardent desire, and stages peer pedagogy to illuminate the inequalities that must be rectified for women to enjoy agency in the sexual marketplace. Its singlewomen vocalize their curiosity and yearning, only to receive a stern lesson from their "sister[s]."[53] Pedagogy works two ways in this carol: some of the maidens celebrate their desires and declare their intention to enjoy the marketplace's opportunities, while the other female speakers instruct their peers to avoid the risks of sexual congress. *The bella* was written by Tudor composer John Taverner (1490s–1545) and survives with music in both print and fragmentary manuscript versions.[54] Echoing the advice given to young women in conduct manuals like *The Thewis off Gud Women*, whose maternal speaker warns, "Na with na yonge men rouk na roune" (Neither mumble nor whisper with any young man) (18), and another whose narrator cautions, "Tayt nocht with men, na mak raging" (Do not dally with men, nor flirt) (215), the admonitory maidens instruct their sisters to avoid physical contact with men, depicting erotic expression as fraught with hazards.[55] The amorous maidens celebrate their beauty and invite young men to engage in corporeal commerce, while their sisters teach them to reject men's bodily wares, invoking the dangers of unwanted pregnancy and social ostracism.

The song is grounded on the double meanings of the celebratory burden spoken by a group of lusty singlewomen:

> The bella, the bella,
> We maydins beryth the bella,
> The bella, the bella,
> We maydins beryth the bella,
> We maydyns berth the bella,
> The bella, the bella. (1–6)

---

53. *The bella* (*DIMEV* 6162), in *XX Songes*, item 6; additional verses are supplied in NYPL Drexel MSS 4183 and 4184, flyleaves. Text references are to lines in the edition in Appendix 1.

54. For more on *The bella*, see Josephson, *John Taverner*, 181–93; Hugh Benham, *John Taverner: His Life and Music* (Aldershot, UK: Ashgate, 2003), 246–48. The carol also survives in fragmentary manuscript form on three parchment pages from the early sixteenth century that were later clipped to fit as endleaves to a set of seventeenth-century songbooks. In NYPL MS Drexel 4183, verso of front flyleaf, and MS Drexel 4184, recto and verso of back flyleaf (*DIMEV* 6876); also David Fallows, "The Drexel Fragments of Early Tudor Song," *Royal Musical Association Research Chronicle* 26 (1993). The incomplete manuscript version of *The bella* features the treble, bass, and alto parts and includes music, while the version printed in *XX Songes* features the bass part only.

55. *The Thewis off Gud Women* (*DIMEV* 5303), in Mustanoja, *Good Wife*, 176–94; *Incipiunt Documenta Matris Ad Filiam*.

The maidens declare that they "take the prize" among women, that their youth and attractiveness render them victorious in an imagined competition for female supremacy, as they participate in a misogynist framework that pits women against one another and ranks them according to their desirability to men.[56] In this sense, they ventriloquize men's fetishization of women's extreme youth, which we saw in *And I war a maydyn*, with its twelve-year-old "wanton wench" brimming with "corage," and which persists in the contemporary pornographic trope of the schoolgirl temptress. This is reflected in the song's verses, where the lusty maidens describe their bodies by ventriloquizing masculine courtly discourse:

> How praty and proper now that we be,
> So comly under kel-la . . .
> We be madyns fayr & gent
> Wyth yes grey & browys bent. (9–10, 12–13)

> [How pretty and attractive we are now,
> So beautiful under our headdresses . . .
> We are maidens fair and shapely,
> With gleaming eyes and arched eyebrows.]

With their shapely figures, bright eyes, and arched brows, they embody courtly beauty ideals.[57] They tout these attributes to advertise themselves on the sexual marketplace, confident that such features will help them reach a favorable bargain.

The burden carries a corporeal valence: with "bella" as a euphemism for vulva, linked to Alisoun of Bath's naming of her vulva as "my bele chose," it means, "We maidens possess the vulva," or, more crudely, "We girls got the pussy," as they repeatedly vaunt their gendered embodiment.[58] As in the songs of other lusty maidens, their self-celebration presents eroticism as having a prominent element of self-love. By using the first-person plural "we," they highlight the part-song's multivocality and speak collectively about single-women's corporeality with bawdy wordplay.

---

56. *MED* s.v. "belle" (n.[1]), 9(a): "**beren the bell**, to be the best, take the prize, be victorious."

57. These elements' status as courtly commonplaces is exemplified in lyrics such as *Gracius and gay* (*DIMEV* 1654), with the lines "Her eyne byth feyr and gray, / Her brues byth well y-bent . . . Her medyll small and gent" (9–10, 12); and *I saw never joy lyk to that sight* (*DIMEV* 2235), with the description "Her brows thay er both brant and bright, / With two gray lawhyng een" (7–8). Duncan, *Medieval English Lyrics and Carols*, 199–200 and 200–1.

58. *MED* s.v. "bell" (n.); s.v. "bel" (adj.), 1(a): "**bel chose, bel chist**." Alisoun twice refers to "my bele chose"; also Minnis, "From *Coilles* to *Bele Chose*," 172–73.

The maidens in *The bella* use marketplace metaphors to express their desires. They characterize their pursuit of pleasure as a choice to sell themselves, declaring, "We be cum for thys intent / Our selfys now for to sell-la" (14–15), and they identify a target market for their wares and invite those customers to draw nigh: "Cum ner, ye yowng men, behold and see" (8). Their peers also draw on mercantile discourse. "Assay you none of [men's] spyce, / For it will make your bely to swell-la," they warn, drawing on the significance of "spyce" as "commodities" (17–18).[59] By using the experiential verb "assay," meaning "to test the quality of [or] the effectiveness of," to name maidens' erotic activity, and by positing them as the buyers in the transaction, they imagine female economic agents testing merchandise before they choose to buy it, and they use mercantile rhetoric to warn their sisters about unwanted pregnancy.[60]

In one version of the song, the didactic maidens twice instruct, "Syster, loke that ye be not forlorn" (Sister, make sure that you are not [sexually] ruined) (20), underscoring the song's staging of same-sex pedagogy.[61] They caution their peers about the misogynist abuse they will suffer if they become pregnant: "For then every man wyl laugh you to skorn / And say kytt hath got a clap under a thorne," they warn (21–22). They articulate the derogatory language hurled at pregnant singlewomen, including the epithet "kytt," a diminutive form of the name Catherine meaning "a lecherous woman" with negative socioeconomic connotations.[62] The admonitory maidens emphasize the pervasive nature of this gendered disparagement and scornful laughter by attributing it to "every man." They portray penises as piercing "thorne[s]" and premarital pregnancy as a violent, painful "clap" (buffet, blow). In this song, women look out for their sisters by teaching them about misogynist social realities. While female voices warning of pregnancy and social stigma could work to regulate maidens' sexuality, they nonetheless stage a model of sisterhood in which women do their best to teach their peers about navigating an unequal world as singlewomen. The lusty maidens' sorrowful, bewildered response to these admonitions—"Alak, wher shal we then dwel-la?," they won-

---

59. *MED* s.v. "spice" (n.[1]), (e).

60. *MED* s.v. "assaien" (v.), 1a(a).

61. The version from the Drexel Fragments twice features this line. *MED* s.v. "forlosen" (v.), 3(b): "to ruin, disgrace, or dishonor (someone); to debauch (a woman)." This admonition is echoed in *The Goode Wif Thought Hir Daughter*, whose speaker warns, "Loke to thin doughters so wele that thei beth nought forlorne" (180). In Mustanoja, *The Good Wife*, 159–72.

62. *MED* s.v. "kit" (n.[2]). The fifteenth-century pseudo-Chaucerian *Canterbury Interlude* prefacing the *Tale of Beryn* features a sexually duplicitous tapster named Kit and points to the term's lower-status associations by invoking "lewd Kittes / As tapsters and other such" (445–46). The proverbial saying "Kytt hath lost her key" refers to a maiden's loss of virginity and is central to the carol *Kytt she wept I axyde why soo*, where it articulated repeatedly to shame a woman for having sex (Whiting, *Proverbs*, K20).

der in the song's final line (23)—challenges the men who would demean them and shows how patriarchal restrictions on their sexuality make the world a hostile place for them to "dwel." Instead of accepting the inequalities that their sisters warn them about, the maidens express dismay with the despairing interjection "alak" and underscore the need for more livable conditions. The two types of female voices in *The bella* emphasize the tensions between desire and danger that inflect many singlewomen's songs. Here, maidens voice their enthusiasm for erotic commerce at the same time that they acknowledge the perils of breaking the rules, and they protest social inequalities that impede their pursuit of pleasure.

Celebrating Wantonness: *If I be wanton I wott well why*

If I be wanton I wott well why (c. 1500) echoes *The bella* in celebrating singlewomen's sexual freedom with unabashed exuberance and female genital obscenity, as its speaker details her reasons for deferring marriage and voices her wishes for the future.[63] It is copied with music in a slender songbook that includes, in several hands, antifeminist carols, male-voiced amorous songs, Latin religious lyrics, and songs in praise of wine. The anthology was associated with the monks of Durham around 1500, and its songs are filled with references to local customs and dialect.[64] The carol's speaker, a self-described "bold" and "wanton" singlewoman, details how her unmarried status allows her to experience unfettered enjoyment, and she uses the genre's characteristic obscene wordplay and mercantile rhetoric to vaunt her vulva's worth.

The woman vacillates between addressing her lover (7) and referring to him in the third person (8), allowing her song to perform the double function of negotiating sex with her male partner and educating her female peers about desire, mutuality, and the joys of nonpenetrative touch. Far from embodying the unhappy singlewoman desperate for marriage, she claims that she will

---

63. *If I be wanton I wott well why* (DIMEV 2101), in BL MS Harley 7578, fol. 105v; Bernhard Fehr, "Weitere Beiträge zur englischen Lyric des 15 and 16 Jahrhunderts," *Archiv für das Studium der neueren Sprachen und Literaturen* 107 (1901): 58. All text references are to the edition in Appendix 1.

64. This songbook comprises folios 83–102 of MS Harley 7578, a collection of several manuscripts bound together. An early seventeenth-century note by antiquary Joseph Ritson on folio 83v describes the songbook's origins: "An oblong paper-book . . . containing the treble part of a collection of old songs set to musick, used within and about the bishop(ric) of Durham, in the time of queen Elizabeth." For more on the manuscript, see Greene, *Early English Carols*, 304; B. Colgrave and C. E. Wright, "An Elizabethan Poem about Durham," *Durham University Journal* 32, no. 3 (1940); Madeleine Hope Dodds, "Some Notes on 'An Elizabethan Poem about Durham,'" *Durham University Journal* 32, no. 3 (1940).

gladly spend *more* time unmarried: "If I be wanton I wott [know] well why /
I wol fayn tary [gladly delay] another year" (1–2), she announces in the opening lines. In using "fayn" (joyfully, eagerly) to characterize her choice to defer
marriage, she signifies that she embraces her single status wholeheartedly.[65]
She celebrates wantonness as a positive attribute that allows singlewomen to
enjoy their sexuality before finding a marital partner. Like the maidens in *The
bella* and *And I war a maydyn*, she boasts of her attractiveness and demonstrates
self-confidence in her declarations about how "prety" and "myrily" she looks
"every day" (12–13). In her discussion of ethical sexuality, Carmody states that
"the first part of the reflective process encourages awareness of one's own feelings and thoughts in contrast to just complying with someone else's desires,"
which is "important for young women who may be subject to a traditional
gender discourse of compliance to another's needs, particularly opposite-
gender partners."[66] This singlewoman articulates ardent feelings of curiosity
and "wanton[ness]" rather than voicing her compliance to another's wishes.
Instead of expressing regret like the speaker in *And I war a maydyn*, she exults
in her experience when she declares, "I am a woman, I may be bold; / Though I
be lyttyll [physically petite, young], yet am I old [mature, experienced]" (9–10).
She presents her right to "bold[ness]" as grounded in her gendered embodiment, for she claims that her femininity authorizes her to be fearless, daring,
and self-assured in her pursuit of gratification.[67] At the same time, she strenu-
ously denies the dangers of living as a young woman in an unequal world:
"I know nobody wyll do me ill [harm / injure me]" (19) she proclaims, insisting that no violence or other harm will come to her.

Like the maidens in *The bella* advertising their genital supremacy, the singlewoman uses obscene wordplay to proclaim her vulva's desirability in the
carol's burden:

My wanton ware shall walk for me
Shall walk fore me
My prety wanton ware
Shall walk for me
I wyll nott spare to play with / tygh yow[68]
He tygh he tygh he tygh he (3–8)

---

65. *MED* s.v. "fain" (adv.).
66. Carmody, *Sex, Ethics, and Young People*, 114.
67. *MED* s.v. "bold" (adj.), 1(a), 2, and 5(a).
68. Here the scribe has written "play ~~wy w^t~~ tygh yow." Since he has crossed out the preposition
"with," we are left with a choice of the two verbs "play" and "tygh," both with the object "yow."

She praises her vulva as a "ware" that is both "prety" and "wanton." She exploits "ware"'s valences of commodity or merchandise offered for sale to portray her vulva as valuable and vendible.[69] She repeats the adjective "wanton" to characterize both herself ("If I be wanton") and her genitalia ("my wanton ware"), drawing on the term's valences of rebelliousness, exuberance, carnal indulgence, resistance to control, and unbridled abandon.[70] In her repetition of "wanton," she appropriates a word often used in male-voiced texts to disparage women and reimagines feminine wantonness as a positive attribute.[71] By characterizing her vulva as "prety" in addition to "wanton," she claims that it is well-proportioned and pleasing to look at.[72] In her declaration that her "prety wanton ware / Shall walk fore me," the speaker draws on "walk"'s meaning "to be well-known, be the center of public attention, circulate."[73] This verb was sometimes applied to the circulation of money, further underscoring the commercial valences of "ware."[74] Like a vendor in the marketplace, the singlewoman advertises her vulva's attractiveness, value, and readiness for circulation.

The carol's burden features the woman's narration of her amorous behavior: "I wyll not spare to play with/tygh yow" (I will not restrain myself from playfully touching you), she declares. The scribe copies both "play with" and "tygh" as actions that she will do with her lover. She presents herself as the agent of both verbs in accordance with the genre's ethos of assertive feminine sexuality, and she insists she will not hesitate to interact amorously with men.[75] With her subsequent threefold repetition of "he tygh," using a suggestive verb meaning "to touch in a playful or teasing manner" or "to give light or playfully rough touches," she celebrates the joys of erotic touch, as she relates how the object of her affections, an unnamed "he," teasingly handles her vulva.[76]

---

69. *MED* s.v. "ware" (n.[1]), 1. "Ware" also names the vulva in *At the northe ende of Selver Whyte*, whose speaker refers repeatedly to her vulva as "my ware" as she narrates her quest for satisfaction, in Duncan, *Medieval English Lyrics and Carols*, 285–86, lines 5, 7, 17, 19, 29, 31.

70. *MED* s.v. "wanton" (adj. and n.); for further discussion of "wanton" in singlewomen's songs, see chapter 5.

71. The C-text of William Langland's *Piers Plowman* (c. 1387) contains the admonition, "Alle wommen wantowen shulleth be war" (4.143), and Edmund Leversedge's *Vision of Edmund Leversedge* (1465) condemns "this wanton women and undiscreet women" who "shew of . . . hir brestis" (show off their breasts) (124/194). Quotations cited under *MED* s.v. "wantoun" (adj. and n.), (d).

72. *MED* s.v. "prati" (adj.), 3(a) and (b). "Pretty" is used similarly in a unique text of Idley's *Instructions to His Son* copied in 1459 by John Newton in Bodleian MS Laud Misc. 416, fol. 18v, where the vulva is named as "prety tytmose."

73. *MED* s.v. "walken" (v.[1]), 7(c).

74. Thomas Usk's *Testament of Love* (c. 1385) contains a reference to "the leste coyned plate that walketh in money" (33.98); cited in quotations under *MED* s.v. "walken" (v.[1]), 7(c).

75. *MED* s.v. "sparen" (v.), 2a(c). In *My ladye hathe forsaken me*, the speaker says of his former lover's carnal appetite, "She sparethe not for ache nor stytche, but allwaye she ys sure" (18).

76. *DOST* s.v. "tig" (v.); *OED* s.v. "tig" (v.), 1a.

She defies the lesson in *The Thewis off Gud Women*, whose speaker warns her daughter, "It is a takine a full women / To tyg and tait oft with the men" (It is a sign of unchaste women / To teasingly touch and play around with the men) (177–78).[77] This maternal voice uses the threat of being classified among "full women" as a tool to discourage flirtation, but *I can be wanton*'s singlewoman defies those injunctions and celebrates the delights of wanton "tygh[ing]."

Frustrated Desire: *Ate ston casting my lemman I ches*

Ate ston casting my lemman I ches (c. 1300) is voiced by a singlewoman who carefully chooses her lover, only to be disappointed by his erectile incapacity, as she articulates the frustration of unfulfilled arousal.[78] This song is valuable for its vocalization of maidens' agency and disappointment, since it teaches young women that not all sex is pleasurable, even when one has carefully chosen her partner. Its manuscript context reinforces its pedagogical import, because the single-quatrain song is embedded in a Latin sermon on Ezekiel 6:11, a prophecy foretelling the laments of the wicked punished for their idolatry, in a fourteenth-century macaronic sermon collection. The preacher introduces the song as "de suo amasio dixit quondam quaedam puella ad iacturam lapidum" ([what] a certain girl said regarding her lover at stone hurling).[79] The switch from Latin to English, from prose to verse, and from the voice of masculine clerical authority to that of the lusty young woman forces the preacher to inhabit the voiced subjectivity of the maiden who articulates her unabashed eagerness and laments her lover's impotence. This song embedded in multiple sermons illustrates how singlewomen's songs could be used for pedagogical purposes by medieval preachers. It illuminates their complicated work of gendered ventriloquism: even as the moralizing voice of the preacher co-opts the *puella*'s popular song from the oral tradition to illustrate his lesson about lament, linking her despairing "Allas" at her partner's fleeting erection to Ezekiel 6:11's "Heu, heu, heu" (Alas, alas, alas) uttered by the sinful in response to "fallynge bi swerd, hungre, and pestilence," we can still hear

---

77. See also similar lines in *Incipiunt documenta matris ad filiam*, lines 215–18.

78. *Ate ston casting my lemman I ches* (*DIMEV* 728), in CUL MS Ii.3.8, fol. 86r.

79. For a transcription and discussion of the song in its manuscript context, see Theo Stemmler, "More English Texts from MS Cambridge University Library Ii.III.8," *Anglia* 93 (1975): 9; for more on the manuscript, see Siegfried Wenzel, *Macaronic Sermons: Bilingualism and Preaching in Late Medieval England* (Ann Arbor: University of Michigan Press, 1994), 133–40.

her staunchly insisting on her right to "chese" her partners, evaluate their performance, and voice her dissatisfaction.[80]

In four lines, the maiden shares the narrative of her short-lived fling:

Ate ston casting my lemman I ches,
And atte wrastling sone I hym les.
Allas, that he so sone fel!
Wy nadde he stonde better, vile gorel?

She relates that she chose her lover—"my lemman"—at a stone-hurling contest, playing on the testicular valences of "ston."[81] In her first-person declaration "I ches," she invokes the consumer's capacity to choose what they want to buy from an array of options. She evaluates her potential lovers based on the physical strength they display in the stone-putting competition, and she makes her choice based on her observation of their bodies. Unfortunately, her joy at her chosen lover is as fleeting as his erection. She applies the grappling connotations of wrestling to intercourse with her use of the suggestive phrase "atte wrastling" and alludes to the link that conduct texts posit between feminine sexual transgression and community leisure activities, illustrated in one maternal warning to "Goe thou noght to wrastelyng, ne schetyng at the coke, / As it were a strumpet other a gegelotte" (Do not go to wrestling matches, nor cock shooting, / As if you were a whore or a loose woman).[82] Like her fellow lusty maidens, the *puella* refers to her "lemman" in the third person throughout the piece, indicating that she is sharing her narrative with her peers, and she teaches them how to select a lover with care. Although her chosen lover fails to perform as she had hoped, the song is important because it educates her fellow maidens about sexual disappointment and asserts the paramount importance of pleasure. Disappointment, often resulting from a lack of verbal communication, is a common reaction to initial sexual experiences,

---

80. Wyclif, *Holy Bible*, 2:512. Other sermon writers co-opt singlewomen's secular songs from the oral tradition for didactic purposes, typically choosing couplets or short snatches of verse in which the speaker voices her regret over sex, dancing, or accepting gifts from suitors. Examples include *Barred girdel wo ye be (DIMEV 753); Weylawey that iche ne span (DIMEV 6215); Waylaway whi ded y so (DIMEV 6218); Nu her is goo wroth (DIMEV 3753);* and *Were that his don for to done (DIMEV 6221).* For more on women's songs in sermons, see Karin Boklund-Lagopoulou, "Popular Song and the Middle English Lyric," in *Medieval Oral Literature,* ed. Karl Reichl (Berlin: de Gruyter, 2012), 564–66.

81. *MED* s.v. "ston" (n.), 2(c) and 14(a).

82. *The Goode Wif Thaught Hir Doughter,* lines 64–65. The male speaker in the carol *In all this warld nis a meryar lyfe (DIMEV 2471)* similarly emphasizes the link between community leisure activities and amorous dalliance when he boasts of how "maydyns gret and small" "cast hyr love to yonge men" "In daunsyng, in pypynge, and rennyng at the ball" (Duncan, *Medieval English Lyrics and Carols,* 302–3, 9–10, 15).

especially for young heterosexual women, and this poem shares that knowledge with female audiences who would have understood the preacher's vernacular interruption to his Latin homily.[83] Another sermon writer frames a shorter variation of this song by claiming that "wilde wommen" sing it "wan he gon o the ring" (when they go on the ring [dance in a ring dance]).[84] This underscores how peer pedagogy might work in practice: living singlewomen, with real bodies and active desires, could have sung this song about the importance of choice and the possibility of disappointment together as they danced with men and evaluated them as potential lovers.

This song stages a singlewoman deploying double entendre—the suggestive terms "ston" and "wrastling" and the erectile verbs "stonde" and "fel"—to voice her desire and dissatisfaction as she educates her listeners about male bodies.[85] She insults her "amasio" (lover) as "vile gorel" (worthless glutton), implying that his weight or intemperance has compromised his erectile capabilities and voicing her anger at his inability to perform. The preacher emphasizes the man's impotence through repetition when, several lines later on the same folio, the sermon switches back into the sexually frustrated singlewoman's voice and reiterates her song's final couplet. "Allas, that he so sone fel, / Wy nadde he stonde, vile gorel?" she says once more, her thwarted arousal reverberating through the sermon. The preacher is forced to vocalize her fury and lament as his own and to identify with the disappointed lusty maiden for his audience's edification, as he serves as the medium through which the fictive girl instructs the maidens in his congregation.

The Erotic Marketplace: *Off servyng men I wyll begyne* and *I pray yow maydens every chone*

The marketplace model for erotic relations is central to *Off servyng men I wyll begyne* and *I pray yow maydens every chone*. In *Off servyng men I wyll begyne* (c. 1450), a carol copied into a Yorkshire Premonstratensian canon's notebook, a singlewoman exultantly details why she is attracted to her lover, a smartly

---

83. Carmody argues that it is especially important for young women to have the language to voice their disappointment and understand that it is a normal reaction (*Sex, Ethics, and Young People*, 23–24, 59).

84. This song also survives as "Atte wrastlinge mi lemman I ches / And atte ston kasting I him for les" in an early thirteenth-century sermon against such songs in Cambridge, Trinity College MS B.1.45 (c. 1250), fol. 41v. The two versions are discussed together in Boklund-Lagopoulou, "Popular Song," 558–59; Reichl, "Beginnings," 207–8.

85. *MED* s.v. "stonden" (v.), 10(e). This verb is deployed elsewhere in its erectile sense by one of the singlewomen in *I pray yow maydens every chone* and by many of the wives in *A Talk of Ten Wives on Their Husbands' Ware*.

dressed urban servant.[86] Like the maiden in *Ate ston casting my lemman I ches*, she does not address him directly, choosing instead to name him in the third person. This suggests that she is addressing other singlewomen and underscores the carol's pedagogical import: she teaches her peers about masculine desirability, and she reinforces her lesson by repeatedly marveling at her own happiness. The song reflects the historical reality that male and female servants, working and living in close proximity to one another, were often one another's sexual partners.[87] The speaker describes her lover as "mynyon trym" (smartly dressed like a court favorite) (6), a phrase denoting a well-dressed and sexually desirable young man or woman, and she repeats the adverb "tryme" (smartly, neatly, finely) multiple times (19, 21) to emphasize how her lover's fashionable apparel constitutes his attractiveness.[88] She methodically describes each element of his appearance and stylish clothing—"his bonet" (13), his "here" (15), "his dublett" (17), "his shertt" (19), "his coytt" (21), "his kysse" (23), "his hoysse" (25), "his face" (29)—beginning with the top of his head and moving down to the tight garment covering his nether regions before traveling back up his body. After proclaiming that "his hoysse [is] of London black" (25), the woman boasts, "In hym ther ys no lack" (27), suggesting with her linking of these lines through rhyme that with regard to his penis there is "no lack." She connects his semblance of masculinity to his desirability: "His face yt ys so lyk a man . . . Who can butt love hyme than?" she asks (29, 31). Like the maidens in *The bella* who depict penises as commodities available for maidens to purchase at their peril, she uses mercantile rhetoric to assign extravagant monetary value to her lover's acts of physical affection, declaring, "His kysse is worth a hundred pounde" (23).

Off servyng men I wyll begyne enthusiastically celebrates urban singlewomen's pleasure, and its exuberance is reinforced by the carol's burden:

So well ys me begone,
Trolye, lole,
So well ys me begone,
Troly, loly. (1–4)

---

86. *Off servyng men I wyll begyne* (*DIMEV* 4208), in BL MS Sloane 1584, fol. 45v. The speaker's lover embodies the "galaunte," a popular fifteenth- and sixteenth-century literary figure embodying reckless urban masculinity.

87. In York in 1417, John Bown caught two of his servants, John Waryngton and Margaret Barker, having sex in an upper room used for hay storage. Angry that Waryngton had already slept with another of his female servants, Bown used threats to force him to marry Barker (Goldberg, *Women in England*, 110–14).

88. *OED* s.v. "trimly" (adv.), 2. See also the carol *Mynyon goo trym* (*DIMEV* 5732), about a smartly dressed London "mynyon" and his mistress, featuring the burden, "Mynyon go trym go trym / And mynyon go trym go trym, / Thys ys a song thes men a mong / Of mynyon go trym" (1–4), in *XX Songes*, item 9.

The phrase "troly loly," a popular song refrain "expressing gaiety or idle abandon," is repeated after each line of the song's verses in addition to recurring
twice in the burden.[89] A performance of this carol would entail thirty-four
repetitions of the phrase, and its function punctuating the woman's description of her dapper servant-lover contributes to its sense of overall jubilation
over singlewomen's amorous delight. Her exclamation "So well ys me begone!"
means "How overwhelmed I am by happiness!" or "How lucky am I!"[90] Like
other lusty maidens, she speaks with conviction regarding her own worth. The
carol assigns monetary value to the man's "kysse" and tells men what consumer goods they need to buy—a "bonet of fine scarlett" (13), a "dublett of
fine satyne" (17), a "shert well mayd and tryme" (19), a "coytt . . . tryme and
rownde" (21), "hoysse of London black" (25)—to attract singlewomen's affection. In contrast to the competing discourses of desire and danger in *The
bella* and *And I war a maydyn*, the woman in *Off servyng men I wyll begyne* celebrates her fulfillment and good fortune with unrestrained jubilance.

These songs of lusty maidens use obscenity to animate the marketplace,
and its practices of self-advertising, bartering, bargaining, and selling, with titillating erotic possibilities. They reflect the mercantile economy's rapid growth
and emphasize women's increased participation in it, even as some of them
confer fictions of parity on a social world still deeply inflected by inequality.
The speaker in *If I be wanton I wott well why* names her vulva as "my wanton
ware," casting it as her treasured commodity; the singlewoman in *Off servyng
men I wyll begyne* boasts that her lover's "kysse is worthe a hundred pounde";
the maiden in *O Lord how swett Ser John dothe kys*, a poem I do not discuss
here, states, "Ser John to me is proferyng / For hys plesure ryght well to pay,
/ And in my box he puttes hys offryng"; and the maidens featured in *The bella*
attempt to "selle" themselves to "yowng men," only to be warned against
"assay[ing]" men's genital merchandise.[91] This metaphor of commercial exchange is most explicit in *I pray yow maydens every chone* (c. 1500), an erotic
dialogue that stages a singlewoman teaching her younger peers about agency
and negotiation.[92]

---

89. *MED* s.v. "trolli-lolli" (interj.).

90. *MED* s.v. "bigon" (v.), 3.

91. *O Lord, so swett Ser John dothe kys*, in Duncan, *Medieval English Lyrics and Carols*, 284–85, lines
14–16.

92. *I pray yow maydens every chone* (*DIMEV* 2248), in CUL MS Additional 7350, Part 1, Box 2, fol.
iiv; Greene, *Early English Carols*, 280. Text references are to lines in the edition in Appendix 1. On the
manuscript context, see Rossell Hope Robbins, "The Bradshaw Carols," *PMLA* 81, no. 3 (1966). A
twentieth-century analogue is African American husband-and-wife comedy duo Butterbeans and Susie's song "I Want a Hot Dog for My Roll" (1927).

In this spirited conversation between a sausage seller and his ravenous customers, set in a bustling marketplace, gendered voices exploit the culinary and
penile senses of "podynges" (sausages) to work out a transaction that is pleasing to both parties. Female desire entails the capacity to bargain and the prerogative of rejection, as the man invites the women to "assey" his merchandise before
they choose to "bey" it. The song ends on an instructive note, as "the yonger
maydes" learn from their older peer who successfully negotiates the purchase
of the sausage seller's ware. Demonstrating its continued currency, the metaphor of "podynges" as penises for sale in an urban marketplace crowded
with eager female consumers is also central to the late seventeenth-century
broadside ballad titled *Joyful NEWS for maids and young women. Being an account of a ship-load of white puddings, brought from a far country, and are to be
expos'd to sale at reasonable rates, for the benefit of old and young women.*[93] This
song celebrates the arrival in London of a ship laden with "fine white Puddings" in a scene similar to the merry, chaotic marketplace in *I pray yow maydens
every chone*: "Young Women they come flocking / To buy this dainty ware."
One of the woodcuts accompanying the ballad depicts a standing female figure
next to a money chest, emphasizing the song's portrayal of women's economic
agency.[94]

I pray yow maydens every chone provides singlewomen with a detailed script
for sexual negotiation. The sausage seller first identifies a target market for his
merchandise, reflecting merchants' increased focus on women as consumers
during the period.[95] Addressing "maydens every chone [each and every one],"
he presents his "podynges . . . plenty" as an answer to the maidens' "nede" in-
dicated by their "grete mone" (2–6). He attributes to them the power "to
bye" and invites them to "cumme heder to [him]" and test out his wares
(5–6). Rather than accosting them, he encourages them to approach him if
they wish. This carol's negotiation script opens with the sausage seller's identification of the maidens' desire—named in insistent corporeal terms as
"nede"—and his awareness that he has the capacity and willingness to fulfill
that need ("I have plenty"). This is followed by a respectful invitation, as he
asks the singlewomen if they want to purchase his "podyng" and welcomes
them to draw nigh. He engages in teasing wordplay with the women as he
insists on employing the gastronomical sense of the term, asking, "Will ye

---

93. *Joyful NEWS for maids and young women* (London: Printed for Philip Brooksby, Jonah Deacon,
Josiah Blare, and John Back, 1688–1692). *Andoille* (sausage) is a figurative term for the penis in medieval French literature: *OEFD* s.v. "andoille" (n.).

94. See the description for the fifth illustration, which includes "a standing female figure" and
"money chest, treasure-chest, money box," Broadside Ballads Online, http://ballads.bodleian.ox.ac
.uk/view/sheet/29957.

95. McIntosh, *Working Women*, 244–45.

have of the podynges that lye on the shelf? . . . Will ye have of the podynges cum out of the panne?" (5, 9). His customers deploy the term's somatic sense when they declare, "Nay, I will have a podyng that will stand by hymself . . . No, I will have a podyng that grows out of a man!" (6, 10). Their insistence on the term's genital connotations underscores these songs' persistent association between women's voices, obscenity, and assertive sexuality. The women argue individually why they, rather than their sisters, deserve the prized sausage: "Therfor I pray yow hartely, / Lett me have hym, for that will I bye," one says, declaring her intention to "bye" and using the adverb "hartely" (fervently, earnestly, fiercely) to characterize the heartfelt intensity of her plea (9–10).[96] Each maiden argues that her need for the sausage is stronger than her peers': "For he may helpe me at my nede, / Therfor I pray yow now let me spede [be successful]," one declares (13–14). Even as she stresses the urgency of her yearning with the temporal adverb "now" and the noun "nede," she refrains from making demands of her partner, instead using the supplicatory verb "pray" to characterize her request.

The song's sexual script places paramount significance on women "assay[ing]" men's wares before they pay. The empowering possibilities for women of this marketplace ethos of "try before you buy," spurred by competition among different vendors for singlewomen's buying power, is reinforced by texts like the comic poem *Lyarde*, which imagines the penis trade at Westmorland's Appleby Fair, where "As wyfes makis bargans, a horse for a mare, / Thay lefe ther the febill and brynges ham the freche ware" (As wives make bargains, a horse for a mare, / They leave there the feeble men and bring home the fresh commodities), and Jean Bodel's Old French fabliau *Li sohait des vez*, which features a fantastical penis market stocked with every kind of cock imaginable.[97] The song's script has singlewomen testing out men's genitalia before they make a commitment to buy it, with one asking its price and having the ability to pay due to the savings she has accrued from working more years than her younger peers.

The carol closes by staging two pedagogical moments illustrating the relationship that the genre posits between sexual education and negotiation. The first is a lesson that the winner of the sausage bidding war directs to the owner of her newly acquired "podyng," demonstrating the efficacy of the song's ne-

---

96. *MED* s.v. "hertili" (adv.)

97. *Lyarde*, lines 45–46; *Li sohait des vez*, in Willem Noomen and Nico van den Boogaard, eds., *Nouveau recueil complet des fabliaux*, 10 vols. (Assen, Netherlands: Van Gorcum, 1983–98), 6:261–72. For more on the penis-market motif in Old French fabliaux, see Bill Burgwinkle, "Medieval Somatics," in *The Cambridge Companion to the Body in Literature*, ed. David Hillman and Ulrika Maude (Cambridge: Cambridge University Press, 2015), 20; Burns, *Bodytalk*, 55–60. I am grateful to S. C. Kaplan for directing my attention to this fabliau.

gotiation script. The second is a moment of peer instruction between "th' elder mayde" and "the yonger maydes." The elder singlewoman pays forty pence for the vendor's sausage after testing its suitability for her needs:

"What is the price?" seyd th' elder mayde.
She spake ffirste, for she had asseyd.
Fourtie pens she gave hym in hande,
& seyd she wold have him to lerne hym stand. (19–22)

Penis jubilantly in hand, she applies masculine pronouns to the "podyng" and collapses the distinction between seller and ware with her twofold repetition of "hym." She voices her eagerness for her partner's arousal with the volitional construction "wold have." She frames her wishes in instructional terms, as she declares her intention for the penis to "lerne" to become erect and depicts herself as the agent of this erectile education. Like the assertive maidens in Middle Scots pastourelles, she teaches her partner about sex using obscene pedagogy.

The song's closing lines depict the younger maidens learning about negotiation from their knowledgeable peer. Their response to her successful transaction demonstrates that they have taken her lessons to heart:

Than spake the yonger maydes every chone,
"Happie thou art, for now thou haste one!
But and we lyve another yere as plese God we may,
We will have eche of us one what so ever we pay." (23–26)

The younger singlewomen recognize that the elder maid's buying power, bargaining skills, testing of merchandise before buying, and self-confident "spak[ing] ffirste" result in her enjoyment: "Happie thou art," they enviously cry, highlighting "happie"'s valences of blessedness and good fortune.[98] They declare their intention to use their newly acquired knowledge the next time they go to market, demonstrating her lesson's effectiveness.

In addition to privileging women's satisfaction and providing a model of successful negotiation, this carol reflects marketplace-based historical realities for medieval singlewomen. The penis-sausage's price of forty pence, an exorbitant sum at the time, is especially provocative. One could read it as the price of a dowry in a competitive marriage market, as a form of male prostitution, or as representing the high symbolic value of enjoyable, carefully negotiated,

---

98. *MED* s.v. "happi" (adj. and adv.), 1.

mutually consensual sex for a singlewoman.[99] Because of their ability to accrue money and exert economic agency, these women have bargaining power in the sexual market. The song's representation of penises as "podynges" reflects urban singlewomen's living conditions, for the women's negotiations with the sausage seller constitute an obscene echo of the transactions between street vendors and singlewomen that occurred daily in English towns. Since many poorer and single urban residents did not have the means to cook food themselves, because a working kitchen was an expensive operation requiring money and space that most singlewomen did not possess, they relied on hot sausages and other "fast foods" sold by specialty street cooks for sustenance.[100]

Songs of lusty maidens imagine the marketplace as a locus of erotic negotiation, a space where singlewomen navigate sexuality's dangers and delights in search of the best deal. The speakers embrace the rhetoric of choosing, buying, bargaining, and selling to articulate the process by which they seek fulfillment of their desires. The maidens in *The bella* proclaim, "We be cum . . . our selfys for to sell-a." Chaucer's Alisoun declares her intention to enjoy the pleasures afforded by the marketplace: "I wol renne out my borel [merchandise] for to shewe," she says (III.356). In contrast, conduct texts imagine the market as a dangerous site of young women's sexual ruin. One mother warns, "Goe thou noght to market thi borell for to selle, / Ne goe thou noght to taverne thi wurchipe to felle" (Do not go to market to sell your merchandise, / Nor go to the tavern to ruin your good reputation), linking the hazards of selling one's merchandise at the market and destroying one's reputation at the tavern.[101] Another illustrates her instructions for modest dress by comparing the maiden who displays her "legys whyte" to a butcher exhibiting raw animal flesh for sale: "The bocher schewyth feyr his flesche, for he wold sell hit full blythe" (The butcher shows off how fair his meat is, because he is eager to sell it).[102] In both instances, maidens' participation in "selling" carries negative sexual connotations, pointing to patriarchal anxieties generated by the freedoms and pleasures that the market affords young women.[103]

---

99. I am grateful to Dyan Elliott and Ruth Mazo Karras for discussing the meanings of the pudding price with me.

100. For the increasing reliance of English urban residents on hot cooked fast food, including "podynges," see Martha Carlin, "Fast Food and Urban Living Standards in Medieval England," in *Food and Eating in Medieval Europe*, ed. Martha Carlin and Joel T. Rosenthal (London: Hambledon Press, 1998); McIntosh, *Working Women*, 243.

101. *The Goode Wif Thaught Hir Doughter*, lines 52–53. Riddy interprets these lines as discouraging the feminine unruliness associated with the stereotype of the "common huckster" in "Mother Knows Best," 75–76.

102. *The Good Wyfe Wold a Pylgremage*, lines 25, 30.

103. Elizabeth Fowler traces how poets use "misogyny . . . to legitimize a critique of the money economy," as "the sexual is constituted in economic terms, and the economic is construed in sexual

These songs' lusty maidens speak in complicated, nuanced ways about desire and power because they educate one another and advocate for a "bold," agency-driven female sexuality, even as they fulfill misogynist stereotypes of young women as incorrigibly wanton and downplay the disproportionate violence that the pastourelles expose. One can read the portrayal of the twelve-year-old "wanton wench" in *And I war a maydyn* as a pernicious fantasy that casts young girls as adults in order to authorize their exploitation, and hear echoes of male-constructed beauty standards in *The bella*. Mediated and shaped as they are by the interests of fathers, clerics, and urban householders, these songs nonetheless voice an irresistible call to pleasure. They represent obscene wordplay and active verbal communication as resulting in satisfaction for both partners. Bennett argues that "it is possible to hear female resistance to male authority in these songs—to hear that, when women speak, they speak in disruptive and rebellious ways."[104] These songs' emphasis on assertive sexuality and confident negotiation was part of a prevalent model of peer education that operated alongside more familiar discourses urging singlewomen to behave cautiously and chastely, allowing us to see a richer lineage of desire and pleasure in young women's sexuality education.

"Ladyis, leir thir lessonis": Married Women's Peer Pedagogy in the Alewife Poem

This same-sex obscene pedagogy is likewise central to lyrics voiced by married women, namely "gossips songs" or "alewife poems," a popular late medieval subgenre tied to women's increased prominence in the brewing industry. In the generations after the Black Death, an uptick in ale consumption coupled with urban population growth led to a thriving alehouse culture in English towns. The alehouse, like the marketplace, was an important site of women's economic advancement because wives and widows brewed ale and ran alehouses, often employing singlewomen as tapsters or barmaids.[105] The alehouse emerges in fifteenth- and sixteenth-century alewife poems as a gathering place for wayward wives, who assemble to drink with their female friends, squander their husbands' money, and engage in raucous, sexually explicit confessional conversations. The alehouse is a locus of transgressive speech, female

---

terms." Fowler, "Misogyny and Economic Person in Skelton, Langland, and Chaucer," *Spenser Studies* 10 (1992): 246, 263.

104. Bennett, "Ventriloquisms," 200; also Burns, *Bodytalk*, 7.

105. Judith M. Bennett, *Ale, Beer, and Brewsters in England: Women's Work in a Changing World 1300–1600* (Oxford: Oxford University Press, 1996); McIntosh, *Working Women*, 140–81.

friendship, and peer pedagogy, a perverse schoolhouse where married women use obscenity to teach one another how to obtain satisfaction and to show, in the spirit of feminist consciousness-raising, that their individual experiences of mistreatment and thwarted desire have collective political import. Second-wave feminists argued that "the purpose of consciousness-raising was to get to the most radical truths about the situation of women in order to take radical action," and we see this same phenomenon in the nineteenth-century sex radical movement, in which hundreds of women all over the United States wrote in to sex radical periodicals with testimonials that "broke the code of silence shrouding their sexual subordination in marriage" and shed startling light on widespread structural conditions.[106] By bitterly bemoaning their lack of satisfaction and limited agency, women in alewife poems critique the institution of marriage itself, using obscenity to arrive at a shared awareness of structural inequalities and to teach one another the importance of women's pleasure. The genre contains its fair share of embedded misogyny, portraying women as duplicitous, prone to drunkenness, incorrigibly foulmouthed, and cruel to their husbands, whose penises they mockingly compare to maggots and slugs. However, these lyrics also demonstrate the pedagogical possibilities of female friendship and knowledge sharing. They show how obscene conversations can shed light on deeply entrenched inequalities, allowing women to comprehend the systematic nature of their dissatisfaction.

Poems from the late fifteenth and early sixteenth centuries like Dunbar's *The Twa Cummars* (c. 1507), Skelton's *The Tunnyng of Elynour Rummyng* (c. 1521), and the anonymous *A Talk of Ten Wives of Their Husbands' Ware* (1453–1500) stage peer-to-peer didactic "counsaile," frank sexual disclosure, defiance of husbandly authority, laughter, and communal alcohol consumption.[107] The genre's linking of female community, obscenity, and education is central to Dunbar's *Tretis of the Tua Mariit Wemen and the Wedo* (c. 1507), where three women deploy pedagogical rhetoric to frame their obscene, wine-fueled conversation as educational.[108] Dunbar draws liberally from popular misogynist discourse to construct his three ladies, who embody antifeminist stereotypes

---

106. Kathie Sarachild, "Consciousness-Raising: A Radical Weapon," in *Feminist Revolution: An Abridged Edition with Additional Writings*, ed. Redstockings of the Women's Liberation Movement (New York: Random House, 1978), 148–49; Passet, *Sex Radicals*, 68–73.

107. Dunbar, *The Twa Cummars* (DIMEV 4495), in *Poems of William Dunbar*, 1:180–81; Skelton, *The Tunnyng of Elynour Rummyng* (DIMEV 5126) in *Complete English Poems of John Skelton*, 186–200; *A Talk of Ten Wives on Their Husbands' Ware*; the related *Good Gossip* carols (DIMEV 3795 and 2274), in Greene, *Early English Carols*, 251–53. Phillips gives an overview and listing of the "alewife group" or "gossips songs" in *Transforming Talk*, 148; for more on these poems, see Bennett, *Ale, Beer, and Brewsters*, 122–44.

108. *The Tretis of the Tua Mariit Wemen and the Wedo* (DIMEV 6134), in *Poems of William Dunbar*, 1:41–55. Text references are to lines in this edition.

of women teaching one another how to cuckold, deceive, disparage, and dominate their husbands, as when the Wedo instructs her married friends to "be as turtoris in your talk, thought ye haif talis brukill" (be meek as turtledoves in your talk, though you have morally weak vulvas) (262).[109] The alewife poem's genre conventions provide a specific purpose for the poem's misogyny, for the women's conversation is recorded by an eavesdropping narrator, who turns to his male "auditoris" (listeners) at the final lines "to forge a community among men who share . . . knowledge" (527–30).[110] This encodes a double model of same-sex education in the poem: women edify one another about men's bodies, women's desires, strategies for obtaining enjoyment, and the importance of marital and erotic "chois," while men teach their peers about women's duplicity and transgressive talk.[111]

Dunbar's women name genitals as "talis brukill," "a stif standand thing" (486), "hard geir [equipment]" (232), "my thing" (389), "his lwme [tool]" (175, 96), "his pen" (135) "his yerd" (130, 220), and "that snaill tyrit" (tired slug) (176).[112] They use obscenity to propose more pleasurable, tenable alternatives to lifelong marriage (56) and to describe their ideal lovers (78–89). The first wife teaches about aged male sexuality by graphically detailing her aged husband's impotence; the second uses her experience to teach how young, vigorous men like her husband can become impotent from excessive sex; and the twice-married widow instructs her "sisteris" about how to pursue pleasure by describing her practices, which include hosting hedonistic banquets for her crew of lovers. She shares how she nips suggestively on the fingers of the men seated on either side of her, leans hard against the man behind her, plays footsie with the one in front of her, and winks flirtatiously at the rest (490–94). Like the singlewoman who explains how she "ches[es]" her lover, Dunbar's women emphasize the positive possibilities of "chois" for women (46, 54–55,

---

109. Bawcutt, "Images of Women"; Wendy A. Matlock, "Secrets, Gossip, and Gender in William Dunbar's *The Tretis of the Tua Mariit Wemen and the Wedo*," *Philological Quarterly* 83, no. 3 (2004). For more on the medieval literary trope of the widow as obscene teacher, see Jan M. Ziolkowski, "The Obscenities of Old Women: Vetularity and Vernacularity," in Ziolkowski, *Obscenity*.

110. Matlock argues that the poem "depicts the 'horrifying' exchange of the knowledge between the women, not only as a warning to men but also as a means for men to penetrate women's exchange, to gain an understanding of women's strategies, to use that knowledge to recuperate any power that women might appropriate, and to forge a community among men who share that knowledge" ("Secrets, Gossip, and Gender," 210–11).

111. Phillips discusses the pedagogical nature of the women's conversation in *Transforming Talk*, 134–46, esp. 140. Cornelius discusses the poem's links to medieval poetic traditions of advice-giving women and notes its double act of same-sex pedagogy, in "Genre, Representation, and Perspective in Dunbar's 'Mariit Wemen,'" *Scotia* 23 (1999).

112. Perfetti suggests that women's heavy drinking, laughter, and obscene jesting work together to challenge and reinforce misogyny, in *Women and Laughter*, 99–125.

75, 208). They ardently express their desire and envision a model of sexuality in which women are knowledgeable, enthusiastic partners.

The women portray their relationship with one another as an intimate gendered bond while using pedagogical rhetoric to frame their alcohol-fueled conversation. They use the language of sisterhood, as when the Wedo addresses her friends as "my sueit sisteris deir" (145).[113] She performs peer pedagogy within the poem and describes it as a habitual practice: "Than said I to my cummaris in counsall about, / 'Se how I cabeld yone cout with a kene brydill'" (Then I said to my council of gossips, / "See how I secured that colt with a sharp bridle") (353–54). She describes a group of "cummaris in counsall," a wise circle of sisterhood, and relates how she used the didactic imperative "se" to teach her lesson about marital power to her peers.[114] The Wedo mimics scholastic disputation when she initiates the discussion: "Reveill," she demands, "gif ye rewit that rakles conditioun . . . Or gif ye think, had ye chois, that ye wald cheis better" (Reveal if you regret that imprudent condition [of marriage] . . . Or if you think, if you had choice, that you would choose better) (43, 46). This bawdy disputation begins with a question posed formally to the disputants, who respond by enumerating their positions on marriage in alternating speeches, as the widow appropriates this academic strategy as a tool for sexual education. Later she asks one wife to share her marital experience and instructs her, "syne my self ye exem on the samyn wise" (then you examine me in the same way) (156). She structures their conversation as one in which the speakers deliver alternating speeches on the same subject and uses "exem" (examine), a term from educational and legal contexts, to name their exchange.[115] This poem imagines sexual education as a reciprocal, relational practice among friends, with women candidly confessing their experiences, listening to one another, asking questions, and providing commentary.

The Wedo uses pedagogical rhetoric to frame her lecture about how to manipulate one's husband and pursue pleasure. She introduces her sexual autobiography as "my preching" (249) and instructs her "sister[s]" (251), "Wnto my lesson ye lyth and leir at me wit" (Listen to my lessons and learn from my wisdom) (257). She concludes by urging, "Ladyis, leir thir lessonis and be no lassis fundin" (Ladies, learn these lessons so that you are not taken for young girls) (503), again using the terms "lesson" and "leir."[116] She frames her "lesso-

---

113. The women use "sister" as a term of address elsewhere in lines 251 and 151.

114. Phillips discusses the pedagogical import of this moment, arguing that "the Wedo teaches her charges the value of trustworthy female companions" (*Transforming Talk*, 142–43).

115. See quotations listed under *DOST* s.v. "exeme" (v.[1]).

116. Phillips notes how the Wedo's speech is a tool of same-sex community-building: "by insuring that her congregation shares a common set of knowledge, the Wedo's confessional instruction ushers these wives into . . . a community of 'cummaris'" (*Transforming Talk*, 143).

nis" as valuable knowledge separating the women from the girls, and she instructs her sisters to "leir" what she teaches them. In response, they laugh merrily and promise to follow her "teching":

> Quhen endit had hir ornat speche this eloquent wedow,
> Lowd thai lewch all the laif and loffit hir mekle,
> And said thai suld exampill tak of her soverane teching
> And wirk efter hir wordis, that woman wes so prudent.
> Than culit thai ther mouthis with confortable drinkis,
> And carpit full cummerlik, with cop going round. (505–10)

> [When this eloquent widow had ended her highly embellished speech,
> The others laughed loudly and loved her greatly,
> And said they should take example of her incomparable teaching
> And work after her words, for that woman was so prudent.
> Then they cooled their mouths with comfortable drinks,
> And chatted just like sisters, with the cup going round.]

The Wedo's obscene confession is characterized as "soverane teching" better than any other. Its objective is realized by her sisters, who promise to "exampill tak" and "wirk efter her wordis." Stressing the didactic valences of "exampill," the women interpret the Wedo's words as "a guide to conduct" and a model for corporeal action.[117] In their promise to model deeds after words with the active verb "wirk," the wives show how obscenity was imagined to shape the speakers' peers' sexual behaviors. Emphasizing the same-sex closeness and camaraderie of their educational process, the woman drink and chat "full cummerlik" in the fashion of female intimates.[118]

Their hearts lightened by their wine-soaked consciousness-raising session, the three women leave with new knowledge about identifying and acting on their desires. While the methods they share entail duplicity and deceit, illustrating the antifeminist commonplace that women are never to be trusted, they nonetheless stage women educating one another about more pleasurable alternatives to their current plights. The *Tretis* and other alewife poems are valuable for imagining how women could adapt pedagogical strategies like disputation for knowledge-building purposes, for they mobilize obscene personal narrative to increase awareness of the larger inequalities that obstruct feminine pleasure, such as denying women the right to "assay" their partners before they marry, lack of marital "chois," and double standards that enable

---

117. *DOST* s.v. "example" (n.), 1.
118. *DOST* s.v. "cummer" (n.[2]).

men like the second wife's husband to be "ane huremaister" (a whoremaster) while punishing the same behavior in women. Dunbar's women demonstrate that sexual education is an ongoing process as valuable for wives and widows as it is for singlewomen. They portray it as a practice that is at once humorous and convivial, that fosters sisterly intimacy and empowers its participants with knowledge.

Lusty Maidens, Guerilla Pedagogies, and Abstinence-Only Education

These songs voiced by lusty women encode a performative pedagogy in which women teach a model of assertive sexuality that is "wanton" and "bold," that advocates "assay[ing]" lovers before making the commitment of marriage, that results in women's "happie[ness]" and acknowledges danger and disappointment at the same time that it celebrates pleasure. Their lessons serve as a valuable counterdiscourse to the teachings about sexuality in the mother-daughter conduct texts, which encourage young women to "just say no." Scholars have shown how this paradigm in the form of contemporary abstinence-only-until-marriage education denies young people "the human right to sexual information" and forecloses the possibility of ethical sex by assigning heterosexual women the role of gatekeepers, eliding the existence of female desire, refusing to acknowledge young people as sexual subjects, and constructing negotiation in primarily negative terms.[119] Since 1982, the U.S. federal government has earmarked over two billion dollars for programming that stresses abstinence until marriage, even though these programs are often medically inaccurate and fail to provide information about contraception.[120] As of March 2018, thirty-seven states required that abstinence be cov-

---

119. Nancy F. Berglas, Norman A. Constantine, and Emily J. Ozer, "A Rights-Based Approach to Sexuality Education: Conceptualization, Clarification and Challenges," *Perspectives on Sexual and Reproductive Health* 46, no. 2 (2014); Hannah Brückner and Peter Bearman, "After the Promise: The STD Consequences of Adolescent Virginity Pledges," *Journal of Adolescent Health* 36 (2005); Carmody, *Sex, Ethics, and Young People*, 41; Douglas B. Kirby, "The Impact of Abstinence and Comprehensive Sex and STD/HIV Education Programs on Adolescent Sexual Behavior," *Sexuality Research and Social Policy* 5, no. 3 (2008); John Santelli et al., "Abstinence and Abstinence-Only Education: A Review of U.S. Policies and Programs" and "Abstinence-Only Education Policies and Programs: A Position Paper of the Society for Adolescent Medicine," *Journal of Adolescent Health* 38 (2006).

120. This earmarking of federal funds for abstinence-only-until-marriage programs was introduced during the Reagan administration and greatly increased by 1996's Title V abstinence-only-until-marriage state grant program, which was renewed in 2009. Sexuality Information and Education Council of the United States, "Dedicated Federal Abstinence-Only-Until-Marriage Programs Funding by Fiscal Year (FY) 1982–2017," May 2017, http://www.siecus.org.

ered in schools' sexual health curriculum, and twenty-five states mandated that schools stress the importance of refraining from intercourse until marriage, in spite of research demonstrating that comprehensive sex education is far more effective at minimizing the negative outcomes of teenage pregnancy, disease, and violence.[121]

I know how necessary it is to resist pedagogies that seek to silence women's pleasure, nullify their desire, and fix them into roles as passive gatekeepers rather than active, ardent erotic subjects. The education I received as a teenager was the model of "abstinence and then some" championed by the Religious Right in the 1990s and early 2000s, when the True Love Waits cult of sexual purity encouraged virginity pledges, purity rings, and chaste courtship instead of the wanton promiscuities of dating and sexual experimentation.[122] In eleventh grade family living class at my Protestant school, the teachers separated the boys from the girls and spent one hour giving us the essentials of sex education. Any sexual activity was grounds for expulsion, so they sought to dissuade us from all experimentation. For us girls, that meant emphasizing that we were tasked with keeping boys' lust at bay because, we were told, "boys are visual creatures prone to temptation." If we rolled up the waistbands of our uniform skirts to make them shorter than knee-length or unbuttoned more than the collar button of our shirts, we were pulled aside for warnings about emulating the notorious temptress in Proverbs 5–7 whose "steps lead [men] straight to the grave" and injunctions that we "not cause our brothers to stumble."[123] We were taught about the shame and regret we would experience if we gave in to temptation, and about the inevitabilities of unplanned pregnancy and vaginal tearing. "Don't hold hands with boys," our teacher said. "Then you'll want to kiss, and then you'll want to have sex. And if you have sex and get pregnant, you will rip and tear down there when you give birth." We shuddered.

---

121. Guttmacher Institute, "State Laws and Policies: Sex and HIV Education," last updated March 1, 2018, https://www.guttmacher.org/state-policy/explore/sex-and-hiv-education.

122. Anke Bernau, *Virgins: A Cultural History* (London: Granta, 2007); Christine J. Gardner, *Making Chastity Sexy: The Rhetoric of Evangelical Abstinence Campaigns* (Berkeley: University of California Press, 2011); Jen Gilbert, "Between Sexuality and Narrative: On the Language of Sex Education," in *Youth and Sexualities: Pleasure, Subversion, and Insubordination in and out of Schools*, ed. Mary Louise Rasmussen, Eric Rofes, and Susan Talburt (New York: Palgrave Macmillan, 2004); Sara Moslener, *Virgin Nation: Sexual Purity and American Adolescence* (Oxford: Oxford University Press, 2015).

123. The current dress code includes a disproportionate focus on young women's modesty and states, "Parents of girls need to support CCA in seeing that young ladies makes [sic] appropriate and modest dress selections." Cornerstone Christian Academy, "Dress Code Handbook Excerpt," accessed November 30, 2017, https://ccacornerstone.com/uploads/1496344014_DRESS%20CODE%20Handbook%20excerpt.pdf.

Many of us, including me, wore purity rings that were gifts from our parents. They served as perpetual reminders that our choices were not our own, that our virginity belonged to God, our parents, and our future husbands. Our education contained no mention of disappointment, of the supreme awkwardness of fitting two bodies together for the first time, of negotiation, of female desire, of anyone's pleasure. Instead, we were instructed that our virginity was the most precious gift we could give to the husbands whom God had already chosen for us. We were admonished that if we had premarital sex—or "fornication," as one teacher called it, since he feared that even uttering the word "sex" would tempt us to do the deed—we would be like a prematurely opened Christmas present or a piece of chewed-up gum. "Can you imagine getting a present on Christmas morning and seeing that somebody else had already opened it? How would you feel, seeing the wrapping paper all crumpled and torn? That is how your husband will feel if you have sex before you marry him," went one pro-purity pedagogical commonplace. "Imagine that your husband asks you for a stick of gum, and you give him a piece that's already been chewed up. Nobody wants that."

But we resisted. Driven by curiosity and the heady tang of rebellion, we asked each other questions, and we shared hushed confessions of the rules we had broken in cars and in basements. We did our best to teach one another the little information that we knew, to expand on our limited body of knowledge. We warned one another about the dangers of unscrupulous boys, like the aspiring youth pastor in the senior class who addressed the student body during worship services and shouted, "I want you all to be *so* on fire for God!," but propositioned younger girls on the side. One of my sister's friends taught the other girls how to give a blow job, using one of the jumbo pickles from the green plastic pickle barrel that sat on the counter in our cinder-block church basement lunchroom. Another afternoon during study hall, three of my friends took matters into their own hands and drove to the Barnes and Noble bookstore at Great Lakes Mall to educate themselves by reading the sex books, only to spot a woman from church. They quickly returned the forbidden books to their shelves and fled.

It is moments like those, where conversations between peers challenge, revise, or augment the incomplete or erroneous things that they have been taught about sex, that we can find the roots of pedagogies that empower individuals as sexual subjects and encourage ethical sexuality. It is time that we take those whispered conversations seriously, particularly in contexts where young women's erotic expression is curtailed, silenced, and cloaked with shame. Our illicit conversations were not enough to teach us everything we needed to know, to make up for the information about sex and safety that had been withheld from us, to save us from assault or unwanted pregnancy, or to wash off the shame, hot and sticky like summertime tar. But they were a start, a form of small-scale guerilla pedagogy, a series of slim but unmistakable glimmers slanting radiant through the heavy blinds meant to block out the sunlight of knowledge. It is important to recover what has been forgotten about same-sex obscenity's efficacy as pedagogy, and to explore its potential for producing knowledge that enlightens and empowers, that reduces the risk of harm and paves the way for pleasure.

CHAPTER 5

Songs of Wantonness

Voicing Desire in Two Lyric Anthologies

I did not expect to shed tears over the two manuscripts that are the focus of this final chapter, but I cried over the Ritson Manuscript (BL MS Additional 5665) at the restricted manuscripts table in the British Library's Rare Books and Music Reading Room. I was transcribing *Be pes ye make me spille my ale*, a dialogue between rapist and victim that ends with the woman wishing fiercely for knowledge that could have stopped her attack. I had read a printed edition of the song many times, but the experience of seeing the survivor's anguished words in their neat brown Anglicana script—even though I knew they were mediated by the male scribe who wrote them—and inhabiting her first-person *I* as I carefully typed the song, letter for letter, affected me in a way I did not anticipate, and my eyes filled with tears. Horrified, I breathed deeply and willed them not to fall, because I did not want to embarrass myself in a reading room full of scholars. My moment of connection with the lyric subjectivity of the fictional rape survivor was marked by messy, ungovernable feeling, and I could not pretend to be an impassive researcher. Instead, my tears betrayed the unruly affective potential of living, embodied subjects encountering voices from the past whose sufferings are recognizable to them. They demonstrated that those who read or perform fictive lyric voices can be affected in unexpected ways.

The next summer, in the sunny upstairs reading room at the Weston Library in Oxford, it happened again. I was transcribing Bodleian MS Ashmole

176's rape narrative *I can be wanton and yf I wyll*, whose speaker fights off her attacker with every tactic she can muster before he finally overpowers her. Once more, the experience of seeing the woman's words in their looping sixteenth-century secretary hand and encountering her voice in all its wrenching immediacy as fresh on that July afternoon as it was five hundred years ago seized me by the heart, and I found myself crying in the reading room among the researchers. Embarrassed by my loss of composure, I attempted to gather myself and kept working.

My experiences transcribing these lyrics, of unbidden tears incited by encounters with the manuscript page, point to the possibilities of affective reading and shed light on the social and pedagogical workings of lyric voice across time. In the act of transcription, words on the page are processed letter by letter through the transcriber's eyes and brain and heart. Transcribing, like scribal copying and vocal performance, requires one to encounter the text with unexpected intimacy, to inhabit the speaker's subjectivity while reproducing their song. The act of transcription, and my own lived experiences as a woman in this world, meant that I identified with the fictive rape survivor whose song was written many centuries ago. I identified with her so deeply, with her fierce struggle and her horrified realization of her own powerlessness and her choice to survive at all costs, that the tears came and I could not stop them.

This final chapter focuses on the potential for educative empathy in two sixteenth-century manuscript anthologies of early Tudor court songs, the Ritson Manuscript and MS Ashmole 176. By "educative empathy," I mean that these lyrics, especially when read in their manuscript context, can encourage audiences to empathize with the victims of harassment, exploitation, coercion, and sexual violence and to use the knowledge acquired from that affective identification for individual and social change.[1] Affect can enable readers to recognize feminist histories of disempowerment and violation, and it carries the capacity to form transhistorical coalitions based on shared experiences of suffering. Ahmed claims that "feminism itself can be understood as an affective inheritance; how our own struggles to make sense of realities that are

---

1. This strategy of using empathy to facilitate learning has been shown to be effective in reducing violence perpetration and is central to numerous programs seeking to combat campus sexual assault. Flood explores the necessity of victim empathy to reducing rape and discusses the role of education and exposure to "sensitizing experiences" like hearing women's accounts of violence in generating empathy in *Where Men Stand: Men's Roles in Ending Violence against Women* (Sydney: White Ribbon Foundation, 2010), 19, 33. See also Erin Casey and Tyler Smith, "'How Can I Not?': Men's Pathways to Involvement in Anti-Violence against Women Work," *Violence against Women* 16, no. 8 (2010); Foubert and Newberry, "Effects of Two Versions"; John Foubert, *The Men's and Women's Programs* (New York: Routledge, 2011); Peter A. Schewe, "Guidelines for Developing Rape Prevention and Risk Reduction Interventions," in *Preventing Violence in Relationships: Interventions across the Life Span*, ed. Schewe (Washington, DC: American Psychological Association, 2002).

difficult to grasp become part of a wider struggle, a struggle to be, to make sense of being," and I argue that we can claim these lyrics as part of an "affective inheritance" of gendered struggle that persists to this day.[2] They depict the first-person experiences of rape survivors and victims of exploitation in vivid, unflinching detail, encouraging audiences to identify with their perspectives, acknowledge them as sexual subjects, and understand how structural inequalities manifest in individual harms. These anthologies' lyrics, which include courtly complaints, pregnancy laments, rape narratives, and impotence songs, are ripe for analysis after centuries of scholarly oversight. They touch on threads running through previous chapters of this book, including the dynamics of rape and consent, the politics of negotiating conflicting desires, the workings of bodily intersubjectivity, and the possibilities of wantonness. Through what Dinshaw calls the "process of touching the past," the communities of affective learning created by obscene lyrics extend across time.[3] These lyrics possess the potential to facilitate transformative learning in the scribes, transcribers, readers, and performers who encounter them in the sixteenth century as well as in our own time.

These two anthologies, which share songs from the same early Tudor court milieu, illustrate how scribal choices have educational import, for they stage competing versions of gendered power and probe the intersubjective violence that results when desires come into conflict under conditions of inequality. Like the pastourelles in the Welles Anthology, which take on richer meaning when read in their manuscript context alongside courtly lyrics, women's songs, and misogynist pieces, these "songs of wantonness" both illuminate and are inflected by the courtly complaints surrounding them. By staging these contrasting perspectives and mobilizing obscenity's educative potential, the anthologies explore the power dynamics in erotic relationships and probe how those dynamics are shaped by physical space, bodily difference, and intersectional disadvantage.

Sharing Spaces: Bodies, Readers, and Communities

Educative empathy is generated by the sharing of three kinds of space in the lyrics of the Ritson Manuscript and Ashmole 176: the material space of the manuscripts, where songs from divergent perspectives share textual territory

---

2. Ahmed, *Living a Feminist Life*, 20.
3. Dinshaw, *Getting Medieval*, 54.

with one another; the spatial dimensions of violence and desire that the songs explore; and the transhistorical space for affective recognition and coalition building that these lyric voices enable. These miscellanies of courtly love lyrics and obscene verse share affinities with other manuscripts circulating in and around the Tudor court, including the Henry VIII Manuscript, which contains songs attributed to the notoriously lusty young king; the Fayrfax Manuscript (BL MS Additional 5465, c. 1500–1501), a songbook containing religious and secular English pieces that was likely used at Henry VII's court or Prince Arthur's court at Ludlow; and the Devonshire Manuscript (BL MS Additional 17492), copied by a coterie of aristocratic women close to Henry VIII and Anne Boleyn in the 1530s.[4] Ashmole 176 and the Ritson Manuscript share multiple lyrics, including the popular devotional carol *Come over the borne, Bessye* and the pregnancy lament *Up I arose in verno tempore*. Both contain courtly songs that contrast sharply with neighboring lyrics about corporeality and violence.[5] These "songs of wantonness" focus on the role of physical space in conflicts between desiring bodies, and they give voice to the perspectives of rape survivors, unwillingly pregnant singlewomen, and victims of harassment.

Joshua Eckhardt examines how the compilers of early modern verse miscellanies frequently copied polite love lyrics and obscene erotic verses together.[6] He argues that this practice became extremely popular in the early decades of the seventeenth century, "particularly among young men at the universities

---

4. I discuss the Henry VIII Manuscript in chapter 3. The songs of the Fayrfax Manuscript are printed in John Stevens, *Music and Poetry in the Early Tudor Court* (London: Methuen, 1961), 351–85; see also Roger Bowers, "Early Tudor Courtly Song: An Evaluation of the Fayrfax Book (BL, Additional MS 5465)," in *The Reign of Henry VII*, ed. Benjamin Thompson (Stamford, CT: Paul Watkins, 1995). For an edition of the Devonshire Manuscript, see Lady Margaret Douglas and Others, *The Devonshire Manuscript: A Woman's Book of Courtly Poetry*, ed. Elizabeth Heale (Toronto: Centre for Renaissance and Reformation Studies, 2012); for more, see Christopher Shirley, "The Devonshire Manuscript: Reading Gender in the Henrician Court," *English Literary Renaissance* 45, no. 1 (2015); Raymond G. Siemens and Johanne Paquette, "Drawing Networks in the Devonshire Manuscript (BL Add. MS. 17492): Toward Visualizing a Writing Community's Shared Apprenticeship, Social Valuation, and Self-Validation," in *New Ways of Looking at Old Texts, V: Papers of the Renaissance English Text Society, 2007–2010*, ed. Michael Denbo (Tempe: Arizona Center for Medieval and Renaissance Studies, 2014). Siemens discusses the Ritson, Henry VIII, and Fayrfax manuscripts together in *Lyrics of the Henry VIII Manuscript*, 9.

5. Cornish's *Adewe adewe my hartes lust* is copied in Ashmole 176 as well as the Henry VIII Manuscript, fol. 23v–24r. Carol Meale notes how the four-line lyric *Alas, to whom shuld I complayne*, one of Ashmole 176's love complaints, is excerpted from a longer political poem linked to Edward Stafford, Duke of Buckingham, who was executed in 1521, demonstrating how lyrics could circulate and be repurposed for different uses. Carol Meale, "London, British Library, Harley MS 2252: John Colyn's 'Booke': Structure and Content," *English Manuscript Studies 1100–1700* 15 (2009): 92; also Boffey, *Manuscripts of English Courtly Love Lyrics*, 84–85.

6. Eckhardt, *Manuscript Verse Collectors*.

and Inns at Court."[7] In proposing a model of "contextual reading," a methodology that I use here, Eckhardt argues that "a poem's full significance . . . may extend beyond its text to the affiliations and resonances that it develops among other texts and in its various contexts, no matter how local or even physical."[8] He claims that "by routinely countering or complementing love poetry with erotic or obscene verse, manuscript verse collectors arguably formed an unrecognized poetic genre" that he christens "anti-courtly love poetry."[9] Eckhardt and Arthur F. Marotti trace how poems "too misogynist or sexually explicit . . . to print," like the enormously popular *Naye phewe, nay pische* voiced by a woman as she is assaulted, were routinely copied alongside courtly lyrics.[10] This is the case in one miscellany copied by a student at St. John's College, Cambridge, in the late sixteenth century, which includes *Naye phewe, nay pische* as fourth in a sequence of five courtly lyrics and songs of coercion that depict "women variously refusing and submitting to men."[11]

Like the manuscript verse collectors whom Marotti and Eckhardt associate with the universities and Inns of Court, the scribes of the Ritson Manuscript and Ashmole 176 several decades earlier copy lyrics from divergent perspectives alongside one another. By clustering female-voiced songs about violence and exploitation and surrounding them with complaints by disconsolate men, the copyists shed light on the inequalities that courtly ideology both perpetuates and elides. In their choice to include the voices of those who are marginalized, victimized, and thwarted in collections that present the aristocratic male perspective as the norm, the scribes create the opportunity for transformative learning, which Patricia Cranton defines thusly: "Through some event . . . an individual becomes aware of holding a limiting or distorted view. If the individual critically examines this view, opens herself to alternatives, and consequently changes the way she sees things, she has transformed some part of how she makes meaning out of the world."[12] Cranton shows

---

7. Ibid., 4. Marotti also discusses "the bawdy and obscene verse so popular in the manuscript system" and locates it in "all-male environments" of educated individuals in London, Oxford, and Cambridge. Arthur F. Marotti, *Manuscript, Print, and the English Renaissance Lyric* (Ithaca, NY: Cornell University Press, 1995), 76–82.

8. Eckhardt, *Manuscript Verse Collectors*, 14.

9. Ibid., 5.

10. Eckhardt discusses the poem on 1–4, and he locates it in thirty-eight manuscripts and provides a transcription at ibid., 173–74. Marotti discusses its popularity in manuscript collections through the mid-seventeenth century in *Manuscript, Print*, 76–78, 268.

11. Eckhardt, *Manuscript Verse Collectors*, 4; Bodleian MS Rawlinson poet. 85, fol. 1–5.

12. Patricia Cranton, "Teaching for Transformation," *New Directions for Adult and Continuing Education* 93 (2002): 64; also Moira Carmody, "Sexual Violence Prevention Educator Training: Opportunities and Challenges," in Henry and Powell, *Preventing Sexual Violence*, 158–69; Jack Mezirow, "An Overview on Transformative Learning," in *Contemporary Theories of Learning: Learning Theorists—in Their Own Words*, ed. Knud Illeris (London: Routledge, 2009).

how, by exposing individuals to perspectives that challenge or diverge from their own, educators can encourage critical reflection and a new awareness of inequalities, and they can spur individuals to consider how to navigate or eradicate those inequalities. By placing disparate perspectives in the same tex-tual space—women's voices articulating the harms of rape and the despera-tion of unwanted pregnancy, men's voices decrying women's sexual voracity and lamenting impotence—the manuscripts' compilers set up jarring contrasts that expose courtly ideology's distortions, even if that exposure was not their original intention.

In addition to functioning as a material space that facilitates learning by pre-senting competing perspectives, the manuscripts provide a transhistorical af-fective space for educative empathy through the relationship between what Dinshaw calls "forms of desirous, embodied being that . . . engage in hetero-geneous temporalities."[13] In copying the words of a first-person *I*, sixteenth-century scribes and twenty-first-century transcribers inhabit that speaker's subjectivity for a space of time until the copying is complete, just as singers embody the lyric persona during performance. Bruce W. Holsinger argues that choosing to view relationships between past and present in terms of empa-thetic connection "will allow us to take seriously the pleasures and pains that the music of the dead . . . continues to produce upon, against, and within the bodies of the living."[14] Obviously not every reader, scribe, or performer of these songs would be moved to tears by them, nor would they all necessarily feel compassion for the singlewoman contemplating infanticide or the tapster assaulted on the job. Nonetheless, these lyrics' strategic staging of marginal-ized perspectives and use of both affective and obscene language have the capacity to mobilize audiences' empathy for knowledge-building purposes.

Since the Ritson Manuscript is a choir repertory for group performance rather than private reading, the parts of women in its rape narratives and preg-nancy laments would have been performed by Exeter Cathedral choristers, young boys who "liv[ed] together in a special house with an adult cleric to look after them" and sang and attended the local grammar school together.[15] Woods shows that English schoolboys learning Latin had to memorize speeches by "unhappy and sympathetic female victims" that encouraged iden-

13. Dinshaw, *How Soon Is Now?*, 4.

14. Bruce W. Holsinger, *Music, Body, and Desire in Medieval Culture: Hildegard of Bingen to Chaucer* (Palo Alto, CA: Stanford University Press, 2001), 348–49. Karl F. Morrison provides a "history of com-passion" in *"I Am You": The Hermeneutics of Empathy in Western Literature, Theology, and Art* (Princeton, NJ: Princeton University Press, 1988).

15. Nicholas Orme, *Education in the West of England, 1066–1548* (Exeter: University of Exeter Press, 1976), 42–55, esp. 44.

tification with victims of sexual violence, such as Claudian's *On the Rape of Proserpina*, which was a cornerstone of the grammar curriculum.[16] They practiced arguing both sides of rape cases in declamation exercises, as "rape scenes function in this tradition as the paradigmatic site for working out issues of power and powerlessness."[17] Fifteenth-century English songs voiced by schoolboys emphasize the master's physical dominance and the boy's vulnerability to sexualized violence: one lyric relates that "my master pepered my ars with well good spede," while another voices resistance but comments on its inefficacy when he laments, "Wat helpeyt me thow Y sey nay?" (What help is there for me, even though I say no?) in his song's burden.[18] The same schoolboys who suffered corporeal violence from their masters could have also voiced the perspectives of marginalized women as choirboys at Exeter Cathedral. While we cannot know how these lyrics were interpreted or understood by schoolboys, their status as pedagogical texts leaves open the potential of young men identifying with disempowered lyric voices through their shared affective experiences of suffering and subjugation.

These manuscripts' lyrics, in addition to enabling transformative learning through their material proximity and possessing the potential to generate empathy across time, explore the role of physical space in erotic relations. By depicting urban rapes in songs like *Be pes ye make me spille my ale* and *I can be wanton and yf I wyl*, they challenge the myth established in Deuteronomy 22 and perpetuated in the pastourelles that "real rape" occurs only in the deserted countryside with nobody to come to the victim's aid, and they reflect the social reality that many women were assaulted in towns and cities.[19] *Hay how the mavys one a brere* stages a scene of harassment in idyllic woodland and depicts the victim's successful escape, portraying the forest as a space of masculine aggression and feminine resistance. In forester songs like *I have ben a foster*, the forest is coded as a site of corporeal violence, erotic activity, and freedom from the strictures of marriage. By refusing to confine sexual violence to a specific space, these songs shed light on its universality. And just as violence is

---

16. Woods, "Rape and the Pedagogical Rhetoric," 71.

17. Ibid., 73.

18. *I would fayn be a clarke* (DIMEV 2232), in Duncan, *Medieval English Lyrics and Carols*, 306–7, line 21; *Wenest thu usch with thi coyntyse* (DIMEV 6184), in Duncan, *Medieval English Lyrics and Carols*, 307; *A Munday in the morenyng van Y up rise*, in Greene, *Early English Carols*, 246, line 2. For more on schoolboys and violence, see Ben Parsons, "Beaten for a Book: Domestic and Pedagogic Violence in *The Wife of Bath's Prologue*," *Studies in the Age of Chaucer* 27 (2015).

19. Dunn discusses urban assaults and notes that, according to legal records, rapes in urban areas appear to be slightly more common than rural ones in later medieval England, although she cautions that there are too few cases to draw substantial conclusions (*Stolen Women*, 64–67). Harding discusses the contemporary politics of narrowly designating certain assaults as "legitimate rapes" in *Asking for It*, 125–38.

not spatially limited in these anthologies, neither is empathy. These lyrics probe the role of shared physical space in educating male audiences, as songs like *Up I arose in verno tempore* and *In wyldernes* stage men listening to maidens' laments in remote woodlands and learning about the anguish engendered by other men's exploitation and abandonment. They portray desiring bodies coming into conflict in spaces like the woodland, the wilderness, and the ale-house. They illuminate the knowledge-building possibilities of many different kinds of space-sharing: songs sharing textual space in a manuscript, bodies occupying physical space with one another, and the uncontainable affective space of identification between real and fictional subjects across time, crackling irresistibly between past and present like electricity.

Songs of Wantonness in Ashmole 176

Ashmole 176's scribe copied four songs about embodiment together on the recto and verso of folio 98. The cluster begins and ends with two bawdy poems about impotence, one from a dejected man's perspective and the other from a frustrated woman's. This corporeal emphasis is made all the more striking by the scribe's choice to surround the folio with courtly complaints in which disconsolate men bewail "the paynes of love" and lament their powerlessness against women's "false love" and "unkyndnes."[20] Through their mutual disruption, the lyrics open up an interpretive space for readerly empathy, for they draw attention to the factors shaping the stark differences between gendered experiences of desire.

Folio 98's four lyrics—*My ladye hathe forsaken me*, an obscene erotic poem; a singlewoman's pregnancy lament titled *Up I arose in verno tempore*; *I can be wanton and yf I wyll*, a rape narrative; and *Let be wanton your busynes*, a short female-voiced erotic lyric or scribal tag—are part of a collection of seventeen Tudor court songs written in a single, practiced secretary hand.[21] Most of the songs were composed in the 1520s, and they were copied together between

---

20. *Sans remedye endure must I*, line 8; *Thoughe ye my love were a ladye fayr*, line 5; *Ah my hart ah*, line 4.

21. On MS Ashmole 176, see William A. Ringler Jr., *Bibliography and Index of English Verse in Manuscript, 1501–1558* (London: Mansell, 1992), 41. This seventeen-lyric booklet is Part III of the largely astrological collection of booklets that comprise MS Ashmole 176. Bernard Wagner provides transcriptions of eleven of the lyrics in "New Songs of the Reign of Henry VIII," *Modern Language Notes* 50, no. 7 (1935). John Stevens includes a brief entry on the manuscript and calls it "the only known late source of the words of early Tudor court-songs" (*Music and Poetry*, 462). I discuss the manuscript and provide transcriptions of folio 98's four poems in an earlier version of a portion of this chapter in "'All the Strete My Voyce Shall Heare': Gender, Voice, and Female Desire in the Lyrics of Bodleian MS Ashmole 176," *Journal of the Early Book Society* 20 (2017).

1525 and 1550.[22] The anthology is a slim booklet of five paper sheets that were originally bound together and circulated on their own.[23] The booklet was later sewn into a larger quarto-size volume together with several other booklets of astrological material, Latin prose treatises on the planets and signs of the zodiac, planetary tables, and nativity charts with birthdates from 1551 to 1631.[24] The seventeen lyrics, which include ten male-voiced love complaints interspersed with songs about lost virility, unwanted pregnancy, rape, and Henry VIII dancing with his young daughter Princess Mary at court, have not captured much critical interest.[25] Their authorship is largely unknown, save for one song by Tudor court composer William Cornish (d. 1523) and another by Henry Howard, Earl of Surrey (1516–47). Eleven of the collection's seventeen songs survive here in unique copies. We know nothing of the manuscript's provenance or early history before the astrologer William Lilly gifted it to the antiquarian Elias Ashmole in 1637.[26]

---

22. Ringler, *Bibliography*, 41. William Cornish, the composer of *Adewe adewe my hartes lust*, died in 1523; *Come over the borne, Bessye*, survives in manuscripts as early as the fifteenth century (Cambridge, Trinity College, MS O.2.53, fols. 55v–56r); and the events described in *Ravyshed was I that well was me*, which features Catherine of Aragon watching Henry VIII dance with Princess Mary and closes with a prayer that God "send [Mary] shortlye a brother to be Englandes righte heire" (12), took place between 1516 and 1527.

23. The five-folio anthology (folios 97–101) appears to consist of two individually folded bifolia (the first sheet is folios 97–98 and the second is folios 99–100), with folio 101 as a single sheet that was sewn at the end of the booklet. A different but roughly contemporary hand has copied a nativity chart with a 1551 birthdate on the remaining space on folio 100r after *Ravyshed was I that well was me*, the collection's final song, and a third, slightly later hand and ink matching the manuscript's subsequent contents has written another nativity chart for 1551 on folio 100v, suggesting that the song booklet was bound with the astrological material by the early seventeenth century. Eckhardt discusses the material conditions of verse anthologies and notes that "verse regularly circulated in small booklets like these" (*Manuscript Verse Collectors*, 16).

24. For a listing of the whole volume's contents, see William Henry Black, *A Descriptive, Analytical, and Critical Catalogue of the Manuscripts Bequeathed unto the University of Oxford by Elias Ashmole* (Oxford: Oxford University Press, 1845), 120–22.

25. The anthology's seventeen songs, in order, are Surrey's *If care may cause men crye* (TM 712); *My ladye hathe forsaken me* (DIMEV 3618.5; TM 1050); *Up I arose in verno tempore* (DIMEV 6118; TM 1785); *I can be wanton and yf I wyll* (DIMEV 2145; TM 635); *Let be wanton your busynes* (DIMEV 3053; TM 882); *Thoughe ye my love were a ladye fayr* (DIMEV 5895; TM 1714); *Alas myne eye whye doest thu bringe* (DIMEV 291; TM 102); *Adewe pleasure welcome mournyng* (TM 68); *Ah my hart ah this ys my songe* (DIMEV 128; TM 82); *Sans remedye endure must I* (DIMEV 4780; TM 1383); *Parting parting I may well synge* (DIMEV 126; TM 1309); *Alas to whom should I complayne* (DIMEV 300; TM 108); Cornish's *Adewe adewe my hartes lust* (DIMEV 221; TM 64); *O what a treasure ys love certayne* (DIMEV 4090; TM 1248); *Come over the borne bessye* (DIMEV 5227; TM 1505); *In a garden underneth a tree* (DIMEV 2447; TM 749); and *Ravyshed was I that well was me* (DIMEV 4440; TM 1349). Eleven of the lyrics are printed in Wagner, "New Songs"; *Ravyshed was I that well was me* is printed in Wright and Halliwell, *Reliquiae Antiquae*, 1:258; variant versions of *Up I arose in verno tempore* and *Come over the borne bessye* from the Ritson Manuscript are printed in Stevens, *Music and Poetry*, 390 and 348; and Cornish's *Adew adewe my hartes lust* in Siemens, *Lyrics of the Henry VIII Manuscript*, 28.

26. According to a note at the beginning of the manuscript, the codex was a gift from William Lilly to Elias Ashmole on November 27, 1637. It belonged to the Ashmolean Museum after Ashmole's

The anthology's courtly lyrics focus on men's "payne"—a word repeated seventeen times in the ten complaints—and women's power. Three disconsolate lovers utter the phrase "she hathe reclaymed me to her lure," using a falconry metaphor to express feminine domination over men, as "reclayme" means "to make tame" or "subject somebody to one's control."[27] The songs emphasize men's "weping eeis" and "paynfull sighes," and they imagine the audience for their laments of lost or unrequited love as comprising chiefly other men.[28] *In a garden underneth a tree* stages this masculine affective community when the *chanson d'aventure* narrator encounters "a man in paynes prest" sprawled on the grass (3).[29] The narrator "ask[s] hym" to share his feelings (8), and he responds with a doleful complaint. The courtly lyrics stand in stark contrast to the songs on folio 98, which shift their focus from men's emotional pain to women's embodied experiences of pregnancy, assault, and thwarted arousal. The courtly complaints, as well as the male-voiced erotic song on folio 98r, assert that women possess all the "pleasure" in heterosexual relationships by holding men "in cure" (in their power), while the three female-voiced "songs of wantonness" on folio 98v complicate this by vividly depicting various factors that constrain women's agency: unplanned pregnancy, sexual double standards, masculine entitlement, and violence.[30]

MS Ashmole 176's four "songs of wantonness"—one voiced by a man, and three voiced by women—are copied together in a self-contained cluster on the recto and verso of the booklet's second folio (98). The recto and verso of the booklet's first folio (97) are occupied by the anthology's longest lyric, the lute song *If care may cause men crye, whye doe I not complayne*. This framing of the bawdy songs through a courtly lens has important implications for how we read folio 98's lyric cluster. *If care may cause men crye* was written by the

death in 1692 until it was moved to the Bodleian Library's collections in 1860. For background on Lilly and Ashmole, close friends who shared an interest in astrology, see Patrick Curry, "Lilly, William (1602–1681)," *ODNB*; Michael Hunter, "Ashmole, Elias (1617–1692)," *ODNB*.

27. The phrase "she hath reclaymed me to her lure" occurs in *Ah my hart ah* (9) and *In a garden underneth a tree* (16). The speaker in *Sans remedye endure must I* tells his beloved, "doutles ye may reclayme me" (10). *MED* s.v. "reclaimen" (v.), 1(b), 2(d) and "lure" (n.[1]), (b). For "payne(s)," see *If care may cause men crye* (2, 10, 51), *Alas myne eye why doest thou bringe* (2), *Adewe pleasure welcome mournyng* (1), *Ah my hart ah* (7, 9), *Sans remedye endure must I* (1, 3, 4, 8, 10, 11), *Parting parting I may well synge* (1, 3, 7), and *In a garden underneth a tree* (3). The speaker in *My ladye hathe forsaken me* claims that he "did take payne" to ensure his lady's sexual satisfaction (5).

28. *Ah my hart ah*, lines 1–2. A few of the lyrics are addressed to the female object of desire, but most refer to "my lady," "my love," or "my sweting" in the third person, imagining an audience composed of the speaker's male peers.

29. Wagner, "New Songs," 455. Text references are from my own transcription.

30. The speaker in *Ah my hart ah* laments, "I have the payne & she the pleasure" (9). *MED* s.v. "cure" (n.[1]), 3(b): "**haven in cure**, to have (sth.) under one's control, have in one's power"; *In a garden underneth a tree*, line 14.

poet-aristocrat Henry Howard, Earl of Surrey, who along with Sir Thomas Wyatt was among the first to write sonnets in England, before being beheaded for treason by an aging and paranoid Henry VIII.[31] It was printed in variant form by Richard Tottel in *Songes and Sonettes* (1557), the earliest printed anthology of English poetry, and survives in two early seventeenth-century printed songbooks and four sixteenth-century manuscripts.[32] The compiler's choice to open his collection with a lengthy complaint about aristocratic male suffering and service directs the codex's readers to think about gendered pain according to courtly paradigms of women's power and men's suffering, only to offer a different perspective on the next folio.

Surrey's complaint establishes the anthology's focus on male audiences and readers, for the speaker addresses his song not to his beloved but to his fellow men. He claims the complaint is a genre where "eche man may bewayle his woe" (2), a homosocial discursive space where men can share with one another their intimate feelings about suffering and desire. By opening the anthology in this fashion, the scribe establishes a model of same-sex affective identification between textual voice and audience. Surrey's speaker, unable to separate himself from the gendered collective, sees his desires in comparison to other men's, exacerbating his dolorous state: "And when I see some have their most desired sight / Alas thynke I eche man hathe well save I most wofull wight," he sighs (19–20).[33]

By copying together folio 98's cluster of mainly female-voiced lyrics about embodiment and bracketing them with complaints about men's powerlessness, Ashmole 176's scribe provides the opportunity for audiences to consider the various factors that thwart desire and obstruct erotic agency: a dearth of reproductive choices, the threat of violence, the absence of knowledge, restrictive codes of sexual conduct, and impotence. The scribe's choices underscore the gap between the lived realities of women's experiences in a world that denies them bodily agency and the courtly fiction of women holding all the power over "helplesse" men.[34] There are several ties other than proximity that

---

31. For more on Surrey's work, see Heale, *Wyatt, Surrey, and Early Tudor Poetry* (London: Longman, 1998), esp. 88; on the poem, see William A. Sessions, *Henry Howard, Earl of Surrey* (Boston: G. K. Hall, 1986), 91–92. The most commonly copied version of *If care may cause men cry* is printed in Amanda Holton and Tom MacFaul, eds., *Tottel's Miscellany* (New York: Penguin, 2011), 41–42. Text references are from my own transcription, which differs significantly from this version.

32. For the print and manuscript history of Surrey's poem, see *TM* 712 and *TP* 825. For a discussion of the song's manuscript circulation in seventeenth-century Scotland, see A. S. G. Edwards, "Manuscripts of the Verse of Henry Howard, Earl of Surrey," *Huntington Library Quarterly* 67, no. 2 (2004).

33. Elsewhere he compares his pain to that of his fellow men and sighs, "amonge them all I dare well say ys none / So farre from joye so full of woe nor have more cause to mone" (3–4).

34. The speaker in *In a garden underneth a tree* sighs, "thus I am lefte alone helpelesse" (12).

link the four "songs of wantonness" on folio 98 and render them a distinct sub-group within the collection. One is gender and voice, since three of the four lyrics are voiced wholly or partially by women, in contrast to the other thirteen lyrics in the anthology, which are all voiced by men. Another link is visual similarity; unlike some of the collection's other lyrics, they are copied without errors, hesitation, or cross-outs, each piece written in long lines punctuated by medial commas and neatly concluded with a "finis" and one or two *virgulae suspensivae*.[35] With their shared focus on explicit sexuality and female subjectivity, they contrast sharply with the anthology's complaints, which are devoid of bawdy corporeal references and focus instead on men's experiences of lost or unrequited love. Finally, all four are addressed to male audiences, and all can be read as pedagogical in various ways. The first is voiced by a man offering counsel to his peers; the second portrays an eavesdropping man listening to a maiden's complaint of unwanted pregnancy in a genre typically read as pedagogical; in the third, a woman delivers a series of imperatives about her bodily sovereignty; and the fourth is voiced by an amorous woman instructing her lover. All four can be read as demonstrating the possibilities of knowledge building through affective identification, because the scribe's selection of these four lyrics, together with his choice to copy them with care in this specific order, illustrates how male audiences could be encouraged to think about violence, power, and reproductive choice with compassion and nuance. They emphasize women's desire and explore its social costs and consequences, illuminating continuities between premodern and contemporary sexual culture. They purport to enlighten male audiences about gendered corporeality and desire, just as the anthology's courtly complainers appeal to their peers with heartfelt expressions of woe.

"Undoubted she desyrethe muche": *My ladye hathe forsaken me*

Folio 98r is occupied entirely by *My ladye hathe forsaken me*, a six-quatrain male-voiced erotic song.[36] Its speaker narrates how his mistress of "this vij yeares and some deale more" (5) abandoned him for a new lover after he became unable to meet her voracious sexual demands. He addresses his fellow men and

---

35. For more on the significance of *virgulae suspensivae* and commas, see M. B. Parkes, *Pause and Effect: An Introduction to the History of Punctuation in the West* (Berkeley: University of California Press, 1993), 303, 307. The other lyrics in the collection are not as free of errors. "Were" is erroneously copied twice in the first line of *Though ye my love were a ladye fayr* on folio 99r, and "blynde" is written, then crossed out, in the first line of *Alas myne eye whye doest thou bringe*, also on folio 99r.

36. The first four lines are printed in Wagner, "New Songs," 452; Harris, "'Al the Strete My Voyce Shall Heare,'" 56–57.

shares his narrative of desire in obscene detail, representing his experiences of sex, mutuality, impotence, and rejection as having the potential to edify his peers. His song is filled with courtly rhetoric of men's service and unstinting devotion, placing that rhetoric in conversation with the anthology's complaints and offering a contrasting perspective on gender and power.[37] He deploys courtly language throughout the song but invests it with explicitly sexual meaning, for he imagines devoted "service" to the lady as entailing regular, vigorous intercourse.[38] He recalls, "Her Servant when I first began, as then she dyd report / For trewe Servyce I bare the name amonge the rowte and sort" (9–10).[39] But according to this man, it is not honeyed flattery and promises of devotion that constitute "trewe Servyce," but rather the ability to provide his beloved with physical satisfaction. He describes a reciprocal relationship where men make careful, attentive efforts for which women recompense them: "with her I dyd take payne . . . and . . . she therfore rewarded me agayne," he relates (5–6).[40] He underscores the mutuality in their relationship with the adverb "agayne" (in return, in exchange), and he uses rhyme to link "agayne" and "take payne" (to make an effort) to emphasize the reciprocity of their coital efforts.[41]

The man addresses his bawdy narrative as a lesson to his peers. Like Lyndsay teaching James about "mowth thankles" in his *Answer to the Kingis Flyting*, he presents his experiences as an exemplum about men's bodies and women's desires. He warns his fellow men that excessive intercourse with a partner as desirous as his former lady leads to a permanent "lack [. . . of] Strengthe" (24), echoing other obscene didactic poems voiced by men who have permanently squandered their potency.[42] He discloses that his lady rejected him due to his impotence when he states, "But nowe she feeles I faynt, with some she dothe acquaynt" (11), characterizing his physical state with a verb denoting enfeeble-

---

37. The speaker in *If care may cause men crye* relates his beloved's "strangenes when I sued first her servant for to be" (32), and he resolves "to serve and suffer pacyently" in the final lines (46).

38. Gaunt, "Obscene Hermeneutics," 88.

39. The aristocratic appellation "my Ladye" appears in lines 1 and 15, and also appears in *O what a treasure ys love certeyn* (2) and *Though ye my love were a ladye fayr* (1). *MED* s.v. "ladi" (n.), 8(a): "A lady to whom a knight pays his homage in chivalric love;—often in direct address."

40. *MED* s.v. "pein" (n.), 7(d); *OED* s.v. "pain" (n.), 5(b).

41. *MED* s.v. "ayen" (adv.), 7(a).

42. These laments for lost virility include *Ich have ydon al myn youth* (*DIMEV* 3685), in Duncan, *Medieval English Lyrics and Carols*, 65; *Elde makith me geld*; *Whan I have plesyd my lady now and than* (*DIMEV* 6328; *TM* 1869); *Burgeys, thou haste so blowen atte the cole* (*DIMEV* 896), in Robbins, "A Warning against Lechery," *Philological Quarterly* 35 (1956): 93–95; and the antifeminist Middle Scots lyrics that I discuss in chapter 2.

ment and exhaustion due to exertion.[43] He purports to educate men regarding women's desire in his song's refrain, where he asserts that his lady seeks a lover "Lustye and full of strength in Labour good at Lengthe" (4, 8, 12, 20). He emphasizes the vigor that he no longer possesses by repeating the descriptors "lustye" and "full of strength" as bodily prerequisites for his lady's next partner, and he insists that she desires a man who is able to persist in "labour" "at lengthe," or "to the full extent, without curtailment."[44] He imagines all his listeners as her potential partners: "Her appetyte ys suche," he relates, "marke who so Lust to trye" (21). With his demand that his peers "marke" (take note, give heed to) his instructions about his lady's "appetyte" before they "trye" her themselves, he portrays his obscene admonition as explicitly pedagogical by choosing an imperative verb common in didactic literature.[45]

It is easy to read this song as misogynist propaganda about women's insatiate desire, since the speaker voices common anxieties about impotence, rejection, and competition with other men that were prominent in the antifeminist verse that proliferated during the late fifteenth and early sixteenth centuries.[46] *My ladye hathe forsaken me* presents women as fickle and insatiable, requiring more sex than any single man can provide and discarding their lovers for new ones once their potency is sapped. This representation of women's voracity and faithlessness is shared by poems like Lydgate's *Prohemy of a Mariage* (c. 1440–60), another man-to-man didactic piece that represents female desire as both unquenchable "appetyte" (91, 391) and physical "sikenesse" (125).[47] Lydgate's clerical speaker says of one woman, "She was hungry and wold have had hir mele" (390). This characterization of women's desire as unquenchable hunger is central to *My ladye hathe forsaken me*, whose speaker names his beloved as "she unsacyate" (20) and declares, "undoubted she desyrethe muche" (18). Similarly, in Dunbar's *Tretis of the Tua Mariit Wemen and the Wedo*, the Wedo teaches her friends how she assesses potential lovers based on whether

---

43. *MED* s.v. "feinten" (v.), 3(a).

44. *OED* s.v. "length" (n.), 14(a).

45. *MED* s.v. "marken" (v.), 8(v).

46. Heale discusses the role of misogyny in courtly verse in *Wyatt, Surrey, and Early Tudor Poetry*, 46–49. She argues that, in the context of the early Tudor court, this enormously popular discourse of misogyny allowed women to "embody, or act as scapegoats for, deep-seated masculine fears and resentments, displacing the competition for royal service into an often antagonistic game-world of amorous service" (48).

47. Lydgate, *Prohemy of a Mariage Betwixt an Olde Man and a Yonge Wife, and the Counsail* (DIMEV 139), in Salisbury, *The Trials and Joys of Marriage*, 103–29. Text references are to lines in this edition. See also Lydgate's *Payne and Sorowe of Evyll Maryage*, another misogynistic didactic poem addressed to "yonge men," on 211–18, and Edward Gosynhyll's *A dialogue bytwene the commune secretary and jalowsye, touchynge the unstablenesse of harlottes* (London: John Kynge, 1556).

they appear to be "forgeit . . . maist forcely to furnyse a bancat / In Venus chalmer" (forged most strongly to furnish a banquet in Venus's chamber) (430–31), while in the Middle Scots fabliau *The Freiris of Berwik*, a woman addresses "hir cunt" to say, "Thir mullis of youris ar callit to ane feist" (These lips of yours are invited to a feast).[48] These poems depict men's fears that women will sap their potency before rejecting them for their more virile peers, and they give voice to anxieties about sexual competition among men.

The speaker in *My ladye hathe forsaken me* addresses his peers with familiarity and appeals to their shared body of gendered wisdom by using two proverbs to illustrate his lesson:

Ye knowe that newe brome Swepeth cleane, as many mens sainge ys,
And hackneyes that be comon oftymes tyred ys
And so shall he be that servethe my Ladye
Although he nowe have strengthe, she wyll hym tyre at Lengthe.
(13–16)[49]

His reference to the collective authority of "many mens sainge" invokes a same-sex oral community of instruction regarding erotic matters. He imagines a common corpus of men's knowledge: "Ye know," he states in his lesson about gendered bodies and desires. He closes his song with a warning to his peers: "Thus he who lacketh strengthe," he cautions, "she letteth him slyp at lengthe" (24). His use of "slyp" here is bawdily suggestive because to "let slip" means "to release" and also "to slide," depicting the lady discharging her lover from his courtly service and invoking the obscene image of a flaccid penis sliding helplessly out of the lady's vagina.[50]

This song's material context in Ashmole 176 opens up interpretive possibilities beyond that of a misogynist man-to-man lesson about women's voraciousness. It depicts a woman with ardent corporeal desires who chooses her partners based on their capacity to fulfill those desires, challenging the courtly complaints' portrayal of women's choices as motivated by cruel "disdayne" and "lacke [of] pytye."[51] Its depiction of women's longing as unquenchable "appetyte" is immediately challenged by the trio of lyrics copied onto the subsequent verso (folio 98v), whose female voices declare that they want far more than a man who is "Lusty and full of Strengthe, in Labor good at Lengthe."

---

48. *The Freiris of Berwik* (*DIMEV* 726), in Furrow, *Ten Bourdes*, 84–109, lines 139, 142.

49. For more on the proverb "a new broom sweeps clean," see Whiting, *Proverbs*, B563. For the phrase "to labor like a hackney," see H6.

50. *MED* s.v. "slippen" (v.), 1(a) and 1(c).

51. *Ah my hart ah*, line 7.

"Alas, quid faciam?": Choice and Complaint in *Up I arose in verno tempore*

The next three lyrics in the anthology, all voiced wholly or partially by women, are copied on folio 98v, and their depictions of desire offer a marked counterpoint to the ravenous lady in *My ladye hathe forsaken me* on the preceding recto. Their presence together on this verso is significant because all the other lyrics in the collection are voiced by men. The pregnancy lament *Up I arose in verno tempore* is the first of the three, setting the tone for the verso's focus on women's voices protesting sexual violence, lack of reproductive choice, and thwarted desire.[52] The scribe pays careful attention to punctuating folio 98v's lyrics, ending each with two *virgulae suspensivae*, in contrast to the single *virgula* he typically writes at the end of the anthology's courtly songs. Alternatively, these similarities could mean that he copied them from the same exemplar. Regardless of their origin, these double *virgulae* encourage readers to pause for an extra moment to digest the lessons in the women's songs on folio 98v.[53] When read together in the order that the scribe has carefully copied them, the songs demonstrate a steadfast belief in the capacity of male audiences to listen to and empathize with women's experiences, and they illuminate the inequalities that curtail women's erotic agency.

Up I arose in verno tempore, copied at the top of the page, is a singlewoman's narrative about sex and abandonment featuring her agonized deliberations regarding her unplanned pregnancy.[54] Like the maidens in other English pregnancy laments, she depicts herself as a victim of clerical predation, underscoring how many clerics exploited their power over young, unmarried female parishioners: "with me hath layne, quidam clericus [a certain clerk]," she says (3).[55] The lyric is macaronic, with the first half of each line in English and the second

---

52. The song's *chanson d'aventure* opening and ventriloquizing of an abandoned maiden's lament also occurs in the lyrics *Nou sprinkes the sprai* (DIMEV 614; Duncan, *Medieval English Lyrics and Carols*, 70) and *In wyldernes* (see below).

53. The only exception to this is *Alas to whom should I complayne* on folio 100r, which is punctuated with two *virgulae*; otherwise, all the anthology's lyrics are punctuated with a single *virgula*. According to Parkes, a single *virgula suspensiva* was "used to mark the briefest pause or hesitation in a text," and "the double form / / was used as a direction for . . . a final pause" (*Pause and Effect*, 307).

54. The pregnancy lament, a popular lyric genre in fourteenth- and fifteenth-century England, is discussed in Neil Cartlidge, "'Alas, I Go with Chylde': Representations of Extra-Marital Pregnancy in the Middle English Lyric," *English Studies* 5 (1998), and Bennett, "Ventriloquisms," 196–97; Cartlidge discusses this lyric at 399. Other pregnancy laments include *Be chance bot evin this uthir day* (c. 1568), in *Bannatyne Manuscript*, 2:358–61; *This enther day I met a clerke* (DIMEV 5679; Greene, *Early English Carols*, 277), *The last tyme I the well woke, Ladd y the daunce a myssomur day*, and *Al this day ic han soght* (DIMEV 393; Duncan, *Medieval English Lyrics and Carols*, 280–81).

55. Harris, "'Al the Strete,'" 57.

half in Latin, the half-lines separated by commas.[56] The maiden speaks in both languages, and she uses the Latin of the clerk who abandoned her to criticize him and critique the lack of choices available to women who become pregnant against their will.

The *chanson d'aventure* opens with a (presumably) male first-person speaker enjoying a springtime morning stroll when he encounters "a mayd, sub quadam arbore" (under a tree) (1) and listens to her song of abandonment.[57] The song's pastourelle-esque opening primes readers to expect the man to behave violently toward the maid, but he listens respectfully to her instead, challenging the myth of natural masculine aggression in isolated natural settings. This is the only time the eavesdropper appears in the song, and his subsequent absence places the focus solely on the maid's complaint. The framing fiction of the *chanson d'aventure*, a popular lyric form in the later Middle Ages, reinforces the song's didactic potential. It renders the maiden's lament as offering the man edification or didactic instruction; Judith Davidoff argues that the genre would have been understood as "a generalized *exemplum* whose *moralitas* would become clear in the poem's didactic core."[58] This lyric stages a maiden's voice teaching a male audience about the results of insufficient sexual knowledge and lack of reproductive options, using personal narrative and affective language. By emphasizing her desperation—"What shal I say?" (3)—and highlighting her grief with the statement "incipio flere" (I begin to weep) (6), the woman encourages listeners to empathize with her plight and to recognize the social conditions that have created it.

The narrator characterizes the woman's lament as "a mayd['s] complayn[t]" (1), both aligning it with and setting it in direct contrast to Ashmole 176's ten male-voiced complaints. The anthology is filled with complaining men: "Alas, to whom shuld I complayne?" wonders one; another sighs, "I may complayne as one in payne"; a third characterizes his song as "paynfull playnt"; and a fourth declares, "with double sorowes complayne me I must."[59] Those complaints bemoan love lost through parting, feminine falseness, or the woman's failure to reciprocate the speaker's affections, whereas this female-voiced com-

---

56. For more on macaronic poetry during the period, see Elizabeth Archibald, "Tradition and Innovation in the Macaronic Poetry of Dunbar and Skelton," *Modern Language Quarterly* 53, no. 1 (1992); Ad Putter, "The French of English Letters: Two Trilingual Verse Epistles in Context," in *Language and Culture in Medieval Britain: The French of England c. 1100–c. 1500*, ed. Jocelyn Wogan-Browne et al. (York: York Medieval Press, 2009).

57. Judith M. Davidoff discusses the genre conventions of the *chanson d'aventure* in *Beginning Well: Framing Fictions in Late Middle English Poetry* (Rutherford, NJ: Farleigh Dickinson University Press, 1988), esp. 36–59. See also Sandison, "*Chanson d'Aventure.*"

58. Davidoff, *Beginning Well*, 59.

59. *Alas to whom should I complayne*, line 1; *Sans remedye endure must I*, line 3; *If care may cause men crye*, line 12; *Adewe adewe my hartes lust*, line 2.

plaint details the social and bodily consequences of the cleric's selfish desire and callous abandonment, forcing the anthology's readers to consider how the differences between men's and women's grievances are shaped by larger conditions of inequality. In addition to denoting a heartfelt expression of grief, as is suggested here through its pairing with the phrase "in suo pectore" (in her breast) (2), the verb "complayne" contains both affective and legal valences, meaning "to bewail, lament, deplore" and "to make a formal statement of grievance, bring a charge."[60] This introduces the maiden's narrative of abandonment and lack of reproductive agency as a legal complaint, or the reporting of a crime committed against her, much as the woman in the verso's next lyric frames her narrative of assault as an act of raising the hue and cry against her rapist. By characterizing the maiden's song as "complayn[t]," the framing speaker not only underscores lyric's affective capacity to encourage audiences to identify with the terror, panic, and sorrow resulting from her unplanned pregnancy, but also highlights lyric's capacity to stage social protest, as the maiden can be read as delivering an official grievance regarding her experience. Her complaint issues a sharp challenge to conditions that allow the unnamed "clericus" to escape unscathed while she prepares to suffer abuse from her loved ones after her condition is revealed.

In the poem's final two lines, the maiden considers how she will proceed with her pregnancy and weighs the options available to her: "with this said child alas, quid faciam [what shall I do], shall I yt kepe, vel interficiam [or shall I kill it], / yf I yt sley, quo loco fugiam [whither shall I flee], I shall lose god and vitam eternam [eternal life]" (7–8). She considers multiple courses of action rather than resigning herself to raising an unwanted child and accepting the accompanying social costs, which indicates that she is framing motherhood in terms of volition rather than biological imperative. She underscores the acute difficulty of her dilemma with the sorrowful interjection "alas," which recurs repeatedly in the collection's courtly complaints.[61] When she considers abortion or infanticide, she renders that option in Latin ("interficiam") as well as in English ("sley"), while she imagines "kepe[ing]" the child in English alone, indicating that the former is the option to which she is giving greater consideration.[62] By vividly detailing the consequences she will suffer for her pregnancy—beatings from her parents, public shaming and ridicule, verbal

---

60. *MED* s.v. "compleinen" (v.), 1(a) and 4(a); *OED* s.v. "complain" (v.), 1(a): and 8(a).

61. See *If care may cause men crye* (9, 37, 53), *Alas myne eye why doest thu bringe* (1), *Adewe pleasure welcome mournyng* (1), *Ah my hart ah* (twice in 7), *Sans remedye endure must I* (12), *Alas to whom should I complayne* (1), and *Adewe adewe my hartes lust* (twice in 2).

62. Bennett and Froide note that "the majority of women accused of infanticide [during the period] were singlewomen" ("Singular Past," 36n77); for cases of abortion and infanticide, see Goldberg, *Women in England*, 119, 122, 123. Laura Gowing provides a historical overview of the issue, albeit with

abuse, loss of playmates—the maiden encourages her eavesdropping listener to have compassion for her desire to avoid those consequences regardless of the cost.

The singlewoman's yearning for tenable choices reflects larger battles for control over women's bodies during the period. Monica H. Green traces the narrowing of women's reproductive options in later medieval medical discourse.[63] She notes that "all late medieval [English] vernacular gynecological texts addressed to women have suppressed information on contraceptives," with scribes either writing these passages in cipher or omitting them entirely in order to limit women's knowledge and restrict their choices regarding their bodies.[64] Indeed, one fifteenth-century translator of the gynecological treatise *The Knowing of Woman's Kind in Childing* states that he "dare not wryte" about contraception or abortion methods "lest sume cursyde calet wold hit use" (lest some accursed whore would use it).[65] He represents his withholding of vital information as necessitated by women's carnal transgressions, blaming his choice to foreclose their reproductive agency on "sume cursyde calet." He holds women responsible for their own lack of knowledge and condemns them to suffer the consequences of this lack. In light of increasingly virulent attacks on women's reproductive choice and access to abortion and contraception in the United States in recent years, this fictional maiden's voice calling on audiences to empathize with her terrified desperation is fraught with especial urgency.

"I crye, / That all the strete my voyce shall heare": *I can be wanton and yf I wyll*

The second lyric copied onto folio 98v, *I can be wanton and yf I wyll*, is voiced by a woman proclaiming her right to "be wanton" and "be merye," before she is brutally assaulted.[66] She challenges her attacker and details her increasingly forceful attempts to defend herself, then promises to stop crying out and "lye styll" (2) in the final line after he has physically overpowered her, as she shifts her focus from preventing the assault to surviving it. While one could read this song as illustrating the myth that women's refusal can be overcome with

---

cases from a slightly later period, in "Secret Births and Infanticide in Seventeenth-Century England," *Past and Present* 156 (1997).

63. Monica H. Green, "Making Motherhood in Medieval England: The Evidence from Medicine," in *Motherhood, Religion, and Society in Medieval Europe 400–1400: Essays Presented to Henrietta Leyser*, ed. Conrad Leyser and Lesley Smith (Aldershot, UK: Ashgate, 2011).

64. Ibid., 189.

65. Barratt, *Knowing*, 60.

66. Wagner, "New Songs," 452–53. Text references are to the edition in Appendix 2.

persistence and brute force, it also illuminates the different forms of women's resistance—physical, verbal, and legal—and demonstrates lyric's capacity for teaching male audiences about the experiences of women living under the unrelenting threat of assault. The woman represents her song as an act of "cry[ing] howe" (1, 7, 12) or raising the hue and cry in response to rape, forcing readers to bear witness to her suffering and rendering them complicit in her legal outcry against her assailant.

This lyric makes bold claims about female desire, asserting a woman's right to be "wanton" and "merye" without being subjected to unwanted sexual attention (1–2) and establishing women as erotic subjects who are entitled to freedom from harm. It also contains messages that can be read as reinforcing rape culture, for it portrays a woman being brutally punished for expressing lighthearted flirtation and sexual playfulness and enables her to be read as "asking for it." It allows for a woman's desperate negotiations with her rapist— she threatens to raise the hue and cry, then "warant[s]" him to come near has long as he remains unseen by others (4), before demanding that he "syt farre from [her]" because he seems dangerous (5) and refusing to kiss him—to be interpreted as "mixed messages" and used to discredit her claims of coercion, if one chooses to read the song in that way. Or it can be read as a literary version of a legal outcry, compelling audiences to serve as witnesses to the speaker's violation. Copied on folio 98v between *Up I arose in verno tempore*, a song about a woman's yearning for tenable reproductive choices, and *Let be wanton your busynes*, about a woman's frustrated lust, *I can be wanton and yf I wyll* voices a woman's desire to express wantonness without fearing violence.

The song opens with the woman confidently articulating her right to engage in merriment without being perceived as sexually accessible, to express lighthearted enjoyment without violation of her bodily sovereignty. She declares in the first two lines, "I can be wanton and yf I wyll, but yf yowe touche me I wyll crye howe / I can be merye & thynke no evell, but yet beware one cometh I trowe" (1–2). She defends her prerogative to be "merye" and "wanton," and she insists that this does not mean that men can "touche" her as they please. She invokes the law on her side, threatening to raise the hue and cry if any man should misconstrue her playful "wantonness" as sexual availability. Her repeated use of the verb "can," with its implications that she is right and justified in her actions, grounds her claim.[67] The stanza's layout on the manuscript page further authorizes her pronouncement of agency: "I can be" begins each of the poem's first two lines, the first-person *I*'s oversized, with circular looped ascenders and long, trailing descenders.

---

67. *MED* s.v. "connen" (v.), 2.

Even as she declares her right to "be wanton . . . [and] merye," the woman expresses a fear of violence as retribution for this expression. She anticipates the unwanted "touche" that she might suffer, twice using the conjunction "but" when she cautions, *"but* yf yowe touche me I wyll crye howe . . . *but* yet beware one cometh" (1–2; emphasis mine). She offers a stern warning to men who presume to touch her without permission, by threatening to invoke the law's protection against rape. Her use of the verb "beware," meaning "to take heed, in reference to a danger," to characterize the man's approach indicates that she immediately—and correctly, as we soon see—perceives him as a potential threat.[68] She repeats "beware" again five lines later when she declares, "me semeth youe should be wylde . . . I wilbe ware of suchelyke wylde men," depicting some men's "wylde[ness]" and refusal to govern their desires as a threat to women's safety (5, 7). "Wylde," which contains valences of wickedness, licentiousness, and lack of sexual self-control, frequently occurs in alliterative pairings with "wanton," another adjective denoting lecherousness and ill restraint that she applies pejoratively to her assailant (6).[69] The speaker's highlighting of her fears of violence alongside her assertion of sexual agency underscores the physical risk that accompanies singlewomen's expressions of desire and points to the power imbalances that some "songs of lusty maidens" elide. It elucidates the inequalities that are occluded in courtly discourse, directly contradicting the anthology's complainers' assertions that women are their "governour[s]," as one man tearfully puts it.[70] The woman acknowledges the fear she feels while living under threat of violence, and she asserts her right to wantonness and merriment in spite of that fear. The subsequent five quatrains validate her fears with chilling specificity when she encounters a man who refuses to respect her desires.

At the same time that it portrays women's resistance to violence and asserts their right to be "wanton" without being "touche[d]," *I can be wanton and yf I wyl* emphasizes the social and legal power of women's voices and underscores the political possibilities of survivor discourse by focusing on the act of "cry[ing] howe" (raising the hue and cry), a response to rape in which the aggrieved party publicly declares that she has been criminally assaulted.[71] In "cry[ing] howe," women's voices acquire formal legal power. Dunn notes that "rape was one of the few crimes that women—even married women—could

---

68. *OED* s.v. "beware" (v.), 1.
69. *MED* s.v. "wild" (adj.), 1(c); *OED* s.v. "wild" (adj.), 7(b).
70. *In a garden underneth a tree*, line 18.
71. *MED* s.v. "heue" (n.[2]), c: "*law.* A loud outcry of alarm raised at the occurrence of robbery, assault, etc." Dunn discusses the role of raising the hue and cry in rape cases in *Stolen Women*, 68. For more on the hue and cry, see John H. Baker, *An Introduction to English Legal History*, 4th ed. (Oxford: Oxford University Press, 2005), 503–4.

prosecute independently," and "cry[ing] howe" was a tool for demanding justice available to any woman with a voice.[72] This understanding of "crying howe" as resistance is reflected in a parliamentary record from 1423 that characterizes "hewe [and] cry" as "resistence making."[73] In the very first line, the woman promises, "yf youe touche me I wyll crye howe" (1), then declares, "I wilbe ware of suchelyke wylde men for when they touche me I doo crye howe" (7). The song returns to the hue and cry in its final lines, as the woman concludes her outcry by telling her assailant after he has overpowered her, "I wilbe styll and crye howe no more" (12).

The speaker invokes the laws that ostensibly protect women from the harm of nonconsensual touch, but she ultimately demonstrates the ineffectiveness of these laws by sharing a step-by-step narrative of her assault that occurs in spite of the fact that she follows legal procedures. Her song serves as an important lesson that the law often does not work in women's lived realities; if a woman can be characterized as "asking for it," a conclusion that rape culture is set up to produce, then the law is useless to her. In telling her story, the woman issues a stinging critique of the law's incapacity to protect her from violence. In addition to exposing the law's ineffectuality and shedding light on the stark gap between legal provision and lived experience, her song positions itself as a formal speech act of legal protest. Her threefold repetition of the formula "crye howe," and her use of it to frame her song, renders the song itself as an act of raising the hue and cry. It serves as testimony to the crime committed against its speaker, encouraging audiences to empathize with her anguish and support her resistance. The song insistently draws attention to the fact that she follows legal procedure and fights back with every strategy she can muster, and yet she is still assaulted.

The woman opposes the man's aggression with words as well as fists. As part of raising the hue and cry, women were expected to produce evidence of resistance to violence, including blood, torn clothing, and other signs of physical struggle. Her deployment of multiple strategies—blunt refusal, negotiation, heartfelt pleading, and physical violence in self-defense—functions as the legal proof victims needed to support their act of "cry[ing] howe."[74] She declares her opposition to sexual contact with the man in no uncertain terms when she insists, "ye may me kyll as soone as kysse" (8), using alliteration to reinforce her equation of being killed and kissed by her assailant. She switches to polite pleading and negotiation by begging, "I pray youe awaie and let me

---

72. Dunn, *Stolen Women*, 53.

73. John Strachey, ed., *Rotuli Parliamentorum, ut et petitiones, et placita in Parliamento*, 6 vols. (London, 1767–77), 4:198b.

74. Dunn, *Stolen Women*, 56.

be" (9), using the supplicatory verb "pray." She calls on the power of public shaming by threatening to testify about her assault: "In faith all the world wyll speake of this," she promises (10), then declares, "I crye, that all the strete my voyce shall heare" (13). She turns to physical aggression as her final tactic in her closing quatrain, where she exclaims, "By God I strike youe with my fyste" (11).

After punching her assailant, the woman chooses survival at all costs in the final line, portraying the decision to survive as its own resistance: "But for all that doe what youe lyst [whatever pleases you], / And I wilbe styll and crye howe no more," she tells her attacker (12). While one could interpret this as signifying her consent, I am more interested in reading the degree to which she is still resisting. She tells her assaulter to "doe what *youe* lyst" (emphasis mine), refusing to voice her complicity in what he is about to do. She recognizes that there are no other means of resistance available to her, because no one has responded to her cries. Since she sees no other options, she makes the choice to survive the assault. Like the anguished pregnancy lament copied just before it on folio 98v, this maiden's song sheds light on the difficult choices for survival that women sometimes must make due to deeply entrenched inequalities, and it can be read as a legal complaint regarding the suffering engendered by those inequalities. In framing her song as an act of "crying howe," the speaker puts the onus on her audience to respond to her rape by bearing unflinching witness to her violation.

Thwarted Desire: *Let be wanton your busynes*

Folio 98's fourth and final lyric, *Let be wanton your busynes*, takes the previous two songs' portrayals of women's victimization in an unexpected direction, for it stages a woman instructing her lover. In this single quatrain, which could be read as either a short lyric or a scribal tag responding to what has just been copied, a woman voices her frustration at her lover's impotence: "Let be wanton your busynes, for in good faith youe are to blame / To put me thus in this distris, Seing that your best lymme ys lame."[75] "Wanton," which appears so prominently in the previous song, here functions as a noun of direct address for the man who has aroused the speaker with his amorous "busynes" but is unable to consummate the encounter due to his penile "lame[ness]"; in this context, "wanton" means "a lustful or lecherous person" or "a flirt."[76] The

---

75. *DIMEV* 3053. This poem can be read in relation to chapter 4's similar four-line singlewoman's song of frustrated desire and impotence, *Ate ston-castinge my lemman I ches*.

76. *OED* s.v. "wanton" (adj. and n.), B. 2.

woman chastises her lover for his failure to please her through penetration, much as the titular lady in *My ladye hathe forsaken me* discards her impotent long-term partner for a more virile one. She emphasizes her displeasure at the man's impotence, using alliteration to underscore the link between the genital term "lymme" and its descriptor "lame" (weak, ineffectual), expressing her irritation by naming his flaccid penis sarcastically as his "best lymme."

The woman's imperative tone and frank voicing of arousal is especially notable coming just after her fellow singlewoman's assertions of erotic subjectivity were punished with rape. She opens her song with a command— "Let be," she orders—and she issues instructions to her lover about how to please her. In characterizing her state of thwarted arousal as "this distris," she echoes the anthology's courtly complainers, who utter sentiments such as "thus mourne I may in paynes allway, both nyght and day in great distress."[77] Like the other desiring voices on folio 98, the woman attaches corporeal significance to the discourse of courtly love that dominates the collection, rendering "distris" a state of sexual rather than emotional suffering.

When folio 98's four lyrics are read in order, they exhibit a circular logic. We can imagine the frustrated speaker in the folio's last lyric as the amorous lady described in its first, as the two poems portray differing gendered perspectives on desire and impotence. *Let be wanton your busynes* can be read as a response to *My ladye hathe forsaken me*, or it can be interpreted as offering an alternate perspective. Even if the lyrics were not necessarily read in order, the scribe's choice to copy the cluster together and embed it within a collection of polite courtly lyrics depicts bodies and desires coming into conflict with one another. In reading folio 98's four lyrics together and tracing how they speak to one another as well as to the anthology's courtly complaints, we see the productive possibilities of scribal ordering in generating compassion by shedding light on the lived effects of sexual difference in an unequal world. In contrast to the courtly lyrics' emphasis on women's power and men's pain, these songs focus on men's and women's experiences of embodied intersubjectivity and use their bawdy didactic potential to generate empathy. The female-voiced songs copied together on folio 98v articulate women's desires—to enjoy satisfying fleshly "busynes," to have control over their reproductive bodies, to flirt and "be merye" without suffering violence—and illuminate the impediments to the satisfaction of those desires. They challenge the portrayal of women's desire in the impotence lyric copied on the recto just before them, with its claims that women most want lovers "Lustye and full of strength, in Labor good at Lengthe." All four lyrics on the folio challenge the anthology's

---

77. *Sans remedye endure must I*, line 4.

courtly complaints about women's absence or hardheartedness by elucidating a far more corporeal, unequal, and violent erotic universe.

Violence and Volition in the Ritson Manuscript

Ashmole 176 and the Ritson Manuscript share two lyrics—*Up I arose in verno tempore* and *Come over the borne, bessye*—from the same early Tudor courtly milieu, and both anthologies illustrate how songs about violence and volition can speak to one another in provocative and edifying ways.[78] Two groups of songs about gendered embodiment copied into the Ritson Manuscript by two different hands demonstrate how scribes' placement and ordering of lyrics can encourage empathy for victims of violence, and they portray knowledge as having the power to prevent assault and defend against exploitation. Like Ashmole 176's folio 98, with its insistent corporeal focus, the Ritson Manuscript contains sites of "lyric disruption" where courtly lovers "Lyfyng in stryf, / Lyvyng yn payn, / Lovyng in vayne" are challenged by the voices of women protesting harassment, speaking back to their rapists, testifying about the destructive effects of sexual ignorance, and contemplating abortion.[79]

The Ritson Manuscript, which was presented by the antiquary Joseph Ritson (1752–1803) to the British Museum in August 1795, is a choir repertory of ninety-seven songs in English, Latin, and French, all with music, copied by multiple hands beginning in the 1460s and ending around 1510.[80] Its contents are diverse and wide ranging, containing bawdy songs, courtly lyrics, and Latin, English, and macaronic liturgical pieces and religious part-songs. It originated in Devon, according to three deeds and receipts in the manuscript dated between 1501 and 1510, and it may have been associated with Exeter Cathedral.[81] It was meant for performance rather than private reading, as the scribes copied many songs in three parts and wrote them on facing versos and rectos in order

---

78. These are the only two surviving copies of *Up I arose in verno tempore*. *Come over the borne bessye* also survives in Cambridge, Emmanuel College, MS 263, fol. ir–iiv and Cambridge, Trinity College, MS O.2.53, fol. 55r–56r.

79. *Alone alone*, folio 140v (*DIMEV* 446), lines 32–34.

80. For the manuscript's background and transcriptions of twenty of its English and macaronic songs, see Stevens, *Music and Poetry*, 338–50; for a more thorough description, see Nick Sandon's introduction to *The Ritson Manuscript: Liturgical Compositions, Votive Antiphons, and Te Deum* (Moretonhampstead, UK: Antico Editions, 2001); for a full edition of the songs with commentary on their musical characteristics, see Catharine Keyes Miller, "A Fifteenth-Century Record of English Choir Repertory: B. M. Add. MS. 5665; A Transcription and Commentary," 2 vols. (PhD diss., Yale University, 1948). For more on Ritson's life, see Stephanie L. Barczewski, "Ritson, Joseph (1752–1803)," *ODNB*.

81. Sandon, *Ritson Manuscript*, iii–iv.

to minimize page turning while singing. Its contents are far more heteroge-
neous than those of Ashmole 176; the English songs and carols, many by local
Exeter musicians including John Trouloffe, Richard Smert, and Thomas Packe,
are interspersed singly and in groups among the religious pieces. Like Ashmole
176, the Ritson Manuscript shares songs with the Henry VIII Manuscript, including *Passetyme with good companye* and related versions of *Y have ben a foster*.

The Ritson Manuscript features two rich sites of interpretive disruption.
The first lyric cluster, containing several songs copied in the same neat, practiced
Anglicana hand, is on folios 53v–69r. It includes lyrics that grapple with the
role of violence in social constructions of masculine sexuality: *Y have ben a
foster*, a song about virility celebrating the choice to forgo marriage; *Be pes, ye
make me spille my ale*, an urban pastourelle variant depicting a rape; and three
courtly complaints that bookend *Be pes* and take on new meaning in light of
its unflinching portrayal of sexual violence. The other song cluster on folios
139v–148r, written in a sprawling secretary hand, examines knowledge's role
in sexual consent and imagines possibilities for escaping inequality. This group
includes a pair of pregnancy laments (*In wyldernes* and *Up I arose in verno tempore*), several courtly complaints, and *Hay how the mavys on a brere*, a dialogue
between an aggressive man and a female songbird that, like the pastourelles,
lays bare the violence undergirding courtly discourse and articulates a powerful fantasy of women's escape from harassment and harm.

Violent Spaces: *Y have ben a foster* and *Be pes, ye make me spille my ale*

The Ritson Manuscript's first song cluster opens on folio 53v with one male
voice's part from *Y have ben a foster*.[82] The speaker is a "foster," a term covering a web of interrelated masculine identities—forest officer, game warden,
keeper of a royal forest, hunter, assistant in the chase—located at the nexus
of violence, power, and sylvan space.[83] His short song about his penis belongs
to the genre of "forester songs" that were popular during the Tudor period
and played a central part in the entertainments at Henry VIII's court during
the early 1520s, including Cornish's sumptuous forester-themed play at Wind-
sor Castle in June 1522.[84] Forester songs celebrate virility by emphasizing the

---

82. *Y have ben a foster* (DIMEV 2175; TM 643), on fol. 53v; Stevens, *Music and Poetry*, 338, and Siemens,
Lyrics of the Henry VIII Manuscript, 112. Text references are to lines in Siemens's edition.

83. *MED* s.v. "foster" (n.[2]), (a).

84. Other forester songs include Robert Cooper's *I have bene a foster* (DIMEV 2176), the anonymous *I am a joly foster* (DIMEV 6503), and Cornish's *Blow thi hornne hunter* (DIMEV 5005; TM 1455),
which were all associated with Cornish's 1522 play and survive in the Henry VIII Manuscript. Greene
discusses the genre and its performance context in *Early English Carols*, 499; also Stevens, *Music and*

obscene double meanings in the technical vocabulary of the hunt and blurring the boundaries between predation and eroticism. They use the forest keeper's rhetoric of authorized violence and the lush descriptive language of the green forest to portray the penis as a bow or arrow, ejaculation as an act of skilled shooting to kill, and the secluded "grenewode" as an idyllic natural space for men's pleasure. With his persistent use of the masculine first-person *I* and refusal to name the object of his genital efforts, *Y have ben a foster* advances a self-centered, singular notion of masculine desire.

This song's use of the forester metaphor for the masculine erotic subject, and its valorization of the forester's predatory violence, illuminates how brute force and power inequalities between embodied subjects are central to literary representations of "natural" masculine sexuality. The genre links masculinity to the verdant forest, a space coded as erotic in fifteenth- and sixteenth-century lyric, with its "greenewode spray" (4) providing inviting shade for amorous encounters.[85] The forest was tied to the court due to hunting's status as courtly pastime and measure of aristocratic masculinity, especially during the early reign of Henry VIII, who, according to a French diplomat in 1515, "care[d] for nothing but girls and hunting."[86] This association between hunting, pleasure, and aristocratic manhood is reinforced in the Ritson Manuscript, which includes two versions of *Passetyme with goode cumpanye*, a convivial song attributed to Henry VIII whose male speaker declares, "woll I / For my pastaunce [recreation] / Hunte, syng and daunce."[87]

Y have ben a foster's white-haired bachelor protagonist reflects on his erotic choices, and he equates "be[ing] a foster long and meney day" to carnal activity outside the bonds of marriage (1). He declares he will give up his livelihood only when he may no longer exercise his genital weapon:

All the whiles that Y may my bowe bende
Shall Y wedde no wyffe,
My bowe bende shall y wedde no wiffe, wiffe.

Poetry, 222, 249. These poems are printed in Siemens, *Lyrics of the Henry VIII Manuscript*, 46–47, 48–49, 38; for more on Cornish's play, see 112.

85. For other songs featuring the erotic valences of the "grenewode" that circulated in the same early Tudor songbook milieu, see Cornish's *Trolly lolly loly lo* (*DIMEV* 6965; *TM* 1774) and *Yow and I and amyas* (*DIMEV* 5363; *TM* 1545), both in the Henry VIII Manuscript, and the anonymous *Smale pathis to the grenewode* (*DIMEV* 3277) from the Fayrfax Manuscript. Siemens, *Lyrics of the Henry VIII Manuscript*, 39–40; Greene, *Early English Carols*, 283.

86. J. S. Brewer, ed., *Letters and Papers, Foreign and Domestic, of the Reign of Henry VIII*, 24 vols. (London: Longman, Green, Longman, and Roberts, 1862), 2:292.

87. *Passetyme with goode cumpanye* (*DIMEV* 4347; *TM* 1312), lines 4–6. This song, which the scribe titles "The Kynges Balade," is copied by two separate hands on folios 136v–137r and 141v–142r, and also survives in the Henry VIII Manuscript, fol. 14v. Siemens, *Lyrics of the Henry VIII Manuscript*, 25–26.

I shall bygges me a boure atte the woodes ende
Ther to lede my lyffe,
Att the wodes ende, ther to lede my lyffe. (7–12)

The speaker compares sex to the archer's action of drawing back the bowstring just before he releases the arrow in hopes of maiming his target, although it is not clear whether he is referring to intercourse or masturbation.[88] His ability to "bende" his "bowe" determines how he "lede[s]" his "lyffe," for he portrays virility as the chief factor governing his manner of existence. He stresses his willful relinquishment of matrimony through repetition, underscoring the nonexistence of a "wiffe" three times in two lines. Instead of marrying, he declares his intention "to lede my lyffe" in the liminal viridian space "atte the woodes ende." His use of the masculine first-person singular, asserting that "I" will build "me" a dwelling to lead "my" life, valorizes individuality over companionship and suggests that the erotic activity he pursues so single-mindedly lacks mutuality. He proclaims his intention to build a secluded woodland sex hut and spend the rest of his life there, using "boure" to denote a dwelling place or shelter from the elements as well as a bedchamber.[89]

    Y have bene a foster's rendering of the forest as the domain of masculine sexuality, where men with weapons have full rights to the bodies passing through it, appears in other sixteenth-century lyrics like the Middle Scots pastourelle *Still undir the levis grene* (1570s), in which a forester encounters a maiden and insists that her solo presence in his territory gives him the right to assault her:

In waithman weyd sen I yow find
In this wod walkand your alone,
Your mylk quhyt handis we sall bynd
Quhill that the blud burst fra the bone.[90]

[Since I find you dressed as a hunter
In this wood walking by yourself alone,
Your milk-white hands I / we shall bind
Until the blood bursts from the bone.]

This poem imagines women's presence in men's sylvan space as licensing violence against their bodies, emphasized by the alliterative linking of "bynd," "blud," and "bone." Similarly, in two pastourelles from the Welles

---

88. *MED* s.v. "benden" (v.), 1(a).
89. *MED* s.v. "bour" (n.), 1(a) and 2(a).
90. *Still undir the levis grene*, in Craigie, *Maitland Folio Manuscript*, 1:360–64, lines 64–67.

Anthology, young women are assaulted in "a forest" and in "the woodes fair and grene" by men who hunt them like prey.[91] These woodland pastourelles illustrate why the forester is such a vexed metaphor for masculine erotic subjectivity: foresters traffic in violence authorized by the space that they occupy. They exist outside the court but are intimately connected to it nonetheless, allowing them to replicate its power hierarchies for their own purposes. Foresters are charged with protecting the king's forest from intruders, and they possess the power to inflict violence on the living bodies who occupy their territory. It is their job to chase, wound, kill, and dismember weaker, more vulnerable bodies (rabbits, foxes, deer), and in the metaphorical landscape of the forester lyric, those animal bodies become women's bodies. The forester derives a thrill from pursuing his less powerful prey, from watching them run for their lives with all their might before he releases the fatal arrow and it is over.

While the masculine violence in *Y have ben a foster* is stylized and eroticized, its effects elided, *Be pes ye make me spille my ale* twelve folios later is far more explicit.[92] The former lyric is set in sylvan space and depicts hunting and nonmarital sexual activity as markers of masculinity, valorizing equally the ability to kill and the ability to fuck. *Be pes* takes place in the storeroom of an alehouse, and it uses unsparing detail to portray the violent effects of the myth that women who sell alcohol are sexually available.[93] *Be pes*, an anonymous three-stanza song with parts for three voices, is a clerk-and-serving-maid ballad, a close cousin of the pastourelle that transports that genre's social-sexual clash from the isolated natural space of the forest or meadow to the back quarters of an urban alehouse, where its debate occurs between a tavern customer and the singlewoman whose job it is to serve him alcohol.

This literary movement from rural to urban reflects historical realities and allows authors to probe the relationship between space, consent, violence, and culpability established in Deuteronomy 22:23–29's decree that a maiden raped in town shall be stoned to death for her assault "for she cryed not, whanne she was in the cytee," while the maiden attacked in the countryside is allowed to go unpunished. This myth invalidates the experiences of urban rape survivors and holds victims responsible for making sufficient outcry to

---

91. *Come over the woodes fair and grene*, line 1; *Throughe a forest as I can ryde*, lines 1.

92. *Be pes ye make me spille my ale* (DIMEV 773; TM 244), fols. 66v–67r; Stevens, *Music and Poetry*, 339–40. Text references are to lines in the edition in Appendix 2.

93. Margaret Aziza Pappano and Nicole R. Rice explore how ale sellers were portrayed as errant singlewomen, their bodies "rendered open and transgressive," in *The Civic Cycles: Artisan Drama and Identity in Premodern England* (Notre Dame, IN: University of Notre Dame Press, 2015), 161–209, esp. 189–94. This stereotype is central to Lydgate's *Ballade upon an Ale-Seller* (c. 1449; DIMEV 4466), in *John Lydgate: The Minor Poems*, vol. 2, *Secular Poems*, ed. Henry Noble McCracken (London: Early English Texts Society, 1934), 429–32.

summon help. *Be pes* challenges this myth by staging the assaulted woman articulating "gret afray" (outcry, uproar), only for her cries to go unheard in the chaotic din of the alehouse. After the Black Death, young women migrated to towns and cities to find work as tapsters and servants in alehouses, and the clerk-and-serving-maid ballad emerged at the end of the fifteenth century at the intersection of cultural anxieties about singlewomen's physical and economic independence, sexual autonomy, and alcohol consumption. Two composed around the same time are Skelton's *Manerly Margery Mylk and Ale* (1490s), copied in the Fayrfax Manuscript, and *Be pes, ye make me spille my ale*.[94] Both songs feature customers who exploit tapsters' work responsibilities to assault them, underscoring how their interlocking identities as women and alehouse workers render them vulnerable to assault and highlighting how popular representations of tapsters as rapacious sex workers, exemplified by the wily, flirtatious Kit in the pseudo-Chaucerian *Canterbury Interlude*, could put women working in alehouses at increased risk of violence.[95]

Be pes opens with the tapster expressing shock when a male customer surprises her alone in the alehouse storeroom, startling her so badly that she spills the ale she has gone there to fetch. This moment of violent workplace interruption illuminates how gender inequality and spatial politics intersect to put working women in danger. McIntosh notes that working in inns and alehouses "render[ed women] vulnerable to sexual advances and social disapproval."[96] Women working in the service industry today can attest to the persistence of these attitudes, because workers whose job it is to provide food, drink, and courteous service are assumed by many male customers to be available for their flirtation and lewd objectification.[97] The tapster orders the man to leave her alone with the forceful interjection "Be pes," meaning, "Silence! Be quiet!"[98] She emphasizes the physical effects of her surprise by noting that his intrusion "make[s] me spille my ale" and interferes with her completion of

---

94. *Manerly Margery Mylk and Ale* is copied with music in the Fayrfax Manuscript, folios 96v–99r, and also survives in Cambridge, Trinity College, MS VI.18.2, where it is copied by an early sixteenth-century hand onto a flyleaf at the end of a printed volume of *The Dictes or Sayengis of the Philosophres* (London: William Caxton, 1477). For a comparison of the two versions, see A. S. G. Edwards and Linne R. Mooney, "A New Version of a Skelton Lyric," *Transactions of the Cambridge Bibliographical Society* 10 (1994).

95. For more on women, alehouse space, and sexual violence, see Hanawalt, "Medieval English Women," 24–26.

96. McIntosh, *Working Women*, 253.

97. This is backed up by research showing sexual harassment to be "endemic" in the restaurant industry. Restaurant Opportunities Centers United Forward Together, "The Glass Floor: Sexual Harassment in the Restaurant Industry," October 2014, http://rocunited.org/wp-content/uploads/2014/10/REPORT_TheGlassFloor_Sexual-Harassment-in-the-Restaurant-Industry.pdf.

98. *MED* s.v. "pes" (interj.).

her job. Her approach to narrating her assault is to voice the effects of the man's actions on her body in methodical, step-by-step detail, requiring the person copying or performing the part to experience the assault along with her.

The song's tooth-and-nail struggle between resistant tapster and aggressive customer gives valuable insight into how rapists' strategies of coercion were imagined. The man exploits the physical constraints of the woman's workplace and the responsibilities of her job in order to corner her, then insists that she abandon her work to have sex with him. He first attempts to shame her for her startled reaction to his unauthorized presence in her workspace by asking reprovingly, "Now thyngke ye this ys a fayre ray?" (Do you think this is a nice state of affairs?) (2). Even though she has entered the storeroom to fetch ale as part of her job, he orders her to "Leff werk" immediately and "abyde awhile" with him (4, 6), placing his carnal whims over her need to earn a living. He normalizes his aggression and reproaches her for wanting to leave his company: "What have ye haste?" (6), he asks when she scrambles unsuccessfully to escape the cramped room. He dismisses her "gret afray" and insists that she will enjoy sex with him once she tries it: "After asay then may ye wette" (After you try it, then you may know), he declares confidently (9). When she continues to refuse, he protests his innocence by pleading, "Why blame ye me withoute offence?" (10). He makes himself the victim by accusing her of "blam[ing]" him unjustly, and his use of "blame" and "offence" puts his actions in the legal language of sexual crime, at once signaling what he is about to do and encouraging audiences to view his behavior as criminal. In the third and final stanza, he abandons all pretense of seduction and moves to direct imperatives: "Cum kys me," he demands. He responds to her refusal by declaring, "Be God, ye shall!" (17). His final words are his command, "Take to gev all, and be stille than!" as he rapes the tapster (21). John Stevens glosses the first half of the line as "Take it upon yourself to make a complete surrender"—the assailant orders the woman to hand over the use of her body even as he takes it by force.[99] With his order to "be stille," he tells her to stop struggling and demands that she be quiet as he attempts to quell her verbal and physical resistance.[100]

Be pes provides a useful catalogue of women's methods of verbal resistance similar to the list of strategies in *I can be wanton and yf I wyl*. After rebuking the man for his incursion into her workspace, the tapster demands that he release his grip on her and dismisses his persuasive speech as fiction: "Let go Y

---

99. *MED* s.v. "yeven" (v.), 4(f): "to offer or allow the use of (one's body to sb.) in a sexual relationship."

100. *MED* s.v. "stille" (adj.), 1(a).

say, straw for yeure tale!" she exclaims (3), using a popular proverbial expression to cast his words of attempted seduction as worth no more than a wisp
of straw.[101] When he demands that she abandon her work to have sex with
him, she asks sharply, "Wene ye that everybody lest to play?" (5), using "play"
to signify "the opposite of work" as well as amorous activity. In her blunt refusal
"Ywisse, wanton, ye shull not yette!" (11), she uses the intensifier "yette"
(further, ever) to reinforce her assertion and echoes the tapster in *Manerly
Margery Mylk and Ale* who denigrates the "wanton clarkis" (2) who harass her
at work.[102] She orders, "Nou, Gode, go hens!" (12), invoking God on her side
and using the temporal adverb "nou" and the spatial adverb "hens" (away,
from here) to emphasize that she wants him to leave their shared space immediately. She issues a series of direct, pointed questions: "What do ye here
within oure spence [storeroom]? / Recke ye not to make us shende? [Do you
not care that you'll destroy us?]" (13–14), she asks, demanding that he account for his actions.[103] She inquires what he is doing in her space ("here"),
uses the domestic plural ("our spence") to emphasize that he has intruded
where he does not belong, and reminds him that his actions harm both of
them. "Nay!" she retorts when he commands her to kiss him (17), then shouts
defiantly, "Be Criste, Y nelle, what see the man?" (By Christ, I will not, what
does the man say to that?) (18). When he begins to assault her, she tells him,
"Ye herte my legge agenste the walle" (19), pointing precisely to where and
how he is causing her pain and using the verb "herte" to characterize his
movements. Her step-by-step narration of the harms of the man's actions as
they occur is important for teaching audiences about the experiences of assault survivors, as she challenges the myth that "rape is a trivial event" for its
victims.[104] As her final strategy, she appeals to his social status, recalling the
inequalities between privileged man and disadvantaged woman that shape
the genre's politics of entitlement and coercion: "Ys this the gentery that ye
can?" (Is this the courtesy that you are capable of?), she asks as he pins her
roughly against the storeroom's wall (20), recalling the connections between
aristocratic masculinity, sexuality, and violence central to *Y have bene a foster*.
She draws attention to their unequal class status, reminding him that he is
exploiting their differences to inflict violence on her.

---

101. Whiting, *Proverbs*, S816.

102. *MED* s.v. "yet" (adv.), 1(a) and 1(d).

103. *MED* s.v. "spens(e" (n.[2]). The association between tapsters, sexuality, and spences also occurs in the Croxton *Play of the Sacrament* (c. 1475) when Colle says of his dissolute master, "He sytthyt
with sum tapstere in the spence" (531); cited in the *MED* entry.

104. Grubb and Turner, "Attribution of Blame," 445.

At this point in the dialogue, there is just enough space at the bottom of the folio for the scribe to copy the song's last four lines. Instead, he chooses to leave the space blank and write them vertically in the right margin:

"Take to gev all, and be stille than!"
"Now have ye leyde me un the flore,
But hadde Y wyste when ye bygan,
Be Criste, Y wolde have schytte the dore!" (21–24)

The scribe's choice to copy the lines this way, forcing the reader to stop and turn the codex to a ninety-degree angle to continue reading or singing the song, imposes a pause in the narrative. Audiences are left in suspense, not knowing whether the tapster will slip free or manage to dissuade her assailant by appealing to his nonexistent sense of courtesy. The tapster speaks three of the final four lines copied vertically in the folio's right margin, leaving audiences with her perspective. The capital letters beginning each of these four lines are far more elaborate and detailed than the song's other capitals, indicating that the scribe has taken special care to add extra pen strokes and flourishes. The tapster continues to narrate her assault in precise and agonizing detail. She portrays education about sexual violence as both prevention and empowerment when she imagines knowledge as having the power to stave off her attack with her use of the popular formulation "hadde y wyste" (if I had known).[105] She envisions an alternate scenario in which she is armed with sufficient awareness of her assailant's intentions to act in her own defense.

The song focuses on the physical logistics of the assault in the "spence"; its cramped layout as a storeroom for food and beverages, along with the necessity of the tapster making frequent solo trips there to fetch the ale she needs to perform her job, are two factors that the man uses to attack the tapster. She underscores how he exploits the spatial particularities of her workplace to facilitate the assault. She protests that he is hurting her leg "agenste the walle," states that he has "leyde [her] un the flore," and voices her ardent yearning for information that could have prevented the assault. In her heartbreaking final line, she imagines a different outcome in which she uses empowering knowledge and physical obstruction to "schytte the dore" against her assailant and prevent him from entering her storeroom.

---

105. *MED* s.v. "witen" (n.[1]), 2. In *Naye phewe, nay pishe*, a woman uses the same formulation to depict women's knowledge as having the power to prevent rape: "Yow marr the bed, you teare my smock, but had I wist, / So much before I woulde have kepte you oute" (14–15).

Be pes and *I have ben a foster* probe the socially constructed relationship between violence and masculine sexuality. In *I have ben a foster*, men's sexual activity is imagined as the beginning of an act of fatal violence, as the slow, practiced drawing of a bowstring before the arrow flies forth and pierces the body of its target. With the masculine erotic subject portrayed as a foster, a man whose job it is to regulate the forest with force and to chase and kill the vulnerable occupants of his domain, the song recalls popular designations of the penis as a "wepene," "launce," "sperys heed," "arwe . . . fyled kene," and "castyng dart" in other poems.[106] *Be pes*, copied twelve folios later in the same hand, highlights the implications of portraying penises as weaponry and depicts the violent result of certain myths about sexuality, namely that women working in the service industry are fair game for sexual aggression and that women enjoy sex once they "assay" it, even if they resist at first.

Be pes is sandwiched between two songs of courtly male suffering, *My wofull herte of gladnesse bareyne* and *Absens of yeu causeth me to sygh and complayne*, and it challenges their portrayals of women's power and men's pain.[107] The speaker in the first lyric claims his sorrow has "enforsed me this complaynte for to make" (2), his use of "enforsed" anticipating the brutal assault that occurs on the next folio, with its valences of rape and violent compulsion.[108] The complaint copied immediately after *Be pes* features similar abdications of male agency and assertions of women's power. Its speaker claims his uninterested beloved has "governaunce" over him (2) and insists he cannot keep himself from expressing his desire for her, though he wishes to do so: "And thogh Y wolde, Y koude me noght refrayne," he sighs (3). This assertion of men's helplessness over their actions is particularly dangerous in light of *Be pes*, which depicts the violent effects of men refusing to "refrayne" from acting on unreciprocated desire.

Emancipatory Space: *In wyldernes, Up I arose in verno tempore*, and *Hay how the mavys on a brere*

Another cluster of lyrics about embodiment in the Ritson Manuscript is centrally concerned with knowledge and consent. In contrast to *Be pes* and *I have ben a foster*, which depict how spatial politics can be used to facilitate violence against women's bodies, these songs focus on space's emancipatory

---

106. *MED* s.v. "wepen" (n.), 2(b) and "launce" (n.), 3(e); for the last three, see Lydgate, *My fayr lady so fressh of hewe*.

107. *My wofull hert of all gladnesse bareyne* (DIMEV 3665; TM 1076), fol. 65v–66r; Stevens, *Music and Poetry*, 339. *Absens of yeu causeth me to sygh and complayne* (DIMEV 208; TM 57), fol. 67v–68r. Stevens, *Music and Poetry*, 340. Text references are to lines in this edition.

108. *MED* s.v. "enforcen" (v.), 1(a) and 1(c).

and recuperative possibilities: woodland and wilderness are portrayed as spaces for men to empathize with women's experiences of exploitation, pregnant singlewomen imagine fleeing to faraway lands to escape social stigma, and harassment victims escape successfully from their tormentors. Their female speakers persistently imagine "other spaces" free of sexual stigma and un-wanted incursion, where they have full bodily sovereignty. These songs are written in a later, messier hand than the previous cluster, its hasty secretary script in sharp contrast to the earlier neat, professional-grade Anglicana hand. On folios 133v–148r, this hand copied four courtly complaints; two versions of Henry VIII's prohunting lyric *Passetyme with good companye*; *Come over the borne, bessye*, which features a recalcitrant woman refusing to "come over the borne [brook]" to the man who repeatedly summons her; two *chanson d'aventure* pregnancy laments, *In wyldernes* and *Up I arose in verno tempore*; and *Hay how a mavys on a brere*, a contentious dialogue concluding the anthology with a powerful portrayal of its female speaker's escape from the aggression authorized by courtly discourse. The women's voices in these songs echo and revise the rhetoric of the male-voiced complaints surrounding them, and they shed light on how women's lack of knowledge constrains their consent.

In wyldernes opens with its male speaker encountering a woman named Besse "alone, / In grete dystres" (3–4).[109] It closely echoes *Up I arose in verno tempore*, copied four folios later with minor variations from the version in Ashmole 176. Both songs are set in idyllic outdoor space, "sub quadam arbore" (under a tree) and "in wyldernes" (in the countryside) (1, 46). In both, the man does not speak directly to the lamenting maiden, and he disappears from the song after establishing his physical presence in the space; this portrays him as a sympathetic (or voyeuristic) listener and points to the role of shared space in facilitating understanding.[110] *In wyldernes*'s first verse survives with music in another early sixteenth-century manuscript, demonstrating its popularity.[111]

---

109. *In wyldernes* (DIMEV 2666; TM 812), fol. 141r; Stevens, *Music and Poetry*, 346–47. Text refer-ences are to lines in the edition in Appendix 2. See also Cartlidge, "'Alas, I Go with Chylde,'" 398–99.

110. *Up I arose in verno tempore*, fols. 145v–146r. The differences between the Ritson Manuscript and Ashmole 176 versions are as follows: Ashmole 176 reverses the order of the poem's middle two quatrains, whereas in Ritson, the young woman first mourns the loss of pleasures before imagining her parents' anger and violence. In Ritson's version, she imagines that "they wyll . . . me sore chast coram omnibus [before everyone]" (11–12), whereas in Ashmole 176, the scribe has written "they wyll . . . me deprave [disparage], coram hominibus [before all people]." In the Ritson Manuscript, she is a "maydyn" who exhibits a greater degree of sexual agency: she narrates, "by cause y lay with quidam clericus" and declares, "Adew plesers." In Ashmole 176, she is a "mayd" who emphasizes her victimization with the phrase "that with me hath layne, quidam clericus," laments her loss of homo-social community with the declaration "Adewe playfers," and articulates an extra "alas" ("with this said child alas, quid faciam") that is absent from Ritson.

111. The first stanza only is copied in BL MS Egerton 3002, folio 2v, a codex of assorted sixteenth-and seventeenth-century papers from the Heath and Verney families. Several long flourishes and

Besse's lament is framed as a "moone" (6, 48), rendering it a legal grievance against lack of knowledge and double standards, much like *Up I arose in verno tempore*'s "complayn[t]." She depicts her first sexual experience as entailing the heartbreaking loss of homosocial community:

"Alas," she seyd,
"Y was a mayde
As others be.
And at-a-brayde
Y was afrayde
Right pyteusly." (7–12)

She claims to have been part of a gendered collective with "other" "mayde[s]" before characterizing her removal as a sudden, agonizing rupture. Her use of the descriptive phrase "at-a-brayde" (suddenly), often deployed in romance to denote violent surprise in battle, portrays her initial sexual experience as an unexpected and painful occurrence. "Afrayde," the verb she chooses to name the encounter, likewise signifies attack and alarm.[112] She reinforces her lack of agency with the descriptor "ryght pyteusly," meaning "in a manner arousing or deserving of pity," which encourages the eavesdropping man as well as the song's audiences to empathize with her plight and view the encounter as not necessarily consensual.[113] Besse relates how she was deceived, impregnated, and abandoned by a smooth-talking aristocratic youth:

A wanton chyld
Spake wordes myld
To me alone,
And me begylyd,
Goten with child
And now ys gone. (13–18)

Her characterization of the young nobleman as "wanton" echoes the derisive epithet that the tapster in *Be pes* voices against her rapist, and in both of these cases, masculine wantonness is predatory and painful for women. Besse characterizes herself as "begylyd" (duped, betrayed, seduced) by the youth's courtly speech, using a verb suggesting sexual trickery and inequalities in power and

wavy lines have been drawn in a different ink under the name "Bes" in the line "Ther fond y bes," a scribal gesture putting visual emphasis on the song's female speaker.

112. *MED* s.v. "breid" (n.), 4(a); s.v. "affraien" (v.[1]), 1(a) and 3(a).

113. *MED* s.v. "pitousli" (adv.), (b).

knowledge.[114] She illustrates how women's ignorance can be used to manipulate them and shows how it compromises their consent, making a powerful case for more comprehensive education and stressing the importance of informed consent.

In contemplating her next course of action, Besse imagines other spaces as entailing emancipatory possibilities: "In ferre cuntre [distant land] / Men wene I be / A mayde agayn" (28–30). She imagines she can escape the stigma of sexual transgression in "ferre cuntre," and she views flight as the most "wyse" choice (24); otherwise, "men" will mistreat her for not being "a mayde." Similarly, in *Up I arose in verno tempore*, the pregnant singlewoman wonders, "If y sley hyt sley, quo loco fugiam?" (whither shall I flee?) (15). She dreams of a place—"loco" (a part of space having definite location)—where she can elude the unjust social consequences of unwed motherhood.[115] Here the scribe mistakenly copies "sley" twice, his error rendering it as the option to which she is giving greater consideration.

In wyldernes echoes the language of the surrounding courtly lyrics and invests it with new meaning. It is preceded by two dolorous love complaints. One man sighs, "She hath me hurt, why shall she not hele / And geve me salfe unto my sore?"[116] The next laments, "With a dulfull chere here I make my mone, / Pyteusly my own self alone."[117] His language is echoed in the opening and closing lines of *In wyldernes* on the facing recto, as Besse describes herself as "myself alone . . . Makyng my moon" (45–48; also 3–6) and uses the phrase "ryght pyteusly" to characterize her sexual experience. Besse's portrayal as "remedyles" (unable to be helped) (5, 47) and twofold articulation of "Alas" (7, 43) closely echoes the refrain, "Alas, alas, what remedy?" repeated four times in *My herte ys yn grete mournyng*, a male-voiced complaint copied four folios before *In wyldernes*.[118] In her description of the aristocratic young man who betrayed and abandoned her, Besse demonstrates how the courtly rhetoric in the anthology's complaints can be used for exploitative purposes. She names her faithless lover as a "chyld," a term meaning "a youth of noble birth," frequently applied to romance heroes.[119] She states that he used "wordes myld"

---

114. *MED* s.v. "bigilen" (v.), 1(a), 2, and 3(b).

115. *DMLBS* s.v. "locus" (n.), 1.

116. *So put in fear I dare not speak* (DIMEV 4944; TM 1437), fols. 137v–140r; Stevens, *Music and Poetry*, 345–46, lines 15–16.

117. *Alone alone* (DIMEV 446; TM 135), fol. 140v; Stevens, *Music and Poetry*, 346, lines 3–4; see also the similar *Alone alone mornyng alone* (DIMEV 447; TM 136) on folios 133v–135r.

118. *My herte ys yn grete mournyng* (DIMEV 3605; TM 1040), fols. 136v–137r; Stevens, *Music and Poetry*, 343–44, lines 3, 7, 11, 15. The speaker in *Alone alone* similarly wonders, "What remedy?" in line 36.

119. *MED* s.v. "child" (n.), 6(a).

(friendly, gracious) to "begyle" her into sex that she did not necessarily want, portraying courtly speech as coercive and deceptive.

The lyric cluster concludes with *Hay how the mavys on a brere*, a *chanson d'aventure* dialogue between a man and a female songbird, which is closely aligned with the pastourelle due to its secluded woodland setting, gendered debate form, and depiction of men's violent entitlement and women's resistance.[120] Although the poem's female speaker is not a woman but a "mavys," a small, nomadic thrush known for its sweet song, she is portrayed in the same language as a pastourelle maiden.[121] Like the anthology's pregnancy laments, the exchange occurs in "the greves [branches] among" (5) in a secluded woodland setting. The mavis sits alone on a dog rose branch, singing "with notes clere" (2). Like the eavesdropping men in the preceding pregnancy laments, the male speaker listens carefully to her song. Unlike them, he initiates physical closeness with her, and he sees her as existing chiefly for his enjoyment: "Y drew me nere / To se her chere" (3–4). The mavis responds to his invasion of her space not with birdsong, but with speech:

> When Y cam ther
> She stode yn fere
> And seyd, "No nere!
> What doyst thou here?
> Hyt ys grete wrong, wrong." (6–10)

She first reacts by freezing up with fear. After he has drawn "nere" uninvited, she orders him, "no nere," using the imperative mood to establish a firm physical boundary. By characterizing his presence as "grete wrong" (crime, unjust or harmful act), the mavis portrays his intrusion into her space and interruption of her song as both harmful and criminal.[122] She repeatedly voices the noun "wrong" in pairs, once on folio 146v and twice on folio 147r, to emphasize that the man's closeness is a violation. Like the rapist in *Be pes* who repeatedly rebuffs the tapster's refusals, he ignores her dismissal. Instead of accounting for his incursion, he insists that she remain near him, echoing the

---

120. *Hay how the mavys on a brere* (DIMEV 2017; TM 591), fols. 145v–147r; Stevens, *Music and Poetry*, 349–50. Text references are to lines in the edition in Appendix 2. For another fifteenth-century debate between a male human and a female bird, see *Disputacio inter clericum et philomenam* (DIMEV 500) and *In a mornyng of may as I lay on slepyng* (DIMEV 2451), two parts of the same poem, printed in Conlee, *Middle English Debate Poetry*, 267–77.

121. MED s.v. "mavis" (n. sg. and pl.); "Redwing (*Turdus iliacus*)," in D. W. Snow and C. M. Perrins, *The Birds of the Western Palearctic*, concise ed. (Oxford: Oxford University Press, 1998), 1228–30.

122. MED s.v. "wrong" (n.[2]), 2a(a) and 2a(d).

rapist's command to "Abyde awhile" as he blocks his victim's escape: "I bade her abyde / And stop a tyde" (11–12), he says.

The mavis refuses him again before using her power of flight to end the encounter: "She seyd me nay / And flo her way" (15–16). This narrative of rejection and escape is doubly meaningful in the context of the collection's earlier lyrics where women are portrayed as bodies to be hunted, where they are cornered and assaulted in cramped urban spaces from which they are physically unable to flee. The mavis has the capacity to follow her verbal refusal ("nay") with corporeal action: she flies "her way," refusing to subordinate her desires to her harasser's and denying him the pleasure of her presence. This song rewrites the anthology's recurring portrayal of women as hunted and overpowered. After the mavis departs, the man curses her for going "her way," underscoring the violence underlying his ostensibly courteous request that she grant him her company:

> Such on as she,
> That away woll flee,
> Yll must she the,
> Wherever she be
> Yn castell strong. (25–29)

He sees her choice to exercise agency and "flee" "away" as a crime, shifting the blame from the "grete wrong" of his unwanted closeness to her choice to leave his presence because he refused to respect her boundaries. He lumps together all who reject men's undesired advances as "such on[es] as she" and declares them universally deserving of punishment. Infuriated by the songbird's choice to leave his presence and frustrated at his inability to detain her through force, he curses her with the proclamation, "Yll must she the" (Evil must she prosper).[123] He stipulates that his curse will follow her wherever she goes and insists that no fortification, not even "castell strong" (built to resist assaults), can protect her from his violent rage at having his desires thwarted.

Hay how the mavys on a brere is the final song in the Ritson Manuscript, and it concludes a collection featuring multiple narratives of victimization by portraying a woman's successful escape from violence. These songs together teach audiences about the possibilities of survival, of saying no, of fighting back even when the deck is stacked mightily against them, and they demonstrate that escape is sometimes possible, that one can "flee her way" and survive unscathed. They speak to recent feminist approaches to fighting rape: Gavey

---

123. *MED* s.v. "then" (v.), 2(b).

highlights the importance of rewriting our standard cultural scripts for heterosexual sex and adopting "an 'attitude of refusal'" to all unwanted contact, and Martha McCaughey argues for a "physical feminism" cultivated by self-defense training as essential to reconfiguring gendered power relations.[124] Fiona Vera-Gray calls for "new ways of inhabiting ourselves" by developing "counterhabits" and speaking out about "the range and extent of women's strategies for coping with, avoiding, and resisting men's intrusions, strategies lived as forms of bodily know-how."[125] She suggests the development of educational initiatives "encouraging women to experience their bodily capacities . . . [and] live their embodied self in a habitual mode of 'I can.'"[126] These lyrics, copied in close proximity by the same hand, feature female voices that loudly decry the destructive effects of sexual ignorance, challenge masculine entitlement, emphasize the importance of informed consent, and seek ways to flee from harm. The Ritson Manuscript's lyrics underscore the importance of voicing the effects of sexual intrusion in all its forms and of imagining new spaces, other worlds where women have bodily sovereignty and the capacity to escape unwanted contact and unjust stigmatization.

Pedagogies of Wantonness

The term "wanton," in all its rich multivalence, is a useful through-line for understanding the lessons encoded in the carnal lyrics of Ashmole 176 and the Ritson Manuscript, as its ever-shifting valences shed light on the pleasures and dangers it entails. I categorize these lyrics as "songs of wantonness" because the word "wanton" recurs repeatedly and constitutes a governing principle for their explorations of desire and gendered embodiment because it meant "lustful (esp. [of] a woman)," "sexually promiscuous," "given to excessive pleasure-seeing," "unrestrained in merriment," and "playful."[127] "Wanton" is a compound of the pejorative descriptive prefix "wan"—meaning "wrongly," "badly," or "mistaken"—and the pedagogical verb "ten," meaning "to teach, train, educate."[128] "Wanton" means, in its most basic sense, "badly taught" or "wrongly educated." The pregnant, abandoned Besse decries how "a wanton chylde / Spake wordes mylde" to exploit her lack of knowledge, and the tapster

124. Nicola Gavey, "Fighting Rape," in *Theorizing Sexual Violence*, ed. Renée J. Heberle and Victoria Grace (New York: Routledge, 2009); McCaughey, *Real Knockouts*; also Cahill, *Rethinking Rape*, 198–207.

125. Vera-Gray, *Men's Intrusion, Women's Embodiment*, 164–75.

126. Ibid., 172.

127. *OED* s.v. "wanton" (adj. and n.), 3 and 4(a); *MED* s.v. "wantoun" (adj.), (c) and (d).

128. *MED* s.v. "wan" (pref.); s.v. "ten" (v.[1]), 5(a).

attacked at work shouts at her rapist, "Ywisse, wanton, ye shulle not yet!" In *Let be wanton your busynes*, "wanton" names a man who is unable to please his lover due to impotence, with "wanton" signifying the promise of feminine satisfaction without the capacity to deliver it. The speaker in *I can be wanton and yf I wyll* asserts her prerogative to "be wanton" (1) by invoking the term's valences of lighthearted enjoyment, and several lines later, she applies it negatively to her rapist when she warns, "by suche wanton men as youe be yonge maydes are sometymes begyled" (6), aligning male wantonness with deceptiveness and overt harm to young women. She presents wantonness as pleasure and danger, as prerogative and threat. While these songs depict men's wantonness as frequently harmful to women, their deployment of the term "wanton," with its connotations of faulty pedagogy, highlights the fact that "wanton" behavior is a product of education; if men can be taught to perpetuate rape culture, they can also be taught more ethical, respectful sexual paradigms. And even though women's wantonness is implicitly attributed to bad education and punished with violence, *I can be wanton* shows how they can still lay claim to it in order to argue for their right to erotic expression. These songs together emphasize the corporeal joys and risks of wantonness, for "wanton" illuminates the full range of valences—pleasure, rebellion, threat, arousal, coercion, and recklessness—that they attach to sexuality.

These lyrics suggest a pedagogical model grounded in wantonness, entailing both learning and unlearning about sexuality. We can read the voices of these women who "desyreth muche" as rejecting teachings that constrain their erotic expression and challenging double standards that punish them more harshly than their male partners. We can hear in them calls for a more comprehensive and compassionate kind of sexual education that gives individuals the knowledge to evaluate risk, respond to aggression, and negotiate for pleasure. These songs' wanton voices, their empathetic charge arcing across the centuries like live wires, teach us to continue fighting, to keep resisting, and to acknowledge the anguish of living under threat. They incite compassion for disadvantaged erotic subjects, for the fleeing prey and not the hunter with his killing arrows. Nearly five hundred years later, women are still fighting to have reproductive agency without interference from male politicians, legislators, and judges. We still cannot laugh and drink and dance without having that used as justification for the violence perpetrated against us. In reading these long-ignored voices of resistance, which challenge readers to empathize with women's experiences of violence and acknowledge their sexual subjectivity, I hope that contemporary audiences can choose to use their lessons to help shape a future full of wantonness and merriment for all.

Conclusion
Obscene Pedagogies, Past and Present

The comic poem *Lyarde* (c. 1430–50) uses obscenity to narrate the travails of "sory swywers" (pitiful fuckers) (112, 115) and "counte betyn" (cunt-beaten) men (60).[1] "Alle the wyfes of this land," frustrated by their husbands' impotence, gather "at assente" (in formal mutual agreement) and petition the king to establish a park where the men can be imprisoned together (19). They institute a yearly market at which women can "mak[e] bargans" and exchange "the febill" husbands for "freche ware" (45–46). The narrator uses the language of commerce and feminine agency to name the wives' sexual activities: "And yitt sall thai be coussid awaye at Appilby Faire" (And yet shall [the impotent husbands] be bartered away at Appleby Fair), the narrator says (44), referring to the borough fair held annually at Whitsuntide and echoing singlewomen's erotic songs with his deployment of mercantile rhetoric to portray women as sexual-economic agents bargaining for satisfaction. Following the patterns I have traced throughout *Obscene Pedagogies*, he concludes by addressing "smalle swywynge men" (infrequently fucking men) (105, 37): "Alle Lyardes men, I warne yowe byfore, / Bete the cownte with your neffes when ye may do no more" (All impotent men, I warn you in advance, / Beat the cunt with your fists when you may

---

1. Melissa M. Furrow, "Lyarde: A Minor Romance Poem in a Major Romance Manuscript," *Forum for Modern Language Studies* 32, no. 4 (1996). Text references are to lines from this edition.

copulate no more), he commands (127–28). With "alle," he stresses the inclusivity of the imagined brotherhood of "men" he is teaching. He uses the verb "warne," meaning "to admonish, exhort, or teach," to introduce his instructions and underscore their pedagogical import.[2] Having already portrayed women's genitalia as responsible for impotence with his obscene epithet "counte betyn man," he urges his peers to "bete the cownte" once they are unable to "do" sexually, replacing intercourse with one-sided aggression. The violence in his lesson is reinforced by his use of the imperative verb "bete," meaning "to strike, smite, buffet, slap, pummel" as well as "to punish somebody" and "to conquer, overcome," to prescribe repeated blows, as he invokes physical force and masculine domination.[3] His emphasis on brutality is underscored by the phrase "with your neffes" to signify that these blows to the vulva ought to be delivered with clenched fists.[4] The speaker teaches his fellow "men" to enact sexual violence and minimizes its harms by conflating "bet[ing] the cownte" with the fists to "do[ing]" with the penis, as he mobilizes obscenity's shock value and pedagogical power to disparage women's genitalia and encourage misogynist violence.[5]

This use of obscenity between men to authorize sexual violence and downplay its damages, prominent in Chaucer's *Canterbury Tales* and Lyndsay's *Answer to the Kingis Flyting*, is not relegated to the premodern past but persists to this day. I close *Obscene Pedagogies* by highlighting how obscenity is marshaled both for and against rape culture and misogyny in our own time, demonstrating how practices of obscene pedagogy from the fourteenth through sixteenth centuries continue to shape Western sexual culture. In October 2016, a recording was released of then-presidential candidate Donald Trump regaling *Access Hollywood* entertainment reporter Billy Bush and several other men with an obscene narrative in 2005.[6] In the bawdy all-male conversation, Trump says of a woman, "I moved on her actually . . . I moved on her and I failed."

"Whoa," says a man's voice.

---

2. *MED* s.v. "warnen" (v.), 4.

3. *MED* s.v. "beten" (v.[1]), 1a(b), 2a(a), and 3.

4. *MED* s.v. "neve" (n.[2]).

5. American hip-hop artist LoveRance's 2011 hit single "Up! (Beat the Pussy Up)," whose chorus features a fivefold repetition of its obscene, violent title, is a contemporary echo of "Bete the cownte with your neffes."

6. David A. Farenthold, "Trump Recorded Having Extremely Lewd Conversation about Women in 2005," *Washington Post*, October 7, 2016, https://www.washingtonpost.com/politics/trump-recorded-having-extremely-lewd-conversation-about-women-in-2005/2016/10/07/3b9ce776-8cb4-11e6-bf8a-3d26847eeed4_story.html?utm_term=.2bc0ab85acbb.

"I'll admit it," Trump continues. "I did try and fuck her. She was married." He goes on to mock the woman's "big phony tits," reducing her to a sexualized body. He boasts of "mov[ing] on her like a bitch"—in fact, he voices the phrase "I moved on her" four times, drawing on its predatory meanings "to approach, especially with the purpose of attacking, trapping, or threatening; to close in on a target or victim"; his peers respond to his tale of attempted conquest with peals of raucous laughter.[7] He says to one man in the group, "Look at you. You are a pussy," using the term "pussy" to police his peer's masculinity much like the emasculating epithet "cokeney" functions in the all-male world of the *Reeve's Tale*'s Soler Hall. Trump brags of assaulting women and teaches his peers how they, too, can exploit their power to assault: "I don't even wait [for their consent]. And when you're a star, they let you do it. You can do anything. Grab 'em by the pussy. You can do anything." His boasts of seizing women's vulvae without their consent, an echo of Nicholas "prively ca[tching]" Alisoun "by the queynte" in the *Miller's Tale*, are punctuated by Bush's laughter and approving declaration, "Whatever you want."[8] Bush's response authorizes Trump's admission of assault by validating it as both humorous and admirable, illustrating how obscene pedagogy operates in homosocial contexts. His reaction is similar to that of Chaucer's Cook, who responds with "joye" and chortles, "Ha! ha!" at the Reeve's tale of nonconsensual "swyv[ing]" (I.4326–27). Trump both boasts of his predation and exhorts his peers to use their power similarly to violate women: "You can do anything," he insists repeatedly, moving from "I" to "you" to instruct them how they, too, "can do anything" to women's bodies that they desire. He delivers his encouragement to "grab 'em by the pussy," an echo of *Lyarde*'s order to "bete the cownte with your neffes," as an imperative command. He uses the obscenity "pussy" to demean other men and boast of assaulting women, its transgressive charge inculcating his same-sex lessons about gender, sex, power, and consent.

The *Access Hollywood* tape was significant not simply because it exposed a powerful man using obscenity to police his peers' masculinity and encourage them to assault women, but also because it forced journalists and audiences to reckon with the taboo status of "pussy," much as Chaucer's repeated deployment of "swyve" tested the tolerance of medieval scribes and readers. The

---

7. Penn Bullock, "Transcript: Donald Trump's Taped Comments about Women," *New York Times*, October 8, 2016, https://www.nytimes.com/2016/10/08/us/donald-trump-tape-transcript .html; *OED* s.v. "move" (v.), "to move in," 2.

8. Sonja Drimmer and Damian Fleming draw connections between the *Access Hollywood* tape and medieval art and literature in "Not Subtle; Not Quaint," *In the Middle: A Medieval Studies Group Blog*, October 9, 2016, http://www.inthemedievalmiddle.com/2016/10/not-subtle-not-quaint.html.

New York Times and *Washington Post*'s websites prefaced the video with the statement, "Editor's Note: This Video Contains Graphic Language," and the *Post* censored the written obscenities as "p—y" and "f—," highlighting the illicit nature of Trump's language.[9] One journalist declared, "Never before has a presidential candidate been caught in a situation so obscene that members of the news media found themselves struggling with and breaking their own rules to cover it."[10] The vehement reactions that the tape's vulgarities elicited from those who heard and wrote about them are testimony to the ever-potent power of the obscene to challenge those who encounter it.

"Pussy" is a fitting note on which to end this book, since the term functions in current usage as a technology of intimidation and discipline to punish men who deviate from strict codes of masculinity. It also names women's genitalia in a manner that is frequently objectifying and demeaning. Trump uses "pussy" twice in the conversation, first as an epithet meaning "an effeminate male, a weakling, a coward" and next as *"coarse slang* [for] the vulva or vagina."[11] "Pussy," which entered English as the Dutch word for *"cat" (poes)* around the turn of the sixteenth century, had meanings both animal and feminine, as it meant "a cat" and "a girl or woman exhibiting characteristics associated with a cat."[12] The double significance is central to a popular erotic song from the early sixteenth century titled *Adew, my pretty pussy.*[13] The song is a bawdy farewell from a man to his former lover, whom he calls "pus" (50, 61, 65) and "my pretty pussy" (1), after she has left him for another man. In the first stanza, addressed to his erstwhile partner, he expresses his displeasure at their breakup, asks for one final kiss, and boasts that "wemen wyll be plenty" in his future (10). The five subsequent stanzas are addressed to his fellow men, as he ends nearly half of the poem's lines with the vocative "syr," illustrating how men used obscenity to teach one another about women's faithlessness

---

9. Farenthold, "'Trump Recorded"; Alexander Burns, Maggie Haberman, and Jonathan Martin, "Donald Trump Apology Caps Day of Outrage over Lewd Tape," *New York Times*, October 7, 2016, https://www.nytimes.com/2016/10/08/us/politics/donald-trump-women.html.

10. Lorraine Ali, "Has Donald Trump Broken the Media?" *Los Angeles Times*, October 9, 2016, http://www.latimes.com/entertainment/la-et-has-donald-trump-broken-media-20161008-snap-story.html.

11. *OED* s.v. "pussy" (n. and adj.), A. 1b and 3.

12. Ibid., A. 2a and 1a.

13. *Adew my pretty pussy* (DIMEV 224; TM 67). Variant versions of the poem's first seven lines are copied twice in a sixteenth-century hand in the margins of CUL MS Ff.2.38, fol. 149r and 179v. The longer seventy-two-line version survives in Bodleian MS Ashmole 48, fols. 137r–38r, a secular verse miscellany compiled 1557–65. For the full version, see Wright, *Songs and Ballads*, 209–11; for a facsimile of the shorter versions and the only scholarly background on the poem, see Frances McSparran and Pamela R. Robinson, eds., *Cambridge University Library MS Ff.2.38* (London: Scolar Press, 1979), xvii, 149r, 179v. Text references are to lines in Wright's edition.

and insatiability.[14] He regales his peers with ribald boasts of drunken sex with his ex-lover: "For she can syt asyde, syr . . . With all her poynts untyde, syr, / When she hath yn her ale" (For she can sit as if on horseback, sir, / With all her clothing unlaced, sir, / When she is drunk from ale), he boasts (41, 43–44). Trump's use of the word "pussy" five hundred years later to brag of seizing women's vulvas without "even wait[ing]" for their consent, coupled with Bush's gleeful giggling and affirmations, illustrates the lasting power of "pussy" as a same-sex educational tool.

In the second presidential debate, two days after the *Access Hollywood* tape's release, Trump excused his remarks as "locker room talk" a total of five times.[15] He linked their obscenity, violence, entitlement, misogyny, and all-male conversational context to sports culture, with its intimate same-sex bonds, emphasis on hegemonic masculinity, and competition with teammates as well as rivals. Sociologist Timothy Jon Curry defines locker room talk as an all-male discourse of "hostile talk about women blended with jokes and put-downs about . . . each other," dominated by "talk about women as objects, homophobic talk, and talk that is very aggressive and hostile towards women . . . [and] promotes rape culture."[16] Trump's locating of his comments within this discourse illustrates locker room talk's instructive capacity and shows that it is not confined to the locker room at all.[17] Like Chaucer's "felawe masculinity" and the flyters' lexicon of insult, locker room talk enables its participants to proclaim their heterosexuality and punish one another for transgressing group norms.

In recent years, this discourse's use of obscenity to foster fraternal bonds and endorse violence has taken the form of explicit recordings exchanged among men, enabling them to boast of their conquests in a digital brotherhood,

---

14. "Syr" ends thirty-four of the longer version's seventy-two lines.

15. "Transcript of the Second Debate," *New York Times*, October 9, 2016, https://www.nytimes.com/2016/10/10/us/politics/transcript-second-debate.html.

16. Timothy Jon Curry, "Fraternal Bonding in the Locker Room: A Profeminist Analysis of Talk about Competition and Women," *Sociology of Sport Journal* 8 (1991): 126, 128. For more on locker room talk and its role in sports culture, see Jason B. Jimerson, "A Conversation (Re)Analysis of Fraternal Bonding in the Locker Room," *Sociology of Sport Journal* 18 (2001) and Curry, "Reply to 'A Conversation (Re)Analysis of Fraternal Bonding in the Locker Room,'" *Sociology of Sport Journal* 18 (2001). Jessica Luther notes how one college football coach used the negative connotations of "pussy" as a tool to motivate his players, in Luther, *Unsportsmanlike Conduct: College Football and the Politics of Rape* (New York: Akashic, 2016), 185–86.

17. For more on sexual violence in sports culture, see Luther, *Unsportsmanlike Conduct*, esp. 43–49 on gang rapes perpetrated by college teammates; also Anna Krien, *Night Games: Sex, Power, and A Journey to the Dark Side of Sport* (London: Vintage, 2014). Peggy Reeves Sanday analyzes the social phenomenon of fraternity gang rape, which refers to "male bonding in sex acts in which the males involved aid and abet the activity," in *Fraternity Gang Rape: Sex, Brotherhood, and Privilege on Campus*, 2nd ed. (New York: New York University Press, 2007).

akin to the competitive obscene storytelling between John and Aleyn in the *Reeve's Tale*.[18] This was the case in September 2016 when, according to the University of Minnesota's Office of Equal Opportunity and Affirmative Action's eighty-page investigative report, at least ten members of the school's football team, along with a high school senior visiting the university as a recruit, gang-raped a twenty-year-old woman in an off-campus dorm in the early morning hours after the first game of the season.[19] According to one player's testimony, one of the men said to his teammates, "You can all go in and fuck if you want to," using obscenity to encourage his peers to assault the woman.[20] The men shared multiple videos of the assaults in a text message group called Empire that included all the team's first-year members.[21] They used the group messages to gloat about their behavior over the course of the night: "Me and the recruit finna double team this bitch," one man announced to his teammates in a message quoted in the report. "I'm sliding in some pussy r[ight] n[ow] lol," he wrote, bragging about his actions and framing them as comic with his use of the jocular acronym "lol" (laughing out loud).[22] Later he boasted, "I took good videos," relishing the opportunity to share his deeds with his brethren.[23] Another man joked about "run[ning] her," using terminology "which generally refers to more than one man having sex with the same woman."[24] One witness reported that "a bunch of guys gathered around one of their phones [and] became excited" while viewing one of the recordings as they experienced the assault as a fraternal collective.[25] The use of obscene digital storytelling to build fraternal bonds and authorize violence is likewise central to the Ched Evans case, when Evans's brother and friend stood outside the window at the Premier Inn, laughing loudly and using their phones to record what they saw.[26]

---

18. Nicola Henry and Anastasia Powell, *Sexual Violence in a Digital Age* (New York: Palgrave, 2017), 117–52.

19. "University of Minnesota–Twin Cities EOAA Report," December 7, 2016, http://kstp.com/kstpImages/repository/cs/files/U%20of%20M%20EOAA%20redacted5.pdf.

20. Ibid., 26.

21. Ibid., 16–17, 24–25.

22. Ibid., 17.

23. Ibid..

24. Ibid.; *OED* s.v. "train" (v.), 23.

25. "University of Minnesota–Twin Cities EOAA Report," 70.

26. This digital "felawe masculinity" is central to numerous multiple-perpetrator assaults involving athletes in recent years, including those perpetrated by Steubenville High School's football team (2012), Baylor University's football team (2012), and Vanderbilt University's football team (2014). For the role of obscene texts and photos in the Vanderbilt case, see Luther, *Unsportsmanlike Conduct*, 143–50. This phenomenon of collective assault and digital sharing is not limited to athletes, as illustrated in the documentary *Aubrie and Daisy* (Netflix, 2015); also Henry and Powell, *Sexual Violence in a Digital Age*, 130–32.

In light of obscenity's continued power to teach humiliation, aggression, homophobia, and rigid masculinity, we must confront how little has changed culturally from Chaucer's band of "felawes" swapping comic tales of assault and Scottish poets exchanging misogynist vitriol about one another's wives to prove their literary supremacy. We must acknowledge the perniciousness and unacceptability of locker room talk regardless of where it occurs, and we must reckon with how this discourse uses obscenity to educate men about sex and power. Now as in the Middle Ages, obscenity is used by some men to teach their peers how to deny another's sexual subjectivity and how to inflict violence on women and other men. It is time to recognize the tight wires running between past and present, humming persistently with an ever-living charge, and say, *No more. Fuck this. We will not stand for it.* Spurred by understanding how obscenity's power has been mobilized to teach lessons that are anathema to ethical sexuality, and by comprehending the full breadth of the suffering those lessons have engendered, it is my hope that we can eradicate them once and for all.

"Pussy" teaches about gender and sexuality because of its social power to subordinate and dehumanize. It is wielded to humiliate men who do not follow certain codes of masculinity. It objectifies women and reminds them of their status as penetrable bodies marked for violence. Several months before the *Access Hollywood* tape's release, I was walking from the subway in the early-evening winter dark. Two men across the street, stocky and broad-shouldered with the swaggering fearlessness of youthful masculinity, shouted out to me. "Pussy," I heard them yelling. "Give us some of that pussy. We want that pussy." When you are a woman and two men are shouting "pussy" at you across a darkened street, the obscenity teaches you that you are not safe, that you are nothing more than a fuckable body part, that you need to be ready to run for your life, fleeing your way like the songbird in *Hay how the marys on a brere*. I keep walking. They follow me, shouting about my pussy. I turn left down the next street. They turn, too. I keep walking, electric with terror and ready to fight, the adrenaline of fear and ironclad determination to escape coursing through my body. Eventually they give up, deciding that they don't need to hurt me, that scaring the shit out of me and reminding me of my relative powerlessness is enough. When I finally get to my friends' house, I am breathless as though I have been running for a very long time. I notice I have lost my scarf along the way, that it fell on the ground somewhere and I did not even feel the cold because I was so afraid.

On January 21, 2017, the day after Trump's inauguration symbolically ratified his obscene lessons in the *Access Hollywood* video, millions of women protested in cities around the world. Obscenity, particularly "pussy," was prominent in the signs brandished by the marchers. Women mobilized it to protest governmental attempts to regulate their bodies and to draw attention to the hypocrisies of male politicians who seek to limit their reproductive agency. They seized the words used to dehumanize them and wielded them to oppose Trump's lessons using his own language. PUSSY GRABS BACK, said many signs that day. NOT YOUR PUSSY, NOT YOUR PROBLEM, said one. MY PUSSY, MY RULES. GONNA MOVE ON YOU LIKE A BITCH. IF I WANTED THE GOVERNMENT IN MY UTERUS, I'D FUCK A SENATOR. IF MY VAGINA SHOT BULLETS, IT WOULDN'T NEED REGULATION. PATRIARCHY IS FOR DICKS. SEPARATION BETWEEN COOCH AND STATE. Like the medieval singlewomen celebrating "the bella" and proclaiming the desires of their "prety wanton ware," the protesters marshaled obscenity's discursive power to make a case for women's bodily sovereignty. Butler notes how "being called a name"—in this case, being reduced to one's "pussy"—"can be the site of injury, and . . . this name-calling may be the initiating moment of a counter-mobilization."[27] She declares that "insurrectionary speech becomes the necessary response to injurious language, a risk taken in response to being put at risk, a repetition in language that forces change."[28] The marchers' obscenity functioned as this "insurrectionary speech," with women wielding the words used to subordinate them, now as weapons for social change.

Obscenity is an effective teaching tool because it provokes a response: it engenders shame and disgust, causing listeners to turn away; it transgresses cultural norms, enabling it to disrupt the social order; and it unites individuals through its illicit charge. I suggest that we respond to its provocation by exploring how its galvanizing charge can be harnessed to protest injustice and shed unforgiving light on persistent inequalities. We can choose to answer its challenge by recognizing how it is used to teach the lessons of rape culture in premodern Britain as well as in our own time, and we can respond with teachings that minimize harm and encourage respect. Instead of using obscenity to subordinate and demean, let us utilize its transgressive power to give voice to those who are marginalized, to engender empathy for those who are wounded, and to consider new paradigms for negotiating desire.

---

27. Butler, *Excitable Speech*, 163.
28. Ibid.

APPENDIX TO CHAPTER 4

Songs of Lusty Maidens

I include full-text editions of the singlewomen's erotic songs that I discuss in chapter 4 because they have never been printed together before, and many are in unglossed or difficult-to-find editions. I base my editions on my own transcriptions as well as on the most recent published editions, and I have added glosses. I have italicized each carol's burden, which was sung at the song's beginning and then repeated after each stanza.

#1—*And I war a maydyn*

BL MS Additional 31922, fol. 106v–107r

	And I war a maydyn	[If I were a maiden
	As many one ys,	
	For all the golde in Englond	
4	I wold not do amysse.	[commit (sexual) sin, do wrong
	When I was a wanton wench	
	Of twelve yere of age,	
	These cowrtyers with ther amorus	[courtiers; amorous affections

(continued)

8	They kyndyld my corage.	[inflamed; sexual desire
	When I was come to	
	The age of fifteen yere,	
	In all this lond, nowther fre nor bond,	[neither freewoman nor bondwoman
12	Methought I had no pere.	[I thought I had no peer/equal

#2—*The bella*

XX Songes (London, 1530), item 6; with additional verse from incomplete, cropped version in NYPL Drexel MSS 4183 and 4184, flyleaves.

	The bella, the bella,	*[The best in its class/vulva*
	We maydins beryth the bella,	*[take the prize/have the vulva*
	The bella, the bella,	
4	*We maydins beryth the bella,*	
	We maydyns berth the bella,	
	The bella, the bella.	
	We be maydins fayr and fre;	[beautiful
8	Cum ner, ye yowng men, behold and see	
	How praty and proper now that we be	[attractive
	So comly under kel-la	[beautiful in our headdresses
	The bella, the bella . . .	[(signal to repeat the burden)
12	We be madyns fayr and gent,	[shapely
	Wyth yes grey and browys bent.	[gleaming eyes; arched eyebrows
	We be cum for thys intent	
	Our selfys now for to sell-la,	
16	*The bella, the bella . . .*	
	Assay you then non of ther spyce,	[test out; commodities
	For it wyl make your bely to swell-la,	
	The bella, the bella . . .	
20	Syster, loke that ye be not forlorn,	[ruined sexually
	For then every man wyl laugh you to skorn	
	And say, "Kytt hath got a clap under a thorne."	[whore; gotten a blow; sharp object
	Alak, wher shal we then dwel-la?	[Alas
24	*The bella, the bella . . .*	

#3—*Ate ston casting my lemman I ches*

CUL MS Ii.3.8, fol. 86r

Ate ston casting my lemman I ches,	[a stone-hurling competition; lover
And atte wrastling sone I hym les.	[at a wrestling match soon I lose him
Alas, that he so sone fel!	
4 Why nadde he stonde better, vile gorel?	[Why didn't he stand better, worthless glutton?

#4—*Off servyng men I wyll begyne*

BL MS Sloane 1584, fol. 45v

So well ys me begone,	[How fortunate am I!
Troly, lole,	[(popular jolly song refrain)
So well ys me begone,	
4 Troly, loly.	
Off servyng men I wyll begyne,	[servant
Troley, loley,	
For they goo mynyon trym,	[smartly dressed like a social climber
8 Troly, loley.	
Of mett and drynk and feyr clothyng,	
Troley, loley,	
By dere God, I want none,	
12 Troly, loley.	
His bonet is of fyne scarlett,	
Troley, loley,	
With here as black as geitt,	[hair; jet
16 Troly, lolye.	
His dublett ys of fyne satyne,	[tight-fitting torso garment; satin
Troly, lolye,	
His shertt well mayd and tryme,	[shirt well-made and smart
20 Troly, lolye.	
His coytt itt is so tryme and rownde,	[coat; smart and round
Troly, lolye,	
His kysse is worth a hundred pounde,	

(continued)

24	Troly, loly.	
	His hoysse of London black,	[hose
	Troly, lolye,	
	In hyme ther ys no lack,	[In him there is no deficiency
28	Troly lolye.	
	His face yt ys so lyk a man,	
	Troly, lolye,	
	Who cane butt love hyme than?	
32	Troly, lolye.	
	Whersoever he bee, he hath my hert,	
	Troly, loly,	
	And shall to deth depart,	
36	Troly, lolye.	

#5—If I be wanton I wott well why

BL MS Harley 7578, fol. 105v

	If I be wanton I wott well why	[If I am lustful, know very well why
	I wol fayn tary another year	[I will happily delay
	My wanton ware	*[My pleasure-seeking commodity*
4	*Shall walk for me, shall walk fore me;*	*[circulate (as money) on my behalf*
	My prety wanton ware	
	Shall walk for me.	
	I wyll nott spare to tygh yow,	*[refrain from playfully touching you*
8	*He tygh, he tygh, he tygh he*	*[He touches, he touches, he touches . . .*
	I am a woman, I may be bold;	[fearless, daring, confident, shameless
	Though I be lyttyll, yet am I old	[petite, young; experienced, mature
	My wanton ware . . .	
12	I am so pretty myne aray,	[in my clothing
	And looke so myrily every day	
	My wanton ware . . .	
	I may well forbear sum man to fynd	[relinquish *or* tolerate, allow
16	Of gentyll nature, loving and kind	
	My wanton ware . . .	
	I wyll be gentyll, com when ye wyll;	[courteous
	I know nobody wyll do me ill	[harm
20	*My wanton ware . . .*	
	If I were wedded, I woll be glade	
	As for the sowrowe that I have hade	[Because of/regarding; sorrow
	My wanton ware . . .	

#6—*I pray yow maydens every chone*

CUL MS Additional 7350, Part 1, Box 2, fol. iiv

Podynges at nyght and podynges at none   [Sausages; noon

Were nat for podynges the world were clene done   [If it were not for sausages, the world

would be completely over

"I pray yow, maydens every chone,   [ask; each and every one

4   Tell me wherfore ye make so grete mone.

Yf ye have nede podynges to bye,

Cumm hether to me, for I have plenty.   [Come hither

Will ye have of the podynges that lye on the shelf?"

8   "Nay, I will have a podyng that will stand by hymself!

Therfor I pray yow hartely,   [I ask you fervently

Let me have hym, for that will I bye."

"Will ye have of the podynges cum out of the panne?"

12   "No, I will have a podyng that grows out of a man,

For he may helpe me at my nede;

Therfor I pray yow now let me spede."   [be successful

"How sey ye mayde, will ye eny more?

16   Speke now betyme, for I have lytyll store.   [promptly; a limited amount

Yet I have one sumtyme I dare say,

A handful and half beside the assey."   • [the "trying-out portion"

"What is the price?" seyd th' elder mayde.

20   She spake firste, for she had asseyd.   [tested the quality

Fourtie pens she gave hym in hande,   [Forty pence; in his hand

And seyd she wold have hym to lerne hym stand.

Than spake the yonger maydes every chone,   [each and every one

24   "Happie thou art, for now thou haste one!

But and we lyve another yere as plese God we may,   [If

We will have eche of us one what so ever we pay."   [no matter what

Finis quod E   [The end, said E

Songs of Wantonness

Oxford, Bodleian Library, MS Ashmole 176, fol. 98r–v (c. 1525–50)

1—*My ladye hathe forsaken me* (fol. 98r)

My Ladye hathe forsaken me that longe hathe bene her man,

Yet she her selfe retayned me and covenunte first beganne.   [engaged me in service; formal agreement

But nowe I have espyed some other she hathe tried,

4   Lustye and full of strength, in Labor good at Lengthe.   [to the full extent

This seven yeares and some deale more with her I dyd take payne,   [make an effort

And cannot say but she therfore rewarded me agayne,   [as a result; in return

But nowe I am forsaken, another she hathe taken

(*continued*)

8   Lustye and full of strengthe, in Labour good at Lengthe.

Her servant when I first began, as then she dyd report

For trewe servyce I bare the name amonge the rowte and sort   [among all the people

But nowe she feeles I faynt, with some she dothe acquaynt   [become exhausted

12   Lustye and full of strengthe, in Labour good at Lengthe.

Ye knowe that newe brome swepeth cleane, as many mens sainge ys,

And hackneyes that be comon oftymes tyred ys,   [hired pack-horses

And so shall he be that servethe my Ladye;

16   Although he nowe have strengthe, she wyll hym tyre at Lengthe.

Undoubted she desyrethe muche in labour to endure,   [Doubtless

She sparethe not for ache nor stytche, but allwaye she ys sure;   [refrains; sharp pain

Thus she unsacyate, hathe obteyned for a mate   [insatiable; acquired

20   Lustye and full of strength, in Labor good at Length.

Her appetyte ys suche, marke who so lust to trye   [note; desires

A springing founteyne she wyll lurche and clearlye drawe hym drye,   [prevent others from using; completely

And as the springe dothe quayle, lykewyse her love shall fayle   [weaken

24   Thus he that lackethe strengthe, she lettethe hym slyp at lengthe.   [releases him

#2—*Up I arose in verno tempore* (fol. 98v)

Up I arose, in verno tempore,   [in the springtime

And found a mayd, sub quadam arbore,   [under a tree

That dyd complayne, in suo pectore,   [a heartfelt fashion

4   Sainge, "I feele, puerum movere,   [the child move

What shall I say, meis parentibus?   [to my parents

That with me hath layne, quidam clericus?   [a certain clerk

They wyll me beate, virgis and fustibus,   [with rods and switches

(continued)

8	And me deprave, coram hominibus. /	[vilify; before all the people
	Adewe playfers, antiquo tempore!	[Farewell, companions from times past
	Full ofte with youe, solebam ludere,	[I was wont to laugh
	But for my mysse, mihi deridere,	[sin, plight; they laugh mockingly at me
12	With right full cause, incipio flere,	[completely justified; I begin to weep
	With this said child alas, quid faciam?	[what shall I do
	Shall I yt kepe, vel interficiam?	[or shall I kill [it]?
	Yf I yt sley, quo loco fugiam?	[If I kill it, whither shall I flee?
16	I shall lose God and vitam eternam." / / finis	[eternal life; the end

#3—*I can be wanton and yf I wyll* (fol. 98v)

	I can be wanton and yf I wyll,	
	But yf youe touche me, I wyll crye howe	[raise the hue and cry
	I can be merye and thinke no evell,	[think no wicked thoughts
4	But yet beware, one cometh I trowe.	[suppose
	Yf any come, in faith I crye,	
	That all the strete my voyce shall heare.	
	Take hede that no man doe youe espye,	[Make sure; sees you
8	And I then warant youe come verye nye	[give you permission; near
	But yf youe come, syt farre from me,	
	For me semeth youe should be wylde,	[It seems to me; sexually undisciplined
	And by suche wanton men as youe be	
10	Yonge maydes are sometymes begyled.	deceived
	I wilbe ware of suchelyke wylde men,	[similar
	For when they touche me, I doo crye howe.	
	Kysse me ye should, I beshrewe me then;	[If you should kiss me, I curse myself
12	By Crist, not for my mother's blacke cowe!	
	Ye may me kyll as soone as kysse,	
	I pray youe awaie and let me be.	[I request you go away and leave me alone
	In faith, all the world wyll speake of this,	[Truly
16	I say, ye play the foole with me.	[you act like a fool with me
	By God, I strike youe with my fyste,	
	I shall make your cap fall on the flower.	[I will knock your cap off your head
	But for all that, doe what youe lyst,	[whatever you wish
20	And I wil be styll and crye howe no more.	

#4—*Let be wanton your busynes* (fol. 98v)

Let be, wanton, your busynes,	[Lecher, cease your amorous activity
For in good faith, youe are to blame	[truly
To put me thus in this distris,	[distress
4 Seing that your best lymme ys lame.	[penis; weak, ineffectual

London, British Library, MS Additional 5665 (c. 1510)

#1—*Y have ben a foster* (fol. 53v)

Y have ben a foster	[forest-keeper, hunter
Long and meney day,	[For a long time
My Lockes ben hore,	[My locks are gray
4 Foster woll Y be no more.	
Y shall hong up my horne	[hunting-horn
By the grene wode spray,	[leafy green branch
My lockes ben hore,	
8 Foster will Y be no more.	
All the whiles that Y	[As long as I
May my bowe bende	[May prepare my bow to shoot
Shall Y wedde no wyffe,	
12 My bowe bende	
Shall y wedde no wiffe, wiffe.	
I shall bygges me a boure	[establish my dwelling-place / bedroom
Atte the woodes ende	[At the edge of the forest
16 Ther to lede my lyffe,	
Att the wodes ende,	
Ther to lede my lyffe.	

#2—*Be pes, ye make me spille my ale* (fol. 66v–67r)

	"Be pes, ye make me spille my ale!"	[Be quiet/still
	"Now thyngke ye this ys a fayre ray?"	[Do you think this is a nice way to treat me?
	"Let go I say, straw for yeur tale!"	[I don't care about your story/words
4	"Leff werke a twenty-a-devell away!"	[Leave your work to the devil!
	"Wene ye that everybody lest to play?"	[Do you think that everybody wants to play?
	"Abyde awhile! What have ye haste?	
	I trow for all youre gret affray	[I suppose in spite of all your great fear/alarm
8	Ye will not make to huge a waste.	[waste this opportunity
	After assay then may ye wette;	[testing-out; know
	Why blame ye me withoute offence?"	[crime
	"Ywisse, wanton, ye shull not yette!	[Truly; lecher; ever
12	A, kan ye that? Nou, Gode, go hens!	[Oh, is that what you're doing?; go away
	What do ye here within oure spence?	[storage room
	Recke ye not to make us shende?	[Do you not care that you'll ruin us?
	I wolde not yette for furty pence	[ever
16	My moder cam in, or that ye wende."	[That my mother came in before you left.
	"Cum kys me!" "Nay!" "Be God, ye shall!"	
	"Be Criste, I nelle, what see the man?	[I will not; what does the man say to that?
	Ye herte my legge agenste the walle;	[You hurt my leg against the wall
20	Is this the gentery that ye can?"	[good breeding; demonstrate
	"Take to gev all, and be stille than!"	[make a complete surrender of your body
	"Now have ye leyde me un the flore,	[Now you have laid me on the floor,
	But hadde I wyste when ye bygan,	[But if I had known when you began,
24	Be Criste, I wolde have schytte the dore!"	[By Christ, I would have shut the door!

#3—*In wyldernes* (fol. 141r)

	In wyldernes	[uncultivated woodland
	There founde Y Besse,	
	Secret, alone,	[secluded
	In grete dystres,	
5	Remedyles,	[Without a solution
	Makyng here moone.	[lament, legal complaint
	"Alas," she seyd,	
	"Y was a mayde,	

(continued)

As others be

10   Ande at-a-brayde   [suddenly and violently

Y was afrayde   [attacked, deeply disturbed

Right pyteusly.

A wanton chyld   [lecherous young nobleman

Spoke words mylde   [friendly, courteous

15   To me alone,

And me begylyd,   [duped

Goten with childe,

And now ys gone.

Now hit is so,

20   Lefe of my woe   [forsake

With gode devyse,   [judgement

And let hym go

With sorow also

And play the wyse.   [act like a wise person

25   Now may I wynde   [wander

Withoute a frynd

With hert onfayn.   [misery in my heart

In ferre cuntre   [distant land

Men wene I be   [Men think I am

30   A mayde agayn.

This young men say,

Yn sport and play,

Go wach a byrde;

Men tellyth yn town,

35   When clothis be downe

The smock ys hyd.

I can not kepe,   [refrain

But soore wepe

All for oon;

40   So fro my hert

Shall he not stert,   [go

Thof he be gon.   [Even though he is gone

Alas, that he

Has thus lefte me

45   My sylf alone,   [Alone by myself

In wyldernes,

Remedyles,

Makyng my mone."

#4—*Hay how the mavys one a brere* (fol. 146v–148r)

	Hay how the mavys one a brere,	[small songbird; dog-rose branch
	She sett and sang	
	With noates clere.	
4	I drew me nere[1]	
	To se here chere,	[face, activity
	The grevys amonge, amonge.	[branches
	When Y cam there,	
8	She stode yn fere	
	And seyd, "No nere!	
	What doyst thou here?	
	Hyt ys grete wronge, wronge."	
12	I bade her abyde,	[I asked her to remain
	And stop a tyde.	[moment
	I shall her gyde	
	To a forest which was brode and wyde.	
16	She sayd me nay,	[said no to me
	And flo her way.	[flew
	She wold asay	[attempt
	To take here pray	
20	That she had lovyd so longe.	
	Whan she was gone,	
	And y alone,	
	Makynge my mone,	[lament, complaint
24	With sorowfull grone,	
	Thus ys my song:	
	Such on as she	
	That away woll flee	
28	Yll must she the	[Evil may she prosper
	Where ever she be	
	Yn castell stronge.	[fortified

1. The second part contains "here" in place of "me."

BIBLIOGRAPHY

Manuscripts

BL MS Additional 5665
BL MS Additional 35286
BL MS Egerton 3002
BL MS Harley 268
BL MS Harley 3362
BL MS Harley 7578
BL MS Sloane 1210
Bodleian MS Ashmole 176
Bodleian MS Laud Misc. 416
Bodleian MS Rawlinson C.813
CUL MS Additional 7350, Part 1, Box 2
CUL MS Dd.5.75
CUL MS Ff.5.48
CUL MS Ii.3.26
CUL MS Ii.3.8
NLW MS Peniarth 356B
NYPL MSS Drexel 4183 and 4184

Printed and Electronic Texts

Abbey, Antonia, and Angela J. Jacques-Tiura. "Sexual Assault Perpetrators' Tactics: Associations with Their Personal Characteristics and Aspects of the Incident." *Journal of Interpersonal Violence* 26, no. 14 (2011): 2866–89.

Adams, J. N. *The Latin Sexual Vocabulary*. Baltimore: Johns Hopkins University Press, 1982.

Ahmed, Sara. *Living a Feminist Life*. Durham, NC: Duke University Press, 2017.

Albury, Kath. "Porn *and* Sex Education, Porn *as* Sex Education." *Porn Studies* 1 (2014): 172–81.

Alcoff, Linda, and Laura Gray. "Survivor Discourse: Transgression or Recuperation?" *Signs* 18, no. 2 (1993): 260–90.

Ali, Lorraine. "Has Donald Trump Broken the Media?" *Los Angeles Times*, October 9, 2016. http://www.latimes.com/entertainment/la-et-has-donald-trump-broken-media-20161008-snap-story.html.

Allen, Louisa. "'Looking at the Real Thing': Young Men, Pornography, and Sexuality Education." *Discourse* 27, no. 1 (2006): 69–83.

———. *Young People and Sexuality Education: Key Debates*. New York: Palgrave Macmillan, 2011.

Allen, Louisa, and Moira Carmody. "'Pleasure Has No Passport': Re-visiting the Potential of Pleasure in Sexuality Education." *Sex Education* 12, no. 4 (2012): 455–68.

Allen, Louisa, Mary Lou Rasmussen, and Kathleen Quinlivin, eds. *The Politics of Pleasure in Sexuality Education: Pleasure Bound*. New York: Routledge, 2014.

Amsler, Mark. "Rape and Silence: Ovid's Mythography and Medieval Readers." In *Representing Rape in Medieval and Early Modern Literature*, edited by Elizabeth Robertson and Christine M. Rose, 61–96. New York: Palgrave Macmillan, 2001.

Andersen-Wyman, Kathleen. *Andreas Capellanus on Love? Desire, Seduction, and Subversion in a Twelfth-Century Latin Text*. New York: Palgrave Macmillan, 2007.

Anderson, J. J. "Two Difficulties in *The Meeting in the Wood*." *Medium Ævum* 49 (1980): 258–59.

Anderson, M. L., ed. *The James Carmichaell Collection of Proverbs in Scots*. Edinburgh: Edinburgh University Press, 1957.

Anderson, Peter D. "James V, Mistresses and Children of (*act. c.*1529–1592)." *ODNB*.

Archibald, Elizabeth. "Tradition and Innovation in the Macaronic Poetry of Dunbar and Skelton." *Modern Language Quarterly* 53, no. 1 (1992): 126–49.Baker, John H. *An Introduction to English Legal History*. 4th ed. Oxford: Oxford University Press, 2005.

Banks, Mary Macleod, ed. *An Alphabet of Tales*. Pts. 1, 2. Early English Text Society, o.s., 126, 127. London: Kegan Paul, Trench, Trübner, 1904–1905.

Bannatyne, George. *The Bannatyne Manuscript*. Edited by W. Tod Ritchie. 4 vols. Edinburgh: Scottish Text Society, 1928.

Barbaccia, Holly. "Remembrance in an Early Modern Woman's Seduction Lyric." *Early Modern Women* 6 (2011): 217–21.

Barczewski, Stephanie L. "Ritson, Joseph (1752–1803)." *ODNB*.

Bardsley, Sandy. *Venomous Tongues: Speech and Gender in Late Medieval England*. Philadelphia: University of Pennsylvania Press, 2006.

Barnes, Ishbel C. M. *Janet Kennedy, Royal Mistress: Marriage and Divorce in the Courts of James IV and V*. Edinburgh: John Donald, 2007.

Barratt, Alexandra. "English Translations of Didactic Literature for Women to 1550." In *What Nature Does Not Teach: Didactic Literature in the Medieval and Early-Modern Periods*, edited by Juanita Feros Ruys, 287–301. Turnhout, Belgium: Brepols, 2008.

———, ed. *The Knowing of Woman's Kind in Childing*. Turnhout, Belgium: Brepols, 2002.

Bates, Laura. *Everyday Sexism*. New York: St. Martin's, 2016.

Bawcutt, Priscilla. "Crossing the Border: Scottish Poetry and English Readers in the Sixteenth Century." In *The Rose and the Thistle: Essays on the Culture of Late Medieval and Renaissance Scotland*, edited by Sally Mapstone and Juliette Wood, 59–70. East Linton, UK: Tuckwell Press, 1998.

———. "Dunbar: New Light on Some Old Words." In *The Nuttis Schell: Essays on the Scots Language Presented to A. J. Aitken*, edited by C. Macafee and Isobeal Macleod, 83–95. Aberdeen: Aberdeen University Press, 1987.

———. *Dunbar the Makar*. Oxford: Clarendon Press, 1992.

———. "Images of Women in the Poems of Dunbar." *Études Écossaises* 1 (1992): 49–58.

Bay, Mia. "Love, Sex, Slavery, and Sally Hemings." In *Beyond Slavery: Overcoming Its Religious and Sexual Legacies*, edited by Bernadette J. Brooten, 191–212. New York: Palgrave Macmillan, 2010.

Beattie, Cordelia. *Medieval Single Women: The Politics of Social Classification in Late Medieval England*. Oxford: Oxford University Press, 2007.

Bédier, Joseph. *Les fabliaux: Études de littérature populaire et d'histoire littéraire du moyen âge*. Paris: Champion, 1893.

Beidler, Peter G., ed. *Masculinities in Chaucer*. Cambridge: D. S. Brewer, 1998.

———. "The *Reeve's Tale*." In *Sources and Analogues of the Canterbury Tales*, vol. 1, edited by Robert M. Correale and Mary Hamel, 23–74. Woodbridge, UK: Boydell and Brewer, 2002.

Benham, Hugh. *John Taverner: His Life and Music*. Aldershot, UK: Ashgate, 2003.

Bennett, J. A. W. *Chaucer at Oxford and Cambridge*. Toronto: University of Toronto Press, 1974.

Bennett, Judith M. *Ale, Beer, and Brewsters in England: Women's Work in a Changing World 1300–1600*. Oxford: Oxford University Press, 1996.

———. *History Matters: Patriarchy and the Challenge of Feminism*. Philadelphia: University of Pennsylvania Press, 2006.

———. "Ventriloquisms: When Maidens Speak in Middle English Songs, c. 1330–1500." In *Medieval Woman's Song: Cross-Cultural Approaches*, edited by Anne L. Klinck and Ann Marie Rasmussen, 187–204. Philadelphia: University of Pennsylvania Press, 2002.

Bennett, Judith M., and Amy M. Froide. "A Singular Past." In *Singlewomen in the European Past 1250–1800*, edited by Judith M. Bennett and Amy M. Froide, 1–37. Philadelphia: University of Pennsylvania Press, 1999.

Benson, Larry D. "The 'Queynte' Punnings of Chaucer's Critics." In *Studies in the Age of Chaucer, Proceedings 1 (1984): Reconstructing Chaucer*, edited by Paul Strohm and Thomas J. Heffernan, 23–47. Knoxville: University of Tennessee Press, 1985.

Berglas, Nancy F., Norman A. Constantine, and Emily J. Ozer. "A Rights-Based Approach to Sexuality Education: Conceptualization, Clarification and Challenges." *Perspectives on Sexual and Reproductive Health* 46, no. 2 (2014): 63–72.

Bernau, Anke. "Medieval Antifeminism." In *The History of British Women's Writing, 700–1500*, edited by Liz Herbert McAvoy and Diane Watt, 72–82. New York: Palgrave Macmillan, 2012.

———. *Virgins: A Cultural History*. London: Granta, 2007.

Beveridge, Erskine, ed. *Fergusson's Scottish Proverbs, from the Original Print of 1641, Together with a Larger Manuscript Collection of About the Same Period Hitherto Unpublished*. Edinburgh: William Blackwood and Sons for the Scottish Text Society, 1924.

Bird, Sharon R. "Welcome to the Men's Club: Homosociality and the Maintenance of Hegemonic Masculinity." *Gender and Society* 10, no. 2 (1996): 120–32.

Black, William Henry. *A Descriptive, Analytical, and Critical Catalogue of the Manuscripts Bequeathed unto the University of Oxford by Elias Ashmole.* Oxford: Oxford University Press, 1845.

Blamires, Alcuin, ed. *Woman Defamed and Women Defended: An Anthology of Medieval Texts.* Oxford: Clarendon Press, 1992.

Boffey, Julia. "The Maitland Folio Manuscript as a Verse Anthology." In *William Dunbar, "The Nobill Poyet": Essays in Honour of Priscilla Bawcutt,* edited by Sally Mapstone, 40–50. East Linton, UK: Tuckwell Press, 2001.

——. *Manuscripts of English Courtly Love Lyrics in the Later Middle Ages.* Cambridge: D. S. Brewer, 1985.

Boffey, Julia, and A. S. G. Edwards. "Bodleian MS Arch. Selden.B.24 and the 'Scotticization' of Middle English Verse." In *Rewriting Chaucer: Culture, Authority, and the Idea of the Authentic Text, 1400–1602,* edited by Barbara Kline and Thomas Prendergast, 166–85. Columbus: Ohio State University Press, 1999.

——. "'Chaucer's Chronicle,' John Shirley, and the Canon of Chaucer's Shorter Poems." *Studies in the Age of Chaucer* 20 (1998): 201–18.

Boklund-Lagopoulou, Karin. "Popular Song and the Middle English Lyric." In *Medieval Oral Literature,* edited by Karl Reichl, 555–80. Berlin: de Gruyter, 2012.

Booth, Paul. "An Early Fourteenth-Century Use of the F-Word in Cheshire, 1310–11." *Transactions of the Historic Society of Lancashire and Cheshire* 164 (2015): 99–102.

Bowers, John M., ed. *The Canterbury Tales: Fifteenth-Century Continuations and Additions.* Kalamazoo, MI: Medieval Institute Publications, 1992.

Bowers, Roger. "Early Tudor Courtly Song: An Evaluation of the Fayrfax Book (BL, Additional MS 5465)." In *The Reign of Henry VII,* edited by Benjamin Thompson, 188–212. Stamford, CT: Paul Watkins, 1995.

Boyd, David Lorenzo, and Ruth Mazo Karras. "The Interrogation of a Male Transvestite Prostitute in Fourteenth-Century London." *GLQ* 1, no. 4 (1995): 459–65.

Boynton, Susan. "Women's Performance of the Lyric before 1500." In *Medieval Woman's Song: Cross-Cultural Approaches,* edited by Anne L. Klinck and Ann Marie Rasmussen, 47–65. Philadelphia: University of Pennsylvania Press, 2002.

Brewer, J. S., ed. *Letters and Papers, Foreign and Domestic, of the Reign of Henry VIII.* 24 vols. London: Longman, Green, Longman, and Roberts, 1862.

Brownmiller, Susan. *Against Our Will: Men, Women, and Rape.* New York: Fawcett Books, 1975.

Brückner, Hannah, and Peter Bearman. "After the Promise: The STD Consequences of Adolescent Virginity Pledges." *Journal of Adolescent Health* 36 (2005): 271–78.

Bruckner, Matilda Tomaryn. "Fictions of the Female Voice: The Woman Troubadours." In *Medieval Woman's Song: Cross-Cultural Approaches,* edited by Anne L. Klinck and Ann Marie Rasmussen, 127–51. Philadelphia: University of Pennsylvania Press, 2002.

Brundage, James A. *Law, Sex, and Christian Society in Medieval Europe*. Chicago: University of Chicago Press, 1987.

Buchanan, George. *Ane Detectioun of the duinges of Marie Quene of Scotts, touchand the murder of her Husband, and his Conspiracie, Adulterie, and pretensit Mariage with the Erle Bothwell. Translatit out of the latine, quhilk was written be G. B*. London: John Day, 1571.

———. *The History of Scotland*. Translated by James Aikman. 4 vols. Edinburgh: Archibald Fullarton and Blackie, Fullarton, 1827–29.

Buchwald, Emilie, Pamela R. Fletcher, and Martha Roth, eds. *Transforming a Rape Culture*. Rev. ed. Minneapolis, MN: Milkweed, 2005.

Bullock, Penn. "Transcript: Donald Trump's Taped Comments about Women." *New York Times*, October 8, 2016. https://www.nytimes.com/2016/10/08/us/donald-trump-tape-transcript.html.

Burgwinkle, Bill. "Medieval Somatics." In *The Cambridge Companion to the Body in Literature*, edited by David Hillman and Ulrika Maude, 10–23. Cambridge: Cambridge University Press, 2015.

Burns, Alexander, Maggie Haberman, and Jonathan Martin. "Donald Trump Apology Caps Day of Outrage over Lewd Tape." *New York Times*, October 7, 2016. https://www.nytimes.com/2016/10/08/us/politics/donald-trump-women.html.

Burns, E. Jane. *Bodytalk: When Women Speak in Old French Literature*. Philadelphia: University of Pennsylvania Press, 1993.

Butler, Judith. *Excitable Speech: A Politics of the Performative*. New York: Routledge, 1997.

Byrd, William. *Songs of Sundrie Natures*. London: Thomas East for William Byrd, 1589.

Cadden, Joan. *Meanings of Sex Difference in the Middle Ages*. Cambridge: Cambridge University Press, 1995.

Cahill, Ann J. *Rethinking Rape*. Ithaca, NY: Cornell University Press, 2001.

Cameron, Jamie. *James V: The Personal Rule, 1528–1542*. Edited by Norman Macdougall. East Linton, UK: Tuckwell, 1998.

Camille, Michael. *Image on the Edge: The Margins of Medieval Art*. London: Reaktion, 1992.

———. "Obscenity under Erasure: Censorship in Medieval Illuminated Manuscripts." In *Obscenity: Social Control and Artistic Creation in the European Middle Ages*, edited by Jan M. Ziolkowski, 139–54. Leiden: Brill, 1998.

Cannon, Christopher. "Chaucer and Rape: Uncertainty's Certainties." In *Representing Rape in Medieval and Early Modern English Literature*, edited by Elizabeth Robertson and Christine M. Rose, 255–79. New York: Palgrave Macmillan, 2001.

———. *From Literacy to Literature: England, 1300–1400*. Oxford: Oxford University Press, 2016.

Caputi, Mary. *Voluptuous Yearnings: Toward a Feminist Theory of the Obscene*. Lanham, MD: Rowman and Littlefield, 1993.

Carlin, Martha. "Fast Food and Urban Living Standards in Medieval England." In *Food and Eating in Medieval Europe*, edited by Martha Carlin and Joel T. Rosenthal, 27–51. London: Hambledon Press, 1998.

Carmody, Moira. "Ethical Erotics: Reconceptualizing Anti-Rape Education." *Sexualities* 8, no. 4 (2005): 465–80.

——. *Sex, Ethics, and Young People.* New York: Palgrave Macmillan, 2015.

——. "Sexual Violence Prevention Educator Training: Opportunities and Challenges." In *Preventing Sexual Violence: Interdisciplinary Approaches to Overcoming a Rape Culture,* edited by Nicola Henry and Anastasia Powell, 150–69. New York: Palgrave Macmillan, 2014.

Carruthers, Mary. *The Book of Memory: A Study of Memory in Medieval Culture.* 2nd ed. Cambridge: Cambridge University Press, 2008.

Cartlidge, Neil. "'Alas, I Go with Chylde': Representations of Extra-Marital Pregnancy in the Middle English Lyric." *English Studies* 5 (1998): 395–414.

Casey, Erin, and Tyler Smith. "'How Can I Not?': Men's Pathways to Involvement in Anti-Violence against Women Work." *Violence against Women* 16, no. 8 (2010): 953–73.

Chambers, E. K., ed. *The Oxford Book of Sixteenth Century Verse.* Oxford: Clarendon, 1932.

Chambers, W., ed. *Charters and Documents Relating to the Burgh of Peebles with Extracts from the Records of the Burgh AD 1165–1710.* 2 vols. Edinburgh: Burgh Records Society, 1872, 1909.

Chaucer, Geoffrey. *The Riverside Chaucer.* 3rd ed. Edited by Larry D. Benson et al. Boston: Houghton Mifflin, 1987.

Cho, Sumi, Kimberlé Williams Crenshaw, and Leslie McCall. "Toward a Field of Intersectionality Studies: Theory, Applications, and Praxis." *Signs* 38, no. 4 (2013): 785–810.

Clinton, Catherine. "Breaking the Silence: Sexual Hypocrisies from Thomas Jefferson to Strom Thurmond." In *Beyond Slavery: Overcoming Its Religious and Sexual Legacies,* edited by Bernadette J. Brooten, 213–28. New York: Palgrave Macmillan, 2010.

Coates, Richard. "Fockynggroue in Bristol." *Notes and Queries* 54, no. 4 (2007): 373–76.

Cohen, Cathy J. "Punks, Bulldaggers, and Welfare Queens: The Radical Potential of Queer Politics?" *GLQ: A Journal of Lesbian and Gay Studies* 3 (1997): 437–65.

Coleman, Robin R. Means, and Douglas-Wade Brunton. "'You Might Not Know Her, but You Know Her Brother': Surveillance Technology, Respectability Policing, and the Murder of Janese Talton Jackson." *Souls* 18, no. 2 (2016): 408–20.

Colgrave, B., and C. E. Wright. "An Elizabethan Poem about Durham." *Durham University Journal* 32 (1940): 161–68.

Collins, Patricia Hill. *Black Feminist Thought: Knowledge, Consciousness, and the Politics of Empowerment.* 2nd ed. New York: Routledge, 2009.

——. *Fighting Words: Black Women and the Search for Justice.* Minneapolis: University of Minnesota Press, 1998.

——. "On Violence, Intersectionality and Transversal Politics." *Ethnic and Racial Studies* 40, no. 9 (2017): 1460–73.

Conlee, John W., ed. *Middle English Debate Poetry: A Critical Anthology.* East Lansing, MI: Colleagues Press, 1991.

Cooper, Brittney. "Intersectionality." In *The Oxford Handbook of Feminist Theory*, edited by Lisa Disch and Mary Hawkesworth, 385–406. Oxford: Oxford University Press, 2016.

Copeland, Rita. *Pedagogy, Intellectuals, and Dissent in the Later Middle Ages: Lollardy and Ideas of Learning*. Cambridge: Cambridge University Press, 2001.

Cornelius, Michael G. "Genre, Representation, and Perspective in Dunbar's 'Mariit Wemen.'" *Scotia* 23 (1999): 17–32.

——. "Robert Henryson's Pastoral Burlesque *Robene and Makyne* (c. 1470)." *Fifteenth-Century Studies* 28 (2003): 80–96.

Cornell, Drucilla. "Pornography's Temptation." In *Feminism and Pornography*, edited by Drucilla Cornell, 551–68. Oxford: Oxford University Press, 2000.

Cornerstone Christian Academy. "Dress Code Handbook Excerpt." Accessed November 30, 2017. https://ccacornerstone.com/uploads/1496344014 _DRESS%20CODE%20Handbook%20excerpt.pdf.

Cottman, Michael. "Historians Uncover Slave Quarters of Jefferson's Enslaved Mistress Sally Hemings at Monticello." *NBC News*, July 3, 2017. http://www .nbcnews.com/news/nbcblk/thomas-jefferson-s-enslaved-mistress-sally -hemings-living-quarters-found-n771261.

Craigie, W. A., ed. *The Maitland Folio Manuscript*. 2 vols. Edinburgh: William Blackwood and Sons for the Scottish Text Society, 1919.

Cramond, William, ed. *The Annals of Banff*. 2 vols. Aberdeen: New Spalding Club, 1891–93.

——. *The Church and Churchyard of Cullen*. Aberdeen: G. Cornwall and Sons, 1883.

——. *The Records of Elgin, 1234–1800*. 2 vols. Aberdeen: New Spalding Club, 1903, 1908.

Cranstoun, James, ed. *Satirical Poems of the Time of the Reformation*. 4 vols. Edinburgh: William Blackwood and Sons, 1890–93.

Cranton, Patricia. "Teaching for Transformation." *New Directions for Adult and Continuing Education* 93 (2002): 63–71.

Crenshaw, Kimberlé Williams. "Mapping the Margins: Intersectionality, Identity Politics, and Violence against Women of Color." *Stanford Law Review* 43, no. 6 (1991): 1241–99.

——. "The 2 Live Crew Controversy." In *Feminism and Pornography*, edited by Drucilla Cornell, 218–39. Oxford: Oxford University Press, 2000.

Crocker, Holly A. "Affective Politics in Chaucer's *Reeve's Tale*: 'Cherl' Masculinity after 1381." *Studies in the Age of Chaucer* 29 (2007): 225–58.

——. *Chaucer's Visions of Manhood*. New York: Palgrave Macmillan, 2007.

Cupples, Jacqueline B., Ann P. Zukoski, and Tatiana Dierwechter. "Reaching Young Men: Lessons Learned in the Recruitment, Training, and Utilization of Male Peer Sexual Health Educators." *Health Promotion Practice* 11, supplement 1 (2010): 19–25.

Curry, Patrick. "Lilly, William (1602–1681)." *ODNB*.

Curry, Timothy Jon. "Fraternal Bonding in the Locker Room: A Profeminist Analysis of Talk about Competition and Women." *Sociology of Sport Journal* 8 (1991): 119–35.

——. "Reply to 'A Conversation (Re)Analysis of Fraternal Bonding in the Locker Room.'" *Sociology of Sport Journal* 18 (2001): 339–44.

Dauney, William, ed. *Ancient Scotish Melodies*. Edinburgh: The Maitland Club, 1838.

Davidoff, Judith M. *Beginning Well: Framing Fictions in Late Middle English Poetry*. Rutherford, NJ: Farleigh Dickinson University Press, 1988.

Davis, Deirdre. "'The Harm That Has No Name': Street Harassment, Embodiment, and African American Women." In *Gender Struggles: Practical Approaches to Contemporary Feminism*, edited by Constance L. Mui and Julien S. Murphy, 214–25. Oxford: Rowman and Littlefield, 2002..

Davis, Norman, ed. *The Paston Letters and Papers of the Fifteenth Century*. Pt. 1. Oxford: Oxford University Press for Early English Text Society, 2004.

Delany, Sheila. "Anatomy of the Resisting Reader: Some Implications of Resistance to Sexual Wordplay in Medieval Literature." *Exemplaria* 4 (1992): 7–34.

Dinshaw, Carolyn. *Chaucer's Sexual Poetics*. Madison: University of Wisconsin Press, 1989.

——. *Getting Medieval: Sexualities and Communities, Pre- and Postmodern*. Durham, NC: Duke University Press, 1999.

——. *How Soon Is Now? Medieval Texts, Amateur Readers, and the Queerness of Time*. Durham, NC: Duke University Press, 2012.

Dodds, Madeleine Hope. "Some Notes on 'An Elizabethan Poem about Durham.'" *Durham University Journal* 33 (1940): 65–67.

Dor, Juliette. "'The Sheela-na-gig: An Incongruous Sign of Sexual Purity?" In *Medieval Virginities*, edited by Anke Bernau, Ruth Evans, and Sarah Salih, 33–55. Cardiff: University of Wales Press, 2003.

Douglas, Lady Margaret, and Others. *The Devonshire Manuscript: A Woman's Book of Courtly Poetry*. Edited by Elizabeth Heale. Toronto: Centre for Renaissance and Reformation Studies, 2012.

Drimmer, Sonja, and Damian Fleming. "Not Subtle; Not Quaint." *In the Middle: A Medieval Studies Group Blog*, October 9, 2016, www.inthemedievalmiddle .com/2016/10/not-subtle-not-quaint.html.

Dubin, Nathaniel, trans. and ed. *The Fabliaux*. New York: W. W. Norton, 2013.

Dunbar, William. *The Poems of William Dunbar*. Edited by Priscilla Bawcutt. 2 vols. Glasgow: Association for Scottish Literary Studies, 1998.

——. *William Dunbar: The Complete Works*. Edited by John Conlee. Kalamazoo, MI: Medieval Institute Publications, 2004.

Duncan, Thomas G., ed. *Medieval English Lyrics and Carols*. Cambridge: D. S. Brewer, 2013.

Dundes, Alan. *Mother Wit from the Laughing Barrel: Readings in the Interpretation of Afro-American Folklore*. Englewood Cliffs, NJ: Prentice-Hall, 1973.

Dunn, Caroline. *Stolen Women in Medieval England: Rape, Abduction, and Adultery, 1100–1500*. Cambridge: Cambridge University Press, 2013.

Dunnigan, Sarah M. *Eros and Poetry at the Courts of Mary Queen of Scots and James VI*. New York: Palgrave Macmillan, 2002.

Dunton-Downer, Leslie. "Poetic Language and the Obscene." In *Obscenity: Social Control and Artistic Creation in the European Middle Ages*, edited by Jan M. Ziolkowski, 19–37. Leiden: Brill, 1998.

Eccles, Mark, ed. *The Macro Plays: The Castle of Perseverance, Wisdom, Mankind*. Oxford: Oxford University Press for Early English Text Society, 1969.

Eckhardt, Joshua. *Manuscript Verse Collectors and the Politics of Anti-Courtly Love Poetry*. Oxford: Oxford University Press, 2009.

Edington, Carol. *Court and Culture in Renaissance Scotland: Sir David Lindsay of the Mount*. Amherst: University of Massachusetts Press, 1994.

Edwards, A. S. G. "Chaucer's *Cook's Tale* 4422." *Notes and Queries* 64, no. 2 (2017): 220–21.

———. "Manuscripts of the Verse of Henry Howard, Earl of Surrey." *Huntington Library Quarterly* 67, no. 2 (2004): 283–93.

Edwards, A. S. G., and Linne R. Mooney. "A New Version of a Skelton Lyric." *Transactions of the Cambridge Bibliographical Society* 10 (1994): 507–11.

Edwards, Suzanne M. *The Afterlives of Rape in Medieval English Literature*. New York: Palgrave Macmillan, 2016.

Elliott, Dyan. *Fallen Bodies: Pollution, Sexuality, and Demonology in the Middle Ages*. Philadelphia: University of Pennsylvania Press, 1999.

———. "Sex in Holy Places: An Exploration of a Medieval Anxiety." *Journal of Women's History* 6, no. 3 (1994): 6–34.

———. "Sexual Scandal and the Clergy: A Medieval Blueprint for Disaster." In *Why the Middle Ages Matter: Medieval Light on Modern Injustice*, edited by Celia Chazelle, Simon Doubleday, Felice Lifshitz, and Amy G. Remensnyder, 90–105. New York: Routledge, 2012.

———. *Spiritual Marriage: Sexual Abstinence in Medieval Wedlock*. Princeton, NJ: Princeton University Press, 1993.

Enders, Jody. *Rhetoric and the Origins of Medieval Drama*. Ithaca, NY: Cornell University Press, 1992.

England, G., and A. Pollard, eds. *The Towneley Plays*. Early English Text Society, e.s., 71. London: Oxford University Press for Early English Text Society, 1897. Reprint, 1973.

Evans, Ruth, ed. *A Cultural History of Sexuality in the Middle Ages*. New York: Berg, 2011.

Ewan, Elizabeth. "Disorderly Damsels? Women and Interpersonal Violence in Pre-Reformation Scotland." *Scottish Historical Review* 89, no. 2 (2010): 153–71.

———. "'For Whatever Ales Ye': Women as Producers and Consumers in Late Medieval Scottish Towns." In *Women in Scotland c. 1100–c. 1750*, edited by Elizabeth Ewan and Maureen Meikle, 125–35. East Linton, UK: Tuckwell Press, 1999.

———. "'Many Injurious Words': Defamation and Gender in Late Medieval Scotland." In *History, Literature, and Music in Scotland, 700–1560*, edited by R. Andrew McDonald, 163–86. Toronto: University of Toronto Press, 2002.

Fallows, David. "The Drexel Fragments of Early Tudor Song." *Royal Musical Association Research Chronicle* 26 (1993): 5–18.

———, ed. *The Henry VIII Book (British Library, MS Add. 31922)*. Chicago: University of Chicago Press for the Renaissance Society of America, 2014.

Farber, Lianna. *An Anatomy of Trade in Medieval Writing: Value, Consent, and Community*. Ithaca, NY: Cornell University Press, 2006.

Farenthold, David A. "Trump Recorded Having Extremely Lewd Conversation about Women in 2005." *Washington Post*, October 7, 2016. https://www

.washingtonpost.com/politics/trump-recorded-having-extremely-lewd
-conversation-about-women-in-2005/2016/10/07/3b9ce776-8cb4-11e6-bf8a
-3d26847eeed4_story.html?utm_term=.2bc0ab85acbb.

Fehr, Bernhard. "Weitere Beiträge zur englischen Lyric des 15 and 16 Jahrhunderts." *Archiv für das Studium der neueren Sprachen und Literaturen* 107 (1901): 48–61.

Fein, Susanna Greer, ed. and trans., with David Raybin and Jan Ziolkowski. *The Complete Harley 2253 Manuscript.* 3 vols. Kalamazoo, MI: Medieval Institute Publications, 2015.

Finch, Emily, and Vanessa E. Munro. "The Demon Drink and the Demonized Woman: Socio-Sexual Stereotypes and Responsibility Attribution in Rape Trials Involving Intoxicants." *Social and Legal Studies* 16, no. 4 (2007): 591–614.

Fine, Michelle. "Sexuality, Schooling, and Adolescent Females: The Missing Discourse of Desire." *Harvard Educational Review* 58, no. 1 (1988): 29–53.

Fine, Michelle, and Sara I. McClelland. "Sexuality Education and Desire: Still Missing after All These Years." *Harvard Educational Review* 76, no. 3 (2006): 297–338.

Finke, Laurie, and Martin Shichtman. "The Mont St. Michel Giant: Sexual Violence and Imperialism in the Chronicles of Wace and Laȝaman." In *Violence against Women in Medieval Texts*, edited by Anna Roberts, 56–74. Gainesville: University Press of Florida, 1998.

Fisher, Keely. "Comic Verse in Older Scots Literature." PhD diss., Oxford University, 1999.

——. "The Contemporary Humour in William Stewart's *The Flytting betuix the Sowtar and the Tailyour*." In *Literature, Letters, and the Canonical in Early Modern Scotland*, edited by Nicola Royan and Theo van Heijnsbergen, 1–21. East Linton, UK: Tuckwell Press, 2002.

Fitzgerald, Christina M. *The Drama of Masculinity and Medieval English Guild Culture.* New York: Palgrave Macmillan, 2007.

Flood, Michael. "Involving Men in Efforts to End Violence against Women." *Men and Masculinities* 14, no. 3 (2011): 358–77.

——. "Men, Sex, and Homosociality: How Bonds between Men Shape Their Sexual Relations with Women." *Men and Masculinities* 10, no. 3 (2008): 339–59.

——. *Where Men Stand: Men's Roles in Ending Violence against Women.* Sydney: White Ribbon Foundation, 2010.

Florio, John. *A Worlde of Wordes, or Most copious, and exact dictionarie in Italian and English.* London: Arnold Hatfield for Edward Blount, 1598.

Forni, Kathleen. "The Antifeminist Tradition: Introduction." In *The Chaucerian Apocrypha: A Selection*, edited by Kathleen Forni, 101–4. Kalamazoo, MI: Medieval Institute Publications, 2005.

Forster, Katie. "Ched Evans: Court Hears What Happened on Night Out as Footballer Cleared of Rape." *Independent*, October 14, 2016. http://www
.independent.co.uk/news/uk/home-news/ched-evans-what-happened-latest
-really-did-trial-admitted-court-footballer-not-guilty-rape-a7361966.html.

Foubert, John. *The Men's and Women's Programs.* New York: Routledge, 2011.

Foubert, John, and Johnathan T. Newberry. "Effects of Two Versions of an Empathy-Based Rape Prevention Program on Fraternity Men's Survivor

Empathy, Attitudes, and Behavioral Intent to Commit Rape or Sexual Assault." *Journal of College Student Development* 47, no. 2 (2006): 133–48.

Fowler, Elizabeth. "Misogyny and Economic Person in Skelton, Langland, and Chaucer." *Spenser Studies* 10 (1992): 245–73.

Fradenburg, Louise O. "The Scottish Chaucer." In *Writing after Chaucer: Essential Readings in Chaucer and the Fifteenth Century*, edited by Daniel J. Pinti, 167–76. New York: Garland, 1998.

Francis, W. Nelson, ed. *The Book of Vices and Virtues*. Early English Text Society, o.s., 217. London: Oxford University Press for Early English Text Society, 1968.

Freedman, Estelle B. *Redefining Rape: Sexual Violence in the Era of Suffrage and Segregation*. Cambridge, MA: Harvard University Press, 2013.

Freeman, Susan K. *Sex Goes to School: Girls and Sexual Education before the 1960s*. Urbana: University of Illinois Press, 2008.

Freitag, Barbara. *Sheela-na-gigs: Unravelling an Enigma*. New York: Routledge, 2004.

Friedman, Jaclyn, and Jessica Valenti, eds. *Yes Means Yes! Visions of Female Sexual Power and a World without Rape*. Berkeley, CA: Seal Press, 2008.

Friedman, John B. *Northern English Books, Owners, and Makers in the Late Middle Ages*. Syracuse, NY: Syracuse University Press, 1995.

Frith, Simon. *Performing Rites: On the Value of Popular Music*. Oxford: Oxford University Press, 1996.

Froide, Amy M. *Never Married: Singlewomen in Early Modern England*. Oxford: Oxford University Press, 2007.

Fuidge, N. M. "Welles, Humphrey." In *The History of Parliament: The House of Commons 1509–1558*, edited by S. T. Bindoff. London: Secker and Warburg for the History of Parliament Trust, 1982.

Furrow, Melissa M. "Lyarde: A Minor Romance Poem in a Major Romance Manuscript." *Forum for Modern Language Studies* 32, no. 4 (1996): 289–302.

——, ed. *Ten Bourdes*. Kalamazoo, MI: Medieval Institute Publications, 2013.

Gardner, Christine J. *Making Chastity Sexy: The Rhetoric of Evangelical Abstinence Campaigns*. Berkeley: University of California Press, 2011.

Gaunt, Simon. "Obscene Hermeneutics in Troubadour Lyric." In *Medieval Obscenities*, edited by Nicola McDonald, 85–104. York: York Medieval Press, 2006.

Gavey, Nicola. "Fighting Rape." In *Theorizing Sexual Violence*, edited by Renée J. Heberle and Victoria Grace, 96–124. New York: Routledge, 2009.

——. *Just Sex? The Cultural Scaffolding of Rape*. New York: Routledge, 2005.

Gilbert, Jen. "Between Sexuality and Narrative: On the Language of Sex Education." In *Youth and Sexualities: Pleasure, Subversion, and Insubordination in and out of Schools*, edited by Mary Louise Rasmussen, Eric Rofes, and Susan Talburt, 109–26. New York: Palgrave Macmillan, 2004.

Goldberg, P. J. P. "Desperately Seeking the Single Man in Later Medieval England." In *Single Life and the City 1200–1900*, edited by Julie De Groot, Isabelle Devos, and Ariadne Schmidt, 117–37. London: Palgrave Macmillan, 2015.

——, ed. and trans. *Women in England, c. 1275–1525: Documentary Sources*. Manchester: Manchester University Press, 1995.

——. "Women in Later Medieval English Archives." *Journal of the Society of Archivists* 15 (1994): 59–72.

——. *Women, Work, and Life Cycle in a Medieval Economy: Women in York and Yorkshire c. 1300–1520.* Oxford: Oxford University Press, 1992.

Goldstein, R. James. "Normative Heterosexuality in History and Theory: The Case of Sir David Lindsay of the Mount." In *Becoming Male in the Middle Ages,* edited by Jeffrey Jerome Cohen and Bonnie Wheeler, 249–65. New York: Garland, 2000.

The Gossips Meeting, Or The merry Market-Women of Taunton (London: For F. Coles, T. Vere, J. Wright, and J. Clarke, 1674).

Gosynhyll, Edward. *A dialogue bytwene the commune secretary and jalowsye, touchynge the unstablenesse of harlottes.* London: John Kynge, 1556.

Gowing, Laura. *Domestic Dangers: Women, Words, and Sex in Early Modern London.* Oxford: Oxford University Press, 1996.

——. "Secret Births and Infanticide in Seventeenth-Century England." *Past and Present* 156 (1997): 87–115.

Gravdal, Kathryn. *Ravishing Maidens: Writing Rape in Medieval French Literature and Law.* Philadelphia: University of Pennsylvania Press, 1991.

Green, Monica H. "Making Motherhood in Medieval England: The Evidence from Medicine." In *Motherhood, Religion, and Society in Medieval Europe 400–1400: Essays Presented to Henrietta Leyser,* edited by Conrad Leyser and Lesley Smith, 173–91. AldershotUK,: Ashgate, 2011.

Greene, Richard Leighton, ed. *Early English Carols.* 2nd ed. Oxford: Clarendon Press, 1977.

Greentree, Rosemary. "Literate in Love: Makyne's Lesson for Robene." In *Older Scots Literature,* edited by Sally Mapstone, 61–69. Edinburgh: John Donald, 2005.

Gregory the Great. *Gregorii magni dialogi,* ed. Umberto Moricca, 2 vols. Rome: Forzani e C. Tipografi del Senato, 1924.

Grubb, Amy, and Emily Turner. "Attribution of Blame in Rape Cases: A Review of the Impact of Rape Myth Acceptance, Gender Role Conformity, and Substance Abuse on Victim Blaming." *Aggression and Violent Behavior* 17, no. 5 (2012): 443–52.

Guttmacher Institute. "State Laws and Policies: Sex and HIV Education." Updated March 1, 2018. https://www.guttmacher.org/state-policy/explore/sex-and-hiv-education.

Guy, John. *Queen of Scots: The True Life of Mary Stuart.* New York: Mariner Books, 2005.

Hall, Joseph. "Short Pieces from MS Cotton Galba E.ix." *Englische Studien* 21 (1895): 201–9.

Hall, Kim F. "'These Bastard Signs of Fair': Literary Whiteness in Shakespeare's Sonnets." In *Post-Colonial Shakespeares,* edited by Ania Loomba and Martin Orkin, 64–83. New York: Routledge, 1998.

——. *Things of Darkness: Economies of Race and Gender in Early Modern England.* Ithaca, NY: Cornell University Press, 1996.

Hall, Rachel. "It Can Happen to You: Rape Prevention in the Age of Risk Management." *Hypatia* 19, no. 3 (2004): 1–19.

Hanawalt, Barbara A. "Medieval English Women in Rural and Urban Domestic Space." *Dumbarton Oaks Papers* 52 (1998): 19–26.

Hansen, Elaine Tuttle. *Chaucer and the Fictions of Gender*. Berkeley: University of California Press, 1992.

Haraway, Donna. "Situated Knowledges: The Science Question in Feminism and the Privilege of Partial Perspective." In *The Feminist Standpoint Theory Reader: Intellectual and Political Controversies*, edited by Sandra Harding, 81–101. New York: Routledge, 2004.

Harding, Kate. *Asking for It: The Alarming Rise of Rape Culture—and What We Can Do about It*. Boston: Di Capo, 2015.

Hardwick, Paul. *English Medieval Misericords: The Margins of Meaning*. Woodbridge, UK: Boydell, 2011.

Harker, C. Marie. "Skirting the Issue: Misogyny and Gender in Lyndsay's *Ane Supplicatioun Directit . . . to the Kingis Grace, in Contemptioun of Syde Taillis*." In *Older Scots Literature*, edited by Sally Mapstone, 266–82. Edinburgh: John Donald, 2005..

Harris, Carissa M. "'All the Strete My Voyce Shall Heare': Gender, Voice, and Female Desire in the Lyrics of Bodleian MS Ashmole 176." *Journal of the Early Book Society* 20 (2017): 29–58.

———. "Inserting 'a Grete Tente, a Thrifty, and a Long': Sexual Obscenity and Scribal Innovation in Fifteenth-Century Manuscripts of the *Canterbury Tales*." *Essays in Medieval Studies* 28 (2012): 1–16.

Hasday, Jill Elaine. "Contest and Consent: A Legal History of Marital Rape." *California Law Review* 88, no. 5 (2000): 1373–505.

Hasler, Antony J. *Court Poetry in Late Medieval England and Scotland: Allegories of Authority*. Cambridge: Cambridge University Press, 2011.

Heale, Elizabeth. *Wyatt, Surrey, and Early Tudor Poetry*. London: Longman, 1998.

Heberle, Renee. "The Personal Is Political." In *The Oxford Handbook of Feminist Theory*, edited by Lisa Disch and Mary Hawkesworth, 593–609. Oxford: Oxford University Press, 2016.

Helms, Dietrich. "Henry VIII's Book: Teaching Music to Royal Children." *Music Quarterly* 92 (2009): 118–35.

Henderson, E., ed. *Extracts from the Kirk-Session Records of Dunfermline from AD 1640 to 1689*. Edinburgh: Fullarton and Mac, 1865.

Henderson, Jeffrey. *The Maculate Muse: Obscene Language in Attic Comedy*. 2nd ed. Oxford: Oxford University Press, 1991.

Hendricks, Jacquelyn. "The Battle of 'Trechour Tung[s]': Gaelic, Middle Sots, and the Question of Ethnicity in the Scottish Flyting." *Fifteenth Century Studies* 37 (2012): 71–96.

Henry, Nicola, and Anastasia Powell. "Framing Sexual Violence Prevention." In *Preventing Sexual Violence: Interdisciplinary Approaches to Overcoming a Rape Culture*, edited by Nicola Henry and Anastasia Powell, 1–21. New York: Palgrave Macmillan, 2014.

———. *Sexual Violence in a Digital Age*. New York: Palgrave Macmillan, 2017.

Henryson, Robert. *Robert Henryson: The Complete Works*. Edited by David J. Parkinson. Kalamazoo, MI: Medieval Institute Publications, 2010.

Higgins, Ian MacLeod. "Tit for Tat: The *Canterbury Tales* and *The Flyting of Dunbar and Kennedy*." *Exemplaria* 16, no. 1 (2004): 165–202.

Hines, John. *The Fabliau in English*. New York: Longman, 1993.

Holsinger, Bruce W. *Music, Body, and Desire in Medieval Culture: Hildegard of Bingen to Chaucer*. Palo Alto, CA: Stanford University Press, 2001.

Holton, Amanda, and Tim MacFaul, eds. *Tottel's Miscellany*. New York: Penguin, 2011.

Honigmann, John J. "A Cultural Theory of Obscenity." *Journal of Criminal Psychopathology* 5 (1944): 715–33.

Horobin, Simon. "Additional 35286 and the Order of the *Canterbury Tales*." *Chaucer Review* 31, no. 3 (1997): 272–78.

——. "A Transcription and Study of British Library Additional MS 35286 of Chaucer's *Canterbury Tales*." PhD diss., University of Sheffield, 1997.

Hunter, Michael. "Ashmole, Elias (1617–1692)," *ODNB*.

Idle, Peter. *Peter Idley's Instructions to His Son*. Edited by Charlotte D'Evelyn. Boston: Heath for the Modern Language Association, 1935.

Ives, Carolyn, and David Parkinson. "Scottish Chaucer, Misogynist Chaucer." In *Rewriting Chaucer: Culture, Authority, and the Idea of the Authentic Text, 1400–1602*, edited by Barbara Kline and Thomas Prendergast, 186–202. Columbus: Ohio State University Press, 1999.

Jansen, Sharon L., and Kathleen H. Jordan, eds. *The Welles Anthology: MS Rawlinson C.813, a Critical Edition*. Binghamton, NY: Medieval and Renaissance Texts and Studies, 1991.

Jasin, Joanne. "A Critical Edition of the Middle English *Liber Uricrisiarum* in Wellcome MS 225." PhD diss., Tulane University, 1983.

Jeffries, Michael P. *Thug Life: Race, Gender, and the Meaning of Hip-Hop*. Chicago: University of Chicago Press, 2011.

Jensen, Robin E. *Dirty Words: The Rhetoric of Public Sexual Education, 1870–1924*. Urbana: University of Illinois Press, 2010.

Jimerson, Jason B. "A Conversation (Re)Analysis of Fraternal Bonding in the Locker Room." *Sociology of Sport Journal* 18 (2001): 317–38.

Johns, Catherine. *Sex or Symbol? Erotic Images of Greece and Rome*. London: Routledge, 1999.

Johnson, Imani Kai. "Dark Matter in B-Boying Cyphers: Race and Global Connection in Hip Hop." PhD diss., University of Southern California, 2012.

Johnson, J. S. *Chesters Roman Fort Northumberland*. London: English Heritage, 1990.

Jones, Malcolm. "Sex, Popular Beliefs, and Culture." In *A Cultural History of Sexuality in the Middle Ages*, edited by Ruth Evans, 139–64. New York: Berg, 2011.

Josephson, David S. *John Taverner: Tudor Composer*. Ann Arbor: University of Michigan Press, 1979.

Joyful NEWS for maids and young women. London: Printed for Philip Brooks by Jonah Deacon, Josiah Blare, and John Back, 1688–92.

Junior, Nyasha. *An Introduction to Womanist Biblical Interpretation*. Louisville, KY: Westminster John Knox Press, 2015.

Karras, Ruth Mazo. *From Boys to Men: Formations of Masculinity in Late Medieval Europe*. Philadelphia: University of Pennsylvania Press, 2003.

——. *Sexuality in Medieval Europe: Doing unto Others*. 2nd ed. New York: Routledge, 2012.

Kearl, Holly. *Stop Street Harassment: Making Public Spaces Safe and Welcoming for Women*. Santa Barbara, CA: ABC-CLIO, 2010.

Kehily, Mary Jane, and Anoop Nayak. "'Lads and Laughter': Humour and the Production of Heterosexual Hierarchies." *Gender and Education* 9, no. 1 (1997): 69–87.

Kennedy, Walter. *The Poems of Walter Kennedy*. Edited by Nicole Meier. Edinburgh: Scottish Text Society, 2008.

Kimball, Elisabeth G., ed. *The Shropshire Peace Roll, 1400–1414*. Shrewsbury, UK: Printed for the Salop County Council, 1959.

Kirby, Douglas B. "The Impact of Abstinence and Comprehensive Sex and STD/ HIV Education Programs on Adolescent Sexual Behavior." *Sexuality Research and Social Policy* 5, no. 3 (2008): 18–27.

Klausner, David N., ed. *The Castle of Perseverance*. Kalamazoo, MI: Medieval Institute Publications, 2010.

Klinck, Anne L., ed. *An Anthology of Ancient and Medieval Woman's Song*. New York: Palgrave Macmillan, 2004.

——. "The Oldest Folk Poetry? Medieval Woman's Song as Popular Lyric." In *From Arabye to Engelond: Medieval Studies in Honour of Mahmoud Manzalaoui on His 75th Birthday*, edited by A. E. Christa Canitz and Gernot R. Wieland, 229–52. Ottawa: University of Ottawa Press, 1999.

——. "Thinking outside the Box: Pastourelle Encounters in Middle English and Middle Scots." Paper delivered at the 47th International Congress of Medieval Studies, May 2012.

Koldeweij, A. M. "A Barefaced *Roman de la Rose* (Paris, B.N., ms. fr., 25526) and Some Late Medieval Mass-Produced Badges of a Sexual Nature." In *Flanders in a European Perspective: Manuscript Illumination around 1400 in Flanders and Abroad*, edited by Maurits Smeyers and Bert Cardon, 499–516. Leuven: Peeters, 1995.

——. "Lifting the Veil on Pilgrim Badges." In *Pilgrimage Explored*, edited by J. Stopford, 161–88. York: York Medieval Press, 1999.

Kowaleski, Maryanne. "Singlewomen in Medieval and Early Modern Europe: The Demographic Perspective." In *Singlewomen in the European Past*, edited by Judith M. Bennett and Amy M. Froide, 38–81. Philadelphia: University of Pennsylvania Press, 1999.

Krien, Anna. *Night Games: Sex, Power, and A Journey to the Dark Side of Sport*. London: Vintage, 2014.

Kristeva, Julia. *Powers of Horror: An Essay in Abjection*. Translated by Leon S. Roudiez. New York: Columbia University Press, 1982.

Krueger, Roberta L. "Misogyny, Manipulation, and the Female Reader in Hue de Rotelande's *Ipomédon*." In *Courtly Literature: Culture and Context*, edited by Keith Busby and Erik Kooper, 383–97. Amsterdam: Benjamins, 1990.

La Tour-Landry, Geoffroy de. *The Book of the Knight of the Tower*. Edited by M. Y. Offord. Early English Text Society, s.s., 2. London: Oxford University Press, 1971.

Lamb, Sharon. "Feminist Ideals for a Healthy Adolescent Female Sexuality: A Critique." *Sex Roles* 62 (2010): 294–306.

Langland, William. *The Vision of William concerning Piers the Plowman.* Pt. 2. Edited by W. W. Skeat. Early English Text Society, 38. London: Early English Text Society, 1869. Reprint, 1972.

Laskaya, Anne, and Eve Salisbury, eds. *The Middle English Breton Lays.* Kalamazoo, MI: Medieval Institute Publications, 1995.

Levine, Lawrence W. "The Ritual of Insult." In *Black Culture and Black Consciousness: Afro-American Folk Thought from Slavery to Freedom,* 344–58. Oxford: Oxford University Press, 1977.

Lewis, Mary. "Work and the Adolescent in Medieval England AD 900–1550: The Osteological Evidence." *Medieval Archaeology* 60, no. 1 (2016): 136–71.

Lord, Alexandra M. *Condom Nation: The U.S. Government's Sex Education Campaign from World War I to the Internet.* Baltimore: Johns Hopkins University Press, 2010.

Lorde, Audre. "The Master's Tools Will Never Dismantle the Master's House." In *Sister Outsider: Essays and Speeches,* 110–13. Berkeley, CA: Crossing Press, 1984.

Luker, Kristin. *When Sex Goes to School: Warring Views on Sex—and Sex Education—since the Sixties.* New York: W. W. Norton, 2006.

Lutey, Tom. "Judge's Remarks about Teenage Rape Victim Spark Outrage." *Billings Gazette,* August 28, 2013. http://billingsgazette.com/news/local/judge-s-remarks-about-teenage-rape-victim-spark-outrage/article_07466a01-c9c1-5538-a9e0-41f296074b27.html.

Luther, Jessica. *Unsportsmanlike Conduct: College Football and the Politics of Rape.* New York: Akashic, 2016.

Lyall, Roderick J. *Alexander Montgomerie: Poetry, Politics, and Cultural Change in Jacobean Scotland.* Tempe: Arizona Center for Medieval and Renaissance Studies, 2005.

Lydgate, John. *John Lydgate: The Minor Poems.* Vol. 2, *Secular Poems.* Edited by Henry Noble McCracken. London: Early English Texts Society, 1934.

——. *A Selection of the Minor Poems of Dan John Lydgate.* Edited by James Orchard Halliwell. London: C. Richards for the Percy Society, 1840.

Lynch, Annette. *Porn Chic: Exploring the Contours of Raunch Eroticism.* London: Berg, 2012.

Lyndsay, David. *Ane Satyre of the Thrie Estaitis.* Edited by Roderick Lyall. Edinburgh: Canongate, 1989.

——. *Sir David Lyndsay: Selected Poems.* Edited by Janet Hadley Williams. Glasgow: Association for Scottish Literary Studies, 2000.

——. *The Works of Sir David Lindsay of the Mount, 1490–1555.* Edited by Douglas Hamer. 4 vols. Edinburgh: Scottish Text Society, 1931–36.

Lyndsay, Robert. *The Historie and Cronicles of Scotland.* Edited by Æ. J. G. Mackay. 2 vols. Edinburgh: William Blackwood and Sons for the Scottish Text Society, 1899–1911.

MacDonald, A. A. "The Bannatyne Manuscript—A Marian Anthology." *Innes Review* 37 (1986): 36–47.

——. "William Stewart and the Court Poetry of James V." In *Stewart Style 1513–1542: Essays on the Court of James V,* edited by Janet Hadley Williams, 179–200. East Linton, UK: Tuckwell, 1996.

Macdougall, Norman. *James IV*. Edinburgh: John Donald, 1989.

MacKay, William, Herbert Cameron Boyd, and George Smith Laing. *Records of Inverness*. 3 vols. Aberdeen: New Spalding Club, 1911, 1924.

MacQueen, Hector L. "Kennedy Family (*per. c.1350–1513*)." *ODNB*.

Manly, John M., and Edith Rickert. *The Text of the Canterbury Tales*. 8 vols. Chicago: University of Chicago Press, 1940.

Mannyng, Robert. *Robert of Brunne's "Handlyng Synne."* Edited by Frederick J. Furnivall. Early English Text Society, o.s., 119, 123. London: Early English Text Society, 1901, 1903.

Mapstone, Sally. "Invective as Poetic: The Cultural Contexts of Polwarth and Montgomerie's *Flyting*." *Scottish Literary Journal* 26, no. 2 (1999): 18–40.

Marchand, James W. "*Quoniam, Wife of Bath's Prologue* D.608." *Neuphilologiche Mitteilungen* 100, no. 1 (1999): 43–49.

Marotti, Arthur F. *Manuscript, Print, and the English Renaissance Lyric*. Ithaca, NY: Cornell University Press, 1995.

Martin, Joanna M., ed. *The Maitland Quarto: A New Edition of Cambridge, Magdalene College, Pepys Library MS 1408*. Edinburgh: Scottish Text Society, 2015.

Matlock, Wendy A. "Secrets, Gossip, and Gender in William Dunbar's *The Tretis of the Tua Mariit Wemen and the Wedo*." *Philological Quarterly* 83, no. 3 (2004): 209–35.

Maxwell, Claire. "The Prevention of Sexual Violence in Schools: Developing Some Theoretical Starting Points." In *Preventing Sexual Violence: Interdisciplinary Approaches to Overcoming a Rape Culture*, edited by Nicola Henry and Anastasia Powell, 105–26. New York: Palgrave Macmillan, 2014.

Mayhew, A. L., ed. *Promptorium Parvulorum*. London: Kegan Paul, Trench, Trübner for Early English Text Society, 1908.

McCaughey, Martha. *Real Knockouts: The Physical Feminism of Women's Self-Defense*. New York: New York University Press, 1997.

McDonald, Nicola. "Games Medieval Women Play." In *Chaucer's Legend of Good Women: Context and Reception*, edited by Carolyn P. Collette, 176–97. Cambridge: Cambridge University Press, 2006.

———, ed. *Medieval Obscenities*. York: York Medieval Press, 2006.

McGuire, Danielle L. *At the Dark End of the Street: Black Women, Rape, and Resistance—A New History of the Civil Rights Movement from Rosa Parks to the Rise of Black Power*. New York: Vintage Books, 2010.

McIntosh, Marjorie Keniston. *Working Women in English Society, 1300–1620*. Cambridge: Cambridge University Press, 2005.

McSheffrey, Shannon, and Julia Pope. "Ravishment, Legal Narratives, and Chivalric Culture in Fifteenth-Century England." *Journal of British Studies* 48 (2009): 818–36.

McSparran, Frances, and Pamela R. Robinson, eds. *Cambridge University Library MS Ff.2.38*. London: Scolar Press, 1979.

Meale, Carol. "London, British Library, Harley MS 2252: John Colyn's 'Booke': Structure and Content." *English Manuscript Studies 1100–1700* 15 (2009): 65–122.

Meier, Nicole. "*The Flyting of Dunbar and Kennedy* in Context." In *Language Cleir Illumynate: Scottish Poetry from Barbour to Drummond, 1375–1630*, edited by Nicola Royan, 61–77. Amsterdam: Rodopi, 2007.

Mezirow, Jack. "An Overview on Transformative Learning." In *Contemporary Theories of Learning: Learning Theorists—in Their Own Words*, edited by Knud Illeris, 90–105. London: Routledge, 2009.

Milburn, Kathryn. "A Critical Review of Peer Education with Young People with Special Reference to Sexual Health." *Health Education Research* 10, no. 4 (1995): 407–20.

Miller, Catharine Keyes. "A Fifteenth-Century Record of English Choir Repertory: B. M. Add. MS. 5665; A Transcription and Commentary." 2 vols. PhD diss., Yale University, 1948.

Miller, Jody. *Getting Played: African American Girls, Urban Inequality, and Gendered Violence*. New York: New York University Press, 2010.

Miller, William Ian. *The Anatomy of Disgust*. Cambridge, MA: Harvard University Press, 1997.

Minnis, Alastair. "From *Coilles* to *Bel Chose*: Discourses of Obscenity in Jean de Meun and Chaucer." In *Medieval Obscenities*, edited by Nicola McDonald, 156–77. York: York University Press, 2006.

Mirk, John. *John Mirk's Festial, Edited from British Library MS Cotton Claudius A. II*. Edited by Susan Powell. 2 vols. Early English Text Society, o.s., 334, 335. Oxford: Oxford University Press for Early English Text Society, 2009, 2011.

——. *Mirk's "Festial": A Collection of Homilies, Edited from Bodl. MS. Gough. Top. 4*. Edited by Theodore Erbe. Pt. 1. Early English Text Society, e.s., 96. London: Kegan Paul, Trench, Trübner, 1905.

The Mirrie Historie of the Thrie Friers of Berwicke. Aberdeen: Edward Raban for David Melvill, 1622.

Mohr, Melissa. *Holy Shit: A Brief History of Swearing*. Oxford: Oxford University Press, 2013.

Montgomerie, Alexander. *Alexander Montgomerie: Poems*. Edited by David J. Parkinson. 2 vols. Edinburgh: Scottish Text Society, 2000.

Montgomerie, Alexander, and Sir Patrick Hume of Polwarth. *The Flyting betwixt Montgomerie and Polwart*. Edinburgh: Andrew Hart, 1621.

Morris, Steven. "Ched Evans Accused of 'Callous Indifference' in Rape Trial Closing Speech." *Guardian*, October 13, 2016. https://www.theguardian.com/uk -news/2016/oct/13/ched-evans-accused-of-callous-indifference-in-trial -summing-up.

——. "Ched Evans Admits Not Asking If He Could Have Unprotected Sex with Woman." *Guardian*, October 11, 2016. https://www.theguardian.com/uk -news/2016/oct/11/ched-evans-admits-not-asking-if-he-could-have -unprotected-sex-with-woman.

——. "Ched Evans Raped Drunk Teenager in Hotel Room, Jury at Retrial Told." *Guardian*, October 4, 2016. https://www.theguardian.com/uk-news/2016 /oct/04/ched-evans-raped-drunk-teenager-hotel-room-retrial-jury-told.

——. "Ched Evans Tells Rape Retrial That Woman Consented to Sex." *Guardian*, October 10, 2016. https://www.theguardian.com/uk-news/2016/oct/10 /ched-evans-tells-retrial-that-woman-consented-to-sex.

——. "Ched Evans Told Police: 'We Could Have Had Any Girl We Wanted.'" *Guardian*, October 6, 2016. https://www.theguardian.com/uk-news/2016/oct/06/ched-evans-told-police-we-could-have-had-any-girl-we-wanted.

——. "Ched Evans Trial: Friends Describe Alleged Victim's Distress the Next Day." *Guardian*, October 6, 2016. https://www.theguardian.com/uk-news/2016/oct/06/ched-evans-trial-friends-describe-alleged-victims-distress-next-day.

——. "Ched Evans Trial: Woman Awoke Confused in Hotel Room, Court Told." *Guardian*, October 5, 2016. https://www.theguardian.com/uk-news/2016/oct/05/ched-evans-trial-woman-awoke-confused-in-hotel-room-court-told.

——. "The Rich Footballer and the Waitress Living at Home: Ched Evans Trial Profiles." *Guardian*, October 14, 2016. https://www.theguardian.com/football/2016/oct/14/trial-profiles-rich-footballer-waitress-living-home.

——. "Second Ched Evans Defence Witness Denies £50,000 Reward Motive." *Guardian*, October 12, 2016. https://www.theguardian.com/uk-news/2016/oct/12/second-ched-evans-defence-witness-denies-payment-motive.

——. "Witness in Ched Evans Retrial Accused of Lying to Earn £50000 Reward." *Guardian*, October 11, 2016. https://www.theguardian.com/uk-news/2016/oct/11/witness-in-ched-evans-retrial-accused-of-lying-to-land-50000-reward.

Morris, Steven, and Alexandra Topping. "Ched Evans: Footballer Found Not Guilty of Rape in Retrial." *Guardian*, October 14, 2016. https://www.theguardian.com/football/2016/oct/14/footballer-ched-evans-cleared-of-in-retrial.

Morrison, Karl F. *"I Am You": The Hermeneutics of Empathy in Western Literature, Theology, and Art*. Princeton, NJ: Princeton University Press, 1988.

Morrison, Toni. *Lecture and Speech of Acceptance, upon the Award of the Nobel Prize for Literature, Delivered in Stockholm on the Seventh of December, Nineteen Hundred and Ninety-Three*. New York: Alfred A. Knopf, 1995.

Mory, R. N. "A Medieval English Anatomy: MS Wellcome 564." PhD diss., University of Michigan, 1977.

Moslener, Sara. *Virgin Nation: Sexual Purity and American Adolescence*. Oxford: Oxford University Press, 2015.

Moss, Rachel E. "Chaucer's Funny Rape: Addressing a Taboo in Medieval Studies." *Meny Snoweballes*, September 14, 2014. https://menysnoweballes.wordpress.com/2014/09/11/chaucers-funny-rape-addressing-a-taboo-in-medieval-studies/.

Munro, Vanessa E. "Constructing Consent: Legislating Freedom and Legitimating Constraint in the Expression of Sexual Autonomy." *Akron Law Review* 41 (2008): 923–56.

Mustakeem, Sowande' M. *Slavery at Sea: Sex, Sickness, and the Middle Passage*. Urbana: University of Illinois Press, 2016.

Mustanoja, Tauno F., ed. *"The Good Wife Taught Her Daughter," "The Good Wyfe Wold a Pylgremage," "The Thewis of Gud Women."* Helsinki: Suomalaisen Kirjallisuuden Scuran, 1948.

Neal, Derek G. *The Masculine Self in Late Medieval England*. Chicago: University of Chicago Press, 2008.

"'Negro Wench' to be sold by Thomas Wiggins." *Princeton and Slavery*. https://slavery.princeton.edu/sources/negro-wench-2.

Nelson, Ingrid. *Lyric Tactics: Poetry, Genre, and Practice in Late Medieval England.* Philadelphia: University of Pennsylvania Press, 2017.

Newlyn, Evelyn S. "The Function of the Female Monster in Middle Scots Poetry: Misogyny, Patriarchy, and the Satiric Myth." In *Misogyny in Literature*, edited by Katherine Ackley, 33–66. New York: Garland, 1992.

———. "Images of Women in Sixteenth-Century Scottish Literary Manuscripts." In *Women in Scotland, c. 1100–c. 1750*, edited by Elizabeth Ewan and Maureen Meikle, 56–66. East Linton, UK: Tuckwell Press, 1999.

———. "Luve, Lichery, and Ewill Women: The Satirical Tradition in the Bannatyne Manuscript." *Studies in Scottish Literature* 26 (1991): 283–93.

———. "Of 'Vertew Nobillest' and 'Serpent Wrinkis': Taxonomy of the Female in the Bannatyne Manuscript." *Scotia* 14 (1990): 1–12.

———. "The Political Dimensions of Desire and Sexuality in the Poems of the Bannatyne Manuscript." *Selected Essays on Scottish Language and Literature*, edited by Steven D. McKenna, 75–96. Lewiston, NY: Edwin Mellen, 1992.

Noomen, Willem, and Nico van den Boogard, eds. *Nouveau recueil complet des fabliaux.* 10 vols. Assen, Netherlands: Van Gorcum, 1983–98.

Novikoff, Alex J. *The Medieval Culture of Disputation: Pedagogy, Practice, and Performance.* Philadelphia: University of Pennsylvania Press, 2013.

Ong, Walter J. *Rhetoric, Romance, and Technology: Studies in the Interaction of Expression and Culture.* Ithaca, NY: Cornell University Press, 1971.

Orme, Nicholas. *Education in the West of England, 1066–1548.* Exeter: University of Exeter Press, 1976.

Paden, William D., ed. and trans. *The Medieval Pastourelle.* 2 vols. New York: Garland, 1987.

———. "Rape in the Pastourelle." *Romantic Review* 80, no. 3 (1989): 331–49.

Pappano, Margaret Aziza. "'Leve Brother': Fraternalism and Craft Identity in the *Miller's Prologue* and *Tale.*" In *Reading Medieval Culture: Essays in Honor of Robert W. Hanning*, edited by Robert M. Stein and Sandra Pierson Prior, 248–70. Notre Dame, IN: University of Notre Dame Press, 2005.

Pappano, Margaret Aziza, and Nicole R. Rice. *The Civic Cycles: Artisan Drama and Identity in Premodern England.* Notre Dame, IN: University of Notre Dame Press, 2015.

Parkes, M. B. *Pause and Effect: An Introduction to the History of Punctuation in the West.* Berkeley: University of California Press, 1993.

Parkinson, David J. "Alexander Montgomerie, James VI, and 'Tumbling Verse.'" In *Loyal Letters: Studies in Mediaeval Alliterative Poetry and Prose*, edited by L. A. J. R. Houwen and A. A. MacDonald, 281–95. Groningen: Egbert Forsten, 1994.

———. "'A Lamentable Storie': Mary Queen of Scots and the Inescapable *Querelle des Femmes.*" In *A Palace in the Wild: Essays on Vernacular Culture and Humanism in Late-Medieval and Renaissance Scotland*, edited by L. A. J. R. Houwen, A. A. MacDonald, and S. L. Mapstone, 141–60. Leuven: Peeters, 2000.

Parsons, Ben. "Beaten for a Book: Domestic and Pedagogic Violence in *The Wife of Bath's Prologue.*" *Studies in the Age of Chaucer* 27 (2015): 163–94.

Partridge, Stephen. "Minding the Gaps: Interpreting the Manuscript Evidence of the *Cook's Tale* and the *Squire's Tale.*" In *The English Medieval Book: Studies in*

Memory of Jeremy Griffiths, edited by A. S. G. Edwards, Vincent Gillespie, and Ralph Hanna, 51–85. London: British Library, 2000.

Passet, Joanne E. *Sex Radicals and the Quest for Women's Equality*. Urbana: University of Illinois Press, 2003.

Payne, Diana L., Kimberly A. Lonsway, and Louise F. Fitzgerald. "Rape Myth Acceptance: Exploration of Its Structure and Its Measurement Using the *Illinois Rape Myth Acceptance Scale*." *Journal of Research in Personality* 33, no. 1 (1999): 27–68.

Perfetti, Lisa. *Women and Laughter in Medieval Comic Literature*. Ann Arbor: University of Michigan Press, 2003.

Perkins-Valdez, Dolen. *Wench: A Novel*. New York: Harper Collins, 2010.

Petrina, Alessandra. "Deviations from Genre in Robert Henryson's 'Robene and Makyne.'" *Studies in Scottish Literature* 31, no. 1 (1999): 107–20.

Phillips, Kim M. *Medieval Maidens: Young Women and Gender in England, 1270–1540*. Manchester: Manchester University Press, 2003.

Phillips, Susan E. *Transforming Talk: The Problem with Gossip in Late Medieval England*. University Park: Pennsylvania State University Press, 2007.

Pierce-Baker, Charlotte. *Surviving the Silence: Black Women's Stories of Rape*. New York: W. W. Norton, 1998.

Pigg, Daniel F. "Performing the Perverse: The Abuse of Masculine Power in the *Reeve's Tale*." In *Masculinities in Chaucer*, edited by Peter G. Beidler, 53–61. Cambridge: D. S. Brewer, 1998.

Pough, Gwendolyn D. *Check It While I Wreck It: Black Womanhood, Hip-Hop, and the Public Sphere*. Boston: Northeastern University Press, 2004.

Powell, Anastasia. *Sex, Power, and Consent: Youth Culture and the Unwritten Rules*. Cambridge: Cambridge University Press, 2010.

——. "Shifting Upstream: Bystander Action against Sexism and Discrimination against Women." In *Preventing Sexual Violence: Interdisciplinary Approaches to Overcoming a Rape Culture*, edited by Nicola Henry and Anastasia Powell, 189–207. New York: Palgrave Macmillan, 2014.

Press Association. "Ched Evans 'Delighted' to Seal Sheffield United Return from Chesterfield." *Guardian*, May 8, 2017. https://www.theguardian.com/football/2017/may/08/ched-evans-sheffield-united-return-chesterfield.

——. "Ched Evans's Rape Victim Had to Change Name and Move Five Times, Says Father." *Guardian*, December 28, 2014. https://www.theguardian.com/football/2014/dec/28/ched-evans-rape-victim-change-name-move-house-father.

Putter, Ad. "The French of English Letters: Two Trilingual Verse Epistles in Context." In *Language and Culture in Medieval Britain: The French of England c. 1100–c. 1500*, edited by Jocelyn Wogan-Browne with Carolyn Collette, Maryanne Kowaleski, Linne Mooney, Ad Putter, and David Trotter, 397–408. York: York Medieval Press, 2009.

Quadara, Antonia. "The Everydayness of Rape: How Understanding Sexual Assault Perpetration Can Inform Prevention Efforts." In *Preventing Sexual Violence: Interdisciplinary Approaches to Overcoming a Rape Culture*, edited by Nicola Henry and Anastasia Powell. 41–63. New York: Palgrave Macmillan, 2014.

Raphael, Jody. *Rape Is Rape: How Denial, Distortion, and Victim-Blaming Are Fueling a Hidden Acquaintance Rape Crisis*. Chicago: Lawrence Hill Books, 2013.

Rasmussen, Mary Louise. "Pleasure/Desire, Sexularism, and Sexuality Education." *Sex Education* 12, no. 4 (2012): 469–81.

Rebollo-Gil, Guillermo, and Amanda Moras. "Black Women and Black Men in Hip Hop Music: Misogyny, Violence and the Negotiation of (White-Owned) Space." *Journal of Popular Culture* 45, no. 1 (2012): 118–32.

Reichl, Karl. "The Beginnings of the Middle English Secular Lyric: Texts, Music, Manuscript Context." In *The Genesis of Books: Studies in the Scribal Culture of Medieval England in Honour of A. N. Doane*, edited by Matthew T. Hussey and John D. Niles, 195–243. Turnhout, Belgium: Brepols, 2011.

——. "Debate Verse." In *Studies in the Harley Manuscript: The Scribes, Contents, and Social Contexts of British Library MS Harley 2253*, edited by Susanna Fein, 219–39. Kalamazoo, MI: Medieval Institute Publications, 2000.

——. "Popular Poetry and Courtly Lyric: The Middle English Pastourelle." *Yearbook of Research in English and American Literature* 5 (1987): 33–61.

Renwick, Robert, ed. *Extracts from the Records of the Royal Burgh of Stirling AD 1519–1666 (1666–1752)*. 2 vols. Glasgow: Glasgow Stirlingshire and Sons of the Rock Society, 1887–89.

Restaurant Opportunities Centers United Forward Together. "The Glass Floor: Sexual Harassment in the Restaurant Industry." October 2014. http://rocunited.org/wp-content/uploads/2014/10/REPORT_TheGlassFloor_Sexual-Harassment-in-the-Restaurant-Industry.pdf.

Revard, Carter. "Scribe and Provenance." In *Studies in the Harley Manuscript: The Scribes, Contents, and Social Contexts of British Library MS Harley 2253*, edited by Susanna Fein, 21–110. Kalamazoo, MI: Medieval Institute Publications, 2000.

Rhoades, Georgia M. "Decoding the Sheela-na-gig." *Feminist Formations* 22, no. 2 (2010): 167–94.

Riddy, Felicity. "Mother Knows Best: Reading Social Change in a Conduct Text." *Speculum* 71, no. 1 (1996): 66–86.

Ringler, William A., Jr. *Bibliography and Index of English Verse in Manuscript, 1501–1558*. London: Mansell, 1992.

Ritchie, Andrea J. *Invisible No More: Police Violence against Black Women and Women of Color*. Boston: Beacon Press, 2017.

Robbins, Rossell Hope. "The Bradshaw Carols." *PMLA* 81, no. 3 (1966): 308–10.

——, ed. *Historical Poems of the XIVth and XVth Centuries*. New York: Columbia University Press, 1959.

——, ed. *Secular Lyrics of the XIVth and XVth Centuries*. 2nd ed. Oxford: Clarendon, 1961.

——. "A Warning against Lechery." *Philological Quarterly* 35 (1956): 90–95.

Robichaud, Paul. "'To Heir Quhat I Sould Wryt': *The Flyting of Dunbar and Kennedy* and Scots Oral Culture." *Scottish Literary Journal*, 25, no. 2 (1998): 9–16.

Robinson, Christine M. "More than One Meaning in *The Flyting of Dunbar and Kennedy*." *Neuphilologische Mitteilungen* 99, no. 3 (1998): 9–16.

Rogers, Cynthia A. "'Make Thereof a Game': The Interplay of Texts in the Findern Manuscript and Its Late Medieval Textual Community." PhD diss., Indiana University, 2015.

Rose, Christine M. "Reading Chaucer Reading Rape." In *Representing Rape in Medieval and Early Modern Literature*, edited by Elizabeth Robertson and Christine M. Rose, 21–60. New York: Palgrave Macmillan, 2001.

Russell, Gareth. *Young and Damned and Fair: The Life of Catherine Howard, Fifth Wife of Henry VIII*. New York: Simon and Schuster, 2017.

Ryan, Rebecca M. "The Sex Right: A Legal History of the Marital Rape Exemption." *Law and Social Inquiry* 20, no. 4 (1995): 941–1001.

Salih, Sarah. "Erotica." In *A Cultural History of Sexuality in the Middle Ages*, edited by Ruth Evans, 181–212. New York: Berg, 2011.

Salisbury, Eve, ed. *The Trials and Joys of Marriage*. Kalamazoo, MI: Medieval Institute Publications, 2002.

Sanday, Peggy Reeves. *Fraternity Gang Rape: Sex, Brotherhood, and Privilege on Campus*. 2nd ed. New York: New York University Press, 2007.

Sandison, Helen Estabrook. *The "Chanson d'Aventure" in Middle English*. Bryn Mawr, PA: Bryn Mawr College, 1913.

Sandon, Nick, ed. *The Ritson Manuscript: Liturgical Compositions, Votive Antiphons, and Te Deum*. Moretonhampstead, UK: Antico Editions, 2001.

Santelli, John, Mary A. Ott, Maureen Lyon, Jennifer Rogers, Daniel Summers, and Rebecca Schleifer. "Abstinence and Abstinence-Only Education: A Review of U.S. Policies and Programs." *Journal of Adolescent Health* 38 (2006): 72–81.

——. "Abstinence-Only Education Policies and Programs: A Position Paper of the Society for Adolescent Medicine." *Journal of Adolescent Health* 38 (2006): 83–87.

Sarachild, Kathie. "Consciousness-Raising: A Radical Weapon." In *Feminist Revolution: An Abridged Edition with Additional Writings*, edited by Redstockings of the Women's Liberation Movement, 144–50. New York: Random House, 1978.

Saunders, Corinne. *Rape and Ravishment in the Literature of Medieval England*. Cambridge: D. S. Brewer, 2001.

——. "A Study of the Book of *XX Songes* (1530)." M. Music thesis, King's College, University of London, 1985.

Scattergood, John. "Courtliness in Some Fourteenth-Century English Pastourelles." In *Reading the Past: Essays in Medieval and Renaissance Literature*, 61–80. Dublin: Four Courts Press, 1996.

——. "The Love Lyric before Chaucer." In *A Companion to the Middle English Lyric*, edited by Thomas Duncan, 39–67. Cambridge: D. S. Brewer, 2005.

Schewe, Peter A. "Guidelines for Developing Rape Prevention and Risk Reduction Interventions." In *Preventing Violence in Relationships: Interventions across the Life Span*, edited by Peter A. Schewe, 107–36. Washington, DC: American Psychological Association, 2002.

Schieberle, Misty. *Feminized Counsel and the Literature of Advice in England, 1380–1500*. Turnhout, Belgium: Brepols, 2014.

Schwartz, Martin D., and Walter S. DeKeseredy. *Sexual Assault on the College Campus: The Role of Male Peer Support*. Thousand Oaks, CA: Sage Publications, 1997.

Seabourne, Gwen. "Drugs, Deceit, and Damage in Thirteenth-Century Herefordshire: New Perspectives on Medieval Surgery, Sex, and the Law." *Social History of Medicine* 30, no. 2 (2017): 255–76.

Seaman, Myra J. "Late Medieval Conduct Literature." In *The History of British Women's Writing, 700–1500*. Vol. 1, *700–1500*, edited by Liz Herbert McAvoy and Diane Watt, 121–30. New York: Palgrave Macmillan, 2012.

Sessions, William A. *Henry Howard, Earl of Surrey*. Boston: G. K. Hall, 1986.

Sexuality Information and Education Council of the United States. "Dedicated Federal Abstinence-Only-Until-Marriage Programs Funding by Fiscal Year (FY) 1982–2017." May 2017. http://www.siecus.org.

Seymour, M. C. "Of This Cokes Tale." *Chaucer Review* 24, no. 3 (1990): 259–62.

Shabazz, Rashad. "Masculinity and the Mic: The Uneven Geography of Hip-Hop." *Gender, Place, and Culture* 21, no. 3 (2014): 370–86.

Sharpe, Reginald R., ed. *Calendar of Coroners Rolls of the City of London AD 1300–1378*. London: R. Clay and Sons, 1913.

Sheidlower, Jesse. *The F-Word*. 3rd ed. Oxford: Oxford University Press, 2009.

Shire, Helena M., and Alexander Fenton. "'The Sweepings of Parnassus': Four Poems Transcribed from the Record Books of the Burgh Sasines of Aberdeen." *Aberdeen University Review* 36 (1955–56): 43–54.

Shirley, Christopher. "The Devonshire Manuscript: Reading Gender in the Henrician Court." *English Literary Renaissance* 45, no. 1 (2015): 32–59.

Shuffleton, George, ed. *Codex Ashmole 61: A Compilation of Popular Middle English Verse*. Kalamazoo, MI: Medieval Institute Publications, 2008.

Sidhu, Nicole Nolan. *Indecent Exposure: Gender, Politics, and Obscene Comedy in Middle English Literature*. Philadelphia: University of Pennsylvania Press, 2016.

Siemens, Raymond G., ed. *The Lyrics of the Henry VIII Manuscript*. Grand Rapids, MI: English Renaissance Text Society, 2013.

Siemens, Raymond G., and Johanne Paquette. "Drawing Networks in the Devonshire Manuscript (BL Add. MS. 17492): Toward Visualizing a Writing Community's Shared Apprenticeship, Social Valuation, and Self-Validation." In *New Ways of Looking at Old Texts, V: Papers of the Renaissance English Text Society, 2007–2010*, edited by Michael Denbo, 113–51. Tempe: Arizona Center for Medieval and Renaissance Studies, 2014.

Skelton, John. *The Complete English Poems of John Skelton*. Edited by John Scattergood. Rev. ed. Liverpool: Liverpool University Press, 2015.

Smith, Geri L. *The Medieval French Pastourelle Tradition: Poetic Motivations and Generic Transformations*. Gainesville: University Press of Florida, 2009.

Smith, Valerie. *Not Just Race, Not Just Gender: Black Feminist Readings*. New York: Routledge, 1998.

Snow, D. W., and C. M. Perrins. *The Birds of the Western Palearctic*. Concise ed. Oxford: Oxford University Press, 1998.

Solterer, Helen. *The Master and Minerva: Disputing Women in French Medieval Culture*. Berkeley: University of California Press, 1995.

Somerset, Fiona. "Censorship." In *The Production of Books in England 1350–1500*, edited by Alexandra Gillespie and Daniel Wakelin, 239–58. Cambridge: Cambridge University Press, 2011.

Spiller, Michael R. G. "Hume, Sir Patrick, of Polwarth (c.1550–1609)." *ODNB*.

Sriranganathan, Gobika, Denise Jaworsky, June Larkin, Sarah Flicker, Lisa Campbell, Susan Flynn, Jesse Janssen, and Leah Erlich. "Peer Sexual Health Education:

Interventions for Effective Program Evaluation." *Health Education Journal* 71, no. 1 (2010): 62–71.

Stavreva, Kirilka. *Words Like Daggers: Violent Female Speech in Early Modern England.* Lincoln: University of Nebraska Press, 2015.

Stavsky, Jonathan, ed. and trans. *Le Bone Florence of Rome: A Critical Edition and Facing Translation of a Middle English Romance.* Cardiff: University of Wales Press, 2017.

Stemmler, Theo. "More English Texts from MS Cambridge University Library Ii. III.8." *Anglia* 93 (1975): 1–16.

Stern, Mark Joseph. "North Carolina Fails to Fix Its Horrifying, Medieval Rape Law." *Slate*, June 29, 2017. http://www.slate.com/blogs/outward/2017/06/29/north_carolina_fails_to_outlaw_rape_after_woman_revokes_consent.html.

Stevens, John. *Music and Poetry in the Early Tudor Court.* London: Methuen, 1961.

Stoltenberg, John. *The End of Manhood: Parables on Sex and Selfhood.* Rev. ed. London: University College London Press, 2000.

Strachey, John, ed. *Rotuli Parliamentorum, ut et petitiones, et placita in Parliamento.* 6 vols. London, 1767–77.

Stuart, John, ed. *Extracts from the Presbytery Book of Strathbogie, 1631–54.* Aberdeen: Spalding Club, 1843.

Sun, Wai Han, Heidi Yin Hai Miu, Carlos King Ho Wong, Joseph D. Tucker, and William Chi Wai Wong. "Assessing Participation and Effectiveness of the Peer-Led Approach in Youth Sexual Health Education: Systematic Review and Meta-Analysis in More Developed Countries." *Journal of Sex Research* 55, no. 1 (2018): 31–44.

Sweeney, Kathleen. *Maiden USA: Girl Icons Come of Age.* New York: Peter Lang, 2008.

Sylvester, Louise M. *Medieval Romance and the Construction of Heterosexuality.* New York: Palgrave Macmillan, 2008.

Taylor, Andrew. "A Second Ajax: Peter Abelard and the Violence of Dialectic." In *The Tongue of the Fathers: Gender and Ideology in Twelfth-Century Latin,* edited by David Townsend and Andrew Taylor, 14–34. Philadelphia: University of Pennsylvania Press, 1998.

Temkin, Jennifer. *Rape and the Legal Process.* Oxford: Oxford University Press, 2002.

Testa, Maria, and Kathleen A. Parks. "The Role of Women's Alcohol Consumption in Sexual Victimization." *Aggression and Violent Behavior* 1, no. 3 (1996): 217–34.

Thomas, Andrea. "'Dragonis Baith and Dowes ay in Double Forme': Women at the Court of James V, 1513–1532." In *Women in Scotland, c. 1100–c. 1750,* edited by Elizabeth Ewan and Maureen Meikle, 83–94. East Linton, UK: Tuckwell Press, 1999.

——. *Princelie Majestie: The Court of James V of Scotland, 1528–1542.* Edinburgh: John Donald, 2005.

Thompson, Krissah. "For Decades They Hid Jefferson's Mistress. Now Monticello Is Making Room for Sally Hemings." *Washington Post*, February 19, 2017. https://www.washingtonpost.com/lifestyle/style/for-decades-they-hid-jeffersons-mistress-now-monticello-is-making-room-for-sally-hemings/2017/02/18/d410d660-f222-11e6-8d72-263470bf0401_story.html?tid=sm_tw&utm_term=.071ee03b88fd.

Tillman, Shaquita, Thema Bryant-Davis, Kimberly Smith, and Alison Marks. "Shattering Silence: Exploring Barriers to Disclosure for African-American Sexual Assault Survivors." *Trauma, Violence, and Abuse* 11, no. 2 (2010): 59–70.

Timmins, T. C. B., ed. *The Register of John Chandler Dean of Salisbury 1404–17.* Devizes, UK: Alan Sutton Publishing for the Wiltshire Record Society, 1984.

Traister, Rebecca. *All the Single Ladies: Unmarried Women and the Rise of an Independent Nation.* New York: Simon and Schuster, 2016.

Transactions of the Buchan Field Club. 13 vols. Peterhead, UK: P. Scrogie, 1913.

"Transcript of the Second Debate." *New York Times,* October 9, 2016. https://www.nytimes.com/2016/10/10/us/politics/transcript-second-debate.html.

Turner, James Grantham. *Schooling Sex: Libertine Literature and Erotic Education in Italy, France, and England, 1534–1685.* Oxford: Oxford University Press, 2003.

Turner, Wendy J. "The Leper and the Prostitute: Forensic Examination of Rape in Medieval England." In *Trauma in Medieval Society,* edited by Wendy J. Turner and Christina Lee, 133–47. Leiden: Brill, 2018.

Turville-Petre, Thorlac, ed. *The Texts of BL MS Harley 913, "The Kildare Manuscript."* Oxford: Oxford University Press for the Early English Text Society, 2015.

"University of Minnesota–Twin Cities EOAA Report." December 7, 2016. http://kstp.com/sports/university-of-minnesota-eoaa-investigative-report-gophers-football-players/4347059/. http://kstp.com/kstpImages/repository/cs/files/U%20of%20M%20EOAA%20redacted5.pdf.

Utley, Francis Lee. *The Crooked Rib: An Analytical Index to the Argument about Women in English and Scots Literature to the End of the Year 1568.* Columbus: Ohio State University Press, 1944. Reprint, New York: Octagon Books, 1970.

van Heijnsbergen, Theo. "The Bannatyne Manuscript Lyrics: Literary Convention and Authorial Voice." In *The European Sun, Proceedings of the Seventh International Congress on Medieval and Renaissance Scottish Language and Literature,* edited by Graham Caie, Roderick J. Lyall, Sally Mapstone, and Kenneth Simpson, 423–44. East Linton, UK: Tuckwell Press, 2001.

——. "The Interaction between Literature and History in Queen Mary's Edinburgh: The Bannatyne Manuscript and Its Prosopographical Context." In *The Renaissance in Scotland: Studies in Literature, Religion, History, and Culture Offered to John Durkan,* edited by A. A. MacDonald, Michael Lynch, and Ian B. Cowan, 183–225. Leiden: Brill, 1994.

Vasvari, Louise O. "Fowl Play in My Lady's Chamber: Textual Harassment of a Middle English Pornithological Riddle and Visual Pun." In *Obscenity: Social Control and Artistic Creation in the European Middle Ages,* edited by Jan M. Ziolkowski, 108–35. Leiden: Brill, 1998.

Vera-Gray, Fiona. *Men's Intrusion, Women's Embodiment: A Critical Analysis of Street Harassment.* New York: Routledge, 2016.

Vernhagan, Hermann. "Zu den sprichwörtern Hending's." *Anglia* 4 (1881): 182–91.

Verweij, Sebastiaan. *The Literary Culture of Early Modern Scotland: Manuscript Production and Transmission, 1560–1625.* Oxford: Oxford University Press, 2016.

Vines, Amy N. "Invisible Woman: Rape as Chivalric Necessity in Medieval Romance." In *Sexual Culture in the Literature of Medieval Britain,* edited by

Amanda Hopkins, Robert Allen Rouse, and Cory James Rushton, 161–80. Woodbridge, UK: Boydell and Brewer, 2014.

Wagner, Bernard M. "New Songs of the Reign of Henry VIII." *Modern Language Notes* 50, no. 7 (1935): 452–55.

Wakelin, Daniel. *Scribal Correction and Literary Craft: English Manuscripts 1375–1510.* Cambridge: Cambridge University Press, 2014.

Wald, Elijah. *The Dozens: A History of Rap's Mama.* Oxford: Oxford University Press, 2012.

Walker, Alice. *In Search of Our Mothers' Gardens: Womanist Prose.* New York: Harcourt, 1983.

Washington, Patricia A. "Disclosure Patterns of Black Female Sexual Assault Survivors." *Violence against Women* 7, no. 11 (2001): 1254–83.

Weisl, Angela Jane. "Violence against Women in the *Canterbury Tales.*" In *Violence against Women in Medieval Texts,* edited by Anna Roberts, 115–36. Gainesville: University Press of Florida, 1998.

Wenzel, Siegfried. *Macaronic Sermons: Bilingualism and Preaching in Late Medieval England.* Ann Arbor: University of Michigan Press, 1994.

West, Lindy. *Shrill: Memoirs of a Loud Woman.* New York: Hachette Books, 2016.

White, Miles. *From Jim Crow to Jay-Z: Race, Rap, and the Performance of Masculinity.* Urbana: University of Illinois Press, 2011.

Whiting, Bartlett Jere. *Proverbs, Sentences, and Proverbial Phrases; from English Writings Mainly before 1500.* Cambridge, MA: Belknap Press, 1968.

Williams, Janet Hadley. "David Lyndsay and the Making of King James V." In *Stewart Style 1513–1542: Essays on the Court of James V,* edited by Janet Hadley Williams, 201–26. East Linton, UK: Tuckwell Press, 1996.

——. "James V, David Lyndsay, and the Bannatyne Manuscript Poem of the Gyre Carling." *Studies in Scottish Literature* 26 (1991): 164–71.

——. "Sir David Lyndsay." In *A Companion to Medieval Scottish Poetry,* edited by Priscilla Bawcutt and Janet Hadley Williams, 179–91. Cambridge: D. S. Brewer, 2006.

——. "Women Fictional and Historic in Lyndsay's Poetry." In *Women and the Feminine in Medieval and Early Modern Scottish Writing,* edited by Sarah M. Dunnigan, C. Marie Harker, and Evelyn S. Newlyn, 47–85. New York: Palgrave Macmillan, 2004.

Williams, Linda. *Hard Core: Power, Pleasure, and the "Frenzy of the Visible."* 2nd ed. Berkeley: University of California Press, 1999.

Wilson, Edward. "A 'Damned F . . . in Abbot' in 1528: The Earliest English Example of a Four-Letter Word." *Notes and Queries* 40, no. 1 (1993): 29–34.

——. "Local Habitations and Names in MS Rawlinson C.813 in the Bodleian Library, Oxford." *Review of English Studies* 41, no. 161 (1990): 12–44.

Woods, Marjorie Curry. *Classroom Commentaries: Teaching the "Poetria nova" across Medieval and Renaissance Europe.* Columbus: Ohio State University Press, 2010.

——. "Rape and the Pedagogical Rhetoric of Sexual Violence." In *Criticism and Dissent in the Middle Ages,* edited by Rita Copeland, 56–86. Cambridge: Cambridge University Press, 1996.

Woolf, Rosemary. "The Construction of *In a fryht as I con fare fremede.*" *Medium Ævum* 38 (1969): 55–59.

Wormald, Jenny. *Mary Queen of Scots: A Study in Failure.* London: George Philip, 1988.

Wright, Thomas, ed. *Songs and Ballads with Other Short Poems Chiefly of the Reign of Philip and Mary.* London: Nichols and Sons, 1860.

Wright, Thomas, and James Orchard Halliwell, eds. *Reliquiae Antiquae: Scraps from Ancient Manuscripts.* 2 vols. London: William Pickering, 1841–43.

Wyclif, John. *The Holy Bible, Containing the Old and New Testaments, with the Apocryphal Books.* Edited by Josiah Forshall and Frederic Madden. 4 vols. Oxford: Oxford University Press, 1850.

——. *Select English Works of John Wyclif.* Edited by Thomas Arnold. Oxford: Clarendon Press, 1869–71.

XX Songes. London, 1530.

Zimmerman, Jonathan. *Too Hot to Handle: A Global History of Sexual Education.* Princeton, NJ: Princeton University Press, 2015.

Ziolkowski, Jan M. "The Obscenities of Old Women: Vetularity and Vernacularity." In *Obscenity: Social Control and Artistic Creation in the European Middle Ages,* edited by Jan M. Ziolkowski, 73–89. Leiden: Brill, 1998.

——, ed. *Obscenity: Social Control and Artistic Creation in the European Middle Ages.* Leiden: Brill, 1998.

INDEX

abjection, 3

Absens of yeu causeth me to sygh and complayne, 219

abstinence-only education (U.S.), 182–85

Access Hollywood, 228–30, 231, 233

Adewe adewe my hartes lust, 194n22, 202n59

Adew my pretty pussy, 230–31

Adoue deir hart of Aberdene, 134

advice poems / carols, 21, 24, 32–34, 86, 151n4

affective connections, 6, 186–88, 197, 203

Agarde family, 64

Ahmed, Sara, 4–6, 7n21, 8–9, 40, 187–88

Ah my hart ah, 195nn27–28, 195n30

An aigit man, twyis forty yeiris, 73–74

Alas, to whom shuld I complayne, 189n5, 201n53, 202n59

Alcoff, Linda, 100, 114

alcohol, 55–58

Al es bot a fantom, 24

alewife poems: and consciousness-raising, 177–78, 181–82; cross-temporal resonances of, 182–85; embedded misogyny of, 17, 178–79; pedagogy of, 151, 179–82

Allen, Louisa, 93n108

All to lufe and not to fenyie, 103–4, 115, 120n60

Alone alone, 222

An Alphabet of Tales, 22, 23

Ancrene Wisse, 126

And I war a maydyn, 159–61, 163, 166, 172, 177, 235–36

Andreas Capellanus, 145n154

Ane Detectioun of the duinges of Marie Quene of Scotts, 139

Ane fair sweit may of mony one, 134, 137–38, 145

Ane Satyre of the Thrie Estaitis, 89

Ane Supplicatioun, Directed . . . to the Kingis Grace, 92n105

Angus, sixth earl of (Archibald Douglas), 84–85

Answer to the Kingis Flyting, 84–96

anthologies. *See* lyric anthologies

antimarriage warnings, 24

antirape education, 107, 115–16, 119–20, 125–26, 147–49

Arthur, Prince of Wales, 189

Ashmole 176: audience of, 196–200, 202, 205; courtly complaints in, 188, 190, 193–96, 202–3, 209; female subjectivity voiced in, 197, 201–9; *I can be wanton and yf I wyll,* 204–8; *Let be wanton your busynes,* 208–10; manuscript context of, 19n80, 193–97, 200, 205, 209–10; *My ladye hathe forsaken me,* 197–200; versus Ritson Manuscript, 186–88, 210–11, 220n110; scribal practices in, 196–97, 201, 209–10; transcribed, 241–44; "songs of wantonness" in, 195–97, 225–26; *Up I arose in verno tempore,* 201–4

Ashmole, Elias, 194

As I stod on a day, 112–13, 143

Ate ston casting my lemman I ches, 168–70, 171, 208n75, 237

At the northe ende of Selver Whyte, 167n69

Audelay, John, 151n4

Audrie and Daisy, 232n26

author: and research, 11, 186–87; subjectivity of, 4–8, 148–49, 183–85, 233

Ballade upon an Ale-Seller, 214n93

Balnavis, John, 73, 79, 89

Bannatyne, George, 75–76

Bannatyne Manuscript: circulation of, 142; flytings in, 73–76, 79, 86n90; pastourelles in, 103, 115, 133n112, 138–39; scribal alterations to, 75–76

Barbour, John, 95

Barclay, Hugh, 69

Barnes, Ishbel C. M., 70n11

Battle of Flodden, 84

Bawcutt, Priscilla, 67n1, 69, 70–71

CPSIA information can be obtained
at www.ICGtesting.com
Printed in the USA
BVHW030135071118
531826BV00001B/12/P